The SCIENCE FICTION FANZINE READER

Focal Points 1930–1960

Edited by
LUIS ORTIZ

nonstop press

THE SCIENCE FICTION FANZINE READER
FOCAL POINTS 1930–1960

Edited by Luis Ortiz

© 2019 Luis Ortiz

First Edition: April 2019
All rights reserved.

No part of this book may be reproduced, stored in a retrieval system, or transmitted in any form, or by any means — digital, electronic, mechanical, photocopying, or otherwise — without prior permission of the publisher.

Acknowledgments for permission to reprint copyrighted materials appear on page 398.

Nonstop Press books may be purchased for educational, business, or promotional use. For information please write: nonstop@nonstoppress.com
or POB 77, Greenwood, DE, 19950-077

Cover and book design by Luis Ortiz • Production by Nonstop Ink

Library of Congress Cataloging-in-Publication Data has been applied for.

ISBN 978-1-933065-67-0 Trade Paper
ISBN 978-1-933065-68-7 Hardcover

PRINTED IN THE UNITED STATES OF AMERICA

www.nonstoppress.com

Set in ITC Cheltenham, Interstate and Airbrush Reverse

Nonstop Press

CONTENTS

INTRODUCTION
WHEN TIME WAS NEW
   Luis Ortiz 9
THE FIRST FAN MAGAZINE
   Forrest J Ackerman 22
FAN MAGAZINES
   H.A. Dittmans, Jr. & W.H. Dellenback 26
BOK ON THE FANTASY SCENE
   Ray Bradbury 32
MY PAL JOHNNY
   Robert A. Madle 35
THE VERSATILE JIM BLISH
   Anonymous 43
HISTORY OF THE SCIENCEERS
   Allen Glasser 47
FANTASY MAGAZINE
   Harry Warner Jr. 53
FANZINE SCOPE
   F. Towner Laney 58
SCIENTI-SNAPS
   Harry Warner, Jr. 63
STRANGE HUNTING
   Anonymous 69
FJ ACKERMAN MEETS WELLS HG
   Bob Tucker 72
FROM THE VALLEY OF THE BLUE MOON
   T. Bruce Yerke 75
CHANGING TENDENCY AMONG FANMAGS
   Jack Speer 79

EARLY FAPA
    Harry Warner Jr. 84
WHEREIN JACK SPEER'S HAIR TURNS GRAY OVER NITE
    Forrest J Ackerman 91
WHEREIN JACK SPEER PARTAKES OF PANTOTHENIC ACID
    Jack Speer 95
BLACK & WHITE REVIEWS
    D.B. Thompson 100
    E. Everett Evans (Edward Everett) 100
    Harry Warner Jr. 101
    F. Towner Laney 101
FUTURIA FANTASIA
    Harry Warner, Jr. 103
CONFESSIONS OF A FANZINE REVIEWER
    Robert Bloch 109
WHAT FAN MAGAZINES?
    Robert W. Lowndes 114
TIGRINA – DEVIL DOLL
    Forrest J Ackerman 119
AN AMATEUR EX-EDITOR SPEAKS
    Manly Banister 122
THE AMATEUR EDITOR
    Walter A. Willis 128
COME IN, THE WATER'S LOVELY!
    Walter A. Willis 130
FILLER 523
    Dean Grennell 133
EDITORIAL Q-ZINE OR F-ZINE
    Don Fabun 140
PURE AS NEW FALLEN SLUSH
    Max Keasler 147
THE PALMER HOAX
    Geoffrey Giles 152
SOME EDITORS SAY
    Andrew Gregg 166
GONE BUT NOT FORGOTTEN
    Bob Tucker 171

THE IMMORTAL STORM
  Ed Wood...176
DEADLINE JOB: Kelly Freas 185
ZINE ARTIST: Lou Goldstone....................................186
ZINE LETTERS 190
  Bob Tucker..190
  Manly Banister 192
  Sam Moskowitz 196
  Letter By A Guy Who Wishes To Remain Nameless...............198
  Richard Sneary 199
THE DEEPER SIGNIFICANCE OF SCIENCE FICTION
  F. Towner Laney... 202
THE FAN FROM TOMORROW
  Walter A. Willis 203
FAN ICONS: Slan Shack..208
WHAT MAKES A FANZINE CRUD?
  Marion Zimmer Bradley....................................... 210
THE READERS ALWAYS WRITE
  Damon Knight... 218
TUMBRILS
  Harry Warner Jr. 220
HOW TO STOP WRITING FOR FANZINES
  Charles Burbee 230
AUTOBIOGRAPHICAL NOTES
  Walter A. Willis 233
A QUESTION OF TITLE
  Walter A. Willis 239
THE FANNISH AUTOBIOGRAPHY OF RICHARD ERWIN GEIS
  Richard E. Geis 244
PEON NOTES
  Charles Lee Riddle 250
THE DAMN THING
  Harry Warner Jr. 252
THE DEATH OF SPACEWAYS
  Bob Tucker 260
SHOPTALK: LETTER TO THE ACOLYTE
  E. Hoffman Price 263

CRACKLE: THE SNAP-ZINE
  F. Towner Laney 271
DELINEATING THE INTERLINEATION
  Bob Tucker 273
123456789? WHAT WAS THAT FANDOM I SAW YOU WITH...
  Ted White..280
SNIDE
  Harry Warner Jr. 288
FAN ICONS: Beanie 293
FANTASTUFF
  Terry Carr... 294
JOEL NYDAHL'S VEGA
  Harlan Ellison 296
A POSTSCRIPT TO VEGA
  Joel Nydahl 300
UP THE GARDEN PATHOLOGY
  Walter A. Willis 303
SLAVE OF THE PIXIE
  Charles Burbee 307
THE IRON CURTAIN DROPS
  Bob Tucker 313
I THINK STF HEROES ARE QUEER
  William Rotsler 321
FILE 13: DIANETICS – FAD OR SCIENCE?
  Redd Boggs..323
DIANETICS: ETC.
  John Larkins... 328
LOVE IN THE CORNFIELD
  Walter A. Willis 336
TOWNER HALL, VOID, ADOLESCENCE AND ALL THAT
  Gregory Benford 341
A DAY WITH CALVIN THOS. BECK
  Ted White..353

WHO KILLED SCIENCE FICTION? 365
   Kurt Vonnegut, Jr. 365
   Raymond A. Palmer 367
   Donald A. Wollheim 368
   Robert Silverberg 372
   Robert A.W. Lowndes 376
MIMEO INK, FANAC, AND PAPERBACKS
   Lee Hoffman 380
ZINE POETRY CORNER: Damon Knight 392
BAH! HUMBUG!
   Robert Bloch 393
Index 399

Science Fiction Fan, vol. 1, #4; Oct., 1936. Ed. Olon F. Wiggins.

INTRODUCTION

WHEN TIME WAS NEW

Luis Ortiz

WALT WILLIS once referred to fanzine publishing as "the lunatic fringe of the lunatic fringe."[1] Willis produced the first few issues of his notable fanzine *Slant* between 1948 and 1953, by the now quaint expediency of hand-setting type, letter by letter, on an abandoned office letterpress. Like many a science fiction fanzine editor before him, Willis started out as a young fan of American pulp magazines. Once hooked, he discovered fanzines and saw the writing on the wall: "Go forth and bring forth your own zine."

Fan, of course, is short for fanatic. Sf fans were especially fanatical. Joyce Carol Oates has written: "Genre fiction is addictive, literary fiction, unfortunately, is not."[2] There have been fans of mysteries, westerns, and romance, but science fiction has always had a special addictive nature. It is quite rare to find fanzines for other fields, published during the period when science fiction fan publications first blossomed. Even if we allow for categories such as popular music and Hollywood stars, there is still no real comparison to science fiction fanzines until much later — and cultural genealogy points to science fiction fandom as part of the main trunk in the fanzine family tree[3].

Science fiction fans wanted to talk about science fiction, evangelize it to the world, fight over its significance, and even write it. Science fiction fans, in true geek-like fashion, also wanted to show off their knowledge to each other regarding the science, the writers, the stories, the artists, the editors, and the magazines. What better place

---

1 "Come In, The Water's Lovely!" *Slant* #4 - Fall 1950.
2 Joyce Carol Oates: "The King of Weird" *NY Review of Books*, Oct. 31, 1996.
3 John-Henri Holmberg has brought to my attention that other fandom zines were begat by sf fans, including the first mystery fanzine (The *JDM Bibliophile*, started in 1965 by Len & June Moffatt); Marion Zimmer Bradley published early circus fanzines; Philip Bronson put out a comic book zine *Scienti-Comics* in 1940; Lee Hoffmann published the folk song zine *Caravan*; Paul Williams' *Crawdaddy* may have been the first rock zine.

to do this than in their own publications.

Part of the charm of fanmags, as they were first called, was their roughness, born out of sheer economic necessity. The physical imperfections were the by-product of the make-do methods used for printing. (For now, we can overlook literary faults from young, immature editors.)

Early fanmags were produced by carbon paper, by using a hektograph or mimeograph, or, as in Willis' case, a letterpress and woodcuts and metal type. In these pre-digital days, a typewriter wasn't even necessary . . . there have been fanzines completely hand-lettered, and even issued as recordings[4].

The most popular early method was the hektograph. A process involving a gelatinous substance that could offset ink from a special master sheet allowing for the duplication of pages of art and text. This was done with a considerable amount of labor and messiness... like a child playing with untinted jelly and magic markers. In a 1940 editorial for the first issue of his zine *Snide*, Damon Knight wrote, "I firmly refuse to apologize for any of the numerous things that are wrong with this issue. Most of them are the fault of the fellow who invented the hectograph, anyway."[5]

The hekto process had a limitation of about 50 pages duplicated before the pull-off became too faint to read. Many fanmag editors shrugged off that 50 page boundary. Hektography was a cheap process...hence it became the first tool of the trade for cash-strapped young editors. A definite step up was the mimeograph, which was able to make hundreds of copies using a stencil. But it was every fan editor's dream to have their fanmag professionally printed. Very few, as we will see, accomplished this.

The Great Depression and the rise of science fiction fandom ran parallel courses. The first sf fanmag, today recognized as such, appeared in May, 1930. *The Comet* (later, *Cosmology*) was a mimeographed club organ for the Science Correspondence Club (later, International Scientific Association), edited by the ambitious, idiosyncratic teenager Raymond A. Palmer (later, numerous pen-names). Its purpose was to champion science and promote science fiction.

---

4 The earliest, *Shangri-La Record Program*, 1941, by Walt Daugherty — containing music, news notes, and a short spoken article. One copy was made and shared by fans.
5 "Editorially Speaking," Damon Knight, *Snide*, #1, May, 1940.

Two other fanmags, *The Planet* (1930) and *The Time Traveller* (1932), both edited by Allen Glasser, may have a better claim to the title of "first real fan magazine" since they were not directly sponsored by clubs.

The term "fanzine" came much later. In the October, 1940, issue of *Detours,* editor Louis Russell Chauvenet coined the word "fanzine": "We hereby protest against the un-euphonius word 'fanmag' ... and announce our intention to plug 'fanzine' as the best short form of 'fan magazine.'" Some fans pointed out that "fanzine" was longer than "fanmag." There had been some experimentation with "fanag", "fzm", and "fan rag", but "fanzine" won out in the end. It just sounded better to the ear. The first use of the shorter form "zine" (written as 'zine), that I have found, is in the December, 1941 issue of Bob Tucker's *Le Zombie*.

You can find avatars of fanzines in the amateur press associations of the early 20th century. H.P. Lovecraft's writings appeared in fanzines during the 1930s, but long before this he was editor and writer for *The Conservative*, an amateur press association magazine that ran from 1915 to 1923 — but this was not a fanmag or fanzine.

In 1876, America's centennial, the National Amateur Press Association, NAPA, was formed in Philadelphia by a confederation of amateur publishers and printers. Members could publish their own journals, or contribute to already established publications, which were distributed among members. The United Amateur Press Association, UAPA, came later, in 1895...Lovecraft belonged to both APAs. His view of amateur publishing would echo later zine editors, " ... amateur journalism has brought me to a circle of persons among whom I am not altogether an alien — persons who possess scholastic leanings, yet who are not as a body so arrogant with achievement that a struggler is frowned upon."[6] This is the mindset of a science fiction fanzine editor.

APAs flourished within the historical corridor between the advent of the first landline telephone, and the time of the first analog home radio sets. At first it appeared as if amateur press publishing was just a vanity sideline for printers. Literary standards were hit or miss.

If one had the resources one could skip the APAs and go it alone. In England, Virginia Woolf and her husband, Leonard, famously joined the ranks of independent amateur printers and publishers when they

---

6 "What Amateurdom and I Have Done for Each Other," 1921.

bought a tabletop hand press in 1917. They had a difficult time learning how to operate the press, or set type, due to the fact that trade schools only took in students preparing for a career in the printing trade.

Under the banner of various APAs, numerous strains of early amateur periodicals, from poetry and fiction to journalism, were published with names like *Rainbow, Nonpareil, Mercury, Stylate, The Sphinx, Phunny Phellow,* and *The Fossil*. These are not much different from the titles of later sf fanzines.[7] The Fantasy Amateur Press Association (FAPA), was late to the game when it was started in 1937 by a group of young science fiction fanzine editors led by Donald Wollheim, inspired by APAs. In the beginning Wollheim thought that FAPA would become a clearing house for all sf fan publishing, but sf fandom was already too big for a FAPA fief, and the impulses of too many individual zine editors did not jibe with Wollheim's plans.

Part of any confusion between amateur publishing and fanzines is the fact that both share many of the same basic elements: mail distribution, low print-run, and unpaid writers. A fanzine is an amateur magazine, but an amateur magazine is not always a fanzine.

APA journals had "subscribers," referred to as members in good standing. SF fanzine editors used the "build it and they will come" adage, and would routinely exchange, and review, each other's fanzines. FAPA followed the NAPA model to some degree, but severely limited its membership to around 50 (again, being the maximum number of good copies possible from hektography), and had a higher activity requirement for editors.

It seems obvious that a science fiction fanzine must be focused on science fiction. But this is not always true. There have been sf zines that never mention or directly talk about sf. So what is a science fiction fanzine? The best answer I can come up with is: running with the pack, including having a shared point of view, interests, and background in reading — especially science fiction.

A focal point fanzine, which suggests a kind of inner circle for fandom with fruitful exchange and reciprocal sustenance, was mostly a rally point for fans. This was where the buzz was for a time…and fannish love and hate played out. Hence the outrage at AMAZING STORIES editor Raymond Palmer trying to push fantasy as true facts; the taking

---

7 Someone needs to do research on overlooked and forgotten "ladies'" and Afro-American APAs.

of sides when Forry J Ackerman debated Jack Speer over racism; bafflement over John W. Campbell, Jr.'s hyping of Dianetics in ASTOUNDING SCIENCE FICTION; the revelation that Lee Hoffman was a girl — and that a girl could edit a focal point zine; the deathwatch for science fiction in Earl Kemp's *Who Killed Science Fiction?*. Then there were the pro/fan contretemps, but, despite the dust-ups, the parade moved on. Even when professionals (I'm looking at you Horace Gold, Ray Palmer, and John Campbell, Jr.) antagonized fans, fans forgave and forgot.

The first focal point fanzine was *Fantasy Magazine* (1934-1937), which originated as *Science Fiction Digest* (1932-1934), which had incorporated people from the earlier *The Time Traveller* (1932). It printed reviews, essays and fiction by fans and well-known professional authors; had a clean, if staid, letterpress appearance, and used little art. It covered the sf scene by printing details of up-coming contents of the pro mags and fan goings-on. Through the years its influence increased, as did its circulation, from a print run of a few hundred to a high of over two thousand. (Most of which were complimentary copies sent to members of the Science Fiction League.) The latter figure was quite unusual for a fanzine — with letterpress it was just as easy to print a thousand copies as a hundred. One of the main attractions of *Fantasy Magazine* was fiction by writers such as Lovecraft, Clark Ashton Smith, Robert E. Howard, Murray Leinster, and Abraham Merritt.

Other focal point zines after *Fantasy Magazine* were: *The Science-Fiction Collector* (1936–1941), *Imagination!* (1937–1938), *Spaceways* (1938–1942), *Le Zombie* (1938–1975, with long gaps between issues), *Shangri-LA* (1941–1987, a club zine), *The Acolyte* (1942–1946), *Vampire* (1945–1947), *Spacewarp* (1947–1950), *Slant* (1948–1953), *Quandry* (1950–1953), *Vega* (1951–1952), *Psychotic* (1953–1955), *Void* (1954–1962), and *Fanac* (1958–1963). This group was the first tier of important zines, but there was also a second tier made up of: *The Fantasy Fan* (1933–1935), *Scienti-Snaps* (1938–1940), *Voice of the Imagi-Nation* (1939–1947), *Science Fiction Newsletter* (1945–1953), *Skyhook* (1948–1957), *Peon* (1949–1957), *Hyphen* (1952–1965), *Yandro* (1953–1985), and *Innuendo* (1956–1960). We can keep adding tiers, including one-shots like Earl Kemp's *Who Killed Science Fiction?* (1960).

Hugo Gernsback performed a good deed for all of fandom in 1934 when he started the Science Fiction League. Hugo saw science fiction as commerce, not literature. The club was an inexpensive way to get free copy and promo for WONDER STORIES. Gernsback even hired teenage fanzine editor and fan Charles Hornig to run the show. The end result was the effective coming together of fans across the country. The league ran its course after a few years, but fans continued to meet, branch out, and put out fanzines.

The cliquishness of sf fans and a sense of finding kindled spirits drove early sf fandom like hi-octane gasoline. There were lone wolves, like Jerry Siegel's *Science Fiction* (1932), yet most early fanzines were sociable enterprises coming out of Chicago, New York, Philadelphia, Newark, and Los Angeles. All places where fraternizing was hard to avoid. But it is the lone wolf fanzine editor that eventually won the day.

There were women sf fanzine editors, including Lee Hoffman, Marion Zimmer Bradley, Lora Crozetti, Judith Merril, Myrtle Douglas (known as Morojo, and thought, at first, to be an alter ego for Ackerman), and a few others. Edythe Eyde, better known as Tigrina to fandom, was living and going to college in San Fancisco when she began writing letters and sending art to *Voice of the Imagi-nation,* edited by Ackerman and Morojo, and other fanzines. Today she is recognized for publishing the first lesbian zine, *Vice Versa*, in 1947.

But early science fiction fandom was mostly a man's world — and a young, outcast man's world at that. So it is not surprising that sex shows up regularly even while that subject was verboten in the newsstand science fiction magazines. As Bob Tucker wrote in a 1941 issue of *Le Zombie*: "It has long been my contention that Man will eventually reach out to the stars, colonize and populate them without help from Woman whatsoever."[8] Bill Rotsler called sf heroes queer. Walt Willis once said that fanzines were a substitute for sexual activity.

Early fans had few sources for science fiction outside pulp magazines. In the comic pages there was Flash Gordon and Buck Rogers, and a few films in the same vein. These did little to sate fans' appetites, or create new cross-over readers for sf — even if Buck Rogers originated in AMAZING STORIES.

A familiar lament of sf fans, on-going to this day, was the degeneration of science fiction in popular media. "But how in the name of all that is held sacred can scientific fiction ever gain anything while it has as its representatives scientifilms, scienticartoons, and pseudo-

---

8 Tucker, *Le Zombie*, (from *Thing* #1*)*, Spring 1946.

science stories?"[9] Sam Moskowitz asked in 1937. "These items have no connection whatever with true scientific fiction, and they should be eradicated from all magazines professing to publish such literature — especially the fan magazines. This can be done, if you fans will cooperate by boycotting these magazines; if you will refuse to pay to view the horror-packed, mechanically-acted melodramas that pass as 'scientifilms'...." Moskowitz also attacked pulp magazines, like DOCTOR DEATH, DOCTOR OCCULT, THE SPIDER, and popular newsstand magazines, that "... have never before printed a science-fiction story, suddenly blossom out with many pseudo-science features of low grade?"

To early fans it would have seemed farfetched that in a few decades science fiction — pseudo or otherwise — would overwhelm much of the media landscape. Today there are tens of millions of self-professed sci-fi fans worldwide (mostly for film, television, and digital gaming). Back in 1952 fans were amazed when an issue of FANTASTIC, featuring fantasy fiction by Mickey Spillane, sold over 200,000 newsstand copies. This was considered a tremendous sell-through.

At the dawn of fanzines, a typical fanzine editor might live in a small room at a boarding house, in a small town. He might have a job as a movie house projectionist, a local newsman, or shoe salesman. That room was sparsely furnished with a wood frame bed, a slat-back chair, a wobbly table that held his old Olympia typewriter, and a hekto pan. The room has homemade shelves made out of box-wood, holding horizontal stacks of AMAZING STORIES, WEIRD TALES, ASTOUNDING SCIENCE FICTION, and fanzines. If a fire had broken out in the house, and had there been time to save only one thing, our editor would have chosen the collection of fanzines and left everything else to burn.

Of course, the town saw him as odd, a strange fish. Lets say he called his zine *Coelacanth*, after the newly discovered, bizarre, four-limbed fish believed to have been extinct for 400 million years. Our zine editor has become well known within sf fandom. Fans traveling across the country will detour through his small town to visit and talk science fiction. He writes most of the copy in *Coelacanth*, and uses pen names to appear to have a staff of more than one. His small town is ignorant of *Coelacanth*, and our editor has a post office box to keep it that way. Every week our zine editor drives 24 miles north to the nearest "big city" with a full newsstand to buy his sf magazines. This

---

9 Moskowitz: *Amateur Correspondent,* vol., 2, #2, September-October, 1937.

scenario could serve as a potted bio of noted zine editor Bob Tucker, or Harry Warner, Jr.

Today it is hard to believe that the usual print-run of many of the fanzines mentioned here was somewhere between 50 and 150 copies. Even with pass-along, it is not likely that more than 500 people in total read any single issue as it came out. But fanzines drove fandom conversations, more so than pro science fiction magazines.

Robert Lowndes, before becoming a pro editor, once made a bold statement: "...there is not today one single fan mag that is dependent upon the continued existence of professional science fiction and/or fantasy magazines...."[10] This was written in 1940, but could just as well apply to any year within the timeframe covered in this book.

As another critic noted, "Fanzines quite rapidly become about fandom itself . . . . Fandom became a parallel world, where Big Name Fans and new arrivals duked it out in social collisions that sometimes mimicked exactly the kind of high school nastiness from which fandom promised escape."[11]

Up to recently, these zines were hard to get to unless your were a collector. Today many old sf fanzines are turning up online, within university pop-culture archives, and for sale on eBay. They appear to be little more than dusty, stapled sheets of paper ephemera. It would be easy to overlook the wealth of science fiction history, wit, youthful *esprit de corps*, and talent embodied in those aged pages.

We must also keep in mind that the paper used in fanzines was cheap pulp stock, the ink fugitive, and many copies were lost or thrown away. It's a wonder that many fanzines from this period have survived, and this is a testament to the bibliophilism of sf fans.

The pieces reprinted here were selected after combing through nearly four thousand fanzines, in print and online. In all this, a few writers and artists stood out: Robert Bloch, Walt Willis, Terry Carr, Bob Tucker, Richard E. Geis, Marion Zimmer Bradley, Ted White, William Rotsler, and Harry Warner, Jr. It was tempting to reprint only these people,[12] all eyewitnesses to the creation of modern sf, but I also

10 "What Fan Magazines?" by Robert W. Lowndes, *Ad Astra*, vol. 1, #5, January, 1940.
11 Johan Kugelberg, "Science Fiction Fanzines Before the Future Got Broken," September, 26 2014, vice.com.
12 Books reprinting some of these authors would be a worthwhile project. There have been a few collections of fan writings: **Fandom Harvest** by Terry Carr, Laissez Faire Produktion AB, 1986, Sweden; and **The Eighth Stage of Fandom: Selections**

sought pieces that show the playfulness of fans, or the validation of science fiction at a time when it looked like it might not survive.

There is a curious incident when John Campbell, Jr., the editor of ASTOUNDING SCIENCE FICTION, published a story[13] in early 1944 outlining the creation of an atomic bomb a year before Big Boy fell on Hiroshima. The story brought FBI men to Campbell's office asking tough questions. Campbell was able to placate the agents by explaining that science fiction was known for far-fetched scientific extrapolations, and the avoidance of stories using publicly available atomic science would be a bigger tip-off to any secret atomic program.

But the G-Men must have missed the August 1941 issue of the fanzine *Fanfare* (out four months before Pearl Harbor) where it was reported that Campbell told a group of fans, "...that the present [European] war is likely to be decided by atomic power. He declared it to be a fact that the U.S. War Dept. has taken over all the cyclotrons in the country in an effort to speed up the discovery, and that all countries possessing cyclotrons are doing the respective same."

Pro sf magazine editors read fanzines. It is there where some of them realized how little they knew about science fiction or its fans.[14] Fanzines spoke with bare-bones immediacy and knowledge, and deployed more raw candor than pro sf magazines were used to seeing. Or as Donald A. Wollheim put it, "By what right ... did incompetents edit [pro] magazines of this specialized field? ... [editors] who may be experts at general pulp editing, but whose knowledge of science fiction didn't equal that of the 35th top fan .... " It took a while for sf fans to find out how much influence they had, or could have.[15]

from 25 Years of Fan Writing by Robert Bloch, (edited by Earl Kemp, with introduction by Wilson Tucker), Advent: Publishers, 1962, Chicago.
13 "Deadline" by Clive Cartmill, ASTOUNDING SCIENCE FICTION, March, 1944.
14 There is also the story of the editors Al and Abby Lu Ashley of *Nova* sending a complimentary copy of the first issue of their zine to FAMOUS FANTASTIC MYSTERIES editor Mary Gnaedinger and getting it returned with a rejection slip thanking them for the privilege of reading their manuscript but it wasn't quite suited to their needs. The editors of *Nova* then rejected the rejections and mailed everything back to FFM (reported in *Nova*, #3, Winter 1942-1943). It should be noted that Gnaedinger did go to fan meetings around NYC, and did understand what fanzines were, so an assistant editor may be responsible for the zine/manuscript confusion. "Editor Meets Fandom" by Mary Gnaedinger, *Sun Spots,* vol. 5, #17, April, 1941.
15 Donald A. Wollheim (1914-1990), *Spaceways*, vol. 3, #4, May, 1941. Written a few months after he became a pro editor at Albing Publications, overseeing COSMIC STORIES and STIRRING SCIENCE STORIES.

Many fans saw sf as entertainment, some saw sf as a refuge, more than a few saw sf as a calling. Eventually they would take over. Lovecraft could have been the first, had he not turned down the editorship of WEIRD TALES in 1924. I will name just a few fanzine kids turn pro: Ray Bradbury, Robert Silverberg, James Blish, Judith Merril, Harlan Ellison, Ray Palmer, Wilson (Bob) Tucker, Julius Schwartz, Donald A. Wollheim, Hannes Bok, Charles Hornig, Robert W. Lowndes, Larry Shaw, Frederik Pohl, Greg Benford, Arthur C. Clarke Algis Budrys, Bob Shaw, Sam Moskowitz, Jack Gaughan, Ted White, Earl Kemp, Marion Zimmer Bradley, Terry Carr, Charles Beaumont, and Damon Knight.

Was it worth the many hours of application building a zine? I think that many zine editors, looking back, would agree that it was. There was a time when you could wow your peers by putting out a good fanzine. Fans knew that editing a popular zine would gain them glory. For a young fan becoming a self-made publisher was quite a boost to the ego,[16] especially when letters and submissions arrived from really big name fans. Ackerman and Warner always encouraged rank beginners. They knew that many fan stars began with laughably bad zines.

Why should we care about these seemingly marginal zines? Are they not just fleeting, sub-pop cultural artifacts? Well, for one thing, science fiction has always been about more than the literature. The common task of these zines, of fifty or more years ago, whether they were run by savants, indigents, eccentrics, outsiders, brawlers, insurgents, or posers, is easy to convey. This was a parish where everyone knew one another and were equally involved in constituting science fiction from the inside out. Or as one sf guru put it: "Underneath all that shoptalk something very important spiritually may be going on."[17]

By 1960, the year in which Xerox introduced its first commercial copy machine, we can see the beginning of the diversification of fanzines. The late 1950s newsstand crash of science fiction magazines seemed to have pushed many mature fans to FAPA, or into creating new sf and fantasy APAs. Young people were getting the fanzine bug via comic books, monster movies, and rock music. Though there were a lot more science fiction zines to come, the golden age of focal point sf fanzines was over.

---

16 AKA "egoboo" in fan talk.
17 Kurt Vonnegut, Jr., "Afterthoughts: Who Killed Science Fiction?" *SaFari*, May, 1960, ed. Earl Kemp.

NOTE ON THE TEXT

FOR CLARITY, the names of fanzines are set in italics, while pro magazines (periodicals with nationwide newsstand distribution) are all caps. So *Imagination!* and IMAGINATION are two different publications with the same name. The first is a fanzine, the latter is a newsstand, pro magazine. The titles of books will be set in bold italics. For the most part, I have tried to keep the idiosyncratic spelling and syntax of many fanzine writers intact. Zine writers and editors would routinely make up words and acronyms (stf originally stood for scientifiction — nothing else), use fandom slang, and abridge commonplace words. Forrest J Ackerman, in his writings, would throw in bits of Esperanto, a language he thought could replace all languages.

Also for the purpose of this book, in general, when I say science fiction I am also talking about the genres of fantasy and horror, or weird fiction, as horror was called throughout the time period covered here[18]. This follows the way many sf fanzines were edited. Fanzine editors knew the boundaries of the various genres, but didn't always care about them. A fan of Robert Heinlein could also be an enthusiast of Lovecraft. In the first issue of *The Fantasy Fan*, September, 1933, Ackerman took issue with combining science fiction and weird fiction in that fanzine. Clark Ashton Smith responded in the following issue, "... Ackerman considers horror, weirdness and unearthliness beyond the bounds of science or science fiction...let me recommend to Mr. Ackerman, and to others like him, a more scientifically open and receptive attitude of imagination. If Mr. Ackerman were transported to some alien world, I fear that he would find the reality far more incredible, bizarre, grotesque, fantastic, horrific, and impossible than any of my stories ..."

This book is directed more at non-fans than fans, but science fiction fans are welcomed. There are many things that I did not get a chance to cover, but this is the first in a series of books that I am preparing about zines. Hopefully, I will get to tell more of science fiction fanzine history in volumes to come.

---

18 Today the term fantastika (promoted by John Clute) is use to cover these genres.

ACKNOWLEDGEMENTS

THIS BOOK would not be possible without the following people, my thanks to all: Nick Certo, Andy Porter, Ned Brooks, Greg & Jim Benford, Laura Freas Beraha, Rich Henshaw, Shelby Vick, Robert Lichtman for some hard to find pieces, Ted White, Joel Nydahl, Joe Siclari, Robert A. Madle, Gary Ross Hoffman, and Robert Silverberg. Special thanks to John-Henri Holmberg and Earl Kemp for reading and commenting on proofs of this book in progress. Extra special thanks and love, as ever, to Karan for everything else.

It has become easier to find fanzines online due to the efforts of sites like fanac.org, eFanzines.com, and the Iowa Digital Library of the University of Iowa, Special Collections Department, Rusty Hevelin Collection of Science Fiction. While nothing will ever take the place of reading an actual paper zine, these online resources are the next best thing. But there are quite a few universities around the country that have collections of old zines, and a visit to one of these repositories will reward you many times over.

The cover art is from *Voice of the Imagi-Nation*, #35 (1944). In that issue editor Forrest J Ackerman writes, "Our cover is a reproduction of the cover for CUENTOS Y NOVELAS, Mexican mag, issue of 21 Nov., 1940, illustrating the feature fantasy novel in Spanish, 'Flor de la Perlas' ('Flower of the Pearls')." No name is given for the artist.

Science Fiction, #3, 1933, cover art by Joe Shuster. Editor Jerome Siegel was inspired by *The Time Traveller*. This was the first time "science fiction" was used in a title of any periodical. Siegel had an even earlier hectographed zine, the one-shot *Cosmic Stories*, published before *Science Fiction*, and also made up of sf stories written by him. Five years later Shuster and Siegel created Superman.

BEHIND THE ZINE

Science fiction has had many midwives, beginning with Verne and Wells, followed by Hugo Gernsback (1884-1967), publisher of the first true sf magazine AMAZING STORIES, and John W. Campbell, Jr. (1910-1971), editor of ASTOUNDING SCIENCE FICTION. But there is also a fan pantheon to which must be added high on the list the name of Forrest J (no period, as was his preference, the J stands for James) Ackerman (1916-2008), a superfan and tireless promoter of sf, who seemed to have been involved in every aspect of the rise of American sf fandom. Ackerman wore the first costume at the first sf Worldcon in 1939, published Ray Bradbury's first story and edited the early L.A. zines *Imagination!*, and *Voice of the Imagi-Nation*, and the iconic monster movie magazine FAMOUS MONSTERS OF FILMLAND. Ackerman is even credited with coining the term sci-fi (he thought that if high fidelity could be shortened to hi-fi then science fiction...), a term deemed by many hard-core fans an "abomination" (author Harlan Ellison most likely first to the gate with this label[19]), and met with derision within sf fandom to this day, but "sci-fi" is still around. Of course, Ackerman was also involved in the very first sf fanzine. —LO

THE FIRST FAN MAGAZINE

Forrest J Ackerman

(from The Fanscient *#2, 1948, ed. Donald Day)*

THE TIME Traveller[20], Vol. 1, No. 1, dated January 1932, was the first of the true fan magazines. Prior to the appearance of this modest mimeographed periodical there had been semi-fanzines such as *The Comet* and *The Planet*, but these were more in the nature of club organs

---

19 Per Ray Nelson in *Trap Door* #23; Dec., 2004, ed. Robert Litchman.
20 Its tagline was "Science Fiction's only fan magazine."

(The Science Correspondence Club and the Scienceers, respectively) than publications aimed at a national audience of unorganized fans.

Creators of the original fan magazine were Mort Weisinger, later for a period to be an editor of THRILLING WONDER STORIES and its companion publications; Allen Glasser, one-time actifan who finally faded from the fan scene; Julius Schwartz, the original science fiction agent; and myself.

The first issue of our historic little publication consisted of but 6 pages, mineoed on one side of the sheet and stingily fastened with but a single staple. Our editorial concluded,"In view of this wide current popularity of Science Fiction, it was deemed advisable to launch a magazine treating all the varied phases of the subject and appealing to the interests of its many devotees. And so came into being *The Time Traveller* —the first and only Science Fiction *fan* magazine.

Featured was a list of all then-known "Scienti-films," and impressive total (for 15 years ago) of 34 titles; a biography of Capt. (later Major) S.P. Meek, an early WONDER contributor; an interview with Bob Olson, another old WONDER standby; news-notes on the stf[21] in production by Flagg, Farley, Leinster, Schachner & Zagat and other fictioneers; a department of Questions and Answers; an article about Otis Adelbert Kline's "Planet of Peril"; and installment of "The History of Science-Fiction" by Mortimer Weisinger; "A day at WEIRD TALES"[22] by Jack (top fan of the time) Darrow; a concealed names poeticontest; and some amazing ads offering at 50 cents apiece, excerpted stf serials, which today are commanding anywhere up to eight times the price.

Undoubtedly the most important article to appear in TTT's pages, was Weisinger's 8-part "History of S-F." "A bit about a Banana" by Allen Glasser vied with the same author's "Looking Forward" as the most entertaining tidbit published in our pages (which later were printed rather than mineoed). Both Follow:

A BIT ABOUT A BANANA (AS CERTAIN WRITERS MIGHT DO IT)

RAY CUMMINGS: This fruit — so strange! Yellow it is, with brown spots. Thick of skin and solid to the touch. Might it be edible? It seemed so. And yet—better to leave it untouched.

---
21 For the longest time science fiction was abbreviated as stf.
22 Iconic pulp magazine that regularly published stories by H.P. Lovecraft, Robert E. Howard, Robert Bloch, and Ray Bradbury.

DAVID H. KELLER: What's a banana anyway? Just an ordinary sort of fruit, tasty but not too easy to digest. While it is undoubtedly superior to wilted lettuce in food value, it is hardly the thing for a regular diet.

JOHN W. CAMPBELL, JR.: Consisting as it does of multiple equilateral surfaces possessing a specific gravity which need not be mentioned here, the banana presents a most interesting study in applied thermo-dynamics.

EDGAR RICE BURROUGHS: Bananas—bah! They are but dainty tidbits for effete over-civilized weaklings; nor would a real man have aught to do with them. Far better the solid meat of the coconut, a fruit worthy of the name.

CLARK ASHTON SMITH: Xantie, mottled with ochre—luscious as a lover's lips, sweet as a siren's song—Who could resist a ripe banana? —Allen Glasser

LOOKING FORWARD

Some future day, time travelers say,
We'll get our food in pills;
Our hair will go, our ears will grow,
We even may sprout gills.

Our clothes will change to garments strange
That now would cause derisions;
And there will be no privacy
Because of television.
From riding much in cars and such,
Our legs will fade away.
We'll never walk, and seldom talk;
At least, that's what they say.

Some people might, with much delight,
Prefer this future sphere;
But as for me, I say wit glee;
"I'm glad I shan't be here!"
—Allen Glasser

The Time Traveller was published for 9 numbers before being combined in November, 1932 with *Science Fiction Digest*.

The Comet, #1, May, 1930. Most early science fiction fanzines like *The Comet*, *The Time Traveller*, and *Fantasy Magazine* used all-type/lettered covers and little art. Jerry Siegel's friendship with Cleveland, Ohio, schoolmate Joe Shuster allowed their zine *Science Fiction* to have more of a visual impact, but we have to wait for the latter half of the 1930s before illustrated covers on sf fanzines became a commonplace sight.

BEGINNINGS

The following piece presents a round-up of sf fanzines extant up to the Spring of 1937. It also lists phantom fanzines heard of but not seen (see "The Versatile Jim Blish" pg. 43). Even at this early date there was a mushrooming proliferation of sf fanmags. The term fanzine did not appear until the 1940s. *The 14 Leaflet*[23] (1935–1937), where this piece originates, was the club zine for the Chicago Science Fiction Club, formally the Chicago chapter of the Science Fiction League[24]. This period of fanzine activity cooled off during WWII, then took off again after the war. — LO

H.A. Dittmans, Jr. & W.H. Dellenback

(from The 14 Leaflet, *vol. 1, #9, Spring 1937,
eds. Walter L. Dennis & W.H. Dellenback)*

FOR THOSE who collect sf amateur publications, as an adjunct to their professional sf collection, we offer this article as an aid. There have been such numbers of these fan mags, as they are called, published in the last few years — the majority mimeographed and hectographed[25], and some few printed — that it is hard to keep track of them. So many of them fold their tents after a few months, as the silent Arabs did, and quietly steal away. We realize that this list is neither complete nor perfectly accurate.

Back in 1930 and 1931 we find the beginner of them all, the

---

23 It had the unique characteristic of having its pages sewn together.
24 See "From the Valley of the Blue Moon," pg. 75.
25 Mimeography entailed printing with ink forced through a wax or plastic stencil cut with a typewriter or stylus. Hectography used special paints and pencils to transfer text and images to a bed of gelatin, then copies can be produced by laying on and pulling off sheets of paper from the gelatin.

large mimeographed *Cosmology*, organ of the *original* International Scientific Association, which began in June 1930 as the *Science Correspondence Club Organ*.

In Jan. 1931, Allen Glasser launched the famous *The Time Traveller*, printed except for issues 1 and 2. After 8 issues, in Sept. 1932, it became *The Science Fiction Digest*, headed in turn by Maurice Z. Ingher, Conrad H. Ruppert, and Julius Schwartz. The name was changed to *Fantasy Magazine* with Jan. 1933 issue. And now, after 39 issues, the best known one of them all has suspended publication.

Jerome Siegel[26] of Cleveland put out 5 issues of *Science Fiction* — mimeographed, Oct. 1932, 1st issue, devoted mainly to stories, 15 cents. A mimeographed story, "Guests of the Earth", preceded the first issue.

We know, too, of William Crawford's *Marvel Tales* and *Unusual Stories*, most pretentious of amateur magazines, issued during 1934 and 1935, 5 of the former and 2 of the latter so far, printed. Mr. Crawford hopes to place a sixth issue of *Marvel* on the newsstands in the fall.

The following are now defunct —

Brooklyn Reporter, G.G. Clark, Brooklyn SFL,[27] Feb. 1935 1st Issue,
  5 issues, mimeographed 10¢
Arcturus, East NY SFL and later Ind. League for S-F, Dec. 1935 1st issue,
  mimeographed 10¢.
The D'Journal, Bob Tucker's SPWSSTFM[28] bulletin, Spring 1935 only,
  mimeographed.
The Polymorphanucleated Leucocyte, Wollheim's anti-SPWSSTFM
  bulletin, a one-sheet affair, mimeographed.
Astonishing Stories, D.A. Wollheim, May 1935 only, hectographed.
Fanciful Tales, D.A. Wollheim and Wilson Shepherd,
  Fall 1936 only, printed 20¢
The Planeteer, Jim Blish, Nov. 1935 1st issue, mimeographed 10¢.
Fantasy Fiction Telegram, John Baltadonis, ?
*The Science Fiction New*s, Dan McPhail, Dec. 1935 1st issue, Oct., Nov.,
  and Dec. 1936 issues were printed and mimeographed 10¢

---

26 Another contributor to Jerry Siegel's fanzine was artist Joe Shuster. The pair would go on to create Superman for ACTION COMICS.
27 Science Fiction League.
28 SPWSSTFM (Society for the Prevention of Wire Staples in Science Fiction Magazines), a mock group that created a fake feud among fans.

Doings of the Lincoln, SFL, 3 issues during 1935, mimeographed.
The Purple Flash, D.A. Wollheim, MY SFL, May 1935 only, hectographed.
The Ink Blot, for Erie SFL members only, 1935.
S-F Review, R.M. Holland, hectographed

The following are still being issued —
The Fourteen Leaflet, Chicago SFL, Nov. 1935 1st issue, 5¢ thru issue 8.
The Phantagraph, D.W. Wollheim, July-Aug., 1935 vol. 4, no.1, before that
    Bulletin of the Terrestrial Fantascience Guild, mimeographed 5¢.
The International Observer, Int. Cosmos Science Club now termed ISA,
    June-July 1935 was vol. 1, no. 10, 1st issue ?, John B, Michel,
    mimeographed 10¢
The Science Fiction Critic, Claire P. Buck, Nov. 1935 1st issue,
    1st issue called *S-F Review*, 1st 2 issues mimeo, rest printed, 10¢.
Novae Terrae, Nuneaton SFL, March 1936 1st issue, mimeographed 5¢.
Scientifiction, Walter H. Gillings Jan. 1937 1st issue, printed 5¢.
Science-Fantasy Correspondent, Willis Conover, Dec. 1936 1st issue,
    printed 10¢.
The Science Fiction Fan, Olon F. Wiggins, July 1936 1st issue, 10¢,
    First 4 were printed, rest hectographed.
Tessaract, C. Hamilton Bloomer, SFAA, April 1936 1st issue,
    mimeographed 10¢.
Science Fiction Digest, Dollens, section in Collector #7,
    Jan. 1937 1st issue.
The Phantasy World, D.A. Kyle, April 1937 1st issue, hectographed 10¢.
Helios, Sam Moskowitz, June 1937 1st issue, printed 5¢.
*Mind of Ma*n, Harry Dockweiler, ?

The following have announced but have not yet appeared —
Fantascience Digest, John Baltadonis
The Science Fiction World, H.S. Kirby, 10¢
The Mutant, Harry Dockweiler
The Atom, Richard Wilson, Jr., 10¢ (2 issues appeared, the last in
    May 1937)
Fantasia, Geo. R. Hahn, 5¢
Phantastique, Bill Miller, 5¢.

The following titles have been seen at times, but no magazines

have ever been published to our knowledge —
Comment, Superfluous Stories, The Comet, Supra-Mundane Stories, Phantasmagoria, Fantasy Mirror, New Zealand S-F Bulletin, Curious, Odd, Fantastic, Bewildering, Nova, and *Grotesque*.

In the above list: H – hectographed, M – mimeographed, P – printed. The prices were the publications values.

The Science Fiction Collector, #10, January, 1937, edited by Morris Dollens Jr., who created early issues by hand-lettering all the text. Dollens also did most of the art.

The Science Fiction Fan, vol. 4, #10, whole #46, May, 1940; cover art by James M. Rogers. *SFF* was edited by Olon F. Wiggins and ran for 55 issues between 1936 and 1941.

Futura Fantasia, #4, Spring 1940; edited by Ray Bradbury; cover art by Hannes Bok.

ART & ZINES

In the following piece Ray Bradbury tells the story of his first meeting with artist Hannes Bok (1914-1964) and subsequent "agenting" of his art work. Bok quickly became a popular pro artist, and sometimes writer, in the sf field. It's very likely that Bok would have broken through into pro ranks on his own, but Bradbury was there to give him an early head start. Bok did most of the artwork for the four issues of Bradbury's fanzine *Futuria Fantasia*. Keep in mind that Bradbury was unknown, and unpublished, at this point. Mentioned in this piece is Forrest J Ackerman (editor of *VOM*), who paid for Bradbury's trip to New York City. —LO

BOK ON THE FANTASY SCENE

Ray Bradbury

(from Le Zombie *#18, December 1939, ed. Bob Tucker)*

I MET HANS in L.A. about Christmas time in 1937. I knew him for three days. He showed me his paintings, we played chess together and enjoyed each others company immeasurable for those short days. Then he went north to Seattle. We Corresponded for a year and a half, two years, until early last Spring when I found out I was going to Manhattan for the [First World SF, 1939} Convention. I wrote Hans and told him this was the chance he needed; to make up six or eight paintings and pen and ink sketches for me to tote along with me to my destination. He agreed and painted. The paintings arrived in Los Angeles about a week before my trip. I packed them in my suitcase and off I went, finally ending up by speaking with Campbell, who like them very much, and Weisinger at THRILLING WONDER STORIES who also liked them

Then on Friday morning in July I went up to Wright at *Weird Tales* with the paintings. My heart was jammed halfway up my throat. Mrs.

Wright, bless her soul, liked them right off, and so did Farnsworth [Wright, the editor of WEIRD TALES]. He looked up at Mrs. Wright and said, "Well, do you think we ought to give the boy a chance?" She nodded. And I jumped, really, for joy and practically pounded the back off Ackerman who had gone along. Wright explained that he had found [Virgil] Finlay in much the same manner, out of town.

So Wright told me he would contact Hans in a few days for some illustrations. He gave me a couple of Finlay drawings and I hurried off to my hotel and wrote Hans a happy (and I do mean happy!) message. Then, a week .... two weeks later, I routed my bus trip up thru Seattle and arrived there early one Friday morning in late July. Hans was waiting at the station for me and it was a grand reunion. We talked about everything; art, science, books. He took me to his apartment and showed me the stacks of paintings he had. It was there that I received my drawings and promises for more, for *Futuria Fantasia*. And it was there that I saw a painting called "Psycho-analysis", worth approximately fifty dollars, that Hans is now completing to send me as my "agent's fee." I can hardly wait for it to arrive from New York.

I spent the whole day with Hans and at midnight left for San Francisco. The next Monday he left for New York.

He's in New York now doing another cover for WEIRD TALES for the February issue, and some interior illustrations. I got a letter from Wright the other day and he shares my exuberance for Bok's work. Here are his exact words: "If you think the first cover by Bok was good, wait until you see his February cover. I only hope the printers can match its beauty."

Only issue of *Bizarre* (formerly *Scienti-Snaps*), Jan., 1941; edited by Jack Chapman Miske & Walter E. Marconette; cover art by Hannes Bok. **Previous page**, *Futura Fantasia* #4, Spring 1940; art by Hannes Bok.

FANZINE GENESIS

These reminiscences of the very early days of fandom and fanzines is by Robert Madle, born in 1920, and at the time of this writing still with us. Here Madle gives us a lucid explanation of how hektography works. He is well known in fandom as a bookseller, and edited *Fantascience Digest* and *Fantasy Fiction Telegram* in the 1930s.—LO

 MY PAL JOHNNY

Robert A. Madle

(from Mimosa *#23, Jan., 1999, ed. Nicki & Rich Lynch)*

JOHN V. Baltadonis, one of the most active fans of the late 1930s, died of lung cancer in July 1998. He was 77 years old. John was born in Philadelphia, in February 1921, and resided in that area all of his life, except for 3½ years in the Army during WWII. Prior to this, he obtained a degree in Art from Temple University and, after the war, supplemented it with a Masters in Fine Art from the Tyler School of Art.

Johnny and I met in first grade at the Vaughn School, in the Kensington section of Philadelphia. We lived within a city block of each other and became the best of friends. This was 1927, during prohibition, and Johnny's father ran a 'speak easy' where beer and liquor was dispensed. It was a very large house, and I have fond memories of all the games we played there.

Both of us, apparently, had learned to read before starting first grade and we soon discovered boys' books. We were friendly rivals in most things we did from the beginning and thus it was we both assembled a worthy collection of such titles as **The Outdoor Chums**, **The Battleship Boys**, and **The Grammar School Boys**. These were the first items we ever collected and those books meant a lot to both of us.

Time went by and soon it was 1930. Several events of "great

importance" occurred. Buck Rogers began to run in January 1930, Tarzan of the Apes appeared in the comics section of "The Evening Bulletin", and a movie was released that shook us to our very foundations – "Just Imagine", starring El Brendel. It was a musical, as were most of the 'talkies' of that early period, but this movie took place in 1980, fifty years in the future! In reality, we had become science fiction fans already.

Johnny was tall, blonde, blue-eyed and handsome, even as a pre-teenager. And he always had to be first in all our activities. So, as he was able to obtain money from his parents (which was a rarity in those days), he had the best boys' book collection, the best chemistry set, the best set of skates. And when he discovered Edgar Rice Burroughs, he was able to buy new books from the bookstores! (They cost all of 99 cents each!) But he let me read them as long as I kept them in perfect condition. I remember that, when reading those pristine copies, I would always remove the dust wrappers.

Then, in early 1931, we discovered S-F magazines. We were in a local junk shop when Johnny found two copies of WONDER STORIES, with marvelous Frank R. Paul covers on them – the December 1930 issue, featuring "The Synthetic Man" by Ed Earl Repp and the April 1931 issue, featuring "The Man Who Evolved" by Edmond Hamilton. Wow! Were we impressed! But we didn't know where to get other issues (remember, we were only nine years old) and it wasn't until the spring of 1933 that we discovered back-date magazines stores and the S-F magazines. And, beginning with the January 1934 issues, we were able to purchase them from the newsstands (this was very neatly accomplished by the method known as "not eating lunch" – and spending our Junior High School lunch money, 15 cents a day, on S-F mags). But back issues were only five cents each (six for a quarter) and we both amassed our early collections in this manner. By this time, Jack Agnew, who is my cousin, joined us and we became a trio. Jack had no choice but to become an S-F fan, too.

In April of 1934, Hugo Gernsback started the Science Fiction League in the pages of WONDER STORIES. This was probably the most important event ever to occur from the viewpoint of S-F and, particularly, S-F fandom. SFL chapters sprang up world-wide. One of these was the Philadelphia SFL, organized by Milton A. Rothman, with the first meeting occurring in January 1935. We attempted to contact

Rothman but received no answer so we assumed he felt we were too juvenile. Little did we realize that Rothman was just a year or so older than us. So, about this same time, we organized the Boys' SF Club, consisting of John Baltadonis, Jack Agnew, Harvey Greenblatt, and me. And we actually produced a 'fan mag', as they were called then, titled T*he Science Fiction Fan*. It was carbon-copied (there were only two or three copies), and featured some S-F magazine reviews plus a short story, "The Atom Smasher" by Donald Wandrei, which was copied from a 1934 ASTOUNDING STORIES. But also featured were the first illustrations by John Baltadonis. They were acceptable – I thought they were excellent – but they gave no hint of the John's latent talent that would propel him to the top of the fan field and make him known as 'The Frank R. Paul of the Fan Artists'.

In 1935, John and I both had letters published in AMAZING STORIES and this time Rothman contacted us! We brought our Boys' SF Club to his home and the first reorganizational meeting of the Philadelphia SFL was held with our group plus Rothman, his fan friend Raymond Peel Mariella, Oswald Train (who had just moved to Philadelphia), and a couple of others who never showed up again.

Baltadonis, Agnew, and I had been working on another carbon-copied fan mag, called *Imaginative Fiction*. After attending the first PSFL meeting, we added a couple of pages and Baltadonis did a remarkable cover (for a 14-year-old). And he had to do it twice, as we made two copies (there were no Xerox machines then!). The three of us then decided we were going to publish a printed fan mag, like *Fantasy Magazine*, to be titled *Fantascience Digest*. We actually bought a press, but had no idea how to set type – and we didn't have any type, anyway! It had taken all we could beg, borrow, or steal to buy the press, so getting type would be another day. But all was not lost; that very week we received in the mail the initial issue of Morris Scott Dollens' *The Science Fiction Collector*, certainly one of the most amateurish fan mags published to that time. It was hand-written – not even typed – but it had illustrations and they were in a blue color! We found out it was done by a process called hektography.

Baltadonis managed to get some more money, did a little research, and called Agnew and I to come over one day to observe his new publishing equipment. We arrived to find that his 'publishing house' consisted of a pound of gelatin, a large rectangular cake pan, a purple typewriter ribbon, and a small jar of blue ink. The gelatin was heated until it became liquid, and was poured into the cake pan and allowed to harden. The typed page was placed face down on the gelatin and allowed to remain for a few minutes until the gelatin absorbed the purple ink, and then removed. A sheet of typewriter paper was then very carefully placed on the gelatin, pressed slightly and pulled off. Eureka! There was a marvelous reproduction of the purple-typed page. With luck, this could be repeated about 50 or even 60 times; thus was born the era of the hektographed fan magazine.

Philadelphia's first fan mag (not counting the carbon-copied ones) was called *Fantasy Fiction Telegram*; it was dated October 1936 and was about 20 half-size pages, all in purple, with blue illustrations, all by Baltadonis, and material by the local group plus an article by the leading fan of the time, Donald A. Wollheim. The original Baltadonis hektographed artwork didn't even begin to suggest the prolific talent he would display in the near future.

John made more trips to the store – the gelatin was called 'Ditto' by the way – and made an amazing discovery, one that would ultimately make him an immortal of early fandom: hektographed ink was available in many colors! From an artistic viewpoint, the possibilities were astounding. The third issue of *FFT* appeared in many colors, and Baltadonis received rave reviews of his artwork (the cover and all interiors). But *FFT* lasted only one more issue, the fifth issue never being completed.

Morris Dollens published the *Science Fiction Collector* for 13 issues, through June 1937 when Dollens announced that would be the last issue. But it wasn't really the last issue. A 14th issue (dated July 1937) appeared and what an issue it was! Sam Moskowitz described it in **The Immortal Storm** as follows:

"In late August of 1937, the first issue of the new *Science Fiction Collector* appeared under the editorship of Baltadonis and staffed by Train, Madle, and Moskowitz. The result set the fan world agog and unified its struggling remnants. For Baltadonis had done the near-impossible; not only was *Collector* ahead of the old insofar as quality of material was concerned, but Dollens' hektography had actually been surpassed. Some of the most important names of fandom were contributors, and in the space of one issue, the *Science Fiction Collector* became the leading representative fan journal."

Sam could have added that the Baltadonis artwork was extremely impressive – and "all in color for a dime." It was at this junction that fandom almost universally recognized Baltadonis as the premier fan artist. Morris Scott Dollens had introduced the varied-colored hektograph fan mag but Baltadonis perfected it. He was not only outstanding in the handling of color and the mechanistic aspects of illustrating – he was also a master of 'figure study', as the following anecdote shows.

Back in 1935, when we graduated from Penn Treaty Junior High School, we had read a letter in WONDER or AMAZING STORIES from Philadelphia fan Raymond Peel Mariella, who mentioned that one of his teachers was an S-F writer who taught at Central High School. We also had read a letter from a Philadelphia writer named Stephen G. Hale who had several stories in AMAZING STORIES, and who was also a high school teacher. It had to be the same writer, we assumed, and both of us attempted to attend Central – to no avail. "You go to Northeast," we were told, and so we did.

But on the first day of art class, we were amazed to realize that Stephen G. Hale (author of "The Laughing Death" and "World's Apart") was our art teacher! He told us he had several other stories awaiting publication (AMAZING STORIES) – but they never appeared. Anyway, one of our first assignments was 'figure study'. So far as drawing was concerned, I was as bad as Baltadonis was good. We came to the deadline, and I hadn't finished the assignment. "Not to worry," said the over-accommodating Baltadonis, "I'll do an extra one and give it to you at class." But it turned out to be a scantily-clad figure study of a female band leader named Ina Ray Hutton. She was drawn wearing short tight pants, and John made sure he disguised nothing. I turned it in and, in the next art period, Hale yelled out, "Madle! Come up here!" I stepped forward in fear and trepidation because I knew he was going to accuse me of turning in someone else's work. But that wasn't it at all – he was extremely angry that I had turned in this "piece of pornography" and that he was considering sending me and the drawing down to the principal's office. But he relented – perhaps because we had discovered his stories a few days earlier.

JVB, as Baltadonis became known in fandom, not only edited and published one of the leading fan journals of this period, but he also conceived of Comet Publications, which comprised all of the fan journals published by the Philadelphia group. At one time, circa 1938-39,

Comet Publications comprised about 15 different fan mags. (It should be mentioned that the 1936-41 fandom was so small that some active fans used only initials. In addition to JVB, there was DAW [Wollheim], FJA [Ackerman], MAR [Rothman], RWL [Lowndes], and RAM [Madle].)

JVB was one of the attendees at the October 1936 meeting in Philadelphia when the New York group came to visit the Philadelphia group. This became known as the 'First S-F Convention', partly because, during the official meeting, Donald A. Wollheim suggested it. JVB was active in producing the annual Philadelphia conference and in helping produce Nycon in 1939 – the First World S-F Convention.

JVB's activity in the 1936-41 period was amazing. He did everything a fan could do – he wrote, illustrated, collected, corresponded, wrote to magazines, organized and attended conventions. During the years 1937-40, he was always voted one of the top fans in the world. In fact, in 1938 and 1939 he was elected as Number One Fan. And this was during the times that active fandom consisted of such as Ackerman, Bradbury, Wollheim, Moskowitz, Tucker, Pohl, Lowndes, and other great names.

Seventeen issues of *The Science Fiction Collector* appeared under JVB's editorship from 1937-41. It was a treasure-trove of early S-F and fandom, beautifully illustrated in multi-color. The final issue was dated Winter 1941 and marked the end of JVB's tenure as an active fan; in reality, the start of World War II in December 1941 marked the end of the grandest of all fan periods.

After the war, Baltadonis rejoined the PSFS for a while, but upon starting graduate work, drifted into inactivity. He did illustrate the Program Book for the Philcon of 1947 and, in 1948, did the dust wrapper and illustrations for New Era's only book, "The Solitary Hunters" and "The Abyss" by David H. Keller. Despite his S-F illustrating talent, he appeared professionally only once when Lowndes reprinted "The Abyss" in MAGAZINE OF HORROR in the 1960s. But his entire career was art-oriented – he taught art in Haverford, Pennsylvania school system for 35 years, then became art programs coordinator for the district until his health forced him to retire.

Our paths crossed occasionally during the late `40s and early `50s when I was attending Drexel University. In 1953 I moved to Charlotte, North Carolina, and later to Washington, D.C., and we rarely made contact. However, beginning in the early `80s, Agnew, John, and I attended Philcons and PSFS Founders' Day dinners, and it was like the old days again. At the Philcons and dinners, John's wife Pat, my wife Billie, and Agnew's wife Agnes learned more than they wanted to when discussions of the old days came up.

John always retained his interest in S-F. He went from reader to collector to fan and back to reader. Fan history will certainly show him as one of the most important members of the 1936-41 period of fandom. (Just look at the indexes of Moskowitz's *The Immortal Storm* and Warner's *All Our Yesterdays* and this becomes quite evident.) It's difficult to accept that John V. Baltadonis is gone – but the memories of the friendship and the numerous hobbies, interests, and activities we shared, will be remembered forever.

Science Fiction Collector, vol. 4, #4; October/November, 1938; cover art by John Baltadonis.

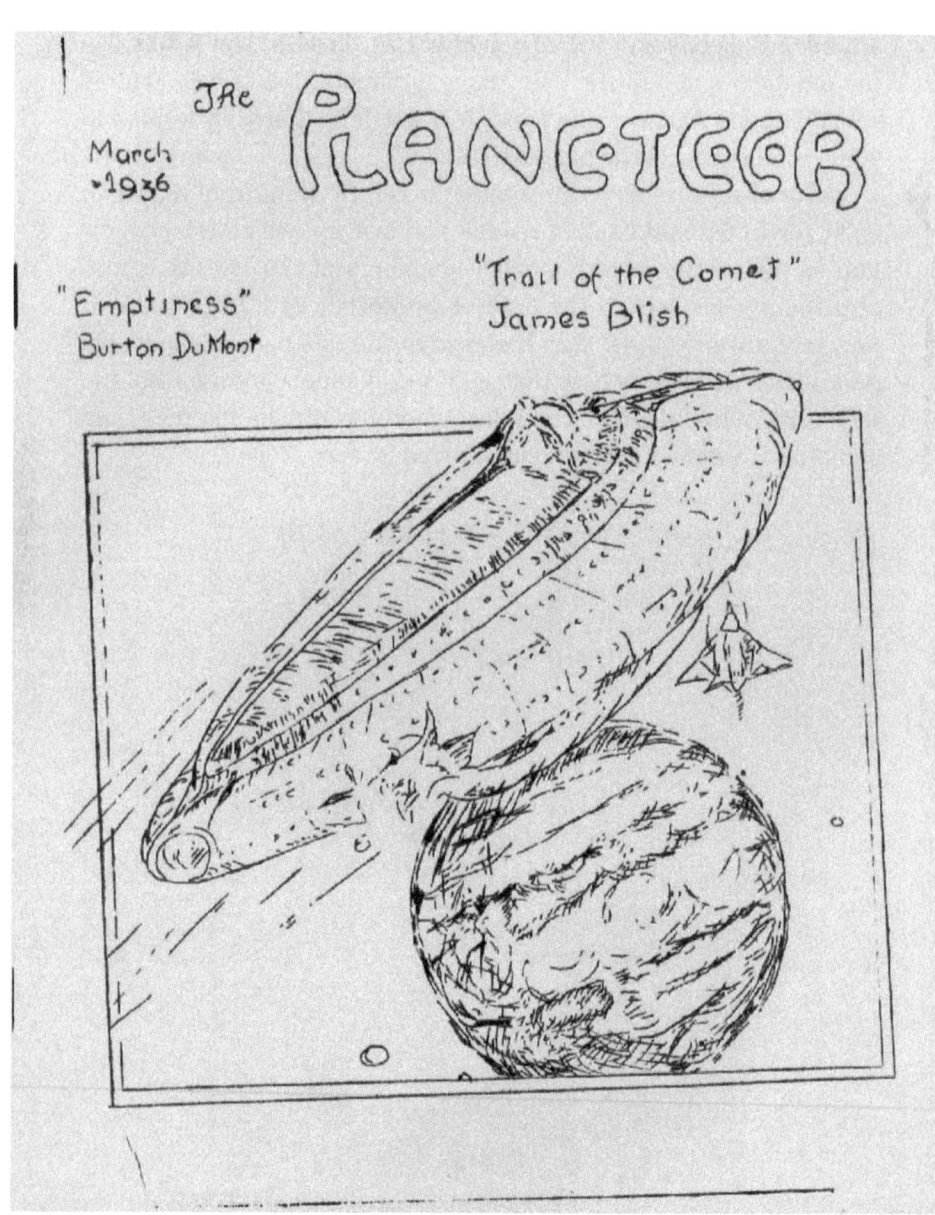

The Planeteer, #5, March, 1936. Published and illustrated by a fifteen-year-old James Blish.

ZINE EDITORS

James Blish (1921-1975) was having letters printed in the pulp magazine ASTOUNDING STORIES in the early 1930s, and had many ideas for fanzines, but being a teenager growing up during the Great Depression, lacked the necessary funds to develope them. Still, Blish was a committed young fan who took any opportunity to produce a fanzine. He also took every opportunity to write science fiction, which eventually found acceptance with pro sf magazine editors. This former fan-turned-pro is the author of three excellent novels, *Cities in Flight, Doctor Mirabilis,* and *A Case of Conscience,* which won a Hugo Award in 1959. Blish is also known for his critical writings under the pen name William Atheling, Jr., and his popular 1970s *Star Trek* books, based on the original series. This early piece may have been written by one of the editors of *Helios,* Moskowitz or Osheroff. At this late date no one knows. —LO

THE VERSATILE JIM BLISH

Anonymous

(from Helios *Volume 1 Number 1, June 1937, eds. Alex Osheroff & Sam Moskowitz)*

JIM BLISH, perhaps fandom's most versatile character, resides at 91 Halsted St., East Orange, New Jersey, Fifteen years old, his age is coincident with that of Bill Miller Jr., well known fan who resides in the second floor of the same residence in the winter, and a few doors away in the summer.

Jim's interest in scientific fiction was aroused about a year and a half ago. The disease was catching, so with Miller as co-editor they turned out the first number of *The Planeteer,* a combination of mimeographing and hektographing. The pair, uninitiated in the field, bought their first story, "The Coal Thief", from Lawrence Manning. Paying five dollars for the same. In answer to a hypocritical letter on Bill's part, T. O'Connor Sloane, editor of AMAZING STORIES, offered to review *The Planeteer* in the book review column. Unfortunately, this number which was to have been printed and contain 60 pages was never completed, due to expiration of available cash. This terminated in a split between Jim Blish and C. Hamilton Bloomer, who was to have combined his *Tesseract* with *The Planeteer*. It also meant a cessation of a series of articles by Jim in the former publication. Disgusted by the turn of events, Jim turned his subscribers over to *the Science Fiction Fan* and signed the rights to *The Planeteer* over to Donald A. Wollheim, who will publish the magazine utilizing the cover title character.

Jim then began working on *Curious Stories*, which was to have been nicely printed and contain material by Lovecraft, Louis C. and Clark Ashton Smith, probably Petaja, and a promise of "The Root Gatherers" by R. H. Barlow. With his usual undecidedness Jim gave up this venture and now has finally decided to publish *Grotesque*. This publication he says will positively appear. It will be hektographed and contain 40 or more pages size 6 by 4 1-2. Will use up *Planeteer* and *Curious Story* material. Only one issue will ever appear. During his short, but versatile period of scientifiction activity Jim has contemplated but never turned out:

1.) *Odd* - No plans.
2.) *Bewildering Tales* - Like Pohl's *Mind of Man*.
3.) *Fantastic* - No plans.
4.) *Nova* - General science fiction content.

Besides *Grotesque* which Jim states will be fandom's weirdest magazine, he is also trying his hand at professional writing. His First effort "Empty City", a collaboration with Nils H. Frome, has been rejected by ASTOUNDING. Another, "Spacecast", is still going the rounds. Blish also has a series of articles on the culture of amoeba running in the *International Observer*.

Shangri-LA, #10, October, 1949; ed. Forrest J Ackerman; cover art by John Grossman.

Voice of the Imagi-Nation, #15, June, 1941; cover art by Frank R. Paul, who was a pro artist working for Hugo Gernsback magazines. *VOM* was preceded by *Imagination!* (1937–1940) and ran from 1940 to 1947. The original image was in color and was converted to line-art by repro/artist Adele.

BEGINNINGS

Allen Glasser (1908-1971) was a very early science fiction and fantasy fan, and a fanzine editor. Fanzines he edited include *The Planet* (1930) and *The Time Traveller* (1932). Donald Wollheim said of the latter,[29] "Several members of the Scienceers had the idea of bringing out a fan magazine to sell to stf [scientifiction] readers as a commercial idea. Edited by Allen Glasser, it was entitled *The Time Traveller*. It was not the official organ of the club. It was not the organ of anything. It was a fan magazine, pure and unattached." It may also have been the first real science fiction fanzine. —LO

HISTORY OF THE SCIENCEERS

Allen Glasser

THE FIRST NEW YORK CITY SCIENCE FICTION CLUB, 1929

(This article first appeared in Joe Christoff's 1950s fanzine Sphere, *and was reprinted in* First Fandom Magazine *#4, June, 1961)*

LONG BEFORE "science fiction" was called by that name, I had become devoted to it through the Mars books of Edgar Rice Burroughs, which I read when I was only twelve. Then I scoured library shelves for the works of H.G. Wells, Jack London, Algernon Blackwood, and the very few fantasy books available at that time.

To me, incidentally, the terms "fantasy" and "science fiction" have always seemed synonymous. I think it's silly, for example, to consider time travel scientific and witchcraft fantastic. One is just as possible — or impossible — as the other; and both make interesting and provocative reading, at least to me.

---

29 *Fan Journalist*, 1945, "The Role of the F.A.P.A." by Donald A. Wolheim.

After finishing all the fantasy books I could find in those early days — there were little more than a dozen then — I discovered that *Argosy* magazine occasionally ran a fantastic serial, which they called "different" or "pseudo-scientific" stories. These I followed with faithful fervor. Some of the novels I recall from that period were ***The Ship of Ishtar***, by A. Merritt; ***The Great Commander*** by Fred MacIsaac; and ***The Return of George Washington***, by G.F. Worts — which will approximate the time for fans familiar with that wonderful ARGOSY era.

WEIRD TALES next engaged my absorbed attention — the first all-fantasy magazine I had ever enjoyed. Then, in 1926, AMAZING STORIES came upon the scene, immediately winning my ardent allegiance.

It was AMAZING STORIES which made me a real science-fiction fan — the kind who wrote letters to the editor, criticized stories, and corresponded with other fans.

However, it was through SCIENCE WONDER STORIES, rather than AMAZING, that I finally made personal contact with other fans in New York City and with them founded the first of all science-fiction fan clubs — The Scienceers.

The exact date on which The Scienceers came into being was Dec. 11, 1929. The founding members, as I recall, were Warren Fitzgerald, Nathan Greenfeld, Philip Rosenblatt, Herbert Smith, Julius Unger, Louis Wentzler, and myself, Allen Glasser. With the exception of Fitzgerald, who was then about thirty, all the members were in their middle teens.

At this point, in relating my activities as a founder of fandom, I should say that most of this account is based on memory alone. Though my recollections of that early era are quite vivid, some minor details ma have been forgotten after so many years. However, I still possess a few treasured clippings from those dawn days of fandom which serve to keep certain basic facts fixed in my mind.

Some readers may dispute my foregoing statement that The Scienceers was the very first fan club in the science-fantasy field. Objectors to that claim may cite the fact that the Science Correspondence Club, founded by Walter L. Dennis of Chicago, existed well before The Scienceers.

While that is undeniably true, I contend that the Dennis organization was — as its name clearly implied — a loose, widespread association of correspondents, with few members ever getting together personally. By contrast, The Scienceers was a tight-knit local group which conducted regular meetings every week. However, I freely acknowledge our debt to Walter Dennis and his Science Correspondence Club as the medium through which several Scienceers' members were brought into our fold.

During the early months of the Scienceers' existence — from its start in December 1929 through the spring of 1930 — our president was Warren Fitzgerald. As previously mentioned, Warren was about fifteen years older than the other members. He was a light-skinned Negro — amiable, cultured, and a fine gentleman in every sense of that word. With his gracious, darker-hued wife, Warren made our young members welcome to use his Harlem home for our meetings — an offer we gratefully accepted.

Early in that year of 1930, Hugo Gernsback's SCIENCE WONDER QUARTERLY conducted a prize contest on the subject "What I Have Done For Science Fiction." My letter about the Scienceers' formation won a prize in this contest and was published in the Gernsback quarterly.

As a result of this publicity, our club attracted the attention of Gernsback's editor, David Lasser, and G. Edward Pendray, who wrote science fiction under the pen name of Gawain Edwards.

Both Pendray and Lasser were members of the American Rocket Society, an organization of mature scientists, engineers, and other professional men.

After attending a meeting of the boyish Scienceers in Fitzgerald's home, Lasser and Pendray invited us to affiliate with their Rocket Society, as a sort of Junior branch. While this offer flattered our juvenile egos, most of us preferred to maintain The Scienceers as an independent group within our own age bracket, rather than become an adjunct to a much more mature organization. Only Fitzgerald, who was closer in age to members of the Rocket Society, joined their ranks.

With Warren's home no longer available for our meetings, we were glad to accept the offer of a new member, Mortimer Weisinger, to meet at his parents' home in the Bronx. There, in a spacious room of their private house, which Mort used for his science-fiction library, The Scienceers came into full flower, attracting many new members through publicity placed in magazines and newspapers by myself, as

Secretary of the club. One paper in particular, the *New York Evening World*, listed our meetings every week during a good part of that year, 1930; and I still have their clippings of our activities.

It was during this period that we published our club monthly, *The Planet*, which was the first paper issued regularly by any local group of science-fiction fans — although it was preceded by *Cosmology*, organ of the Science Correspondence Club. Some authorities on fandom, including Robert A. Madle, consider *The Planet* the pioneer of all the multitude of amateur publications that have waxed and waned in the fantasy field since our club paper set the pattern 30 years ago.

Editor and creator of *The Planet* was myself, Allen Glasser. I also cut all stencils needed for each issue of four or five pages. Mimeographing was done by Philip Rosenblatt, who never received full credit for making the paper's publication possible. Most of our members contributed items to *The Planet*, including reviews of professional science-fantasy magazines which then numbered only four.

Six monthly issues of *The Planet* were published, from June to December, 1930. Since I do not have a single copy left for reference, there is little more I can tell about our club paper. But I do recall that it attracted readers far removed from the Bronx. One was Gabriel Kirschner in Temple, Texas, and another was Carlton Abernathy in Clearwater, Florida — both of whom tried to start branches of The Scienceers in their home towns.

By the end of 1930, dissension among our members caused the club to split into two factions — the smaller group continuing to meet at the Weisinger home while the larger group, led by myself, held regular sessions at the home of Nathan Greenfeld, in another part of the Bronx.

Rather farcically, both factions retained the name of "Scienceers" and both continued to attract adherents. Notable among the newcomers during this schismatic period were Julius Schwartz, who teamed up with Weisinger; and William Sykora, joined my own group.

This separation lasted for nearly two years; but by the start of 1933, all members of The Scienceers had reunited at the Greenfeld residence, where they continued to meet until more mature interests drew them away from the club one by one ... and The Scienceers became only a legend in the annals of fandom.

Fantascience Digest, vol. 3, #3, whole #15, Nov.-Dec. 1941; cover art by John V. Baltadonis; eds. Robert A. Madle, Rust Barron, & Jack Agnew. Here is the iconic fanzine cover concept of nude woman and beast. Similar covers appears on *ScientiFantasy,* Spring 1949 (page 57); *Inside,* March, 1957 (page 209); and *Fantasy Times,* November, 1948 (page 237).

Fantasy Magazine, #25, September, 1934; cover by Clay Ferguson. Most issues were printed by William L. Crawford after Conrad H. Ruppert dropped out in September, 1935. Crawford would later publish *Unusual Stories* and *Marvel Tales*. FM was the most popular fanzine of the time (with a print-run up to 2,000), but never got beyond a paid subscriber base of 200.

ALL OUR YESTERDAYS

We will hear a lot from Harry Warner, Jr. (1922-2003) in this book. To really understand the history and personalities behind sf fanzines one must read his essays on various zines written under the umbrella title of "All Our Yesterdays" (later collected as a book under that title), and his *A Wealth of Fable*, which presents a history of 1950s fandom. No other historian has made a deeper study of sf fanzine culture. Warner also published *Spaceways* from 1938 to 1942 (see "The Death of Spaceways," pg. 260) and the FAPA zine *Horizons* (252 issues between 1939-2003!). Through his fanzines and many essays one can see his personal recipe for an effective sf fanzine: personality, skillful writing, perspective, civility, and clarity. ¶ *Fantasy Magazine* is a continuation of *Science Fiction Digest*, which began in September of 1932 before becoming *Fantasy Magazine* in 1934. The editors wanted to include weird fiction along with sf. In the following piece Warner writes about the first focal point sf fanzine, and we hear about Ray Palmer for the first time. —LO

Harry Warner Jr.

(from Opus #5 — June 1952)

THIS TIME, children, we are going 'way back', close to the very beginning of time, back to the days when hardly anyone existed except Forest J Ackerman. In other words, this is going to be about the most famous of all fanzines, *Fantasy Magazine*. *Fantasy Magazine* began in the depths of the nation's depression years early in the 1930s and it continued existence until late in 1936.

Those were the days when a complete collection of all fanzines ever issued could be fitted into a dresser drawer neatly, and all the prozines that had ever appeared would take up only two or three feet of shelf space.

Most of the people who put out *Fantasy Magazine* benefited by their training to become important in the prozine field. Julius Schwartz, long its managing editor, became one of the top-notch agents in the field. Ray Palmer was its literary editor. Mort Weisinger, former THRILLING WONDER STORIES editor, an associate editor, and Forest J Ackerman, now agenting as madly as Schwartz, was movie editor.

There were thirty eight issues of *Fantasy Magazine*, if my calculations are more accurate than they were for *Golden Atom*, printed on paper nearly the size of today's average pulp magazine, and ranging up to sixty pages in size.

There has never been a fanzine since which came so close to representing the combined attention and interests of all fandom. It wasn't a one man publication like all the best fanzines since. It was the corporate expression of the leading fans of the day, the average of their ideals. And when it finally collapsed, its disintegration became the official point at which First Fandom ended.

Fandom has never been the same since, despite varying attitudes from year to year, there has never been the same attention to the professional magazines and authors on the part of fans. Never quite as much dignity, earnestness and freshness of attitude. Other big, special issues of fanzines have contained more material, better material, than the fourth anniversary issue of *Fantasy Magazine*. But even today it's hard to imagine a single fanzine containing a line-up like this: Eando Binder, Jack Williamson, Edmond Hamilton, Raymond Z. Gallun, John Russell Fearn, H.G. Wells, Walter H. Gillings, Festus Pragnell, Stanley G. Weinbaum, Raymond A. Palmer, H.P. Lovecraft, George Allan England, and most of the leading fans of the day.

More than 2,000 copies of the fourth anniversary issue were mailed out, giving it perhaps the biggest circulation of any fan publication in history. It's still worth hunting today, for such tidings as the Weinbaum story, a short-short which isn't fantasy but probably hasn't been anthologized anywhere, "Graph", Lovecraft's long obituary for Robert E. Howard, and "The Great Illusion", a story written by six of the top notch authors of the day, put together by writing the last section first, then sending it to the next author who wrote something to lead up to the last section, a process that was repeated five times.

The earlier issues are rarer but more typical of *Fantasy Magazine*. For instance, in the June 1934 issue, Ray Palmer gives a biography of himself that contains hints of the ambition that he almost fulfilled, and the mysticism that eventually emerged as Shaverism:

> "At the age of seven...I jousted with a truck in the middle of the street. The truck won; and landing on my head, folded me up to a permanent height of 4' 8." I'm still folded. Followed years and years in hospitals. Passed the time reading thousands of books. Acquired a vocabulary thereby, and the deed was done. All I needed was a typewriter. Santa Claus brought that. Wrote "The Time Ray of Jandra" and went to the sanatorium for another year. That brought 1932... Sharpest memories of this period were: the ghastly face of a dead room-mate staring up into the full moon from where he had fallen on the floor in a flood of blood, the 18 pound fish I caught in a lake where "there were no fish", and the rendezvous with a dream I actually kept — to my horror upon realization of the truth. Intentions: to make my living by writing, and by writing alone. (Editors please note) And to ferociously endeavour to turn out fiction worthy of comparison with the best."

The April 1935 issue of *Fantasy Magazine* was dedicated to WEIRD TALES. Naturally, it had to include a biographical sketch of H.P. Lovecraft, still alive. F. Lee Baldwin wrote it. Some nuggets of information from this sketch. HPL's first story was written when he was seven, entitled "The Noble Eavesdropper", about a cave of robbers. He liked, of his fiction, "The Colour Out Of Space" better than anything else. HPL preferred Abe Merritt, Price, C.L Moore, Robert E. Howard, Clark Ashton Smith, and Frank Belknap Long among his contemporaries in the fantasy writing field.

Oddly enough, he liked the realist school in non-fantasy fiction, naming Balzac, Maupassant, and Zola, but believed that the French are best equipped to do this realism. His musical preferences: Victor Herbert, and old Negro cakewalk ditties. It took an average of three days for him to write a story.

Julius Schwartz wrote a monthly column, "The Science Fiction Eye" in those days, devoted mostly to the chatter about stories that were and were not coming out in the prozines in the near future. (In those days, the authors gave him lists of stories they had sold, and also lists of stories which had been rejected by each magazine, which he cheerfully printed.) And any of those columns is enough to make a completist collector go wild. For instance, the May 1935 issue's column tells of a science fiction series of novels in a magazine called TRUE GANG LIFE, each of them written by Ralph Milne Farley in collaboration with some other stf writer like Palmer or E. Hoffmann Price. Weinbaum was supposed to be the collaborator in the Oct. 1935 issue. British SF of those days included S. Fowler Wright's "War of 1938" in the Sunday Dispatch, and "Boys of 2035" by Carl Hagen in the SUNDAY PICTORIAL. And a woman's magazine called *Home*, was publishing an SF serial by Geo. Worts, entitled "The Last Man On Earth."

For a bit of prophetic defining, you can turn to the April 1935 issue, and read what Donald A. Wollhcim had to say about the "third class" of impossible stories which are neither SF or weird in nature. He was writing this a couple of years before John W. Campbell, Jr. got together the first issue of UNKNOWN. Remember:

> "Pure fantasy is known to everyone in its juvenile version as fairy tales. But it does not stop at the juvenile. Unknown, apparently, to most people, it extends into adult fiction in an almost pure form in a few infrequent books and authors. While it is true that science fiction and weird fiction are also derived from tie juvenile fairy tale, it is equally true that their form and style have changed greatly. This is not so with pure fantasy. Pure fantasy is that branch of fantasy which, dealing with subjects recognizable as non-existent and entirely imaginary, is rendered plausible by the reader's desire to consider it as such during the period of reading."

Even back in those days, some science-fiction items came high. An advertisement in the June 1934 issue, offered BLACK CAT magazines at $1 per copy. On the other hand, Clark Ashton Smith was trying to get rid of new copies of "Ebony and Crystal", a collection of his writings for $1, half the original price. Incidentally, a true, all-out fan must have originally owned most of my copies of *Fantasy Magazine*. I got them second-hand, and the margins are liberally bedecked with comments like "true, true", and even a subscription expiration notice in one copy has been faithfully preserved.

ScientiFantasy, vol. 1, #3, Spring 1949; eds. Bill Kroll and John Grossman; cover art by Joe Krucher. An ambitious little mini-zine which was heavily illustrated with art by Joe Arfstrom, Jack Gaughan, Russ Manning, Bob Dougherty, John Crockroft, Hannes Bok, John Grossman, D. Bruce Berry, Ralph Rayburn Phillips, and Bill Kroll. Four issues appeared between 1948 and 1949.

FANZINES IN PROFILE

Harry Warner, Jr. said in the May, 1959, FAPA issue of Terry Carr's *The Stormy Petrel*, "If someone were to take a poll to determine the ten most important fans of all time, I would unhesitatingly put Francis T. Laney in this list, and he wouldn't go into the tenth slot, either." Sf historian Sam Moskowitz had a different viewpoint, calling FTL a self-styled " reincarnation of the critical side of Ambrose Bierce....by nature a bully....[who] found in fandom many fans unable to protect themselves . . . ."[30] Moskowitz was mainly talking about Laney's one-shot memoir *Ah! Sweet Idiocy!*, which rained fire on what Laney considered the less appealing aspects of 1940s L.A. fandom. It was enjoyed mostly by those fans not mentioned within its pages. Laney's main target was homosexual fans (see "Tigrina–Devil Doll," pg. 119). ¶ Laney's *The Acolyte*, a H.P. Lovecraft weird fiction zine, was a fan favorite during its 14-issue run between 1942 and 1946. Other FTL zines of note include *Fan-Dango* and *Wild Hair*. —LO

F. Towner Laney

(from Spacewarp 37, 1950. ed. Art Rapp)

OF ANTIQUARIAN INTEREST ONLY ...

WHEN THIS column appeared in its other incarnation, a frequent criticism leveled against it was that I didn't go far enough back, spent too much time talking about comparative recent fanzines which too many of the readers had in their own accumulations. So this time I'm going to reach.

The Time Traveller, it says, "Vol. I, No. 1, January 1932, 10¢ a copy, $1 per year. Allen Glasser, Editor; Julius Schwartz, Managing editor;

---

30 *Fanhistorical* #3, Aug., 1980. Edited by Joe Siclari.

Mortimer Weisinger, Forrest J Ackerman, Associate Editors." It consists of six pages mimeographed one side only and fastened with a single staple in the upper right hand corner.

Before we examine the rest of the file, it is rather fascinating to mull over the fact that the second associate editor of this magazine is the same Forrest J, Ackerman of whom you may have heard today. 18 long years ago, this man was publishing fanzines. It would be interesting to know what percent of WARP's readers were yet unborn when all this happened. This would be mighty significant. (Don't ask me what it would signify.)

Anyway, *The Time Traveller* published a total of nine issues, the last a very abbreviated one which announced that it was combining with *Science Fiction Digest*. This, of course, is the magazine which later changed its name to *Fantasy Magazine* and kept publishing clear up into 1937. Under its three names, this fanzine unquestionably was one of the three or four most important items of all fannish time, both from the incredible influence it has as a focal point for the fandom of its day, and through the plethora of bibliographical information which was always featured and which makes a file of it of definite value to even the modern collector.

The Time Traveller itself is no more than a beginning. It is much easier to note format details — such as the fact that all but the first two issues were printed, or that most issues carry the sub-title "Science Fiction's Only Fan Magazine" — than to review the contents. Like so many fanzines, past and present, *The Time Traveller* doesn't have any contents worth noting.

The editorial method is a blend of house organ and high school paper. There is a gossip column or so. Questions-and-Answers department. A joke department with such monstrosities as "LINUS: 'Who was that lady I saw you with last night?' FORRY: 'That was no lady; that was my robot!'" Let us draw a merciful veil over such crud.

A serious item from "Among Ourselves" in the very first issue is much more quote worthy: "President Hoover, according to our Washington correspondent, is a Science Fiction fan. That accounts for a lot of things."

And for some reason I derived great pleasure out of learning (in #3) that the editors considered "Spacehounds of IPC" the "most pointless" of all stf-tales.

But for the most part, *The Time Traveller* consists of stodgy short items about this story and that author. A serial article, "The History of Science-Fiction" by Mortimer Weisinger, is a sketchy resume of "literary" stf, starting with the ancient Greeks — but for the most part *TTT* tells us that "A. Merritt is working on two new novels", or that "Charles Cloukey was only 16 years old when his first story ... was ... published in AMAZING."

Still and all, this is a rare old item. I have seven of the nine issues (lacking 6 and 7). The first person to send me a ten dollar bill may have all seven. (Hey, this is not an ad. Or is it?)

A PLUG FOR WILLIE.

While I'm in this mercenary mood, I'd just as well try Arturo's patience a little more, and run off at the mouth about the best single issue of any fanzine to appear in the past year. I'm referring to the 5th issue of *Masque*, published for FAPA by William Rotsler, the man who walks like a bulldozer. There are something like 80 pages in this melange of line-blocks, lithography, mimeography, and Coswalesque ditto work. About half the issue is art, half text, and it features every "member" of the Insurgent Element[31] except Widner. The address is Route 1, Box 638, Camarillo, Calif. It is priceless, but I imagine 35¢ would fetch you a copy — that is, if any are left.

MELANGE

I fully intended to haul *Sweetness and Light* under the Fanzine Scope this time, but when I just reread, for perhaps the twentieth time, this great fanzine, I realized that I just don't have what it takes, either in space or time. Half the savor of this glorious publication lies in its illustrations, and it came to me that enough of you have not seen them to warrant stenciling a bunch of them. So sometime during the next four or five months, I'm going to see if I can't prepare 8 to 12 pages of *SaL* reprints, which Art can include in WARP in lieu of my column, or else publish separately as a memorial brochure.

Has something happened to the fanzine field, or merely to F. Towner Laney? Back in the days when I was a fan, the week hardly

---

[31] These were more fun loving L.A. fans who rebelled against the science-fiction-as-a-way-of-life minded fans like Ackerman. The insurgents included Charles Burbee, Bill Rotsler, and Francis T. Laney. See "The Deeper Significance Of Science Fiction," pg. 202.

passed that I didn't receive a half-dozen fanzines. Now, with the exception of FAPA, I doubt if I average two fanzines a month. Any of you who publish are invited to send me your magazine. I will gladly exchange my FAPAzine, *Fan-Dango*, on an all-of-yours for all-of-mine basis, for any fanzine which is even remotely readable, and which is published with any degree of regularity. I have also been known to write stuff for fanzines. Who knows — I might write something for you.

Fantasite, vol. 2, #4, 1942; ed. Phil Bronson; art by Arthur H. Osterlund.

Scienti-Snaps, vol. 1, #3, Summer 1938; cover art by Walter E. Marconette.

FANZINES IN PROFILE

Here Warner mentions the flood of pro sf magazines in 1939 with a record 8 different mags crowding newsstands. Bob Silverberg,[32] some 13 years later in *Spaceship* #20, named 1952 the "Year of the Jackpot" with 30-odd pro sf mags (157 collective total issues for the year) straining sf fans' reading budget. Silverberg goes on: "This, gentlemen, is the Boom. Thirty prozines, a hundred hardcovers a year, a dozen or so movies, ten million fanzines. A thousand people at the World Convention... prozines with the circulations of 200,000... folks like Mickey Spillane entering our field... *Life* devoting pages to flying saucers...." Today, if you can find a newsstand, there are 3 professional sf mags available — if the dealer cares to stock them. —LO

Harry Warner, Jr.

(from Innuendo *#8 — August 1958, ed. Terry Carr)*

WHEN YOU read "The Immortal Storm[33], you get a firm impression that immediately after the collapse of *Fantasy Magazine*, fandom entered a period during which nothing emerged from the hectographs and mimeographs but invective, broadsides, propaganda, and feudfare. It was pretty nasty, in truth, at the end of the 1930s, but there were a few fanzines that sailed through fandom's stormy seas with as much regard for the high-breaking waves of feuding and politicking as an ocean line pays to the disturbance that a motorboat kicks up in the surrounding waters, One such publication was Walter Earl Marconette's *Scienti-Snaps*.

---

32 Bob would grow up into Robert Silverberg, a SFWA Grand Master of Science Fiction.
33 A history of early fandom by Sam Moskowitz, see "The Immortal Storm," pg. 176.

It thrived during the last years of this century's fourth decade, and it was one of the rare instances in which a fanzine really expressed the actual personality of its editor. Walt was as calm, good-natured, and friendly a fan as has ever existed, well-built physically in sharp contrast to the two-dimensional proportions of so many of us, and slow and steady in his motions. He plunged into the troubled waters of fandom from time to time, having no fear of getting his feet wet in these agitated pools, but the waters magically calmed, as a rule, when his presence was felt. He doesn't loom really large as a driving force in the fandom of his day, but it's quite possible that he did more for the field than is generally supposed, simply because he was there, living proof that an intelligent individual could find pleasure in fandom and could contribute to it without sharing in the silly fusses that were shaking up New York City, British fandom, and a variety of other areas. *Scienti-Snaps* first consisted of a half-page format, hectographed publication, which was distinctive for the overlapping protective covers of construction paper that were stapled around the fanzine itself. The inevitable handicaps of the hectograph apparently disturbed Walt's desire for neatness and precision, so he converted to a full-page, mimeographed format after the first half dozen issues. The mimeographed issues are quite beautifully done, with a startling resemblance to *Skyhook* in the general appearance, but they lost the wonderful advantage of Walt's hectographed art work. There has never been anyone like him in fandom, for the ability to create distinctive, self-sufficient decorative illustrations with hectograph pencils. I don't think anyone else ever learned how to get quite the pastel shades that he managed from this intractable medium.

In fact, the hectograph process was the joy and despair of most fans in those days when money was so scarce and fandom so small. Jack Speer was considerably wider-eyed in those days, and described in the fourth issue of *Scienti-Snaps* the wonderful things that he had seen when be explored the Washington office of Ditto Duplicators:

> "I was amazed at the extent to which the hectograph of my childhood had developed. There was one mechanism that looked and worked like a mimeograph: turn the crank and out came copies (I understand that the rotary duplicator isn't as hard on the hecto compound as flat reproducing). The jelly for use with these rotary

machines was a thin film on a heavy sheet of paper that is supposed to be just as good as the much deeper layers in the pan hecto, This paper hecto ($1 per sheet) can also be used flat; I was shown a $4 film-o-graph which makes the flat duplicating job as simple as possible. However, what was called a "portable" unit (40 some-odd dollars each!) made it even simpler to operate: A housetop-shaped thing fits over the hecto sheet, one side holding the supply of paper. In the other side you insert a paper, turn the crank, which runs a roller across the paper (which meanwhile has mysteriously been laid out on the hecto) to get it flat, then pulls it up and hands it to you......Ditto still had tray hectos in which the gelatin is a beautiful amber (when new) rather than the traditional green, at $2.75."

The first issue of *Scienti-Snaps*, incidentally, may mark the only time in the history of fandom that a fanzine also attempted to boost a postage stamp business. "Scienti-Stamp Collectors, Attention!" an advertisement declared. "To all interested in looking over a selection of my fine approvals I will send a nice packet for a dime. Contains big set of 1937 Fr. Equatorial Africa, plus many others." WEM apparently was a philatelist and fan simultaneously, a combined avocation that not even Laney could achieve.

It should not be assumed that *Scienti-Snaps* was entirely sweetness and light. Dick Wilson had a fanzine review column in the third issue which did not pull punches:

> "Ho, Moskowitz! Have at you! Of all the poorly printed, messy, badly illustrated, hard-to-read ungrammatical, *et cetera*, *ad. infinitum* fan journals, *Helios* is it. .... *Cosmic Tales* is in a class, and about on a par with *Helios*, Its format is of the sloppiest. It's illustrations... are, altogether without sufficient exception, quit awful. ... Good articles and stories at times find their way into the magazine, tho the errors that are typographed into them are enough to cause the tears to stream from the author's eyes. We know from experience."

The late Henry Kuttner, even then among the best prozine authors, still took time to write quite delightful items. "Idle Thoughts on Spinach" in volume 2, number 4 of *Scienti-Snaps*, was devoted to spoofing the articles discussing the purpose of science fiction that turned up in every other fanzine in those days. Henry wrote:

> "This business of groping for a purpose, and finding, perhaps, the wrong one, has frightening implications. I remember the distressing case of Belshazzar Weet, a promising intelligent young man of seventeen. "The War of the Worlds" proved his downfall. After finishing that novel he remained for some time in a semi-comatose state, brooding; and eventually decided, to his own satisfaction, what the purpose of "The War of the Worlds" was. As a result, he captured a termite (which he named Daisybelle) and fell passionately in love with the creature. Neglecting his studies, he lavished expensive presents upon the termite, and spent hours composing odes in her honour. This went on interminably, but Daisybelle was unmoved. She had become infatuated with a rascally wood-louse named. Edward, who did not return her affections. As a result of this triangle, Daisybelle fell into a decline and died; Mr. Weet committed suicide by precipitating himself from a fearful height on to an ant-hill; and the wood-louse, Edward, went to New York and thereafter vanished. I cannot help but feel that Weet took life somewhat too seriously."

Jack Chapman Miske, one of the most fabulous of all older-generation fans, wrote a two-part biography of Merritt[34]. Some quotations from volume 2, number 6, might be of interest today. Miske is quoting the remarks of Merritt:

> "*Argosy* paid me probably the highest rate they ever paid any writer, but that is to be expected of one whose mere name is magic. However, let it be made clear; Merritt is willing to write and sell his work to the fantasy publications. There are minor considerations, but they are perfectly reasonable: it was not the later price, however, that made me send my stories to the *Argosy*, Possibly, unfortunately, I do not have to write for a living. I write solely to please myself, and for those who like to read what I write. The *Argosy* realized this, and

---

[34] Abe Merritt (1884–1943), a highly successful and popular author who wrote *The Moon Pool* (1919), *Seven Footprints to Satan* (1928), and *Burn Witch Burn!* (1933), among other fantasies. In the 1940s he even had a pro magazine named after him. Today Merritt's fantasies are mostly forgotten, along with the writer.

> printed my stories without change of a single word, I had, and have, a certain sentimental interest in *Argosy*. Bob Davis, when he worked as its editor, bought my first yarns. The stories built up an interesting audience, young and old and of all kinds. This response interested me greatly – was a real reward for the labour of writing, for to me it is a labour. I write slowly – or in fits and starts. Sometimes a hundred words in a week; sometimes five thousand words between ten at night and four in the morning. Sometimes a month will go by without my writing a word. I gave my stories to *Argosy* solely because of this freedom to write what I wanted to write and because of this audience, which, oddly enough, seems still to be appreciative."

The first anniversary issue of *Scienti-Snaps*, in February, 1939, contained a queer combination of good and bad prophecy, in the form of an article by James Avery on the burning question of the day, how in the world the nation's science fiction readers could support the flood of new prozines, which had brought eight titles to the news-stands, in comparison with the former three titles:

> "For all this flooding of fantasy it is my own belief that, by the end of 1939, the field will be once more as clear as it was at the beginning of 1937, with perhaps a few improvements in the then existing magazines. And now a prediction that will no doubt startle some, and cause a number of others to shake their heads sagely! If things keep on as they have for the past three months, it wouldn't surprise me a bit if the Honourable Hugo Gernsback[35] will again publish a science fiction magazine as he promised in his editorial in *The Science Fiction Critic* for June, 1936. Mark my words, if there is the remotest possibility of a dime being made in the fantasy field, Gernsback will re-enter science fiction once more!

Charles R. Tanner, another fellow who was commuting between prodom and fandom in those days, published in volume 2, number 5, a rather ingenious parlay of a parody. It began:

---

[35] Publisher and editor of the first science fiction magazine AMAZING STORIES, started in April, 1926. By 1930, Gernsback had lost rights to AMAZING in a bankruptcy. He would return to sf publishing, for the last time, with 7 issues of SCIENCE-FICTION PLUS in 1953. Sam Moskovitz was managing editor.

> "You are old, Author William," the Young Fan said.,
> "And your cheques are uncommonly fat,
> "Yet your tales grow more infantile, month after month.
> "Pray what is the reason for that?"
> "In my youth," said the old man, "I wrote pretty tales,
> "Nor gave much attention to slants
> "But they always came back marked rejected, so now
> "I write what the editor wants,"

And if you think that those were the good old days when it was safe to do anything you pleased, as long as it didn't conflict with a written law, we find in the same issue Robert W. Lowndes, decrying the fact that freedom to advocate unpopular causes in this country wasn't combined with freedom to take action to back up that advocacy:

> "Advocation will not be too difficult – (although, for example, many people have found themselves very much behind the eight-ball for the simple advocation of birth control. Vested interests concerned.) – but when advocation becomes action (the first step of which is thorough explanation of all points) then you will find censorship and suppression raising their hydra heads in total disregard for our Bill of Rights, Constitution, and any and every other right the American people are supposed to possess."

Scientifantasy, #3, Spring 1949; art by Joe Krucher.

FANZINE BITS & PIECES

As we will see later, a few writers like Bob Tucker, Walter Willis, and Bob Bloch developed fannish humor into an artform. In the early days fanzines were mostly serious, but in the following piece from 1935 we have an example of humorous fiction by someone who preferred to remain anonymous. Julius Schwartz was editor of *Fantasy Magazine*. After 1944 he edited *Batman, Justice League*, and other comic books for DC Comics. Literary editor for *FM* was Ray Palmer (who would go on to edit AMAZING STORIES, 1938-1949). Forrest J Ackerman (FAMOUS MONSTERS OF FILMLAND, 1958-1981) was Scientifilm Editor. Any one of the editors of *Fantasy Magazine* could have had a hand in the following. Note: It was a simpler time. —LO

STRANGE HUNTING

Anonymous

(from Fantasy Magazine *#32, July 1935, ed. Julius Schwartz)*

A TRAVELING SALESMAN was diligently engaged shaving the stubble from his face in a hotel off Broadway one a.m. when an insistent knocking at the door interrupted him. He opened the door to find an excited stranger.

"Can I help you?" He asked.

"Yes, yes!" The newcomer exclaimed. "I am in search of a sound."

"Come in," invited the puzzled host. "I don't know what you mean. There's a Long Island Sound nearby, people upstairs make a lot of unseemly sounds, and I can sing a bit—"

"It was in here," thundered the visitor, "and I want it."

Satisfied that the man was harmless and that an asylum attendant would arrive eventually, the salesman invited his guest to be seated.

"My name," said the excited fellow "is Jack Johnston."

"The fighter?"

"No, and I'm not crazy," the guest went on. "I'm a radio author and —"

"And not crazy?" Suggested the host, with arched brows.

"I stage the 'Buck Rogers in the 25th Century' at WABC," went on Mr. Johnston. In a broadcast in a few days we will use a psychic ray, and we can't find a sound effect for it — that is, we couldn't, but you have one. I heard it as I was going by your door. And I want it."

"Yeah," the salesman said, "I get you now. I know the program, and the sound was my electric razor."

"I want a ream of quarto of a subtle yellow-brown shade suggestive of ancient (even sacred) parchment, and yet possessing that indefinable elan that one associates with a progressive cleverly humorous fanmagazine."

Hyphen, #6, Jan., 1954; ed. Walt Willis; cartoon by Bosh.

Centauri, #4, Summer 1945; cover by E.T. Beaumont. One of the fanzines out of the LA. area. Beaumont was a joint pen name for artists Wilma Bellingham and Charles McNutt (1929–1967), whose art appeared in WEIRD TALES and other pro mags. McNutt edited *Science Fiction Jr.* in 1942 and later became the writer Charles Beaumont and contributed stories and scripts to the original *Twilight Zone* tv show.

FANZINE BITS & PIECES

Mr. Sci Fi, Forrest J Ackerman, did meet H.G. Wells when a group of L.A. science fiction fans, including Robert Heinlein and Morojo, went to hear a lecture by the famed author. You might believe from the following piece that it was all just a bit of fan fiction made up by funny guy Wilson (Bob) Tucker (1914-2007), who is best known in early fandom for the multiple death hoaxes that fandom created around him. One of his "deaths" took place at a movie theater fire (he was the projectionist who fell asleep), and caused him much grief. His 1940s Fanzine titled *Le Zombie* (aka *The Ghoul's Gazette*) is a reference to his return from the dead. —LO

FJ ACKERMAN MEETS WELLS HG

Bob Tucker

(from Le Zombie #37, Mar. 1941, ed. Bob Tucker)

OUT IN Los Angeles number one fan Ackerman and party went to listen to Wells' lecture. Ackerman had to correct the gentleman several times when Wells forgot his own writings and mentioned contradictory futures for the world.

Once Wells sneezed and changed future history. Instead of a war in 1975 we will now have a depression. Ackerman swallowed a cough drop and almost changed it back, but not quite. If the janitor later hadn't forgotten to sweep under the last row of seat, there would have been a rocket flight in 1944.

Ackerman obtained the Wells autograph on the fly leaf of *Star Begotten* and Wells had Ackerman, in turn, put his signature on a copy of the first issue of *Imagination!*. Wells expressed envy that Ackerman had worked himself to position of number one fan, while he (Wells) could only cop seventh place in Art Widner's popularity poll.

Morojo [Myrtle Douglas, co-editor of *Voice of the Imagi-Nation*] astounded H.G. by informing him that *War of the Worlds* had been printed in Esperanto down in Brazil. Wells showed his appreciation by promising to make her the heroine of his next novel, "Blupington of Blup Blups Again."

Walter J. Daugherty was there too, but he kept his mouth shut.

House ad for Bob Tucker's *Le Zombie* c. 1940s.

Shangri-L'Affaires, #17, (house organ of the Los Angeles Science Fantasy Society) August, 1944; cover art by Lora Crozetti. The first 13 issues appeared as inserts in copies of *Voice of the Imagi-Nation* and other zines. The first independent *Shangri-L'Affaires* was the December, 1941 issue. It was *Shangri-L'Affaires* for 38 issues, between December, 1941, and November, 1947. The name changed to *Shangri-LA* with the Jan.-Feb., 1948, issue.

FANZINE GENESIS

Many of the fanzines out of Los Angeles in the late 1930s into the early 1940s came out of the club called the L.A. Science Fantasy Society, founded in Feb. 1936, whose early members included Forrest J Ackerman, Ray Bradbury, T. Bruce Yerke, and Ray Harryhausen. Regular guests included Robert A. Heinlein, Jack Williamson, and Henry Kuttner. One critic called L.A. the " . . . hot-bed of fandom. One bed with too many occupants."[36] In 1940 there was a realignment of club resources and various fanzines left the nest, but still made use of the club mimeograph, like college kids going back home to have their laundry done. It is easy to spot one of these early L.A. fanzines from the tint of green ink used in the club's mimeograph. For more on Yerke see "The Damn Thing," pg. 252. —LO

FROM THE VALLEY OF THE BLUE MOON

T. Bruce Yerke

(from Shangri-LA #1, *[first issue untitled, as insert in* VOM*] Mar., 1940, eds. Forrest J Ackerman & Morojo [Myrtle Douglas])*

OH, YES, another bit of information, having to do with the means by which you, the reader, are absorbing the printed information here. In short, why did *Shangri-La* come to pass? Reasoning was thus:
  (1) Various individuals are now publishing a whole flock of magazines in Shagri-LA.
  (2) If we could all get together, we should be able to issue another magazine comparable to *Imagination!*.
  (3) Well, lets do it.

---

36 "Dirty Old Kepner" by George Ebey, *Diablerie*, February, 1944.

And so, after a few weeks of running madly about, and equally as mad actions right in the Little Brown Room, *Shangri-La* was born. In an effort to cut down on treasury expenses, and to clear the way for an all-club publication, the club withdrew financial support from the three magazines which carried the tile of LA SFT Publications. Then all attention was turned toward getting out the first issue of *Shangri-La* by the first of April.

Subsequent discussion disclosed that Ackerman would continue to publish *Voice Of The Imagi-Nation* on his own (money?). More discussion revealed that Bradbury would publish *Futuria Fantasia* on his own money. Daugherty will publish *The Rocket* on his own money. Hodgkins will publish *Sweetness and Light* and perhaps *Mikros* on his own money. Freehafer will publish *Polaris* on his own money, and we are all happy because the club leases out the mimeograph.

The club? That brings in another mix-up, for at the time of this writing, the club has no name. And how did this sorry mess come to pass, you ask? Well, it seems that a number of years ago a fellow [Hugo Gernsback] used to publish a magazine called WONDER STORIES, and a fellow called Hornig[37] started a Science Fiction League, and the league crawled along for years and years. Then another worry came in. A fellow boy the name of [Frederik] Pohl started a magazine and a club called the Science FIctioneers. Well, the little group out on the Pacific Coast didn't want to give up either of the two clubs, but it was known to all and sundry as the Los Angeles Chapter, Science Fiction League, and it couldn't be a chapter of both of them at once as people would be calling the Thing of the Coast first the one name and then another. Therefore the people concerned decided to affiliate themselves with both clubs, but to change their name to something less specific. Summarily dropping the old name, they discovered they could not decide on a new one, and needed time to think it over, and now — *We Are Nameless!*

---

37 Seventeen year old sf fanzine editor Charles Hornig was installed by Gernsback as the editor of WONDER STORIES in 1933 and soon afterward the magazine sponsored the Science Fiction League, where sf fans could form local clubs around the country. This led directly to the blossoming, and eventual branching off, of sf fandom and their fanzines. Before the SFL, fans only learned of each other by the letter columns in sf magazines that printed letter writers' names and full addresses. The first chapter of SFL was formed in Brooklyn, NY. Los Angeles was the fourth chapter.

Orb, vol., 2 #2, 1951, ed. Bob Johnson; cover art by Ralph Rayburn Phillip (1896-1974). Its motto was "An eye on fandom". In *Destiny* #8, Spring 1953, Manly Banister wrote that Phillip called his art a "mystic-psychic-cosmic" jumble.

Fantasy Digest, #1, 1939; ed. Louis Russell Chauvenet; cover art by Walter Earl Marconette. *FD* was an imitator of READERS' DIGEST, reprinting the best material from various current sf fanzines.

LOOKING BACK

Jack Speer (1920-2008) was, like Ackerman, an early Big Name Fan. *Up to Now*, his chronicles of early sf fandom, was the first history of fandom published. The following excerpt talks about important fanzines from the period. *Up to Now* was superceded by Sam Moskowitz's idiosyncratic ***The Immortal Storm*** in 1951. To date no one has attempted the daunting task of writing a similarly comprehensive account of fandom beyond 1940 — though Harry Warner has tried to fill in the gaps in his informal history of 1940s fandom titled ***All Our Yesterdays***. —LO

CHANGING TENDENCY AMONG FANMAGS

Jack Speer

(Up To Now: A History Of Fandom As Jack Speer Sees It, 1939)

THE FIRST newcomers were Harry Warner, Jr., and Jim Avery. All during the Second Fandom,[38] of course, there had been a few new ones drifting in all the time, but the almost total lack of contact between the fan world and the professional magazines with their wider circulation made such neophytes few. Dale Hart definitely belongs to the Second Fandom, But, tho they were almost "old timers" by the time the full rush of new fans arrived, Warner and Avery belonged to the new day. They appeared rather without warning, dropping postcards to various fans, soliciting material for their proposed hektographed magazine, *Spaceways*. Warner was to do the typing, in Hagerstown, Md, and Avery the hektoing, in Skowhegan, Me. It was, ultimately, to the good of *Spaceways* that the hekto broke down and Warner was forced to purchase a mimeograph. In the more distinguished mimeo

---
38 See "123456789? What was that Fandom I Saw You With..." pg. 280.

format, *Spaceways* was immediately in the top rank.

Under the influence of support from the pro magazines for fandom, and a wider appeal in fan magazine material, many new names began to show up in reports of the meetings of the new Queens SFL[39] (phenomenally successful reincarnation of the Taurasi branch of the GNY fission), credited for items in Nell, in readers' departments of fan magazines, and elsewhere, tho but a comparative few of these have become "active" fans at this writing. There were several feminines among the newcomers. In the past, girl fans had usually been sisters or cousins of the male fans, and these neophytes, largely in Queens, were not exceptions. One amusing exception to this rule was Peggy Gillespie, who, it finally leaked out, was not Jack Gillespie's sister, but the family cat, with Dick Wilson and amateur astronomer Abe Oshinsky doing the ghost-writing.

Besides the new fans, quite a few of the men prominent in the First Fandom reappeared, some, such as Ray Palmer, as successes in the pro field (at the same time that many newer fans were scoring successes as authors), others, like Bob Tucker, as active fans. Bob had a letter published in Brass Tacks[40], and apparently was immediately deluged with letters asking him to return to fandom. He did so, lining up especially with Warner, Avery, and Wiggins, and began turning out reams of humorous and unhumorous publications. Some of these returns of the oldsters began as early as the Newark Convention[41], but few became as active again as Tucker.

The boys were getting older, too. Early in 1938 fans had been vastly surprised to hear of the birth of Olon Wiggins' second daughter. Bob Tucker had a family. Ackerman proudly announced he'd come of voting age and registered as a Socialist. Leslie Perri, illustratrix for Pohl's *Mind of Man* and Robert Lowndes' *Le Vombiteur*, etc, and Fred Pohl began to be mentioned as possibly fandom's first matrimonial match; altho some married couples had afterwards begun work in the fan field together, such as the R D Swishers, whose *S-F Check-List* undertook to list all fanmags actually published or even proposed.

And at the same time that some old-timers were returning, certain of the prominent men of the Second Fandom were forced to re-

---

39 Queens, NY, branch of the SF League, later the Greater New York branch.
40 The letter column of ASTOUNDING SCIENCE FICTION.
41 Held at the Slovak Sokol Hall in Newark, NJ, on May 29, 1938.

duce their activities. The results of Ackerman's employment have already been mentioned. Osheroff was forced to completely discontinue his, probably due to parental pressure, and Taurasi took over his *Fantasy Scout* as one of the myriad supplements to *Fantasy News*. Wollheim's retirement has been dealt with. Speer, on a Thanksgiving trip to visit Kuslan in Connecticut and return via Nell's first birthday party (she passed away half a year later, and Wilson began issuing *Escape*), ran his car into a telephone pole, and the resulting financial burden, parental pressure, and loss of typewriter in the shuffle forced him to cut his activities to a minimum. Baltadonis, attending college, had practically no time for fan activities any more. Ted Carnell, high-ranking British fan, announced that after the 1939 British Convention he would have to give up most of his fan activity—reason: newly married. Claire P Beck, the gloomy hermit of Lakeport, Calif, hitchhiked to New York to visit, where he fell in with Michel's crowd; after his return he announced an end to the *SFCritic*, and lapsed.

The change was reflected in the fan magazines. *Spaceways* was the trailblazer, as its pages were filled with gossip about forthcoming science-fiction, short science stories by both amateurs and professional writers, and almost no "fan" material such as characterized the Second Fandom. Its editorial policy of no controversial material on politics, religion, etc (jeered at by the submerged liberals), was quickly picked up by new and renascent fan magazines thruout the country. *Fantascience Digest*, Madle at the helm, rising to the fore with the *SFCollector's* virtual disappearance, went into mimeoed format and took *Fantasy Magazine* as its ideal. Bob Tucker, a member of Cosmic Publications now, issued a yearbook listing all stf stories in the stf mags and ARGOSY during 1938. *Imagination!*'s mimeographed format was widely copied, but by magazines of an entirely different type in interest. Gossip about collector's items, pro-mag line-up, author interviews, observations on the flood of new professional sf magazines that gave such an impetus to the change in fandom, were the order of the day, and discussion about sociological systems, religion, etc, rigorously tabooed in most of the leading fan magazines.

The old-line fans now justified their claims to the title of "science fiction" fans by showing that they had not forgotten what they had once known about it, nor lost contact. There was almost a feeling of relief as they turned to something they could be sure they were good in. Practically no one attempted to buck the tide completely; even the *SFFan* began featuring more articles on stf books, etc, to pad out the material written mostly by the Quadrumvirate, which consisted of monotonous repetitions of the Michelist theory[42] thinly veiled as biographies and exchanges of compliments.

"The official organ of the mutual admiration society of Wollheim and Company" the new British school described the SFFan. For in Britain, too, a new race had arisen. Disgusted with the lack of appreciation given *Novae Terrae*[43] by lethargic Britishers and Americans, Hanson had finally given it up, and by the time of the 1939 British Convention, the SFA monthly organ was *Satellite*, a humorous magazine modeled along American lines by the new English fans.

Even that stronghold of subversive propaganda, the FAPA, came thoroughly under the dominance of the new order. Controversial material dwindled to fractional proportions; strong literary efforts were put forward, the Swisher *Check-List*, Miske's *Chaos*, Speer's Sustaining program, Michel's *Futurart*, LA's *Sweetness and Light*, and so far, far into the night. A definite date for mailings was established under Rothman, till he moved to Washington/DC to work.

Another exception to the prevailing trend was the rising popularity of fan fiction — fiction in which the principal characters are fans— either synthetic, type characters, or actual personages. *Cosmic Tales*, under Kuslan, was foremost in this; and "Mickey" also calls to mind another exception to the main current. Tho the leading fan magazines were practically all of the "Fantasy Magazine" type, in the second level were "fanny" kind.

---

42 After John Michel, a fan who held pro-Marxist views and tried to get fans to work together towards a scientific, socialist, world utopia. This was pre-WWII (1937-1940) — essentially Michelism held that the fight against totalitarianism was something that forward looking sf fans should embrace. Donald Wollheim said of Michelism, " . . . it is not a party or a club, it is a state of mind . . . ." — ["The Michelist Movement," *The Science Fiction Fan* #48, July, 1940.] New York fans, calling themselves Futurians, including Wollheim, Robert A. W. Lowndes, Cyril Kornbluth, Frederik Pohl and Michel, with this state of mind were barred from the first Worldcon in 1939 by the more conservative group running the show: Moskowitz, William Sykora, and James V. Taurasi.
43 One of the earliest British sf fanzines, with its first issues in March, 1936.

Phanny, vol. 3, #4, Spring 1945; edited and cover art by D.B. Thompson.

ZINE EDITORS

FAPA is the Fantasy Amateur Press Association, created by a group of sf fans including Donald Wollheim, in August, 1937, as a sf version of mainstream amateur press associations. It works as a sort of syndicate where one over all editor collects the various fanzines sent in by its members and combines the whole into one mailing that goes out to all members. FAPA is still an on going concern to this day. Robert Silverberg, an active member since 1949, said of it, "... I came into FAPA ... as a teenager .... I had been reading science fiction for a couple of years at that time, and I was under the delusion that FAPA was an organization devoted to the serious discussion of sf, a delusion that was pretty well obliterated by the time I had finished reading my first mailing (#49, November, 1949). Obviously a lot of FAPA's members did read science fiction, or at least once had, and some of them collected it seriously and some of them were deeply interested in its themes and methods (these two groups, I quickly saw, were pretty much mutually exclusive) but nobody did much talking about sf in FAPA, nor—certainly not!— did anyone publish his own amateur sf stories there, something that I myself started out by doing. (The older members benignly tolerated it but tactfully set me straight before long.)"[44] — LO

EARLY FAPA

Harry Warner Jr.

(from Fanvariety *#11 — August, 1951)*

THE RAREST thing from the fantasy collector's standpoint is a complete file of FAPA mailings. My guess would be that there aren't more than three or four of the critters in existence. Only two or three

---

[44] *Trap Door* #23, December, 2004, ed. Robert Litchman.

people have held membership in the organization since its formation, and it isn't likely that many other fans have managed to get hold of all the mailings. I lack the first halfdozen myself, but if any philanthropic soul would like to cause another complete file of the FAPA to come into existence, he can do so quite easily, simply by sending me those first six mailings.

The first couple of years of the FAPA weren't productive of such large mailings. But the publications compensated for the lack of bulk by means of extreme energy. There were half a dozen violent disputes going at all times about organizational matters, most of them purely theoretical disputes about what might happen if the constitution were interpreted in such a fashion. There were a couple of dozen publications in the June, 1939 mailing, half of them one or two-sheeters, and out of all the editorial credits in these fanzines, I find only two names of people who are still active today. James V. Taurasi was listed on the masthead of *The Fantasy Amateur*, because he was secretary treasurer of the organization, and Bob Tucker was represented with a couple of publications.

This mailing contained the third issue of the *SF check-list*. I think that this was the most herculean research job in the history of fandom. R. D. Swisher, a New Englander who had never shown any other wild tendencies, conceived the bright ides that it would be nice to publish a list of all fanzines that had ever been published. He had a good collection of them, he got some other prominent fans to help him, and setting up a card index file, he went to work. If memory serves me, he went through the alphabet twice in five years of publishing the *SF check-list*. Then he found to his horror that his indexing was slipping behind the onslaught of fanzines in the 40's. He struggled feebly for a time, then quietly gave up. There have been so many fanzines since Swisher's activity that it's hard to imagine the prospect ever being brought up to date again.

The *SF check-list* listed the titles, editors, size, nature of reproduction, and dates of issue of every fanzine. It even included fanzines which were announced but never appeared. It ferreted out three different fan publications which had used the same title *Science Fiction Review* - up to early 1939. Some idea of the difficulties that confront you when you try to do some indexing like this can be found on the quotation under *Supermundane Stories*:

> "Probably one of the most unusual fan magazines ever issued was the first issue of *Supermundane Stories*...No two copies of the magazine were identical. Each and every one contained different illustrations, articles, ads, set up of stories. Cover and illustrations done in hand, therefore, no two copies of this issue are identical. Some pages titled Oct, some Dec-Jan."

This particular publication was issued by a Canadian fan, Nils H. Frome, and the best Swisher could do was to publish two separate descriptions of it, from varying descriptions given by Dick Wilson and Don Wollheim.

In case anyone in the audience feel Swisher left off, let me give some indication about the size of the job. This issue in 1939 required 16 pages to go from *Science Fantasy Movie Review*, to *Unusual Stories*. Remember that fanzines didn't begin until the early 30's and that they never reached the numbers in the 30's that the attained in the 40's.

Ackerman had a little publication in this mailing which contained an advertisement to sell some books. The price and titles give a good idea of how inflation has hit the fantasy book market in recent years. For 15 cents, Forry was offering "The Hamphenshire Wonder or The Diamond Lens." Two bits would bring you one of the **Not at Night** series, Haggard's rather scarce "Witch's Head", or a couple of Marie Corelli novels. Listed at 35 cents apiece were such titles as "Woman Alive", "Sugar in the Air", and "The Green Man of Kilsona." Wells' "The Croquet Player" and "The Man Who Could Work Miracles" were each offered at 40 cents.

The long line of evolution that has ended in the creation of Laney and Burbee began back in the late 30's when *Sweetness and Light* exploded in this FAPA mailing. On the editorial board were Russ Hodgkins, Fred Shroyer, Jim Monney, Art Barnes, and, of all people, Henry Kuttner. Debunking, satirizing, and shocking were their principal aims. Much of their material seems mild today, but a decade ago this sort of approach to fandom was like a bucket of cold water in the face. Here are some excerpts from "That Odour in the Back of the Book", Don Ellis' dissertation on the fellow who writes letters to the prozines.

> "You have read his letters hundreds of times. He takes himself with fantastic seriousness, self-righteously blasting every story in

an issue as utterly unfit to print.... Occasionally he deigns, with pontifical condescension, to praise highly. "Wellman", he says loftily, "shows some promise of developing into a fairish writer. Keep up the good work." This kindly pat on the back by the Great Critic, to a professional author who has spent days or weeks, is enough to make anyone seethe.

"Harsh and ruthless criticism has its place. Voltaire's pen was a scalpel. But Voltaire served a higher purpose because he knew what he was talking about; he was merely an exhibitionist. The pipsqueak scarcely ever knows anything about literature. 'Gee,' he is apt to observe, 'that's swell. The hero tears down the Empire State Building and kills all the Martians. What a brain.' Of course, of the principles of good writing he knows nothing; he will brashly condemn a piece of literature (which he does not understand) and tout to the skies a bit of lousy hack work. But he will never admit he's wrong. How could he? To do so would wreck the lovely psychological structure of ego he had built up. He visualized himself as the Supreme Critic, the discriminating reader who prefers High-Class Stuff (meaning science fiction) to stories published in COWBOY STORIES, ARGOSY, SATEVE POST, or AMERICAN MERCURY. The pipsqueak throws himself headfirst into stf, and in his absorption he loses sight of the fact that he's just a dumb kid in so many cases. Naturally there are exceptions, but this article is not written about the exceptions. It's the typical fat-headed pipsqueak I wish to excoriate. He's a child attempting to sit judgement."

Each issue of *Sweetness and Light* contained several "Meet the Gang" features, The drawings of these typical people were an important part, but the description can stand alone. For instance:

> This is Horation M. Thirkwoddy
> He is slightly lacking in musculature
> His gluteus maximus is callused
> By long hours spent sitting
> Reading Science Fiction
> And thoughtful Books on Fictionized Science

> Naturally he feels the Literary Life
> Is Ultima Thul
> To be attained only by the Brainy Few
> His magnificent cranium
> Contains
> A large soggy mass
> Of Suppressed Desires
> The existence of which, however,
> He will not admit even to himself
> He is protected by strong armour of
> Self-esteem
> And his strength is as the strength
> Of ten because his heart is pure.

Jack F. Spear distributed the first and probably the last linoleum block fanzine through this mailing. It was *Z.Z. Zug's Gazette*. It was simply one sentence written - or carved - on a, linoleum block, created in an effort to get last place on Swisher's *Check-List*.

If he reads this, it may make him feel as old as the hills, because in that 1939 mailing was a publication celebrating Tucker's tenth anniversary in science fiction. It was entitled *Invisible Stories*, and most of the contents were closely akin to that famous book, "What I know about Women." However, there was wordage on the covers. Tucker explained:

> "In 1929, Argosy published a Ray Cummings yarn entitled "The Brand New World." Tucker read it. Tucker fell. Since that time he has been labelled by the handle sf fan."

On the back cover was a description of the front cover:

> "Our cover subject this issue (reproduced on the front hereof) is reminiscent of the old WONDER STORIES of the Charlie Hornig and Hugo dynasty. Ah, for those good old days. The covers were usually by Paul. Not that that mattered any, for you usually couldn't see them anyway. Hugo had the cover so cluttered up with his name, his signs, his disguises and such that very little of a brilliant yellow Paul sky could be seen. "We chose the second October issue, 1934,

as representing the best cover of this dynasty. That is it which you see reproduced (or a reasonable facsimile) on the front of this publication. Notice the glaring yellow sky, typical of Paul, and the particular era. In the background can be seen purple coated figures, running for a green spaceship, pursued by red and orange monsters from the stone age. The only colour Paul and Wonder did not use in those days was black.

"We didn't have room to crowd in, across the top, that streamer that Hugo plastered up there, announcing his magazine to be "The Cream in Your Coffee" or words and music to that affect."

Needless to say, *Invisible Stories* did not possess any drawing at all on the front cover.

YHOS, #5, FAPA, December, 1942; ed. Art Widner; art by Virginia Anderson.

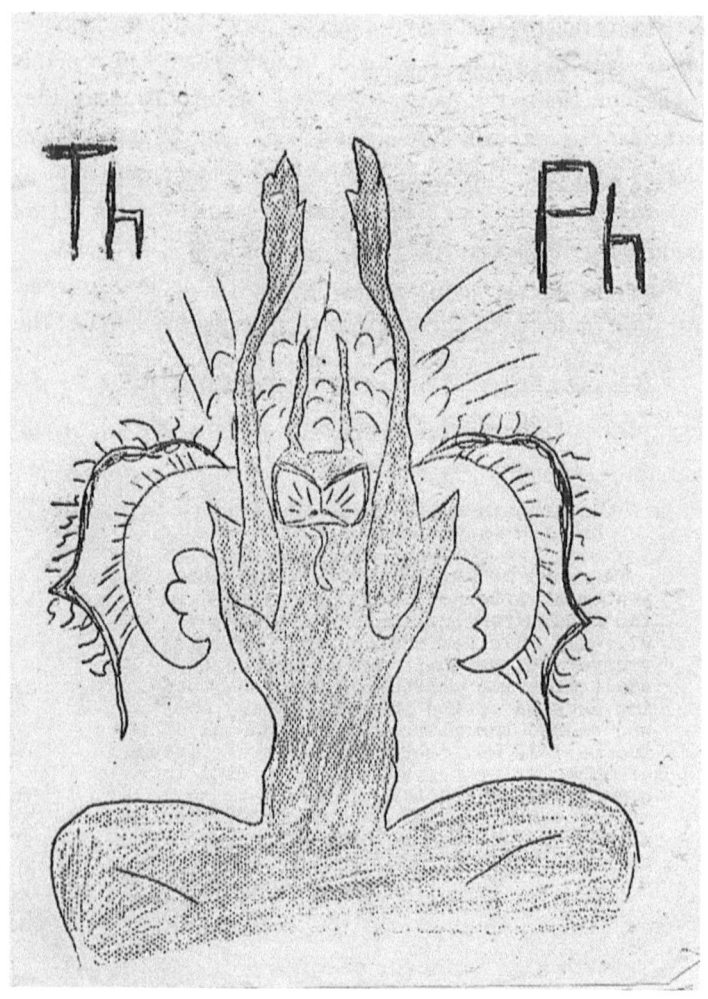

The Phantagraph, 1945; ed. Donald A. Wollheim (1914–1990). By the early 1940s editor Wollheim called *The Phantagraph* "The Oldest Fan Magazine Still Published." There was some cheating since *The Phantagraph* came out of many combined zines that Wollheim had a hand in: *The Terrestrial Fantascience Guild Bulletin* (the first issue appeared in May, 1934), *Science Fiction Review, Fantastory, Mind of Man, The Time Traveller, Science Fiction Weekly, The Planeteer, Curious Stories, Queer*, and others. The July-August 1935 issue was the first issue edited by Wollheim as well as the first printed issue, a large 8-page job produced by amateur publisher William Crawford. In 1936 Wollheim helped organize the first science fiction convention in Philadelphia, and the following year was instrumental in forming the Fantasy Amateur Press Association (FAPA). As an editor he worked for Avon and Ace Books before starting his own publishing house, DAW, with his wife Elsie in 1971. Today DAW is run by his daughter Elizabeth (Betsy) R. Wollheim.

BLACK & WHITE

Black & White was the name of a one-shot fanzine[45], that appeared in the 1944 summer mailing of FAPA. It had been slated to appear in *Nova*, then *En Garde!*, but with race riots going on around the country it was considered a better idea to bring it out as a stand-alone zine under the restricted circulation of FAPA[46]. Now there have been many debates over the years in fanzines, and at times these debates were marginally tied to science fiction. The topic here is racism. Ackerman's p.o.v. is that of a science fiction fan looking towards the future. Speer's is something else. Of course, we have to take into account the time and place for all of the following, even if it opens a window onto an ugly landscape. One would think that this debate would have evolved somewhat 75 years later. —LO

WHEREIN JACK SPEER'S HAIR TURNS GRAY OVER NITE

Forrest J Ackerman

(Black & White, *Published By Nova Press For FAPA, Summer 1944*)

JACK SPEER, as is fairly common knowledge in fandom, is color blind. Would to Stf that he could not distinguish between white and black! But he can and does—to my great regret.

My good friend Jack Speer, and I say that not sarcastically but sincerely, would, I presume, embrace and welcome as a brother a "man" from across space or time, be he 8 feet tall with green scales, tentacles and 4 eyes, or a floating brain sustained by a helium skin-sac. Any amicable conception of Paul, Bok, or Finlay,[47] no matter how

---

45 From Nova Press, run by the duo of Al and Abby Lu Ashley of Battle Creek, Michigan. They were also behind *Nova* and the FAPA fanzine *En Garde!*.
46 *En Garde!* #8, December, 1943, eds. Al and Abby Lu Ashley.
47 Frank Paul, Hannes Bok, and Virgil Finlay, all artists working for pro pulp zines.

repellant a monstrosity, would be greeted and treated like a friend—like Kinnison and Worsol, for example. But Jack balks at a specimen of homo sapiens pigmented black.

Jack Speer is intensely anti-negro. And I have just found the first colored science fiction fan!

In a recent letter, Speer ("with Liberty and Juffus for all") told me in all sobriety and apparent self-satisfaction of a heinous action. He and a white woman (sic) had to sit opposite a "boogie" in a dining car of a train. "We choked up, looked around for some place to move to, which there wasn't so had to content ourselves with making audible remarks, bolting the rest of the dinner, and getting away as soon as possible" — and seems to have been quite proud of their conduct! Damme if I shouldn't say, "Served 'em right!" if they got indigestion. Alas for the inhumanity of man to man—unquote. "The world is full of people, and the people are full of prejudice." Such uncivil conduct I consider despicable, heartless, cruel, censurable. Bad behavior for an average individual; for a science fiction fan, an actifan, in fact, in my estimation, one of the top 10 stfans . . . . Incredible!

On our way to the Nycon, Morojo and I felt distinctly uncomfortable, embarrass to be members of such a country, when we passed through a certain state wherein seats in the coaches were partitioned temporarily and marked "For Colored Only." We resented this, we did not like to think any colored people were blaming *us* in their minds, looking at us accusingly. Beyond personal, selfish considerations, we considered the situation fundamentally unjust.

Now I personally do not *relish* the company of negroes, I admit I've a measure of squeamishness about associating with same. But this mental maladjustment I conscientiously attempt to overcome. All it is, I think, is that, subconsciously, I feel because a man is black he's dirty. Balderdash, of course. But one has to contend with one's thalamus!

While a Negro would not be sexually attractive to me, and I should not expect to have any intercourse with an Oriental or perhaps several other races radically different from the white, certainly I need not snub them in matters of normal activity: eating together, conversing, commerce, sport, etc. This is not to imply sexual relationships are not normal—please let us not go off on a sophisticated tangent.

If Jack is not aghast long before now, here is the part where I confidently expect his red hair to fade at least to pink: I HAVE EATEN

BUTTERED POPCORN FROM THE SAME BAG WITH THIS COLORED FAN! NB: I felt no ill after-effects.

I hope to Stf that my colored fan friend never reads these words. I should want him to know, tho, that this Jack Speer, of Washington, DC, is not representative of fandom, at least, I trust and believe not, and in fact may not be entirely responsible for his own conduct. Is the bent branch to blame if a wild wind or a ruthless hand twisted the sapling? I think there are extenuating circumstances; that Jack has been hypnotized by environment.

In the near future I intend to inform the LASFS of my discovery of this Negro fan, and ask if the club would have any objection to my inviting him to meetings. I do not expect opposition. Should opposition arise, I'd be aroused — dammit to hell, I can promise you I'd be so boiling mad I'd be ready to make an issue of it then and there: either we admit this fan or *I go*! But that would be melodramatic and unproductive of the desired result. Conceivably, if I do not flatter myself, there would be capitulation. But certainly it would be begrudged. I shouldn't want that. But I prefer to prophecy that when the time comes the members will rather think it a little odd of me to question that they might raise any objection, as tho I should know better. In that case I shall be very proud indeed of the fangelenos. But I must know for certain.

Wm R Twiford should have sent Jack Speer an autograft copy of his (obnoxious) book, **Sown in the Darkness–A.D. 2000**. This is a novel Tremaine published in the days of the comet. It is one of the most dastardly damnations ever perpetrated, in my opinion. Equaled, probably, only by that British abomination, **Concrete**, of the sickening future religious revival.

"The Negro," twaddles Twiford, "should have been left in Africa to go the way of the untamed tiger, the gorilla and the lion, into final extinction. If he had been left to do this, his soul would have come back to this earth and be dwelling here today in a white body!" Metaphysical moronity!

"If such ultimate outcome was not the plan of the all-wise Creator, then why has He endowed the white race with superior intellect?" It is to retch.

"If God thought black to be beauty, why did He not paint the lily that way?" Surely you, my readers, see the superficial, the ridiculous reasoning of this nauseating nonsense. Such mad-talk to me is revolting, horrendous and infamous. It really makes me quite incoherent with revulsion and rage, the evil idiocy of it!

Now fans are supposed to know things like relative viewpoints, and that to gorgeous hard ebon panther people living in caves hollowed from coal, a woman's pink body, descended from the ape, would be a thing of soft, bleached and blasphemous obscenity—unless the panther were a fanther.

I suppose Jack Speer agrees with the sentiments of "Sown." I doubt he considers it God's Divine Will that the Negro should be abolish, but I daresay he would consider the prospect most desirable. If I may say so without seeming patronizing or superior, I think Jack has a Blind Spot on this subject. What can we fellow fans say to him to show him the lite? I presume I'm writing to a sympathetic audience: I should be a disillusioned fan indeed were this article to raise a storm of protest against me.

The Negro servifan's name is Vincent Williams. He's a LA reader. As a passifan, he's been reading omnivorously the past 3 years. ASTOUNDING is his favorite. He likes Heinlein, also "Lefty Feep" yarns. He reads WEIRD TALES too. And saves his mags, claiming quite a collection including back numbers he's bought. He'd like to try his hand at writing, particularly playwriting and radio-scripting, of the stf and fsy variety, of course. He knew me by reputation—or repute. I hope to be instrumental in introducing him to fandom. I favor women and "foreigners" in fandom—STF alone the magic password, the Open Sesame—and I earnestly hope you all will accept the concept of a dark-skinned brother.

Simultaneously, what the devil are we going to do about Jack?

BLACK & WHITE – CON'T.

Here is the rebuttal from Speer. Such as it is. —LO

WHEREIN JACK SPEER PARTAKES OF PANTOTHENIC ACID

Jack Speer

(Black & White, Published By Nova Press For FAPA, Summer 1944)

I DOUBT THAT he is the first Negro fan. Some time back, I believe Julius Unger said that an officer of one of the early stf clubs—Scienceers or something like that—was colored.[48] If this is correct, I would say that one more deserves the title of fan; I would call Williams a scientifictionist.

In the letter 4e refers to, I said that the ground for my attitude was objection to intermarriage, which is best prevented at present, since we have no eugenics laws, by a psychological barrier. For reasons which he may consider sufficient, 4e disregards this in writing his article.

Anyway, you can guess from that what my policy on the extraterrestrials would be. Making the improbable assumption that creatures physically so different mite yet have the same number of chromosomes as man and be capable of interbreeding, I would still welcome them prima facie if it should be simply a matter of exchanging diplomats, scientists, and commercial representatives, and even making some scientific mating experiments. But if the e-t's[49] were slated to come live among us, and eventually intermarry, by the hundreds of thousands, I'd want to know what kind of genes they would contribute to the stock common.

---

48 See "History of the Scienceers" by Allen Glasser, pg. 47.
49 This is a very early use of "ET" for an extraterrestrial alien.

The pigment of the skin is not important, except as the most noticeable sign of the race. The other distinctive physical characteristics tend towards a presumption that Negroes are closer to the Neanderthal than Caucasians. But the real test as to equality must be of intelligence.

It is well known that blacks average definitely lower on intelligence tests than whites do. Unfortunately, there are some environmental differences mixed in with the inborn traits, which make all present-day tests less than completely reliable, but in my judgement these differences are utterly insufficient to account for all the disparity in scores, made on tests of intelligence, mark ye, not information or education. Example of the basis of my judgement: In the 201 files (alphabetical), which are now manned almost entirely by Negroes, large posters have been put up on the walls, showing simply the alphabet, for these blacks to refer to. Especially when you consider that they must have been (public-school) educated and literate to have gotten into CAF work, you can't ascribe inability like that to lack of opportunity or incentive; it's unadulterated intellectual deficiency.

It is quite possible, since natural selection preserves the characteristics with survival value and discards those that are anti-survival, that the makeup of the Negro race is better suited for survival in certain environments than that of the Caucasian; but in the civilization which the Occident builds and hopes to build, the most needed element is intelligence, and that's something we've got to work for, regardless of what the 18th Century Rationalists said about all men being created equal. Exceptions like Booker T Washington, George Washington Carver, and the two stfists in question, in no way disprove the general rule that Negroes show lower in inherited brainpower than average whites. But all of this is pretty far-flung reasoning. Obviously it's not going to be much of a deterrent to a great many people; it may not be even for our type if it remains simply the recognition of an intellectual abstraction. So I have built up, to some extent by artificial means, tho the natural reaction to Negroes assists, an emotional bar against contacts with them beyond a certain limit. More of this anon.

I expect that I am indeed in the minority here, since most fans are idealists leaning to the Left, and since the majority of them, like the majority of Americans, live in the North and West where the problem is not acute. In many such places the small Afro element could probably be absorbed with little noticeable deterioration — But don't forget that there are millions of them below the Mason-Dixon line and coming North every year, and quick to marry the mulattoes and quadroons that are the first stages in any amalgamation.

Maybe there's no possibility of you yourself marrying another race. But your example helps shape the mores. There are people in the lower mental classes, and people who care nothing for what society will be like a few generations from now, who will conclude that if you can mix with them politically, economically, intellectually, et cetera, you can mix socially too. I can't think of any case where races have lived together for a long time and stayed distinct. The emotional bar mentioned slows down the process: thousands cross the color line every year, but a much smaller proportion in the South, where social disapproval is unequivocal. What reasons are there for anyone to marry outside hiser race? I guess in recent times the main reasons have been a mistaken idea that it will help racial understanding, desperation because no other spouse can be found, and perhaps in some cases on the level of "it gives me what I want." When we have dependable measurements of individuals' heredity, together with laws on the subject, then will be the time to consider each individual case on its own merits; until then, the rather slipshod color line method will have to do to hold miscegenation to a minimum. Incidentally, isn't it the strangest sort of inconsistency to find an author going out of his way to defend miscegenation at one place in a story of which the central ideal is racial improvement—miscegenation which Heinlein himself admits would tend to deteriorate stock.

Ackerman is being absurd, and knows it, in putting me behind the straw man of Reverend Twiford. In sooth, a stronger case might be made by negrophiles if we were religious, the fatherhood of God over all of us often being said to imply the brotherhood of all men.

The J is right in feeling that there was pride in the account of the incident on the train, but the pride was in the straightforward, objective reporting; the incident itself was simply unpleasant.

I didn't intend to debate this issue publicly while we have a war on. The thing doesn't have to be settled immediately, though of course the sooner the better, other things being equal. Other things aren't equal in war time, tho, and I think it's better policy not to go seeking troublesome points.

I don't get his phrase "He and a white woman (sic)." In the letter I said "Mrs. Eskridge and me." "A white woman" would be a slightly improper way to speak of my sister.

It is suggested that I have been hypnotized by my environment in this matter. A bit of autobiography is in order:

The small town in the South-West where I was brung up is predominately Anglo-Saxon. There were half a dozen or a dozen Republicans, two German households, and one Jewish family, whereof the son was the best companion I could find in school, tho I disliked his extreme extroversion. No Negroes could settle there; the policy was "Don't let the sun set on you inside town", but I didn't know there was such a policy until about the time I was twelve years old, and the only case I have heard of where it was enforced was when the banker's wife wanted to keep a colored maid. And as far as my home town environment was concerned, Negroes were non-existent.

In our summer trips to the paternal home in Florida, of course, we did see quite a lot of darkies. There were a lot of them in Oakland, and they kept perfectly to their place. We liked Fanny and Charlie. I never knew there was a Negro problem till '38.

My first unpleasant notice of them was when I was in Oklahoma City, but these were of no import. Once you get to Washington, tho, you have to decide pretty quick where you will stand. I took Psych my first semester here; the War Department has supplied other supporting data since then.

A third of the Capital's normal population is colored. That makes it ethno-geographically a southern city. But the laws are dictated by Congress, where the North-West is supreme, so the only official segregation is in the schools. On common carriers and in many department stores there is a mixture; in amusement places and eateries the managerial policy is to exclude one race. Exceptions of course are government theaters and cafeterias. Even in the latter, however, they invariably eat at different tables.

Kiplinger's book on Washington describes pretty well the general attitude. We don't like having the Negroes here. They're responsible for most of the crime and other things that give the city a low desirability-rating as compared to the white cities of Southern California and the Middle East. But there are few flare-ups, and in general we go our way and they go theirs. The only occasions for active dislike are those in which the blacks push their claims to equality, like the dining-car episode.

Oh—incidentally, an item mentioning Pfc Ack-Ack and a colored soldier is slated for the next Fictitious But Definitely. Nothing especially objectional about it; I just want to say that it was thunk up before this debate materialized.

Another item in the letter which the "J" doesn't mention tells of a time when I ate at the same table with a Negress. The sponsor and program director of a church group had invited her to speak. None of us liked it, but thot it better not to precipitate a scene. So don't expect me to get up and walk out if Williams shows up at a convention. But don't expect me to welcome him with open arms, either.

"Remove that lipstick! It makes you look like one of those disgusting Earthlings!"

Sun Spots, April, 1941; cartoon by Bronson.

BLACK & WHITE – CON'T.

There was a heartening response to *Black & White*. —LO

D.B. Thompson

(Phanny, *vol. 3, #3, December 1944*)

AS FOR the race question and emotionalism, it seems queer that Speer should see fit to make that criticism. Perhaps he is so used to taking an objective view of other matters, that he actually can't discern the emotional basis for his statements on this subject. His search is not for unbiased data on the subject, but for evidence of any and all sorts, however specious, which will support his convictions; a procedure which is not only unscientific, but foreign to his usual procedure. So the principal opponents of inter-racial breeding are those who consider one race superior to the other?

E. Everett Evans

(Timebinder, *vol. 1, #1, 1944*)

THAT IS the idea that is expressed in our own national ideology – "ALL men are created equal." Yet even we of America have not been willing, as a whole, to face that fact. We do not want to think that ALL men are equal – we want to feel that some, even in our own country and among our own citizenry, are NOT our equals. We do not give full equality, either socially, educationally, economically or politically – especially politically – to quite an astounding percentage of our citizens. We have our negro and our Indian problems – problems because we will not face that fact squarely, courageously and honestly. We have our slum districts, our "poor white trash", our sharecroppers and tenant farmers, because we are not willing to admit that these people are our equals. And therefore, we will not allow them the chance of becoming our equals.

Harry Warner Jr.

(Horizons, vol. 6, #20, September 1944)

BLACK & *White* – Wherein Speer seems to be soundly bested in an argument for the very first time. I refuse to believe that the Harlem Negroes are of lower intelligence than the first and second-generation Italian immigrants, or those of several other races.

F. Towner Laney

(Fan-Dango, vol. 2, #3, Whole #7, Winter, 1944; ed. F. Towner Laney)

SPEER'S COMPLETE inability to use his otherwise passable, if not brilliant, mind whenever he is confronted with the race problem is a source of never failing wonder to me. How did he get into the brain trust? Through his discussions on the negro question?

Imagination!, vol. 1, #9, June, 1938; cover art by Ray Bradbury, announcing a new pro sf mag. It is curious that Bradbury did little art for his own fanzine, *Futuria Fantasia*. Of course, he had his friend Hannes Bok helping out with art.

ZINE EDITORS

You don't have to be a big science fiction fan to have heard of Ray Bradbury, or even read his fiction. But fanzine readers were seeing Bradbury's first writings — and artwork — long before anyone else, in his fanzine *Futuria Fantasia*, which also showcased the early art of a friend of his — Hannes Bok (see "Hannes Bok on the Fantasy Scene," pg. 32). The following piece came out before *The Martian Chronicles* and *Fahrenheit 451* were acknowledged as classics. Bradbury did eventually become a "really important writer." This is another "All Our Yesterdays" piece by Warner. —LO

Harry Warner, Jr.

(from Fanvariety #10 *— July 1951, ed. Max Keasler)*

MOST OF us know that Ray Bradbury was once a pure and simple fan, before he discovered the way to sell stories. But how many fans in the field today realize that he was also a fanzine publisher? Bradbury put out a little fanzine named *Futuria Fantasia* during his Los Angeles days. I find four issues of it in my Los Angeles file, which appeared during late 1939 and early 1940. There may have been a copy or two after these four — it would take a person with a better memory than mine to be sure[50].

Futuria Fantasia had little to distinguish it from a hundred other fanzines of about the same period. Its standard of material may have been just a trifle higher than the average. The general appearance is quite neat, but that was a characteristic of Los Angeles magazines of

---

50 There were only the four issues.

those days, and there were many fanzines coming out of LA during those years. *Futuria Fantasia* contains the green ink which nourished the LA mimeographs in those days and each issue contained up to 20 standard letter sized pages, with a variety of stories, poems and articles. Each of the four issues contains a book cover, three of them mimeoed, the other reproduced by a halftone.

One sure thing, you'd never guess that it was Bradbury writing the editorial for the first issue: "The best laid plans of me, it seems, are destined for detours or permanent and disappointing annihilation upon the road to accomplishment." It goes on in this murky, forced, style for a full page, explaining why the fanzine appeared a year later than originally scheduled. It also reveals that even though Bradbury lived at 1841 South Manhattan Place, he couldn't spell Manhattan without the use of an e.

If Bradbury ever should become a really important writer, these publications of his youngest youth are going to be studied by the research men and the biographers. So it's really a shame that it's almost impossible to determine whether Bradbury wrote certain items which are credited to other people. Guy Amory, listed as the writer of a biography of Kuttner, may have existed. However, Ron Reynolds appears to be Bradbury in disguise, and as a result, a couple of the stories in *Futuria Fantasia* become important.

Best of them is probably "The Piper", which may be the very first of the Bradbury stories about Mars to see print. If it is really Bradbury's fiction, it is surprisingly good, in comparison with the majority of the sophomoric stuff he was writing in those days. It isn't too far from the atmosphere of the published stories about Mars, either, although it doesn't quite fit into the future history pattern of The Martian Chronicles, "The Piper" brings in a man from Venus: "He's crazy, that's what. Stands up there piping on his music from sunset until dawn." The Piper plays on a world – Mars — which has been conquered and brutified by earth men. A little boy who is the "last pure Martian alive" learns that millions of these degraded Martians have their residence "out there, beyond the mountains, in the caves, far back in the subterrance." The man from Venus has also been ill-treated by the earthmen. The concluding paragraph's meaning probably was more clear to Bradbury than to the reader of the story, but it appears that the Piper's music one night causes these brutalised

Martians to revolt against the earthmen. It's an interesting combination of Bradbury's present style and the work of a boy obsessed by adjectives, these final paragraphs:

> "Swirling, jumping, running, leaping, gambolling, crying — the new humanity surged to man's cities, his rocket, his mines. The Piper's song! Stars shuddered. Winds stilled. Nightbirds sang no songs. Echoes murmured only the voices of the ones who advanced, bringing new understanding. The old man, caught in the whirlpool of ebon, was swept down, screaming. Then up the road, by the awful thousands, vomiting out of hills, sprawling from caves, curling, huge fingers of beasts, around and about and down to the Man Cities. Sighing, leaping up, voices and destruction!
>
> "Rockets across the sky!
>
> "Guns. Death.
>
> "And finally, in the placid advancement of dawn, the memory, the echoing of the old man's song.
>
> And the little boy arose to start afresh a new world with a new mate.
>
> "Echoing, the old man's voice:
>
> "Piper, pipe that song again! So he piped, I wept to hear!"

A new day dawned. Compare this with "The Pendulum" in another issue, probably by Bradbury since it isn't credited to anyone. This is the somewhat gruelling account of a man who invents time travel, accidentally kills a lot of famous scientists while trying to demonstrate it, in revenge he is imprisoned in a transparent pendulum connected to his time machine, lives through the centuries in this imprisonment until robots take over and earth and humans vanish, and finally is found dead by visitors to earth from another planet. To get this series of events into fewer than 2,000 words is quite a feat, but that's about all that can be said in favour of the story. One paragraph will be enough:

> "He hadn't minded it so much at first, that first night. He couldn't sleep, but it was not uncomfortable. The lights of the city were comets with tails that pelted from right to left like foaming fireworks. But as the night wore on he felt a gnawing in his stomach,

that grew worse. He got very sick and vomited. The next day he couldn't eat anything."

Bradbury didn't make any claims to be a great writer in those days, In the third issue's editorial, for instance, he wrote: "Unlike Finlay, who draws pictures from poems, we procure pictures from Bok and write poems about them. In fact, I blushingly admit, I even wrote a ten thousand word novelette around that little creature on the cover of the first *Futuria Fantasia*…which, no doubt, will have its share of rejections very soon, in which case I will foist on my poor unsuspecting public, both of them, this story now titled 'Lorelei'."

In this same issue appeared "The Syphomic Abduction", and apparently another Bradbury yarn. This one shows him completely under the spell of the dictionary. It's a story about the effect that music had on a fellow who liked to turn it up loud and stick his ear against the loudspeaker. I think that this single paragraph will suffice:

> "Beneath me was a limitless tract of grey slime which rose and fell torpidly as with the breathing of a somnolent subterranean thing. The moonlight burned brightly on it, and crawling across it from some remote place came – trees snaky-rooted things whose prehensile branches bore, instead of leaves, flexible lenses…They left behind them red trails on the slime, and excrementory ribbons of thin blue vapor streamed from their topmost appendages. Occasionally they paused to feed, focusing their lenses upon the gelatinous ground, which became luminously white under the concentrated light. The sucking mouths of the serpentine roots absorbed this matter, and red viscosity seeped into the eaten places, greying rapidly under the moon's effulgence, chemically affected by it."

Taken as a whole *Futuria Fantasia* could hardly be a clue to the fact that Bradbury would go out and sell stories at a great rate in the next couple of years. It was slightly higher than average fanzine, but part of its quality could be laid to the fact that it was produced in Los Angeles, where any fanzine had the advantage of expert help and assistance from more experienced fellows. Bradbury did manage to get quite a bit of stuff by professional writers and the semi-pros. His friendship with Bok was responsible for the covers and interior illustrations, of course. But there was also material by Henry Kuttner, Emil Petaja, Robert A. Heinlein, J. Harvey Haggard, and some lesser lights. The moral would seem to be that even the most inconspicuous fan writer today may be living off his typewriter in the next decade. But it's also well to remember that there have been hundreds of other guys who started off exactly the same way as Bradbury — and didn't end up the same way.

Incidentally, as far as I know, these issues of *Futuria Fantasia* have not yet acquired any real market value. But if you happen to have the publication in your collection, I'd recommend hanging onto it. About thirty years from now, there's, going to be a Bradbury surge, like the ones that hit Lovecraft and Keller, and the collectors will be greedy for these items, or any of the many fanzines published around the same time containing contributions by Bradbury.

Fantasia, vol. 1, #1, Jan., 1941; art by Damon Knight. See "Snide" for more on Knight.

A Bas, #9, Nov., 1956, an early Canadian fanzine edited by Boyd Raeburn; art by Patterson.

FANZINE LIFE

Today, you can't mention Robert Bloch's (1917-1994) name without also mentioning the Alfred Hitchcock film *Pyscho* (based on Bloch's novel). But pre-*Psycho* Bloch was already a BNF in science fiction fandom, and wrote for many fanzines and pro mags. So it was natural for him to become a fanzine reviewer. Here, Bloch attempts to define what a sf fanzine is, and his definition is as good and any. Bloch got his start in WEIRD TALES, and his early fiction was influenced by the writings of his friend and mentor H.P. Lovecraft. —LO

CONFESSIONS OF A FANZINE REVIEWER

Robert Bloch

(from Leer, *no #, Dec. 1956, ed. Charles Lee Riddle)*

A YEAR AGO, I was a plain, ordinary monster.
Today I am a bug-eyed monster.
And I owe it all to reading fanzines
One year as conductor of "Fandoras Box "in IMAGINATION has done the trick. my eyes have bugged out after perusing the contents of several hundred hectographed, mimeographed, multigraphed, and printed periodicals. Some were big, some were small, some were issued regularly, and others were so irregular they seem in need of Lydia Pikham's Compound[51].

It has been my duty to comment upon them in my regular department, and comment I have. I cannot pretend to have applied the standard techniques of reviewing and/or criticism. Nor have I ever "rated"

---

51 Old-fashioned, herbal-alcoholic "women's tonic" for relief from menstrual and menopausal symptoms. Lydia Pikham was also a hoax name used when suggesting remedies for fans' ills.

them with stars, asterisk's or numerals.

Frankly, I'd seem such a task impossible, to say nothing of unfair. Because there are no abstract or even components to characterize a fanzine.

In order to clarify that statement, just ask yourself the simple, unvarnished question, "What is a fanzine?" Or, if you prefer, varnish the question first. Varnish it, paint it, cover it with shellac, gild it as you may — the question had only one answer.

A fanzine (science fiction variety) is a magazine prepared by a science fiction fan and addressed to other fans.

Beyond that, there is no least common denominator.

Said fanzine can consist of a single hectographed sheet of paper — or it can run into scores or even hundreds of pages, elaborately invested with typeset, color reproduction, and coated stock for photographs. Said fanzine can be produced by a 14-year-old or a septuagenarian.

And, most significantly, there is *no uniformity of content.*

Our definition — and deliberately so — says only that science fiction fanzine is prepared by a fan and addressed to fans. There is nothing which stipulates that the contents of same have anything to do with science fiction.

And if you're a confirmed reader (or a *bar-mitzvah*-ed reader) in the field, you'll realize that in many instances fanzines do not necessarily concentrate on fannish topics or even include them.

In fanzines today, you'll find feuds and nudes, hot rods and cool cats, political arguments about religion and religious arguments about politics. In some fanzines, the accent is on the editorial ME and in others the accent is on the editorial MEOW. Some fanzines reflect the tenor of a Debating Society; some, a Ladies' Sewing Circle; some a session of the Gag Writers of America, and still others sound like a recording of a barroom brawl.

So, how are you going to compare them?

Lacking comparison, critical evaluation is impossible, save on the basis of personal preference. And this in itself doesn't lead to sound, objective reviewing.

I am just a naïve little boy, 39 years old. And when some jaded sophisticate of 16 comes along with a witty dissertation of sex, alcohol, and philosophy, the chances are that our opinions may not coincide. It would be both unsound and unfair for me to set up arbitrary standards of judgment.

So I make no pretext of actually "reviewing" what I read. All I can do and try to do, is indicate what appeals to me personally. And to encourage efforts which I think hold promise of future improvement.

What appeals to me personally? Again, no common denominator. I like some fanzines which are strongly editorial — items such as *Grue* and *Skyhook*, for example. Can you possibly imagine an issue of *Grue* which did not reflect the personality of Dean Grennell?

On the other hand, I also like some fanzines in which the editorial-personality seems quite submerged: examples being *Inside* and *Peon*. This does not mean that these magazines aren't expertly edited (indeed, they owe their success to editorial skill and selectivity) but the influence of the editor seem unobtrusive and the material is more objectively presented.

On the other hand (happen to have three, you know), I also like some magazines that reflect the spirit of a group or a clique: *Hypen, Canadian Fandom, A Bas,* etc. Or — a variant of same — letterzines such as *Hodge-Podge* which seem to operate in an artificial *milieu* or frame of reference, depending entirely on correspondence.

What don't I like in fanzines?

Sloppiness. Sloppiness of physical production, sloppiness of presentation sloppiness of content. I have *never* (and remember, this is my personal opinion) seen a good fanzine in an atrocious format. When an editor can't lay out material and reproduce it legibly, when he cannot correct errors in spelling, punctuation and grammar, chances are he cannot select good material either. Or get it in the first place.

But again, you won't find this view reflected very strongly in my comments. And there are several reasons why I do not choose to "blast the crudzines" in my column.

Now, anyone who has ever taken on the role of reviewer of critic knows this to be so "clever" and "amusing" in name-calling, and one can easily gain a reputation for a "caustic wit." Moreover, in many circles, one acquires a concurrent status for being "honest" and "forthright" and full of "high standards of critical integrity."

The easiest way to attract attention to one's self is to yell "It stinks!" and then go on, with a series of ridiculing remarks, to tell why. But I do not believe that it is the function of a reviewer to call attention to himself; not in his reviews, anyway.

Furthermore, twenty-odd years of fanzine-reading have taught me the danger of issuing such opinions. For I can recall all too many instances where I have read crudzines, and apparently hopeless ones, edited by youngster who grew up to be talented adults. I have read vile contributions by feckless youths (myself included) who eventually emerged as polished professionals (myself not necessarily included). I have also seen downright lousy fanzines blossom into top-rank publications over the course of the years.

The important factor in such changes was not, I am convinced, outside criticism. It was the emergence of mature self-awareness on the part of the individual involved.

Now even the worst crudzine requires a lot of effort to produce. Even the shabbiest contribution must be sweated over in the writing. All too ofter — when a neo is involved — a volley of harsh, superior criticism or snide ridicule is enough to tip the balance and cause the editor or contributor to give up.

The editors and contributors who learn through trial and error, through their own objective comparison of their to that of others, will improve voluntarily and inevitably. The others will fall by the wayside, because nobody will subscribe to their magazines or read and print their material.

But the fanzine reviewer who elects to be a Supreme Arbiter runs the risk of either stifling potential progress or some day looking like a fool when the object of his criticisms confutes him. Some of the learned, omniscient fanzine reviewers of the past may just possibly feel a little silly today when they remember how they spent the latter years of the 1930s ridiculing the puerile fanzine contributions of a sniveling little neo by the name of Bradbury. And — much more important — it is just possible that there were a couple of more fans in the field with equal or even greater potential who didn't persevere as Bradbury did, but dropped out because some Fearless Critic told them their work smell and that there was no hope for them.

As it is, there's enough of such criticism, within the pages of the fanzines themselves, to serve as goad, check, stimulus or retardant.

Again, overall objectivity is impossible. How can you "rate" the first efforts of an adolescent by the same standards as those of an adult? How can you assess the quality of a fanzine addressed to neos in the same way you asses the content of a 'zine by and for adults? How can you encompass the divergent interests, attitudes and goals of an English fake-fan, an earnest Continental, a Dedicated APA member, a saucerian believer, a rocket enthusiast, a frivolous femme-fan, a dianetician, a kid who worships Campbell and an idiot who believes in Tucker?

All I can do, personally, is to say what appeals to me — personally. And to attempt to convey some of my approbation to potential readers and/or subscribers. At the same time, I attempt to avoid mention of the illegible or the ill-natured efforts which crop up. I don't want to damn them but at the same time, I don't want to falsely recommend them to a trusting readership.

But I do believe it is a mistake to play Jehovah, complete with thunderbolts, in the fanzine field.

And I'd like to say — but I can't, there's no time, another batch of those $&&#()*@ "zines" have just come in from Hamling's office and I've got to start reading ....

Hyphen, #12, December, 1954; ed. Walt Willis; art by George Charters. (See also "Fan Icons: Beanie" page 293.)

FANZINE TALK

> Lowndes has an interesting take on the relationship between pro science fiction magazines and fanzines. For more on Lowndes see "Who Killed Science Fiction?" pg. 376. —LO

WHAT FAN MAGAZINES?

Robert W. Lowndes

(from Ad Astra, *vol. 1, #5, January, 1940; ed. Mark Reinsberg)*

THE TIME has come when the simple term "fan magazine" can no longer describe aptly the general outlay of amateur publications issued by active lovers of imaginative fiction. Mainly, this is because there are now several distinct types of amateur publications issued by these "fans" and that the original concept of the "fan mag" has greatly changed.

What was the concept? It was, roughly, an aid to the professional magazines. The original "fan mag", not counting those organs of pioneer science correspondence societies which dealt mostly with experimental and scientific articles, dealt in biographical sketches of stf writers, editors, artists, etc., occasional stories, by these writers," service departments" where old time ARGOSY etc stf was listed, forecasts on current policies, lineups,and acceptances of the various writers and general chatter about authors and in reference to their better-known stories. There were, as well, semi-scientific articles. These original fan magazines were entirely dependent upon and subordinate to professional magazines. They were real scientifiction magazines.

When, however, the situation in professional magazines became such that their quality was greatly reduced and they were irregular in appearance, this function of the amateur fan publication, began to wither away. It did not completely die, but it did gradually begin to be replaced. And, while fiction by imaginative fiction enthusiasts appeared to a greater extent, the accent gradually fell upon organizations of these fans. Thus, we had the 2nd type of magazine, one which was primarily an aid to some particular fan-organization. It did, very naturally, cater to the professional publications, but was not dependent upon them. Where ever the professionals failed them, there was ample material in the organization and activities of the enthusiasts themselves. These magazines were real "fan" magazines.

A subsidiary of this general type was the magazine issued by a single fan, independent of any particular organization. These consisted of fan-chatter, controversies, personalities, service departments, discussions of the professional magazines. But these amateur publications were by no means dependent either upon the professions magazines, nor upon any particular fan organization.

The last type to appear was, the amateur publication, in the FAPA, mostly, issued by an enthusiast of pseudo-scientific and or weird-fantastic fiction which ignored the professional magazine entirely and fan-organizations . . . as well. It was really an independent magazine, good, bad, or indifferent depending upon the editor's capabilities both in the technical field and in obtaining material.

There were, and are, publications which combine to a certain extent all these main features. But, the most interesting thing is this: there is not today one single fan mag that is dependent upon the continued existence of professional stf and/or fantasy magazines, and very few which are dependent upon any particular fan-organization. Thus, the original "fan magazine" is a thing of the past.

As this writer sees it, there are in existence now three general types of these amateur publications (these types somewhat similar, but not equal to, the original fan magazines). And, of course, there are the in-betweens, those things which analysts find so deucedly annoying and wish that they could safely ignore.

First: the "catholic fan magazine." This type covers science fiction and/or fantasy, from as far back as possible to date,caters to no particular publication, covers the field in every possible way: books, leaflets, articles in non-stf magazines, comics, etc. No possible source of imaginative exploitation is closed to it. Prominent example: *Spaceways*.

Second: the "fan news-gossip magazine." This is devoted primarily to the individual fans or fan-groups, and, while running news of the professionals, can get along very well without them. Prominent example is: *Le Zombie*.

Third: the independent literary magazine, offered for subscription, published for the sheer purpose of exploiting the editor's urge for creation. It features stories, poetry, articles, and whimsy by other enthusiasts of imaginative fiction, has little or no interest either in professional publications or in fan organizations. Examples: *The Fantast, Escape, Sweetness and Light, Futuria Fantasia*, and *Polaris*. While none of these examples are as yet full-breed in this type, they most closely resemble it and they are, I believe, fore-runners of that type of "fan magazine" which will most endure.

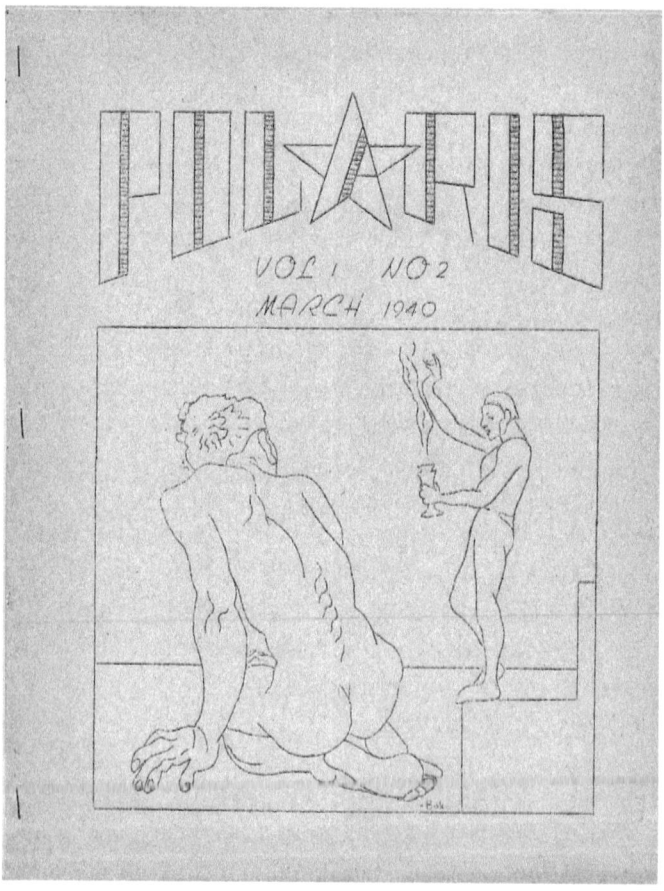

Polaris, vol. 1, #2, March, 1940; ed. Paul Freehafer; cover art by Hannes Bok.

Toward Tomorrow, #2, Summer 1944; edited by James Kepner, who was a member, and later president, of the Los Angeles Science Fantasy Society at the same time as Tigrina (see next page). He was one of the people attacked by Laney in issues of *Shangri-LA* and *Ah! Sweet Idiocy!*. Before *Toward Tomorrow* Kepner had plans to publish a zine called *The Gay Fan*. He was talked out of this by sympathetic friends. Kepner would later become prominent as an early gay rights advocate.

ZINE PEOPLE

Tigrina (Edythe Eyde, 1921–2015) began to write letters to *Voice of the Imagi-Nation*, the "mirror of fandom," in early 1941 while attending a women's college in San Francisco. It wasn't long before she met *VOM* editor Ackerman, who invited her to visit L.A. She eventually moved there and became a regular at Los Angeles Science Fantasy Society meetings. Eyde and Fojak (as she called Ackerman) used to pal around, even once visiting Edgar Rice Burroughs in his home in Tarzana. In the June 19, 1945, issue of *Fanews,* #166, there was an "Open (Heart) Letter to Tigrina" from Ackerman calling her a "beautiful phantasy treasure" and proposing marriage. In the response that appeared in *Fanews* #170, Tigrina let him down gently.[52] Ackerman soon became aware of her attraction to women. By 1947 Eyde had become secretary to the LASFS club. That same year she took what she had learned from sf fandom and anonymously began *Vice Versa*, which is today recognized as the first lesbian zine. Ackerman contributed to *Vice Versa* under the pen name Laurajean Ermayne. At the time the publication of *Vice Versa* could have put Eyde behind bars. Laney wrote *Ah! Sweet Idiocy!* to strike out at the homosexuals in the LASFS club, but somehow had a blind spot for lesbians. Which is just as well. ¶ I get the sense that Tigrina's embrace of the occult lies more in society and church rejection of her sexual orientation than any true affinity to satanism. One letter writer in *VOM* called her perverted for her advocacy of black magic and she defended herself, "I know that my interest in the Backs Arts is, to a certain extent, a rebellion from the exceedingly 'straight and narrow path' that I have sometimes been forced to tread. But it seems that merely because some of us do not react to different situations in the exact manner that the majority of the people do, we are 'perverted and queer'[53]." —LO

---

52 The editor of *Fanews*, Walt Dunkelberger, commented, "We wish only to state that both letters were received through the mail from the individuals who wrote them and to the best of our knowledge no hoax is being perpetrated." *Fanews* #170, July, 1945.
53 *Voice of the Imagi-Nation*, #25; Oct., 1942.

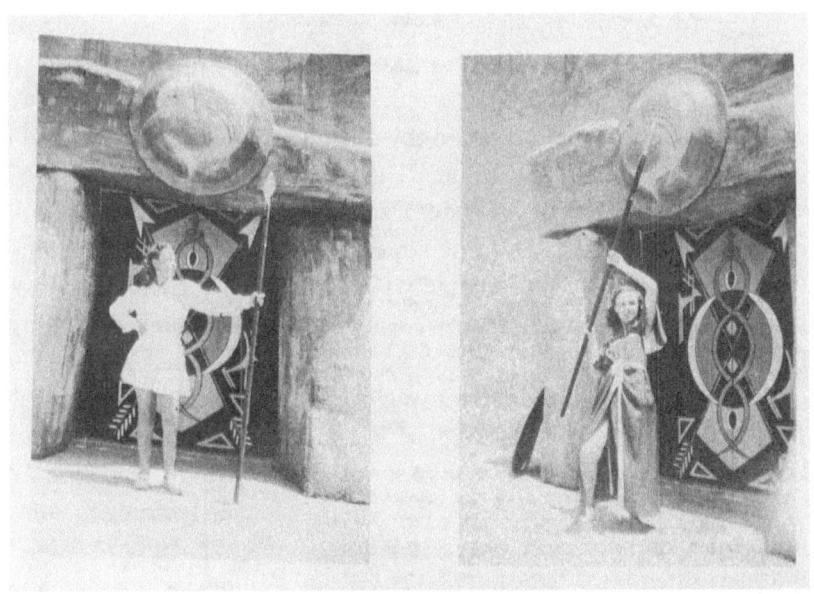

TIGRINA - DEVIL DOLL

Forrest J Ackerman

(from VOM, *#19, Nov. 1941, eds. Forrest J Ackerman &*
Morojo [Myrtle Douglas])

FURTHER INFO on the mysterious miss (above) who shakes a mean spear! The figure "13" figures prominently in her life. She has 13 cats (& an injured lil owl she found on the campus & is nursing back to health, named "Banshee"). She has 3 addresses, all of which end in 13. Her first drawing to appear in a fan mag (*Eclipse* #4) was published on pg. 13. I met her on the 13 of the month. She used to be 13 years old. Other items: Her college curriculum consists of violin lessons, advanced course in musicianship, French, survey of the literature of music, philosophy, speech & drama, and string quarter. She is studying esperanto. But let Tigrina speech for herself in this symposium of letters received from her in the past 6 weeks…. "I have wonderful room this year (at — *College*). I managed to bring what few books on magic, witchcraft, etc., I have, with me without getting a single word of disapproval from my parents. That was because I supervised the packing myself this time. I eve managed to smuggle in my Ouija board and I also brought a small table (altar). The walls, of course are decorated with pictures of Bela Lugosi. I have also hung a Chinese gong outside of my room as a doorbell. And when one enters, an artificial spider, hung on an almost invisible horsehair, gives the victim a friendly(?) greeting and frightens her out of her wits, unless she likes that sort of thing, like we Fantasy Fans. Oh, yest, I also brought some black candles 'in case the lights go off some stormy night,' as I explained to my mother." Tigrina was born under the sign of Scorpio. Maybe she is a zombie? She wonders, for her life-line is practically non-existent. She learned to read & spell when she was 3, "But when it came to learning to write, it was quite a different thing, I was left-handed and I used to begin at the right side of the page and end at the left, writing backwards." She sent a petition to *Shangri-LA* to be circulated among the imagi-natives to secure signatures for the guest starring of Bela Lugosi on an "Inner Sanctum" program. Attending a symphony orchestra concert at her college, after the signed petition had been returned. "I was amazed to see that a friend of mine, whom I had not seen for a long time, was a member of this orchestra. My friend is also interested in the Occult and Science Fiction. I showed him my petition and obtained his signature. When he read over the list of names and saw Fojak's, among the other Los Angeles fans, he was much surprised. He said he used to know you and asked me if you still lived in San Francisco. It is a small world after all, isn't it?" Have you all decided when the convention will take place? (*Not yet, honey chile; watch Pacificonews for announcement.*[54]) How I wish I could be down there then, or any time, for that matter! — I was happy to hear that Fojak had not been drafted. I was afraid for awhile that he was going to join one too many clubs."[55]

FOLLOW THIS GREAT FEATURE — "TALES OF TIGRINA" — EVERY ISSUE EXCLUSIVELY IN THE VOICE!

---

54 Pacificon came off in September, 1946, after a wartime hiatus.
55 Ackerman was indeed drafted, but was stationed near L.A. as an Army staff sergeant. He never saw action or got overseas. His younger brother, Alden Lorraine Ackerman, was killed at the Battle of the Bulge.

The Nekromantikon, first issue Spring 1950; ed. Manly Banister.

BEHIND THE ZINE

Manly Banister was the editor of *Nekromantikon* (1950–1951), a fanzine that ran weird fiction in imitation of pro magazine WEIRD TALES. Copying pro mags appealed to some fanzine editors, but the non-profit ethos of fanzine publishing meant no money for writers, which led to many sub-par, amateurish stories — but after all, it was a labor of love for all parties involved. *Nekro* did feature early fiction by future pros Marion Zimmer Bradley, David R. Bunch, and Wilson [Bob]Tucker. —LO

AN AMATEUR EX-EDITOR SPEAKS

Manly Banister

(from Slant #7, Winter 1952-1953, ed. Walter A. Willis)

NOTICE PLEASE, that I call myself an amateur ex-editor-NOT an ex-amateur editor. The distinction is considerable. An amateur is one who does something for the pure love of it. When I was an amateur editor, I was such for the love of it. Now that I am an amateur ex-editor, the condition still obtains. I love being an ex-editor.

Almost anyone with two or three holes in his head can be an editor. Ex-editing, on the other hand, is a sublime art. Any editor can become an ex-editor simply by stopping up the holes in his head with ground-up contributors. To avoid a lumpy effect, graft over the bumps the hides of those readers every editor flays in his sleep

Since it is so much fun being an ex-editor, why did I ever become an editor in the first place? Well might you ask. The one is contingent upon the other. None can know the pure joy of loafing without having worked.

But all that aside. My principal aim in writing this is to be of service to my fellow men-to that proportion, at least, which senses a restless hankering to edit. Let me make plain that I refer to amateur editing in all instances-pro-editing is a world apart; I know nothing about it (but it must be a pretty good go, to judge from the way the old die-hards keep hanging on year after year).

You to whom I speak are those who have heard the call, or are about to hear it. You feel an incompleteness of living. You seem to think that there is a place for you in the world, if you could but find it. You startle at the rustle of paper, the bang of a typewriter is music to your ears, the smell of printers' ink is a heavenly essence compounded of spikenard and myrrh. The skids are greased under you; you wait only for somebody to cut the rope.

For the day will surely come when you will square your shoulders, lift up your head, fuse a sparkle into your eyes, and cry out: "I will publish a magazine!"

From the inner depths of your own consciousness, a Voice speaks. "You wonderful fellow you!" It says.

From East and West, from North and South, comes the answering voice of the multitude to whom you have made known your intention: "Whuffor?"

Well, hell, am-eds are a dime a dozen-did you expect to be received with breathless excitement?

When I made my first world-shaking announcement in this fashion, I sat back and waited to receive the applause.

I got three dirty cracks from three disinterested individuals. Nothing more.

I broadcast an appeal for manuscripts from a population supposedly frothing at the mouth to appear in print. What happened? I took a leaf from the book of the better pro-eds and jammed the first issue with my own crud under a variety of pseudonyms, plus a little extra stuff I was able to cadge from some very close acquaintances.

Perhaps some of you saw that first issue of The *Nekromantikon*. It was quite fancily illustrated with linoleum cuts. Those lines! I spent hours carving out the stuff to make the result look as much like authentic drawings as possible. I selected the best cover stock I could find on short notice. And the mimeography was lousy.

After publication, results flowed in. "Anybody knows," said one correspondent, "that you should never try to print line-work with lino blocks. That medium is supposed to be used only for a block effect."

By James White! I swore. (James White had not yet begun his own to-become-famous lino artwork,[56] but I swore in the future tense).

Another bellyache concerned the lousy covers—they fell off in the hands. This from a young am-ed whose whole mag disintegrated in my hands.

Somebody else wrote in ecstasy, mentioning one of my pseudonyms. More from this fellow, he says, but that so-and-so (mentioning another of my pseudonyms). he should drop dead.

But everybody thought the mimeographing was wonderful. I thought, and still think, that it smelled. It was bad. A composite of half a dozen different brands of stencils. But everybody agreed on the one point that the mimeographing was excellent, so I took hope. At least, here was an amateur zine you could tell what was in it, besides ink.

The cost of that first issue was 27 per copy, and there were 250 of them. I gave half of them away, and peddled the other half at two-bits a throw.

I was launched. Briefly, the clanking press was stilled, the mimeograph crouched sullenly like a silent A.B. Dick in the corner. Through the long nights, the stapler slowly cooled from the heat of its labor

But the more I nursed the blisters on my fingers and thought of those egregious lino blocks, the more I thought to hell with it. There must be an easier way, I thought, and I considered the possibilities of zinc engravings for future illustrations. I had once made a tour through an engraving plant, and there was nothing to the process, it seemed to me, which could not be learned with determination and ten years of experience.

It was about this time I got a letter from some foreigner telling me about the troubles he was having with his zine. It was a terrible book, he said, but he was sending me a copy anyway, but not to judge too harshly, etc. etc. The foreigner, of course, was Walter Willis, and the lousy zine he mentioned was *Slant*. When the magazine arrived a few days later, Walter became definitely established in my mind as the world's most modest man. The mag was little in size, all right, and the printing could have been improved - but the glinting thread of pure genius ran through the entire work. Beg pardon—two geniuses. I was captivated by the marvelous concepts embodied in those razor-bladed "wood-cuts" of James White. I pride myself that I recognized in

---

56 For early issues of Walt Willis's *Slant*.

the beginning what certain pro-eds and fans did not wake up to until later issues of *Slant* had been published.

(NOTE TO WALTER: The above constitutes fee in kind as payment for the publication of the herewith article. Please tear off coupon at bottom of page, endorse it back to me, and file with Lloyd's of London. MB)

Now, let's get back to this other interesting fellow—me. But why should I go into detail about the process of photo-engraving? There are simply too many details, as I found out, to bore anyone with the recital of them. I should, however, like to mention an initial difficulty which I solved with great neatness, and it may be of help to anyone desiring to take up engraving. In some musty tome or other, I read that the next step after fixing the image on the zinc plate is to "immerse in 20% nitric acid solution and swab gently with a pad of cotton." I swabbed and swabbed and nothing happened, except that all of my body hair fell out. It occurred to me, then, that perhaps it was the zinc I was supposed to immerse, and not myself. As later experiment proved, this was the case.

Enough of technical matters. Let us get to the fun of the business. One day the mailman staggered up to my door and deposited a basketful of manuscripts. Heavens to Betsy! I thought (cleaning up the expression), fandom is certainly WILD about *Nekro* !

I read through script after script happily accepting this one, joyfully rejecting that one with the terse comment: "We can't print everything, you know." This kept up for days. The manuscripts poured in. But one funny thing — I couldn't find the names of the writers in any of the numerous lists of fans. Who were these people?

Then, one day, the horrid secret came to light. I received a printed card from A Certain Writer's Magazine That Shall Not Be Named. It said, to this effect: "Here is a sample of your listing as we have been running it. Please check, make any necessary corrections, and return." That listing looked to me as if it were set in 72-point type, though actually it was something less than six. There was poor little *Nekro*, listed with all the hot-shot paying professional markets…and the blurb concluded: "Payment by arrangement." How this came about is too long a story to tell, and I don't know most of it myself anyway.

I fell upon my knees. I wept tears of chagrin. I tore my hair and beat my breast. My God! My files bulged with accepted Scriptos. I could only write letters of apology and permit the authors to withdraw their creations. Before I could get started on this project, the postman brought another dismal burden. But this one contained three acrid and injurious epistles wanting to know when in hell that "payment by arrangement" was forthcoming. Just because those authors were nasty, I sent back their pieces (which weren't very good anyway) without notes of apology. To the others, I crawled as the lizard crawls upon its belly, limbs akimbo. One expressed his own apology in reply and requested the return of his manuscript. The others generously consented to permit their work to continue toward publication. I am still not completely recovered from the shock of this experience.

One of the oddest manuscripts that I ever received was really a lulu. The author was congenitally incapable of spelling, and his punctuation was fragmentary, to say the least. The script was single spaced, and the lines ran from the top edge of the paper to the bottom edge, and from the left edge to the right, so that every inch of the paper was filled with typewriting. When a word arrived at the right margin, what was left was carried to the next line at the left margin, even if it were only one letter. In some cases, when the last word of a problematical sentence ended at the right, the period began the next line to the left. It would not have been funny if the script had been prepared by some Smarty-Pants. Actually, it was high humor because it was written in honest ignorance, and would have been well worth publishing just for laughs had not my Christian nature come to the fore and bade me refrain.

One character I am not about to forget is one who wrote to me several letters in quick succession, recommending himself highly as a literary artist. The fact that his letters sounded like drivel could have nothing to do with it, for most literary men, when writing personal letters, sound like fugitives from a chain-letter-gang. This gizmo told me all about his agents and his contacts with various editors, and gave me to believe he had a few rejects which were "too good" for pro pubs and would like to see them published.

All agog, I told him to forward his stuff for a look-see. He had, he said, written a story that was word for word in a great many places identical with a certain story written by a well-known name author. He wrote another story so closely like another name author yarn later published, that he accused the editor who had rejected his story of copying it and putting a "house name" on it. His letters were full of stuff like this.

And the wonderful story came. It was terrible, and I told him so. So he wrote me an 8-page letter telling me what was wrong with me. "You are frustrated," he said. And this was the very truth, for I sweated with frustration of a desire to clobber the cuss.

Now, gentle reader, you know in some part the reason for my enjoyment of ex-editing. Another of its joys, besides affording respite from the freaks and vicissitudes of inclement chance, is the opportunity to cultivate quietly the finer things, the nicer people, and so on, it was my fortune to meet while editing... only then I didn't have time for them.

I hope I have discouraged no one from editing a magazine. This has not been my intention. It is great fun...while it lasts. And by the way...if any of you would-be editors think photo-engravings would dress up your mag nicely, please contact me. I have a complete outfit of very fine photo-engraving equipment...For Sale Cheap!

Macabre, #2, June, 1948; cartoon by Don Hutchison.

FANZINE NUTS & BOLTS

The following two editorials, from Walter A. Willis's (1919-1999) great *Slant,* relates the unique printing method of that fanzine. As Willis explained: "My father was a printer, and I have reverted to type." No messy mimeo or hector presswork here, just good old, hand-set letterpress type and woodcuts. (Early issues of *Fantasy Magazine* also used hand-set type.) Eventually, even Willis had to turn to the simpler mimeo way of fanzine production. Very few fanzine editors have tried to imitate *Slant's* presswork since. .—LO

THE AMATEUR EDITOR

Walter A. Willis

(from Slant *#3 - Spring 1950, ed. Walter A. Willis & James White)*

SOME READERS have asked for information on amateur printing. We use what is known as a flat-bed quarto machine. Ours was junk, but a new one costs about ₤6:10. The bed, where the type is placed, is about the size of this page[57]. Two people can run off about 100 copies per hour. Type consists of little rectangular sticks of metal. Size is measured in points, and there are various shapes of letters in all sizes. It is sold in 'founts' containing all the letters in the proportion they are used in English. Naturally the bigger the letters the more a fount costs, but a fount of this type, which is 10 pt. Gloucester Bold Condensed, is about ₤2. It contains one hell of a lot of letters but you really need another half font for a page of this size because about a third of your type is ALWAYS left over.

The type is set up in a little adjustable tray called a 'composing stick', and tightened up by adjusting the spaces, which come in 5 sizes. This is known as 'justifying' the line. When several lines have

---

57 Aprox. 6" by 9".

been set up you grasp the unstable mass firmly and lift it into the bed. (This is a nerve-wracking operation.) You can set up type about as fast as one-finger type-writing.

As for illustrations, I can only tell you what we do, which we're sure is all wrong. James does the woodcuts with a razor blade on plywood. You can use lino but James would rather have plywood. That's all I can tell you so far but we hope to develop as we learn. Photo-engraving, for example.

In SLANT 4 I hope to discuss some of the more general problems of the fan editor.

Slant #4, Autumn 1950; multi-color wood-cut cover art by James White.

BEHIND THE ZINE

This is the follow-up to the previous piece. Walt Willis really came to sf fans' attention when he started writing the column "The Harp that Once or Twice"[58] for Lee Hoffman's *Quandry*. —LO

COME IN, THE WATER'S LOVELY!

Walter A. Willis

(from Slant #4 - Fall 1950, ed. Walter A. Willis & James White)

WE LIKE it here on the lunatic fringe of the lunatic fringe, but think well before you start a printed zine unless like us you have no choice. People not only expect more from print, they think you must be a bit upstage, and you can't be controversial because you publish seldom enough to be attacked with impunity. Besides, handsetting is hard work, and reviewers tend to voice this profound thought instead of casting about for something nice to say: the implication is that of Johnston's remark about the woman preaching, 'Sir, it is like a dog walking on its hind legs. It is not done well, but you are surprise- to see it done at all.' Another thing is that handsetting tends to make your style terse and cryptic. This is bad, because the only people who read fanzines carefully are rival editors and BNFs looking for their own names.

Well, whether your zine is mimeoed, printed, handwritten, or carved on lumps of stone, you'd better have some stories or something to keep the cover from getting torn in the mails. You could ask people who write for other zines I suppose. (Being unsure of the ethics of this I have never done it myself, except for European authors in American zines whom I consider fair game.) But it's long odds they will come up with something rejected by another fanzine. Fanzine re-

---

58 A line from James Joyce's ***Ulysses***, which refers to the harp as an Irish symbol.

jects can be pretty bad; and if you return material, however nicely, it is a law of nature that the author will never speak to you again. So better write the entire first issue yourself. This is customary, but don't make it too blatant. And don't worry if it's not all good. Every zine may contain one really bad item to encourage the authors. This can be overdone, but bear in mind the immortal words of *The American Courier*. 'The *Courier* is forced to admit that it prints in each issue poems that should never see print, yet they do serve a purpose in that they make readers appreciate the really good poems with which each issue is sprinkled.' Poignant, isn't it, Mr. M?

After your first issues you will probably be delighted with letters like this: 'Dear Sir thank you for your fanzine I thought it was very good, much better than X, all the stories were very good especially Y, Z was good too but I think I read something like it before, the illustrations were very good I don't know how he does it with just a razor blade I'm sure I'd never have the patience.' In time even this heady stuff begins to pall, and the law of diminishing returns applies strictly to fanmags: so unless you improve you will attract less and less attention until you fold your mag and silently steal away. Tamam Shud.

Hyphen, #15, Nov., 1955; eds. Chuck Harris & Walt Willis; cartoon by Arthur Thompson riffs on the saying in sf fandom that "It is a proud and lonely thing to be a fan." This tag line originated from the final line in a W. McFarlane story, "To Watch the Watchers," in the June, 1949, issue of ASTOUNDING, about a spaceman on Mars, and Rick Sneary is given credit for using it first, substituting "fan" for "man."

Abstract, #9, 1955; ed. Peter J. Vorzimer; cover art by Ron Cobb.

BEHIND THE ZINE

Dean Grennell (1923-2004) was one of the names associated with the pseudo-Seventh Fandom that began in Harlan Ellison's Cleveland home in 1953 (see "123456789? What Was That Fandom I Saw You With..." pg. 280). Grennell stated his fannish philosophy in *Skyhook* #25, Autumn 1957: "The fan press sometimes seems to lean a shade heavily to discussions of conventions, feuds, fannish projects, polls, and power politics, with relatively little discussion of science fiction itself . . . I say there is excellent reason to discuss science fiction in magazines . . . not because it is the Fitting and Proper Thing to Do, but because it is rather good fun." Grennell's fanzine, *Grue* "The Fan's Magazine" (1953-1958), was a play on the name of the pro magazine TRUE: THE MEN'S MAGAZINE. Besides writing and editing, Grennell's artwork was a familiar sight in many 1950s fanzines. Grennell used filler numbers for many of his pieces, and published an all-filler zine so that zine editors could cite a number and readers could look up the appropriate filler. —LO

Dean Grennell

(from Abstract *#9, January, 1955, ed. Peter J. Vorzimer)*

LAST INSTALLMENT we discussed the more mechanical aspects of producing a readable fanzine. This time I propose to talk about the more-or-less psychological phases of fan-editing — how to maintain a smooth-running, well-oiled relationship with readers and contributors. Though it may be true that I don't always practice what I'm about to preach, it is equally true that your path will be measurably smoother if you do as I say and not necessarily as I do.

To begin with, let's recognize the basic difference between the fanzine and the prozine. A fairly popular prozine may run to a circulation of 100,000 or more. The average fanzine has a "press-run" of about 75 to 250 copies. There are a few fanzines that print up to 1500 copies but we're not concerned with them here. If their editors don't know what they're about they will soon be out of the game, litho charges being what they are.

The fanzine editor is personally acquainted, to varying degrees with nearly everybody he sends his magazine to. In most cases he has carried on correspondence with them at some time or another. If he is a knowing sort of fan-ed, he gradually builds up in his imagination a sort of *gestalt* compounded of the preferences, prejudices and foibles of his entire readership. A pro-ed tries to do the same thing but the vastly greater diversity of his readers makes the chore much more difficult.

So let's say, for the sake of hypothesis, that you are editing a magazine that goes to 150 people. You want the magazine to be popular and, with this in mind, you want the readers to enjoy it.

Does that sound a little obvious, put that way. Perhaps it is, but if one is to judge by some of the fanzines that turn up, it's a point that many a fan-ed never sees. How can one hope to please his readers with a fanzine composed chiefly (or entirely) of such tasty ingredients as imitation prozine stories, so trite and dull that they wouldn't rate a second glance at SPACEWAY; book and movie reviews, at once ponderous and pretentious and shallow as dew in a birdbath; ads from someone who has the September 1953 issue of PLANET to sell (no front cover) and wants to buy the June 1954 issue of BEAUTY PARADE. Those are but three samples of the guff of which crudzines are made.

But fan-eds continue to hopefully accumulate 6 or 8 pages of such material and mimeo them with indifferent skill onto the cheapest paper they can buy. They send them out to all the fan-eds whose addresses they can find, with invitations or demands to trade publications. They send them out to all the pro's whose addresses they can find with invitations or demands (the latter seems preferred) for material. And then they sit back and become understandably puzzled and hurt by the lack of any kind of reaction.

"So what," you ask, "are they supposed to put in their magazines if they want to titillate the reader's interest?"

That's a good question and I'm glad you asked. Happily enough, I have what I think may be the answer in one word. Egoboo.

There is nothing — absolutely nothing — that makes a reader feel at home in a fanzine like seeing his own name mentioned a place or two somewhere in the pages. Even though he may try to give the impression that he is possessed of becoming modesty, in his secret heart each of your readers is fairly fond of himself. If you give him the impression that you share his fondness, a bit of that *selbstliebe* will spill over onto you and your magazine.

All of this is quite basic in the human-relations field and I am stating it rather baldly, I suspect. I confess to a bit of misgivings over the possible effects of revealing trade secrets like this. Can't help but wonder if Pete's and my mutual readers will scan *Grue* with a new eye after reading it. But the truth of the matter, so help me, is that *Grue's* readers are fairly apt to find egoboo cropping up every ish or so because I honestly like them. If a fan-ed doesn't like his readers the fact is damnably difficult to conceal and if such is the case, why bother to put out a magazine in the first place?

But that, as I said before, is the prime difference between a fanzine and a prozine. Campbell, for example, can't work in little references to his readers because a mere listing of their last names would fill the whole issue. But scan through any of the more popular fanzines and you'll find passing mention of several of their readers in every issue. This is not mere coincidence but a clear case of cause and effect.

But what's the objective behind all this mutual back-scratching? Why worry about what the readers think? Isn't it, after all, *your* magazine, to do with as you like? What do you hope to gain?

If those are your questions, then maybe you look at things differently than I do. But I figure that even the most successful of subzines can't expect to take in much more than enough to cover the cost of the materials that go into it. You'll never get money for the countless hours of work that go into even a mediocre sort of fanzine. Face this fact squarely and recognize it for the basic law of nature that it is.

When you plant your ink and staples and paper and stamps and cultivate them with the best job you can possibly do of arranging the ink upon the paper, I can only presume that you're hoping for a harvest of comment — both in the form of letters and reviews in other fanzines and the occasional friendly prozine that deigns to notice the fan press. I imagine it must be pretty discouraging to send out a whole issue of a fanzine and get nothing back but a couple of postcards. I wouldn't know, thank Foo.

So we'll work on the assumption that you're primarily interested in comments coming back via first class mail. Those are the cream of the fan-ed's egoboo. Those are his wages for the weary hours spent slaving over a hot mimeo.

But before we go into the matter of extracting the most letters of comment from your investment of time and materials I'd like to note that there is an inescapable law of diminishing returns at work here, forever preventing a fanzine from getting too big and too good. The catch is those self-same letters just mentioned.

You see, nearly every one of those letter-writers is going to want some sort of direct answer to his letter of comment. And about the time you get to the point where you are cranking out 150 copies and getting back 75 letters something has *got* to give. Even if your magazine comes out every three months, it simply isn't in the cards to answer 25 letters a month and still keep your magazine coming out with its high standards unimpaired. Even if, by really superhuman exertion you answer the letters of comment a certain percentage of the readers will reply to your answer and you will shuttle back and forth forever like a small boy who must use a dixie cup to carry water back and forth for an elephant. Sooner or later you must perforce neglect some of your correspondence if you're going to keep the magazine going and the person neglected will stomp off in a snit, perhaps canceling his sub and making room for some newcomer to take you over the same weary hurdle all over again.

It can go the other way too. Some fan-eds make a conscientious effort to answer each and every piece of mail that comes in, even if it means neglecting their magazine. The end result of this course is that after the magazine dies a death of attrition the correspondence will eventually peter out and vanish. Gafia[59] lies down this path but there are fates worse than Gafia.

But enough of such morbid topics. You still want a sensible amount of comment on your magazine and you want to know how to get it. The answer, as previously noted, is to give your readers a feeling of participation in the magazine. One of the best ways to do this is to maintain a department of letters from readers. Here again the path is not entirely

---

[59] Get away from it all.

free of pitfalls for the unwary. A letter department can be one of the most interesting things in a fanzine or it can be one of the dreariest.

Encourage readers to shoot off on tangents by printing tangential material and comments that readers made in letters of comment about the previous issue. It is well to minimize the amount of comments where the readers merely say "I liked 'Lunar Schooner' in your last issue," or "For cripes' sake, 'Lunar Schooner' stank! The author should be shot!" Such comments are an invaluable aid to the editor in steering a course designed to please the majority of readers but they make dull fare for the rest of the readers.

And it's a good idea to make an effort toward including a little from everybody rather than two or three pages from just a few people. If you have a letter column and Joe Fann writes you a letter, he expects to see it in your next issue. Skip him a time or two and he will say to heck with that guy — he doesn't print my letters anyway. Here again there is a law of natural selection at work. Writers of the less-stimulating letters tend to be winnowed away in time. But I mustn't let that observation go without noting that you will inevitably lose some of the best ones and forget to include others you should have used. I doubt if there is a more efficient letter-loser in the business than the writer of this article.

So much for your steady readers, but what of the new reader and subscriber? Somebody sends you the price of your next issue — what do you do about it? Do you just file away the address, pocket the coin and forget it till it's time to mail out the issues? Alas, I'm afraid I'll have to confess that such is frequently my own procedure but I know better. It's not the right way to do things.

It's not so bad if the money arrives just as you're on the point of mailing out an issue. But if there's going to be a month or so between the time you get the money and the time your new customer gets his issue, then it's a very good idea to acknowledge it with some sort of thank-you note. Aschnouck as it turned out later, sent a barely literate card listing his subscription schedule as "3/25¢, 6/50¢, 9/75¢, 12/$1 ..." on up around 48/$4 or thereabouts. Thank foo I only sent him a quarter because he only had three issues left in him at that time.

I resolved in those days, that if I ever got to publishing a mag myself I'd always write a welcome-note to new subbers. But alas for good intentions, I haven't always been able to make it. The fact remains that it's a very good idea if you can swing it.

I had intended to take up the matter of dealing with contributors and prospective contributors in this installment as well. In fact, the filler number was chosen with that theme in mind. This is the same thing that happened last time when I started out with #97 and wound up with a column that should have been headed #87. Oh well ... drop by next issue and we'll make another stab at it.

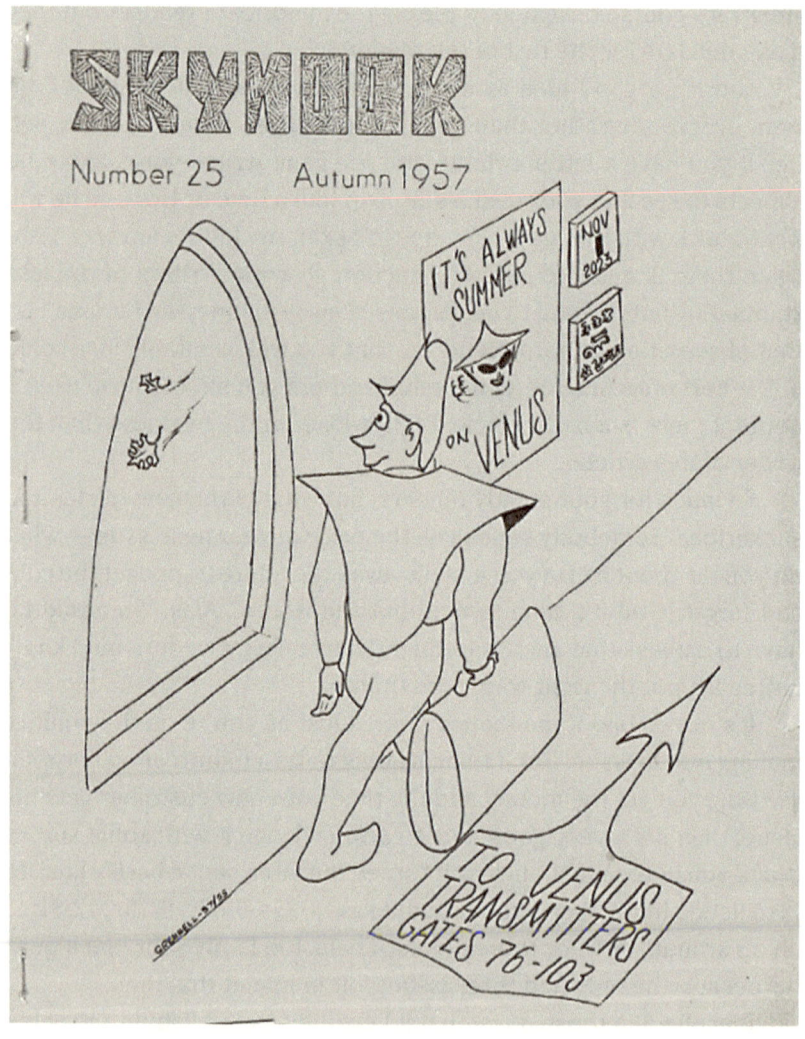

Skyhook, #25, Autumn 1957, eds. Red Boggs & Marion Z. Bradley; art by Dean Grennell.

Fascination

a guy can make a lot of goofs in the zine publishing field, as did Tom Piper when he was twelve and put out REASON, but the one who profits by these mistakes will have the better magazine. Such is the case with Tom and his new magazine, FASCINATION.

for top-notch fan-fiction from the best amateur writers, buy a copy, or be the wiser and order a sub to.....

```
          F A S C I N A T I O N
             c / o      Tom  Piper
             6111 Vista de la Mesa
             La  Jolla, California
```

are you a Neurotic?
are you a Paranoid?
are you a Schizophrenic?
are you a Manic-Depressive?

well, all in all, if you're crazy..PSYCHOTIC is for you!

PSYCHOTIC, reputed by many to be the best all-round fanzine in the U.S. has columns by Harlan Ellison, V.L. McCain, Terry Carr, Bob Stewart, and many others. Stories by almost every good fan author, and many other wonderful features......only one thin dime!

```
        RICHARD E. GEIS
        2631 N. Mississippi
        Portland 12, Oregon
```

is fandom's leading humor magazine. With photo-offset reproduction, HA! out-ranks them all. Send 15¢ for a single copy, or $1 for six issues!!

Here's what they say about "HA!" :

BOOB STEWART: HA! Stinks!
TERRY CARR: This is Humor?
TOM PIPER: "HA!"
LARRY BALINT: "AH!"
RON ELLIK: My Ghod!

Fanzine ads for *Fascination*, *Psychotic* and *HA!* from *Abstract* #1, January, 1954.

139

BEHIND THE ZINE

At the time, *Rhodomagnetic Digest* (early 1950s) was considered one of the quality sf zines or, as one critic put it: " . . . it actually discusses the things fans of science fiction are purportedly interested in."[60] *Rhodomagnetic Digest* began life as the clubzine for the Elves, Gnomes, and Little Men's Chowder, Science Fiction, and Marching Society before going its own way. Rhodomagnetism was a made-up science from Jack Williamson's sf novel **The Humanoids**. *RD* had 21 issues (plus a final "special") from 1949–1952, then was revived for two issues in 1962. —LO

EDITORIAL Q-ZINE OR F-ZINE

Don Fabun

(from Rhodomagnetic Digest *#18, 1952; ed. Don Fabun)*

THE DECEMBER '51 issue of Bob Silverberg's *Spaceship* No. 15 has at last struggled through the snows at Emigrant Gap and lies palpitating on our desk. The issue is reviewed elsewhere in *Rd* so I won't go into it here except to call your attention to pg. 25, where, under the heading "Backtalk (A Review of 1951)" Mr. Silverberg says:

> 1951 was a big year for fanzines, with quantity predominating and quality the keynote. But, in an era where fanzine tendencies are toward the up and up, leaning toward litho format, it's refreshing to note that the outstanding fanzine of 1951, *Quandry*, is but a mere mimeo publication which has to depend on the sparkle and personality for its popularity, rather than on the $$$ its editor lays out each issue. . .

Now the point at issue here is the apparent thought behind the

---

60 "Fan Pubs" conducted by Jerry Burge, *Cosmag* vol. 3, #2, Sept., 1952.

last sentence. The argument would seem to run like this:
1. There are two types of amateur publications in the fan field; quality magazines and fan magazines.
2. Of the two, only "fan" magazines are truly representative of fan publication.
3. The "quality" magazines achieve their effects because they spend a lot of money, whereas the "poor" fan magazine editor has to make up with good copy what he lacks in finances.

Somewhat the same idea, differently expressed, can be found in Greg Calkin's new *Oopsla* (Vol. 1, No. 1) in the "Slush Pile" review column and in Rog Phillips' article "How to Pub a FMZ and stay sane." It is also vaguely behind the controversy in Lee Hoffman's *Quandry* no. 16 concerning the abandonment of the slang "Chicon" in favor of the more dignified "Tenth Annual Science Fiction Convention." Commenting on the name change, Morton D. Paley in *Quandry* adds, "No one bothered to ask whether fandom wants a respectable convention."

To me, these are straws in the wind that indicate that there is a gap widening between what we are pleased (and probably wrongly so) to call the more "mature" element among science fiction readers and the vociferous, but usually adolescent, "true fans" who seldom, it seems to me, even read science fiction and even less often comment intelligently on it.

In many respects, the "true fan" groups represent a cult. In common with many other more or less spontaneous movements, they have invented an esoteric vocabulary that prevents "outsiders" from knowing what they are talking about and helps to conceal the fact that the "fans" frequently don't know what they are talking about, either.

The manipulation of this esoteric terminology takes place in "fanzines" which, by definition, are mimeographed, leaning heavily towards revealing the amazing fact that there are two sexes, and sometimes, if the editor runs out of material, even mention science fiction.

But there must also be a fairly large group of people who actually read science fiction, who are quite capable of spelling out big words like "magazine", and who attach no special significance to the fact that four letter words can be printed on a mimeograph machine.

These same people feel that it is possible to hold a convention for the purpose of discussing science fiction, meeting authors and publishers in the field, and exchanging ideas. It isn't absolutely necessary to hold a convention for the sole purpose of showing how drunk one can get, or for telling others how many old magazines one has in the attic.

In short, the old style fan is perhaps passing like the dodo; disappearing into that special limbo that now holds the old-style space opera, the bug-eyed monsters, and all the rest of the toys of the infancy of science fiction.

It is a passage that is already reflected in the professional magazines of the field. They are better printed, on better paper; by and large they are printing stories that have some intellectual content. The art work is better; the non-fiction articles are sharper and better informed. The field now supports three quite good magazines, the larger publishing houses are putting some effort and money into printing or reprinting (for the most part) the better science fiction stories.

No, the difference between the "quality" fan magazines and the "true" fan publications is more likely one of attitude than of money, and of the amount of work that is put into it. The attitude differs in that the "quality" magazine is attempting, through the best artwork it can get and a wide range of subject matter and presentation, to reach those science fiction readers who would not be caught dead at a convention, who actually read not only science fiction, but possibly a wide range of other types of literature as well; and to whom the true fan appears as a rather glorified bobby sox type.

The field of imaginative literature is very wide. There is room — and to spare — for every type and degree of reader awareness, for every approach and presentation in publication. And, to the extent that they are published by science fiction readers for science fiction readers they will all be "fan" magazines.

Fantasy Book, #2, 1947; cover by Crozetti. Another fanzine trying to imitate pro science fiction magazines. **(next pg., top left)** *Helios,* #2; July, 1937; ed. Sam Moskowitz. **(top right)** *Fantast,* July 1942; a British zine. **(bottom left)**: *Fanciful Tales,* Fall, 1936; Donald A. Wollheim and Wilson Shepherd conceived of this 50-page printed magazine of science and weird fiction. Wollheim edited, and helped financially, while Shepherd did the actual printing. One issue appeared. **(bottom right)** *VOM,* #25; October, 1942; eds. Forrest J Ackerman & Myrtle Douglas; with cover art by Ray Harryhausen.

Voice of the Imagi-Nation #23, June 1942; back cover by Turner; eds. Forrest J Ackerman & Morojo (Myrtle Douglas). The anonymous caption to this reads: "…. Not being acquainted with the British stencil and whether it'd fit our American made mimeo, we sent Harry several of our own stencils in requesting a drawing. About 3 weeks later, when we practically had forgot about them or unconsciously thot of them as nearing their destination, they turned up back at Box 6475, mark 1 & 1/2 ¢ due! Of all the @-#!?! things to do! So we stuck the extra postage on and hastily re-mailed it. Few days later, back again. Stamp fell off or some darn thing. Meantime, Turner received letter advising stencils on way, wonders where on earth or under the Atlantic they are. Eventually: 'How do you guys manage to draw on these godawful stencils? British stencils are sensible; they're white and if you draw on them using a carbon backing sheet, it's easy to see what you're up to. But with yours…well, you're working in the dark all the time — literally and metaphorically! It took a bit of getting used to, but I think my first effort is passable.' Passable? Well-nigh unsurpassable! pal, from what we can make out on the stencil. And no one who's seen the stencil has been able to pass her by or Turrner way. LET THERE BE LIGHT!"

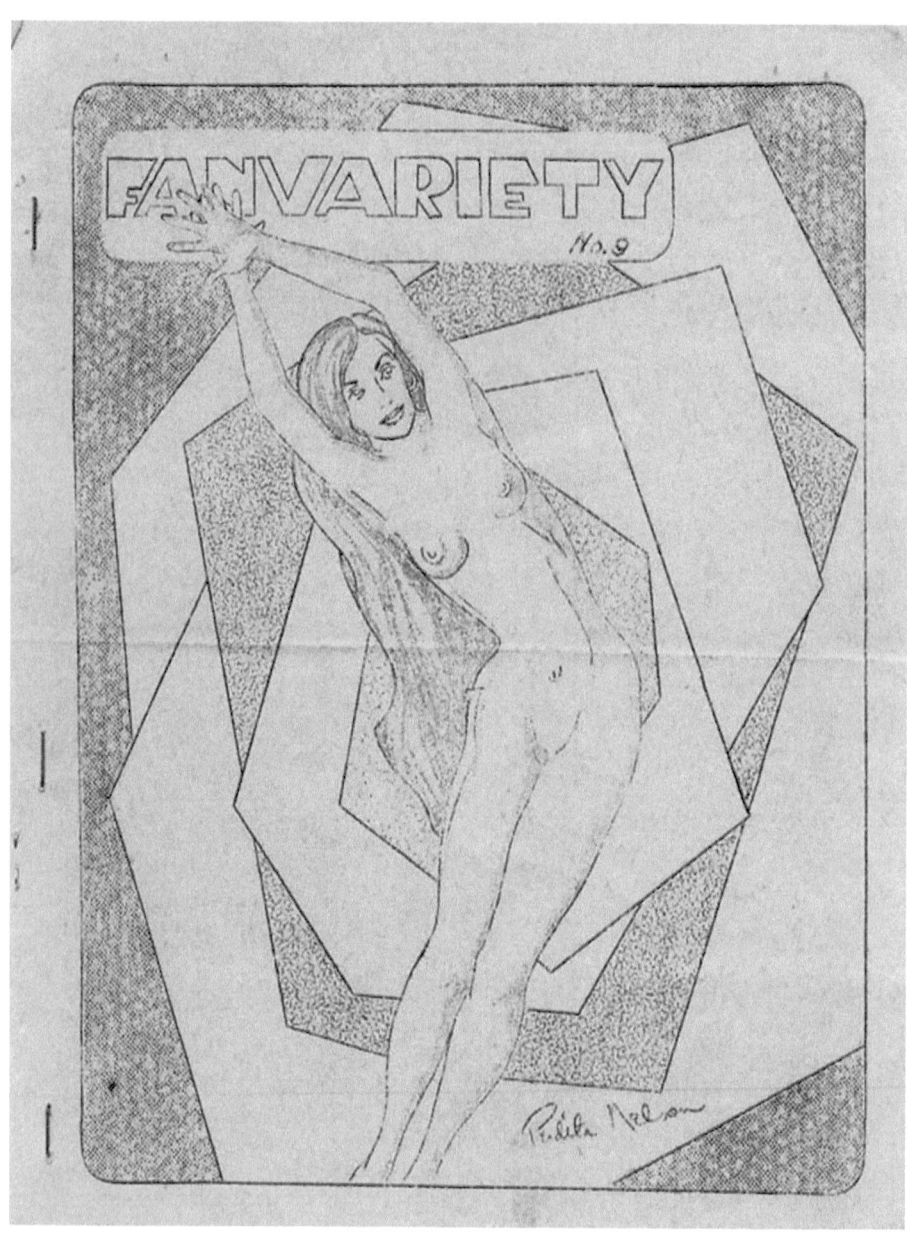

Fanvariety #9, June, 1951; ed. Max Keasler; cover art by Perdita Nelson, who was married to Ray Nelson for a time during the early 1950s. In *Void* #21, April, 1960, Harry Warner said of *Fanvariety*, "By my standards, it was a very good fanzine because it was fun to read and did no particular harm, two qualities which seem to me the most important good things that a fanzine can possess."

FANZINES IN PROFILE

There have always been a lot of nudes in sf fanzines, which is not surprising considering the makeup of sf fanzine editors — teenagers and young (mostly single) men — and how each fanzine was vying for attention from other fans and fanzines. When it became known that the postal authority was threatening to ban a few fanzines (including *Incinerations, Fanvariety, Odd,* and *Opus*) from going through the mail due to what they considered indecent content (usually illustrations), Russell K. Watkins (editor of *Dawn*) took it upon himself to propose a "Crusade to Clean Up Fandom" and suggested that fanzines should be limited to three or four "approved" organs. Of course, this met with a bit of opposition from a lot of fans, including Max Keasler (co-editor of *Fanvariety*, who would boast that he never read sf). On the other hand, there were a few editors that signed onto Watkins' crusade, but let's not go there. —LO

PURE AS NEW FALLEN SLUSH

Max Keasler

(from Quandry *#15, November, 1951; ed. Lee Hoffman)*

WELL, RUSS, Lee said she would like to get this little discussion off to a nice start. So here I am with a smile on my lips and a song in my heart.

You state *Fanvariety* is one of the "uncleanest" fanzines. May I ask how you know that cause I can't ever remember sending you copies. Or do your best friends tell you. Reason I never sent you a copy is that you are most certainly that type of fan I don't want reading *Fanvariety*. I'm looking for an open minded fan, not one with holes in his head. I think I once got a copy of your fanzine when I bought a batch from another fan. I read it too and as I said I never bothered to exchange. I don't know what ever happened to the copy. Must have used it to slip-sheet *Fanvariety*.

Fanvariety is not a stf fanzine and it was never intended to be one. It was first started to publish material that deals with any topic. This could be science-fiction, religion, music, weird, fantasy, good housekeeping, politics, and yes, sex. That's S-E-X. I hope this isn't over your head.

I also think *Fanvariety* was as bad as *Incinerations*, but what if it was, so what? We've toned it down lately. Not cause we wanted tho, but because the post-office told us to. We twist no one's arm to read *Fanvariety*. I guess those first 9 issues were the last of the red-hot fanzines. They will all have to go now and I'm truly sorry to see it.

Early 1960s fanzine cartoon by William Rotsler (1926–1997), who was one of the most prolific sf fanzine artists between the mid 1940s and his death in 1997. His art and cartoons appeared in hundreds of fanzines. Dean Grennell, in his zine *Grue* (#28, May, 1956), said of him, "I wonder, sometimes, if it's possible for two fans to discuss sex without bringing Rotsler into the conversation."

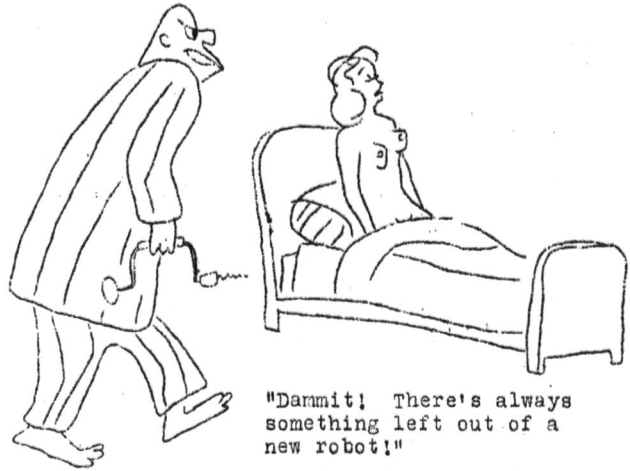

"Dammit! There's always something left out of a new robot!"

Fanac #21, July, 1958; cartoon by Ray Nelson (aka R. Faraday Nelson) who, along with Bill Rotsler, were the premier sf fanzine cartoonists during the 1950s–1960s.

As for your rather gosh-wow-boy-oh-boy idea about consolidating fanzines into 2 or 3 fanzines. That is the biggest fugghead statement since someone wanted to start a Slan Center[61]. Fandom is a hobby, not a way of life, at least not to me. Those fanzines you're talking about wouldn't hold water. Fans have their "professional fanzines" already and some of them are edited by fans. They are called something like prozines or pulp. That have fiction by fans, fan news, etc. But fans still turn to fanzines like they are today. Do you know what has made all great fanzines? It's elementary, my dear Watkins. Do you know what made *Le Zombie, Spaceway, Time-Traveller, Science-Fiction Digest, Shaggy, Fan-dango, Spacewarp* and the other few greats? It was the single personality of the editor and his choice of material. Personality, I said. Maybe you'd better look that up. I can wait.

I'm afraid you'll also find me uh ... what was that phrase you used? Very cute, I think, "downright ornery." You can ask my readers and they'll agree with you. I'm downright ornery. So what? I'm happy as well as downright ornery. Also a bad speller and slightly nearsighted.

This is one editor that doesn't print in *Fanvariety* what my readers like. What goes in *Fanvariety* is what Bill Veneble and I want, not the readers. Since they do very little about footing the bill, I don't care if they like the material or not. If they like it, that makes it nice.

61 A place where fans live cooperatively.

If not, that's too bad. They're welcome to cancel their subscriptions or exchanges. Once I quit running what I like in *Fanvariety*, I'll stop publishing the magazine. You can ask the NFFF about that if you like.

I don't consider profanity a decent language. Personally I don't care for it, cause anyone can curse. I like something original, clever, even funny. If someone can write an article and be at least a little bit original, I'll print it. Whether it has to do with stf, religion, or sex. If I didn't like something in a fanzine I wouldn't read it. I most certainly wouldn't say just because I didn't like a bit of material, no one else should read it, even if they do like it. That's what you do, cause you and your CCF gang don't like "unclean" material (to coin another one of your sappy terms) no one else should. Well, I don't care much for you. Should I ignore you like I always have or should I organize a LET'S CLEAN UP RUSS WATKINS CRUSADE?

Since your Rebuttal is a clean-up crusade I would suggest you call it, "Through Fandom with Mop and Pail." As you said, Russ, everyone's tastes differ from another person's so let's just let it rest at that. That's why they print more than one magazine, you know. Thought I'd pass it on to you. Little things like that are nice to know.

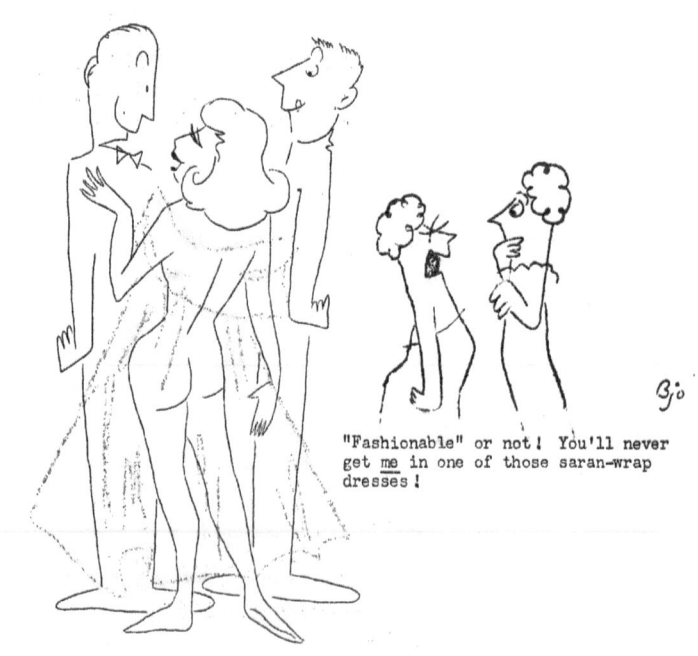

"Fashionable" or not! You'll never get me in one of those saran-wrap dresses!

Shaver Mystery Magazine, vol. 2, #4, 1948; art by Virgil Finlay, who was a pro artist popular with sf fans. He did not create art directly for fanzines, but *Shaver Mystery Magazine* would use art from Ray Palmer's OTHER WORLDS.

HOAXES, DIGRESSIONS & FEUDS

The piece that follows, from the British fanzine *Fantasy Review*, gives a good account of the Palmer/Shaver fracas (aka "Fan-Rap-War") that roiled fandom during the 1940s. Sf fans rebelled when Palmer, as editor of AMAZING STORIES, attempted to pass off Richard Shaver's fiction (about an underground super-race's manipulation of humans) as non-fiction. Palmer was an early advocate for UFOs and after leaving AMAZING in 1949 began the "non-fiction" FATE (later sold, and still publishing), to cover his more mystical (some would say commercial) publishing interests, and the sf magazine OTHER WORLDS, which evolved into FLYING SAUCERS FROM OTHER WORLDS, then finally just FLYING SAUCERS. —LO

THE PALMER HOAX

Geoffrey Giles

(from Fantasy Review *#17, Winter 1949; ed. Walter Gillings)*

"Science fiction is . . . pregnant with wonderful possibilities for development into a new and infinitely beneficial type of literature . . . To achieve (its) purpose (it) must contain actual scientific facts and ideas not based on unfounded theory. Thus it is up to the writers of this fiction to include . . . real science and sound reasoning in their stories . . . It is in the production of more accurate and better science fiction that I am now greatly interested . . . " — "What I Have Done to Spread Science Fiction" —Raymond A. Palmer

TWENTY YEARS ago, when he wrote to SCIENCE WONDER STORIES telling "What I Have Done to Spread Science Fiction," and collected $100 in a Gernsback propaganda contest for his pains, Raymond A. Palmer, secretary of the Science Correspondence Club, was a young Milwaukee, Wisconsin fan who had been converted in 1926 by a copy of AMAZING STORIES he had bought at a drugstore newsstand. Little did he suspect, as he succumbed to its pure delights, that he was destined to become editor of that same magazine — or, rather, of a magazine with the same title. Nor that he was to be assailed by its once devoted readers for deserting the principles he had laid down and degrading science fiction with the unfounded theory and false reasoning of the so-called Shaver Mystery.

By 1938, when the Ziff-Davis Publishing Company of Chicago acquired the decrepit pioneer of sf magazines [AMAZING STORIES], with a view to re-vamping it in the same way that *Wonder* had been made over into THRILLING WONDER a couple of years before, the name of Ray Palmer had come to mean something in sf circles. Having stimulated correspondence between hundreds of fans and authors, he had launched the first of all fan magazines, *Cosmology*, subsequently to join in the production of *Science Fiction Digest* (later *Fantasy Magazine*) with Mort Weisinger (who became THRILLING WONDER's assistant editor[62]), Julius Schwartz (leading sf writer's agent of the 1930s), and Forrest J Ackerman. As Literary Editor, he originated the famous "Cosmos" serial and reported on current trends in a feature titled "Spilling the Atoms," signed with the well-known initials RAP. He also contributed a five-part serial, "The Vortex World," himself.

As a writer of fiction, however, he did more in other fields than in fantasy, where he had made the grade in WONDER STORIES with "The Time-Ray of Jandra" (Jun. 1930). A member of the Milwaukee Fictioneers, to whom he introduced the late Stanley G. Weinbaum (whose Memorial Volume he supervised all too soon afterwards), he churned out material for detective, western and adventure magazines under his own and other names[63]. With such a wide experience for a comparatively young man, such a record in the sf field, and such enthusiasm as he always displayed whatever he tackled, he was just the man Editor B.G. Davis wanted to pep up AMAZING. Or, as RAP himself put it, looking back after two years of directing its altered course and that of FANTASTIC ADVENTURES, which he started in 1939:

---

62 Weisinger (1915–1978) went on to become the editor of Superman comic books.
63 Self-confessed pseudonyms: Rae Winters, A. R. Steber, Alexander Blade, Wallace Quitman, Morris J. Steele. Palmer has also said that he had a lot to do with the actual writing of Richard S. Shaver stories in AMAZING. [Footnote from original fanzine.]

"I succeeded in deluding him into committing the magazine into my tender care ... You can imagine how I felt. Here at last I had it in my power to do to my old hobby what I had always had the driving desire to do . . . the power to destroy, to create, to remake, at my own discretion." He was "determined to make the worst magazine . . . the best in the field"; and in spite of sf's recent invigoration by ASTOUNDING and THRILLING WONDER, which he had heartily welcomed, he found ample scope for his new powers. "Half-baked ideas, screwy science, and pedantic, unprofessional writing. Not one professional author's touch glittered from the . . . dung heap of gadgets, theories and interplanetary travelogues. There wasn't a living, breathing character, emotion (or) adventure in the whole lot." [64]

EMOTION AND "HACK WORDS"

It was a "tremendous task" to get the sort of stories he thought were needed from authors who, in spite of their plentiful ideas, "didn't know what a plot was." The contents of his first (Jun. '38) refurbished issue, which he whipped up in a fortnight, were far from satisfying him: "Only (John Russell) Fearn ('A Summons from Mars') was any good." He readily agreed with the fan who immediately decided: "Your revised AMAZING STORIES stinks." Yet circulation climbed as for two years he strove to teach a new roster of old and new writers what he thought his readers if not the protesting fans, wanted — stories full of human interest, in which the emotional problem was more important than the science; although, to start off with, the cover carried the slogan: "Every story Scientifically Accurate." Stories, too, which were simply told with the "hack words" he advocated, rather than the "pretty, high-sounding phrasing" which some of his most difficult authors (e.g., Robert Moore Williams) insisted on putting into the MSS. he rejected.

But the fans were quite intractable. They squawked, loudly and resentfully, in their mimeographed critiques, against the blatantly juvenile appeal of the Ziff-Davis magazines; the repulsively hideous cover BEMs; the scrawly, sexy interior illustrations; the old fashioned, overlong story-titles; the puerile humor and, not least of all, the ram-

---

64 In an article, "Palmer Tears His Hair," published by William Lawrence Hamling in his amateur magazine, *Stardust* (Nov., 1940). [footnote from original fanzine]

blings of RAP in "The Observatory." Whatever he had accomplished as a fan as an editor, *Spaceways*' "Star Treader" [column]; regretted, Palmer was "a pathetic flop." Again, as he saw it himself in retrospect: "All through those two years, the fans swung their axes at my head. Not only did my magazine stink, but I too . . . I was a traitor to science fiction . . . I dragged the 'literature' of sf down into the dirty, filthy fen of 'hack' pulp . . . I printed tripe. I ground good sf writers into the dirt."

What riled him most was that all the time they actually denounced him for trying "to sell AMAZING STORIES. And I have! I have taken the worst magazine in all sf history and brought it up to the peak of sales. I have pleased my publishers immensely." So he consoled himself; while, at the same time that he discounted the reactions of an estimated 200 fans, he reminded them of his continued championship of their cause, their likes and dislikes, their organized activities. "In every instance, where it was sensible, I gave (them) what they asked for. And no editorial office in the country is as open and extends as hearty a welcome to the visiting fan as does Ziff-Davis."

Such items as Weinbaum's novel, "The New Adam" (AMAZING, Feb.-Mar. 1943), new Edgar Rice Burroughs tales. Willy Ley articles, and Paul's back cover conceptions of extra-terrestrial life, were not unacceptable to the fan reader, as AMAZING and its even more flamboyant sister-mag progressed—or careered-through the next few years. But the fans did not ask for the Shaver Mystery, which in 1945 came as the final insult to their long-suffering intelligence. Richard S. Shaver's Lemurian fantasies, which began to monopolize both magazines, were fair enough, as Ziff-Davis material went; but to be expected to accept them as truth — or as "racial memories" with a foundation of actual fact — was too much. To them, it was the Shaver Hoax, Lemurian alphabets and other "proofs" notwithstanding: to a *Fantasy Times* commentator, these were so much "idiotic flapdoodle and mystical balderdash." The whole unhealthy business was dismissed as a stunt to revive dwindling circulation by attracting the lunatic fringe to the Palmer magazines; and if such was his aim, the decent thing would be to disassociate them from the legitimate sf field. To put it more bluntly — which the *Fantasy Times* headline did: "Scram, Mr. Palmer!"

THE NEW SF?

But RAP had become used to fandom's hard knocks. Not only did he fulfill critic Thomas S. Gardner's early prediction that his new policy would prove such "an outstanding success ... that the Lemurian hoax will go on for years, possibly becoming a permanent esoteric feature Of AMAZING STORIES,"[65] but he had the audacity to suggest that this was "the new sf" which was going to revolutionize and vastly extend the field. Such "flagrant disregard" of fandom's disapproval by "our own little two-bit dictator ... who would turn sf into a plaything for every semi-sane crackpot who ever dreamt he was a Lemurian" could not be permitted to go unchallenged. A meeting of the Queens (New York) Science Fiction League solemnly passed a resolution expressing the opinion that the Shaver "Cave" stories actually endangered the sanity of their readers, and bringing the menace to the notice of the Society for the Suppression of Vice. A fan conference in Philadelphia discussed a proposal that a 1,000-signature petition be organized to get the offending magazines banned by the Post Office; but this project did not meet with approval, although speakers were unanimous in denouncing the Shaver Mythos' as paranoiac.

There was even a suggestion that Editor Palmer had been taken off to a mental institution, which was subsequently revealed as a deliberate hoax perpetrated by RAP himself, with the connivance of assistant editor William Lawrence Hamling, former editor of *Stardust* and a successful recruit to AMAZING's staff of writers. According to Hamling, fandom had passed up a great chance to enlarge its circle by its uncompromising attitude; but it only railed against the Shaver Hoax with redoubled vigor, while Palmer reiterated time and again that, according to the Pennsylvanian steel worker who claimed to remember Lemuria, the stories he welded from his ancestral memories were "based on true conditions as yet beyond the ken of ordinary men."

The only reasonably certain fact that emerged was that the business had indeed been good for circulation. When fan Gordon M. Kull, returning in blissful ignorance from the wars, called on him to find out what all the fuss was about. RAP claimed that the sales of AMAZING had gone up by 50,000, almost overnight, following the presentation

---

65 "Calling All Crackpots! An Analysis of the Lemurian Hoax", *Fantasy Commentator*, Spring 1945. [Footnote from original fanzine]

of the Mystery as "something new in science fiction" without any expectation of its devastating effects. By that time, he had received such a mass of "evidence" in support of Shaver's premise (that the descendants of the Lemurians still live in their subterranean lairs) that he was practically persuaded of the truth of it. Yet he wanted desperately to be friends with fandom; he thought their animosity towards him was blinding them to the good stories he was using, apart from those of Shaver and his imitators (who knew a good thing when they saw it).

The occurrence of such material (especially by Chester S. Geier and Rog Phillips) had been duly noted, however, by the more impartial critics. Nor did the fans fail to observe that, apparently as reward for his circulation-raising tactics — whether calculated or fortuitous — RAP had been promoted to editorship of the whole Ziff-Davis pulp magazine set-up, Hamling taking his place as Managing Editor. And when, at the end of 1947, he made a real gesture of friendship by initiating a new department devoted to their [fans] activities in AMAZING, the fans wisely decided to let bygones be bygones, even though they would still have no truck with Shaver. As an ambassador of his goodwill, RAP sent out Roger P. Graham, who was to conduct "The Clubhouse" [a fanzine review column] under his Rog Phillips pen name; his likeable personality endeared him to the fans on sight, and ensured their ungrudging cooperation. "We wish Mr. Graham... good luck," *Fantasy Times* Editor James V. Taurasi patronized, "and hope that the day is not too far off when AMAZING STORIES can once again return to the sf fold."

A CHALLENGE TO 'FATE'

That was two years ago; since when there have been indications that the Shaver Mystery, having served its purpose and remained insoluble, was going to be abandoned. But its unwholesome aroma, and the writings of Shaver, lingered in both AMAZING and FANTASTIC; while the problem of the "deros" received further impetus in other quarters, notably in the magazine of the Shaver Mystery Club, formed to continue the "investigation" when it looked as though AMAZING was about to drop it. Extensive book publication of the longer works of Shaver and other Ziff-Davis writers exploiting the "Elder World" theme has also been embarked upon. The appearance of FATE, 'whose points of similarity with the Palmer magazines were obvious in spite of its different imprint and nonfiction content, afforded an opportunity to attract further notice to the first of these works through its advertising pages; though it was not until the magazine had been running well over a year, during which it concerned itself with such matters as the Flying Saucers, lost planets and ghostly visitations, that it took up the "challenge" of Shaver in response to a reader's letter (in the Jul. 1949 issue).

"If Richard S. Shaver has anything, we'll print the truth about it. If he hasn't, we'll print that too ... To us it seems amazing that no one has seen fit to present the facts about a subject that hits our mail as often as this one does." Thus Editor Robert N. Webster's comment, right next to an ad for the Shaver Mystery Club. And, having "put a writer on Mr. Shaver's trail," in the November issue he promised to run an article on the theme: "Is the earth hollow . . . honeycombed with vast caverns inhabited by living beings? Or is there another answer to the mystery created by Richard S. Shaver, one of the most unusual pulp writers in America today? Puzzle with us over THE SHAVER MYSTERY."

Simultaneously, OTHER WORLDS: SCIENCE STORIES, newly launched by the publishers of FATE (Clark Publishing Co., Chicago), featured in its initial (Nov. 1949) issue "The Fall of Lemuria," by Shaver, and offered for the future his "Kingdom of the Gods," a "tremendous new tale from the thought records of the dead race who once inhabited the lost caverns of the Earth," inaugurating a "new series of the world's most imaginative and stimulating stories." Suggesting that the Mystery, however insoluble, was still good for much more cogitation. And for some more editorial teasing; for, as Editor Webster observed: "Mr. Shaver as some of you well know, puts a certain verisimilitude into his writing, and in all sincerity claims it is not entirely fiction. We don't take any stand on that ... "

What has all this to do with RAP? This time, Editor Palmer has hoaxed fandom well and truly — and, again, has been his own exposer. On the eve of the appearance of OTHER WORLDS, he took the 200 fans assembled at the Cincinnati World Science Fiction Convention by surprise by appearing amongst them, for the first time for many years, and letting them into his stable secrets. Mouths and eyes opened wide as he blandly announced that he was no longer Editor of the Ziff-Davis magazines, having resigned his position because of disagreements over editorial policy during the past two years. He proceeded to reveal that he and Robert N. Webster are in fact, one and the same person, and that the Clark Publishing Co. now belongs to him.

He went so far as to express his own preference for the type of sf published by ASTOUNDING, while promising that, as from the third issue of his new mag, he would give readers of OTHER WORLDS the type of sf he really believes in. But editor-publisher Palmer was not done with the Shaver Mystery. The whole business, he insisted in his talk to the fans, is so convincing that he believes in it as much as Shaver believes in every word he writes: he himself has "heard the voices," and "everything that happens to Shaver is bad." It must, therefore, be true. However, as truth the Shaver Mystery should properly be presented by a magazine like FATE; as for his other stories, they will be used in OTHER WORLDS as long as they're science fiction. So, having made them a present of OW's first cover painting (depicting a luscious snake-woman from the Shaver novelette), which got auctioned off for $32, RAP made his excuses and departed, to the accompaniment of every indication from his audience that he wasn't, in their estimation, such a flop after all.

NO MORE PARANOIA

What of AMAZING and FANTASTIC? Their new editor, Howard Browne, was not slow to issue a statement concerning future policy. Both magazines, he said, will attempt to give "fandom and other readers" the kind of sf and fantasy they have been requesting "for so many years," but neither will become "a pseudo-scientific journal." The same story elements, which RAP held so important, will remain paramount, but the scientific interest will not be neglected. At the same time, the "comic book type of (story) will be weeded out as quickly as possible, (and) all the type of mysticism that borders on paranoia will not be published by us."

Requesting fandom to withhold judgment until changes in policy can take effect (with the February issues), Editor Browne welcomed suggestions and criticisms, adding: "Our writers are not going to 'write down' to the readers, nor are they going to impugn the basic laws of science by offering as truth the babblings of befuddled minds." Whereupon *Fantasy Times*, its expressed hope of two years ago showing promise of realization, wished the new editor all success and the objects of its former opprobrium a healthy future as "outstanding sf magazines."

As yet, fandom's reactions to OTHER WORLDS are not forthcoming; but Editor "Webster" appeared to be playing safe. "Our policy," said he, in an editorial mentioning six of its competitors by name, "is sf at its best." Of ASTOUNDING he frankly admitted: "We like its editor John W. Campbell, and we think he's tops when it comes to putting up-to-the-minute science in the stories ... and he's always careful to be 100 per cent accurate in his science data." Of "Ray Palmer's AMAZING": "There's a mag we cut our eye-teeth on. It's given us countless hours of pleasure and quite a few surprises." Each story in his first issue, he tried to show, might well have appeared in one of "our older competitors (to which) we nod with respect": Shaver's piece in AMAZING, of course; Rog Phillips' "The Miracle of Elmer Wilde" in ASTOUNDING; G. H. Irwin's "Where No Foot Walks" (written to order around its title) in *Planet*; John Wiley's "Venus Trouble Shooter" in THRILLING WONDER or STARTLING. "But . . . we intend to beat each one at its own game by giving (our) readers exactly what they want ... the best stories that money can buy and the best editing that 26 years of experience in the field can give ..."

On the face of it, it seemed that RAP, with a FATE full of weird and wonderful mysteries, and an OTHER WORLDS full of amazing, startling, astounding science fiction, was going to make the best of all possible worlds henceforth.

Fantasy Advertiser #10, 1954; art by Jack Gaughan.

Shaver Mystery Magazine, no issue #, 1947; cover art by Richard Shaver. At one point in early 1948 Palmer sent word to fans (through Rog Phillips) that he was going to publish proof (with photos) of the Shaver mystery in AMAZING STORIES, but then announced that it would stop printing any more Shaver material since AMAZING was a fiction mag.

Fantasy Advertiser, vol. 4, #5; Nov., 1950; back cover art by Jack Gaughan, which shows a cover within a cover. (Jonbrian is a pen name based on his first and middle names, John Brian.) Gaughan would go on to work for all the major pro sf mags and book publishers, and won Hugo Awards as best fan and best pro artist in 1967 — the only person to ever win these awards in the same year. Gaughan was also the first fan artist to sell art to ASTOUNDING. (**insert**) Front cover, with art by Neil Austin.

Psychotic #22, Dec.1967; cover art by Bill Rotsler. A continuation, after a 12-year hiatus, of the fanzine Richard E. Geis started in July 1953.

Fanfare #8, Feb., 1942; Ed. Art Widner, Jr.; art by Roy Hunt, showing Lovecraft's Cthulhu.

Fantastic Worlds #5, Fall, 1953; eds. Sam Sackett & Stewart Kemble; cover art by Neil Austin. A self-styled "literary magazine in the fields of science fiction and fantasy."

PROS & FANS

It appears that there was, at times, a somewhat contentious relationship between fanzine editors and pro science fiction magazine editors that grew more strident during the 1950s. (Ray Palmer, of course, always had a special love/hate relationship with fans.) The general viewpoint of a few pro editors was that fanzine fans, and sf fans in general, made up a tiny potion of their readership and were therefore not worth any special efforts at appeasement. This subtle love-hate viewpoint towards sf fans is voiced by pro editor H.L. Gold (GALAXY) in the following piece, who somehow manages to blames sf fans for the demise of sf magazines. I have found little information about Andrew Gregg. —LO

Andrew Gregg

(from Rhodomagnetic Digest *#20, 1952; ed. Don Fabun)*

ON MARCH third I sent out a form questionnaire to 15 editors of science fiction and fantasy magazines. There were 22 questions which were intended to furnish the basis for an article entitled, "The Editors Say." Now over a month later, six editors have responded, and the article is entitled "Some Editors Say."

They were returned, honestly filled out, by William L. Hamling of IMAGINATION; Jerome Bixby, of THRILLING; Ed Ludwig of *Fantastic Worlds*, a new "little" magazine, Anthony Boucher (also for J. Francis McComas) of THE MAGAZINE OF FANTASY AND SCIENCE FICTION; and H.L. Gold of GALAXY. Paul W. Fairman of IF, demurred by saying he hadn't been in "the game long enough to answer intelligibly." Either he didn't read as far as the second page or he doesn't know what he wants in his magazine or how much he pays.

What follows should not be construed to be the opinion of all prozine editors. But if they have differing opinions, or if they take offense, by God, they can send my questionnaire back! The following is based on what these five editors say. (For objectivity, not clarity, all my statements and comments from now on are in parenthesis).

They have read fanzines, usually to keep abreast of current fan news, opinions and trends, although some like fanzines for the fun they get out of them, Fanzines come in all classes. Their editors seem to get a lot of enjoyment out of putting them out, but don't put enough effort into them to attain a quality format. In fact, some of them are downright sloppy!

As for the most popular fanzine, that's *Slant*, because it has a fresh approach, high quality of writing and wit, and Walt Willis. Next is the *Science Fiction Newsletter* & *Fantasy Times*, for accurate reporting and the latest fan news. After that is *Rhodomagnetic Digest* for intelligence, liveliness, and good production, although it is sometimes too controversial.

Quandry is next because it is generally mature and interesting. *Peon* is more mature and unpretentious than most, and is more discriminating in its choice of material. Others specially mentioned were *Fantasy Commentator, Fantasy Advertiser, Destiny* and *Fan Faire*. (Note to other fanzine editors; don't feel discouraged. They may read yours, and there are ten other editors that might like your mag).

In these editors' opinions, the percentage of active fans who read their prozines range from a half of 1% for IMAGINATION, to "under 10%" for GALAXY. An average active fan comes in all shapes and sizes. A good number are in their middle teens, with above average intelligence and imagination, but too many tend to be slightly confused in a neurotic sort of way, a bit snobbish about science fiction and emotionally immature.

An inactive fan, reading but not writing or participating in fandom, is more mature, and often hasn't time to participate actively because he also has to earn a living. An inactive fan reads what he likes and follows no fads. As for the feuds sometimes carried on between fans, Hamling thinks they do nothing but hurt science fiction. Bixby says they are "usually preposterous" and Boucher, laconically, "Nuts!"

Boucher and Gold, editors of higher quality magazines, don't have readers' columns because the majority of their readers don't want them. Hamling and Bixby have them because the readers want them and because they think it helps circulation.

As for writing, most of the professional writers are not fans, of course, but, since sf is so radically different in many ways from other fiction, the best sf stories are by fans. The worst material that Thrilling Pubs get is from fans, while Ludwig says that "fan material submitted is five times better, usually, than the material submitted by non-fan readers of writers' magazines." (However, most good material submitted to any magazine comes through agents, irrespective of whether the writers are fans or not).

Seeing your work in a fanzine may give you courage and objectivity, but few fanzines are particular about the quality of the material they print, and you'll get no editorial aid from them. If a fan is really interested in pro writing, he should try an agent or a magazine that helps and encourages beginning writers. The most promising fanzine writers now are Tony Duane, Tom Covington, Lin Carter, Jan Romanoff, Lee Hoffman, Herman S. King, Walt Willis, Clive Jackson, Russel Branch, Vernon McCain, Bob Silverberg, and two others, Joe Kennedy and Len Moffat are already on their way.

If you're sending stories to the following magazines, here are their "pet peeves."

IMAGINATION: Nice suspense and action opening and good build-up towards climax, then writer suddenly decides to get cute with a twist that leaves whole story up in the air but is veddy, veddy stylish.

THRILLING WONDER: SUPER SCIENCE: Slice-of-life and mood-piece stuff.

Fantastic Worlds: Postage due on manuscripts; also sending in mss. without first checking to find out what kind of material the magazine uses.

FANTASY & SCIENCE FICTION: The plot of the man who-is-dead-all-the-time-and-doesn't-know-it.

GALAXY: Any story that lacks literary skill.

According to the editors, the reasons why most stories are rejected are:

IMAGINATION: They're just not good enough.

TWS-SS: It doesn't have a real strong story. If it had one and still bounced, it wasn't an interesting, plausible, or well-written story.

Fantastic Worlds: The idea is too trite. Editor Ludwig said he had received, in three days, "seven humorous stories of the devil arriving on earth, and 14 stories about the hero seeing a strange old man who, the climax reveals, has been dead for 73 years."

Summing up the prozines attitude toward fans, Horace L. Gold, who saved GALAXY last year by finding new backers, should be quoted:

"When sf was fighting for a toe-hold, fandom kept it alive. For that, if for nothing else, sf owes fandom a great debt.

"Today, however, with sf becoming increasingly widely accepted, organized fandom can present a genuine danger to an editor or publisher. Active fans obviously write more and demand more than those who are inactive, and any number of magazines have made the mistake of construing those opinions as general ones; the result? Count the number of magazines that have gone out of business.

"Understand this . . . fandom is the unshakable, dependable core of sf readership, the people we can rely on for steady sales, and for this reason has supportive value that rates appreciation ... when not in direct conflict with those of the majority of readers.

"For, you must recognize, non-active readers are undeniably the major market and they are the ones who ultimately decide whether a magazine is to be a success or a failure. Magazines that have depended entirely upon fan sales have failed; witness the appalling number that have suspended publication.

"A realistic assessment would be about this: fans are exceedingly important to the success of a magazine, but their special requirements can be economically suicidal when granted at the expense of the general readership.

"Do I like fans? Love 'em! But as a professional editor and writer, I have to consider the demands of fandom and those of non-active readers, and follow the ones that produce the greatest effective results. A deplorable commercial attitude, no doubt, but I'd rather have a live magazine that arouses fans' ire than a dead one that reaps their encomiums and ultimate condolences."

(And there you'll find more information than a million questionnaires would unearth!)

Le Zombie #66, Dec., 1968; cover art by Ronald Clyne. "Jiant" 30th Anniversary Issue. There was a gap of ten years between issues 65 and 66. An ad for *Le Zombie* from a 1939 issue of *Funtasy*: "The other day a man dead and supposedly buried three years walked into a public library and demanded to read the latest LE ZOMBIE. 'The Ghoul's Ghazette.' It's just the thing to take with you on that trip to Valhalla!"

THE FANZINE LIFE

Bob Tucker was possibly the most prolific of fanzine writers. His first fanzine in 1932 was *The Planetoid* (Walt Willis said of it, "No first issue is a true criterion of a fan-ed's worth .... Tucker's first fanzine was by all accounts one of the worst ever published."). Tucker later published *Le Zombie* (one of the best zines ever) for 67 issues between 1938 and 1975; five electronic issues, #68–72, in 2000–2001, and was still writing fanzine pieces (sometimes under the pen-name Hoy Ping Pong ... "the Chinese Buck Rogers") well into the 21st Century. Tucker, like Robert Bloch, was a certain kind of actively socializing, hard-drinking, poker playing fan – who eventually started writing some well received science fiction novels, and first-rate mysteries. According to Tucker, *Le Zombie* presented in its pages "(as fans), many names now firmly entrenched on higher planes of art and literature: Robert Lowndes, Charles Hornig, Don Wollheim, Damon Knight, Larry Shaw, Fred Pohl, Ted Carnell, Ted Dikty, Erle Korshak, Forrest Ackerman, Ray Bradbury, Ronald Clyne, Richard Wilson, Frank Robinson, Hannes Bok, Dave Kyle, E.E. Evans, Milton Rothman, Dorothy Les Tina, Cyril Kornbluth, Charles Tanner, John Christopher Youd, Harry Warner, Sam Moskowitz, Bill Hamling, and ... ah well, you name it, chances are we had it."[66]—LO

GONE BUT NOT FORGOTTEN

Bob Tucker

(from Quandry *#16. December 1951; ed. Lee Hoffman)*

THE KEY turned in the lock for the last time, a dirty old hand reached forth to draw out a few letters and a smeary fanzine from the cramped confines, the little metal door bearing familiar numbers

---

66 *Le Zombie* #64; Jan., 1955.

was slammed shut and immediately an impatient spider began spinning a web behind the door. Slowly the key was handed across the counter to a misty-eyed clerk. Box 260 was done. After twenty full years of yeoman duty handling many thousands of postcards, letters, fanzines, magazines, telegrams, bills, advertisements and a bottle of mouthwash, Box 260 was retired into limbo. Its glory shall live forever.

The closing of the box was a simple ceremony. A few postal employees stood around in a tight, silent knot while I picked out the final pieces of mail; the postmaster himself placed a small black ribbon over the face of the receptacle, and the same clerk who rented the box to me two decades ago now received the battered key with a half-hidden display of emotion. He blew his nose rather loudly and rattled his pocket change to divert attention from his emotional display. Unknowing spectators at the stamp window gawked at the silent little group about the box, not realizing that a chapter of history had come to an end. After a moment of respectful silence the postmaster nodded his head and the employees scurried back to their jobs, treasuring the golden moment in their hearts. We shook hands solemnly, the postmaster and myself, and then I left the building with many a backward glance at the little metal door. The box had known my grimy hands for the last time.

Twenty years ago last summer — about June 1931 — I first knew the pangs of active fandom. I had been reading ARGOSY for perhaps a year and a half, and once in a while a stray copy of WEIRD TALES left behind by some traveling roadshow — for some queer reason the actors and actresses who played town seemed to like WEIRD TALES and conveniently left old copies in the theater for me. Sometime during the summer of that year I began reading ASTOUNDING and almost at once discovered the fan letters in the back of the book. I picked out two or three people who requested correspondents, bought myself an eleven-dollar typewriter, borrowed a few dimes to buy stamps and stationery, and sat down to make myself a fan. It cost only two cents to send a letter then. Their answers came back rather quickly, and just as quickly I discovered I had a nosy landlady. I was living in a boarding house where all incoming mail was deposited on the hall table for claiming, and the sweet old lady was overly curious about my "foreign" mail. "Foreign" because it came from out of state. To avoid the prying eyes and clacking tongue of the sweet old bitch I hied myself to the post office and rented a box; something not too easy to accomplish because I was a minor and they were a trifle suspicious as to why a mere child should need a postal box. Finally number 260 was assigned to me, and number 260 remained mine until a cold and snowy day in November, 1951, just over twenty years later. Happily, I was no longer a child. After paying fifty cents a month for two decades, I figured I owned at least one brick in the building.

They wouldn't let me take it home with me, even though I threatened to take my trade over to the opposition.

At this late date I no longer remember the name of my first correspondent nor what happened to him in the years gone by, although I do recall he lived in Jersey City, griped continually about local politics, and boasted a pretty sister. If the picture he sent me was his sister. During the following winter he introduced me to the first big time fanzine, *The Time Traveler*, and I shelled out hard cash to subscribe, wondering if I was doing a foolish thing. I was earning the staggering sum of seven dollars a week, living at the boarding house on four of it, and buying clothes typewriter and whatnot with the remaining three, leaving precious little for fanning. I wonder now what I went without to get the subscription, and I wonder too what the nine issues would repay me now if I had saved them? Let that be a lesson to those who are tempted to throw *Quandry* away with a sneer.

It goes without saying that when you possess a typewriter, you immediately begin writing fiction. I began writing fiction. I probably helped to put the former editor of ARGOSY in the old folk's home, undoubtedly added many gray hairs to the head of Farnsworth Wright,[67] and may have been one of the reasons T. O'Conner Sloane quit editing. It also follows that when you possess a typewriter, you grind out a fanzine. I ground out a fanzine. It was called *The Planetoid*, it was a midget-sized printed monstrosity, it lasted two issues in the winter of 1932-33, and today when bibliographers mention it they are careful not to mention who published it. Which makes them and myself quite happy.

And after twenty years of Box 260, I became acquainted with — and sometimes met — an unbelievable number of queer ducks. Most of them I now recall with a grin:

---

67 Wright was editor of WEIRD TALES; Sloane was editor of ASTOUNDING.

1) There was an atheist semi-fan in Texas who sent me anti-Bible tracts until one day I bundled them all up and sent them back with a note to stop bothering me. He promptly reported me to the post office for enclosing a letter in fourth class mail.
2) There was a young visitor from Indianapolis who startled the waitress of my favorite restaurant by ordering oatmeal and Coca-Cola for breakfast.
3) There was another visiting fan from Hawaii who startled me and my household by coming downstairs at five in the morning and demanding to take a shower — instantly.
4) There was the strange letter that appeared in the box one day bearing a message from a big name editor; the big name editor said he was coming to town and asked me to meet him. I waited about six hours and two or three trains, in vain.
5) There was the young Chicago fan who was taking a trip, with me, and whose mother not only demanded to see my auto insurance, but made me promise to see that junior took a bath every night — before she would let him accompany me.
6) There was another Chicago fan whose brass and guts has pushed him onto the fore today: visiting me once and finding me not at home, he calmly found a ladder and climbed up to force open a window, crawled through, helped himself to a bath, my bathrobe and a cigar before I returned.
7) There was the fat bundle of magazines I received from an unknown somebody in South Africa — the post office let me look at it — but which I didn't claim because the somebody had included a letter and I would have had to pay about two dollars in postage.
8) There was one letter, the prize of them all, which was sent to me by mistake by a streetwalker in a neighboring city. She desired employment in Bloomington and requested that I consider her application to "work" in my house. The letter contained her description, accomplishments and requirements. She was an all-around American girl.
10) There was the visiting soldier-fan who had written that he was coming by while on leave, and did, only he arrived in the middle of the night and threw stones at my window to awaken me.
11) There was the visiting Western fan, on his way to New York where he became an editor, who complained to me the next morning because his bed was underneath a window and because "the damned

birds" kept him awake with their chirping.
12) There were dozens and dozens of catalogs and booklists received from "special" bookstores in England — "special" because someone had put my name on a mailing list of people wanting erotic and under-the-counter literature.
13) There were the mysterious series of postcards from all across the country, signed "Joe Fann", which started that name on the road to fame after I passed the cards on to fandom.
14) There was the pleading letter received from the mother of a very young would-be fan, wanting me to write to her son and persuade him to drop fandom — and stop spending money on magazines — because it was not meant for him.
15) There was the strange character living in Iowa who had fancy letterheads printed, proclaiming him to be: Author, Columnist, Critique; and who sent me samples from his father's button factory.
16) There was the naive somebody out west — I have the impression it was Oregon — who mailed me a dollar and asked me for a copy of *Le Zombie*. I was so flattered I mailed back the magazine and the dollar.
17) There was the mouthwash. Away back at the beginning of this diatribe was mentioned a bottle of mouthwash. I found that in the box one day, a little amber bottle of Listerine stuffed in with the usual mail. I never discovered how it got there, who put it there, nor why. It had not been mailed to me as a sample because it was not wrapped nor packaged, merely a naked bottle waiting there to taunt me with its mystery. I removed the mail and left it — and the next day it was gone.

And so this summer, after those twenty years of accumulative memories, the volume of incoming mail grew so heavy that the window clerk began dropping hints. He opined that I could use a larger box. I held off for I was planning on moving to Florida this winter, but when the Florida plan collapsed, I let his sweet talk and muttered threats sway me. Box 260 came to a glorious end.

My new address is Box 702. The number lacks magic.

LOOKING BACK

Sam Moskowitz (1920-1997) was not a shy man. At many sf conventions his booming voice could be heard way beyond any hotel room he was in. (Robert Bloch called him "decibel-happy."[68]) Moskowitz was an early organizer and founder of sf fandom, fanzine editor (*Helios* 1937-1938), and managing editor of Hugo Gernsback's last genre magazine SCIENCE FICTION PLUS (1953), but he is primarily knows as an sf historian and his *The Immortal Storm* remains the essential thesis of the formation of early science fiction fandom despite the fact that it is one-sided, dry and overly serious, full of faulty research, and treats the first decade of sf fandom like the rise and fall of the Roman Empire. —LO

Ed Wood

(from Science Fiction Digest, *Sept. 1952; ed. Henry W. Burwell Jr.)*

OUT OF the aptly termed microcosm, which is science-fiction fandom, has come one of its few lasting contributions. If there is any document, which is at one and the same time, a sourcebook, handbook, and history of fandom, it is *The Immortal Storm*. The wealth of detail, the technical competence, the overall objectivity make it the *sine qua non* of fandom, past, present, and future. Sam Moskowitz has made of this history of fandom, a living vital moving story of which no-one can tell the end.

In writing history, the writer is circumscribed for he has certain events and personalities to deal with. He cannot draw on his imagination, for he will be attacked by the people concerned, if he includes misinformation. Also, he must be familiar with the events he deals

---

68 *Le Zombie* #62; Jan., 1955.

with, or have access to source material. The perspective must be correct, for he must choose the vital, from a mass of inconsequential information. The good and the bad must also be reported for to expound upon the pleasantly memorable and to exclude the skeletons in the closets would not merely be dishonest, but more important, it would be a distortion of history, which would be very hard to eliminate.

The Immortal Storm must have had a very long gestation period. In the September 1940 issue of the fan magazine *Van Houten Says* the following appears:

> Sammy Moskowitz has in his possession a manuscript which, if printed, will do fandom no good. It's a screwball thing about the Futurians, called "The Immortal Storm" or "Blitzkrieg Over Fandom.

In a letter to this writer, Moskowitz has pointed out that this "Immortal Storm" was a parody on the Futurian - New Fandom episode[69], and not by any means a serious article. Yet there is no doubt that he thought about the historical details and the incidents to a great extent before putting them on paper.

Many people will compare *The Immortal Storm* with Jack Speer's "Up To Now" or his "Fancyclopedia." Perhaps a quote from Speer himself will settle the first:

> "Ungraciously, I have to register a dissent to F.T. Laney's opinion that *Up To Now* was less biased & more accurate in details than *The Immortal Storm*. As he comes up into events in which he par- took, Sam may become guilty of more slanting: but, so far, aside from some scarcely noticeable prejudice for Ackerman, he has remained commendably impartial and the factual research in *The Immortal Storm* is out of "Up To Now" class entirely." (From *Vampire* #8)

The *Fancyclopedia* being arranged in an encyclopedic format suffers from all the advantage, and disadvantage of same. Sadly out of

---

[69] New Fandom was a group of fans led by the "benevolent dictatorship" of Sam Moskowitz. Heart and soul of this new group was Taurasi's weekly *Fantasy-News,* and the official club magazine *New Fandom*. There was an ongoing power struggle in New York City fandom (1938-1940) between New Fandom and Don Wollheim's more left-leaning Futurian group.

date now, had the *Fancyclopedia* been kept up to date with yearly or bi-yearly revisions, it would be invaluable. As it is, to find something in the *Fancyclopedia*, you must know what to look for. Many of the important events of early fandom are dealt with in small detail and any interested person must seek additional information elsewhere. Moskowitz has, in almost every case, added enough minutiae that a complete picture can be obtained from *The Immortal Storm* with no necessity for seeking source material.

The value of this history to present day fandom is not that it details the doings of a certain group of young people ten to twenty years ago but rather in it's details of fan magazines, the organization and decline of fan clubs, the deadly and sterile results of feuds, the universality of the problems in fandom. It is, in some ways, amazing to think that so many words are expended upon problems which a few years can toss into utter oblivion. And when the same problem comes up a few years later, a new generation of fans takes up with fanaticism and vigor the facets of this "crushing" item.

The tragedy of more than one fan publisher is detailed here. Near the end of Chapter 14, speaking of Olon F. Wiggins and his *Science Fiction Fan*:

> " . . . . Wiggins mailed out three hundred sample copies to fans who had not seen the magazine before. Not even one postal acknowledgement — let alone a subscription! — came back. The bitter truth became apparent. There were simply not enough interested fans to support a printed journal.

While this may be an extreme example, it was repeated many times in the first decade of fandom and is not unknown today, in a time when science-fiction is much more popular and is, in the minds of some, becoming respectable (whatever this term may mean). It is a tribute to the pioneer fan magazine editor and publisher that they put out so many magazines of worth. Perhaps lacking the neatness of today's average publication, but showing an enthusiasm sadly lacking today, they are among the tragedies of the microcosm, and though small compared to the vast stage of world problems, the hurt was felt none the less deeply.

If one tried to sum up the many lessons listed in *The Immortal Storm*, they perhaps could be said to add up to this: COOPERATION -

PROGRESS - ANARCHY - APATHY.

The Immortal Storm as it stands, is incomplete. Ending with the conclusion of the first World Convention in 1939, it does not stop at a natural break, which would be a time when a definite era of fandom was over. Later editions may well extend the story to December 7, 1941, or even later. At this date, informed fans know what has to come next, the reaction against New Fandom, the second and third Conventions, the outbreak of World War II & the virtual collapse of British Fandom, the Cosmic Circle[70], etc. Whatever point Moskowitz selects there is little doubt that future historians of fandom will use it as a starting point. No-one can add more to the territory already covered except the personal memoirs (should they ever be written) of Wollheim, Palmer, Ackerman, Lowndes, and a few others of the period.

The reputation of many professionals may suffer a little when read about in *The Immortal Storm*, but that should teach the importance of placing oneself on record in print. Since no-one can tell what importance the years to come may place on one's statements, it is impossible to avoid treading on what one writes, in long range terms, would tend to eliminate many of the trivialities that bother some of our esteemed professionals today.

The names of the fans of yesteryear seem like a rollcall of the professional field today. Fandom has given editors, illustrators, agents, and writers to the field, and will perhaps continue to do so. Irrespective of the final assessment of fandom, *The Immortal Storm* shows clearly that, in spite of false trails, stupid and incompetent leaders, obscure means and ends, fandom has been a group having an importance out of all proportion to its size. To all future fans, it will serve as a guide thru the complex early era of this science fiction fan movement.

All histories are tragedies in the last analysis since the stage remains essentially the same, while the characters change. To the old guard, those few hardy souls that have remained when so many have gone, it will bring back memories of the younger days. The present fans should contemplate whether their contributions to fandom will endure among the members of the microcosm, or if they shall be among the nameless many. History can record and judge achievements, both positive and negative; it cannot record nonentities.

---

70 A dubious network of fan clubs, created during WWII, led by Claude Degler, who believed fans were star-begotten super beings.

Nova #3, Winter 1943; eds. Al Ashley, Jack Wiedenbeck, E.E. Evans and Abby Lu Ashley.

(**above**) *Stardust,* vol. 2, #1, Sept., 1940; ed. William L. Hamling. (**next pg., top left**) *Fantasy Advertiser,* vol. 3 #2, July- 1948; cover art by Henry Ernst. (**top right**) *Magnitude,* #2, Summer 1955; cover art by Ron Cobb. (**bottom left**) *Phantasy World,* #3, April, 1937; ed. & art by Dave Kyle. (**bottom right**) *Alchemist,* #1, Feb., 1940; cover art by Damon Knight.

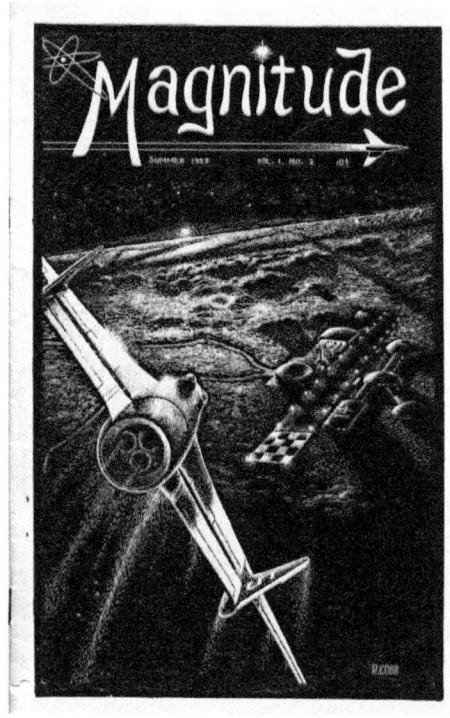

Venus, vol.1, #1, June, 1944; ed. Lora Crozetti. An L.A.-based zine instigated by Forrest J Ackerman one afternoon when he casually said to Crozetti: "Why don't you put out a fanzine."

House ad for *Fantasy Advertiser*, Oct., 1947; art by O.G. Estes, Jr.

Science Fiction Times, #278, Sept., 1957; eds. James Taurasi, Ray Van Houton, Frank Prieto; art by Frank Kelly Freas (1922–2005), a popular artist who appeared in many of the pro science fiction and fantasy magazines at the time.

ZINE ARTIST: LOU GOLDSTONE

Fantasia, v. 1#3, July 1941; art by Lou Goldstone (1920–1983). Illustration for Goethe's *Faust.* Goldstone may have been the best artist working in sf fanzines during the 1940s. He also edited *Fantasia,* a fine zine that had 3 issues from 1940 to1941.

Voice of the Imagi-Nation, Nov., 1945; art by Lou Goldstone. Goldstone at this time was drawing the Tigerman feature for Street & Smith's **Super-Magician Comics**, with scripts signed by E(dna) M(ayne) Hull, very likely science fiction author AE van Vogt. E. M. Hull was van Vogt's wife at the time, and sometimes collaborator.

Fantasia, #2 April 1941; edited and cover art by Lou Goldstone. This issue featured red, blue and green lino-block printing, lithography, and mimeography.

Voice of the Imagi-Nation-, #50, Spring 1947 (final issue,); cover art by Lou Goldstone. The cover illustrates the "cast" of "futurian fantasy" novel *The World Below* by S. Fowler Wright, a favorite book of *VOM* editor Forrest J Ackerman.

ZINE LETTERS

Voice of the Imagi-Nation ran many nude illustrations ("vomnudes") that had little to do with sf. This was a predilection of editor Forrest J Ackerman, and a few letters in *VOM* took him to task for this. Most fans took Ackerman's side, like Jimmy Kepher (in *VOM* #29, 1944): "I did a little checking, and in the last ten issues of *VOM*, I found only sixteen and three halves nudes, one and a half of which were male. (The halves relating to drawings of only the upper portions of the body, rather than to hermaphrodites) and five and one half semi-nudes. This totals up a surprisingly mediocre average of two per issue, with one out of four being male or else semi-clothed. Ye Gods! Is that what the fans are doing all that howling about?"—LO

Bob Tucker

(VOM #30, March 1944; eds. Forrest J Ackerman & Morojo [Myrtle Douglas])

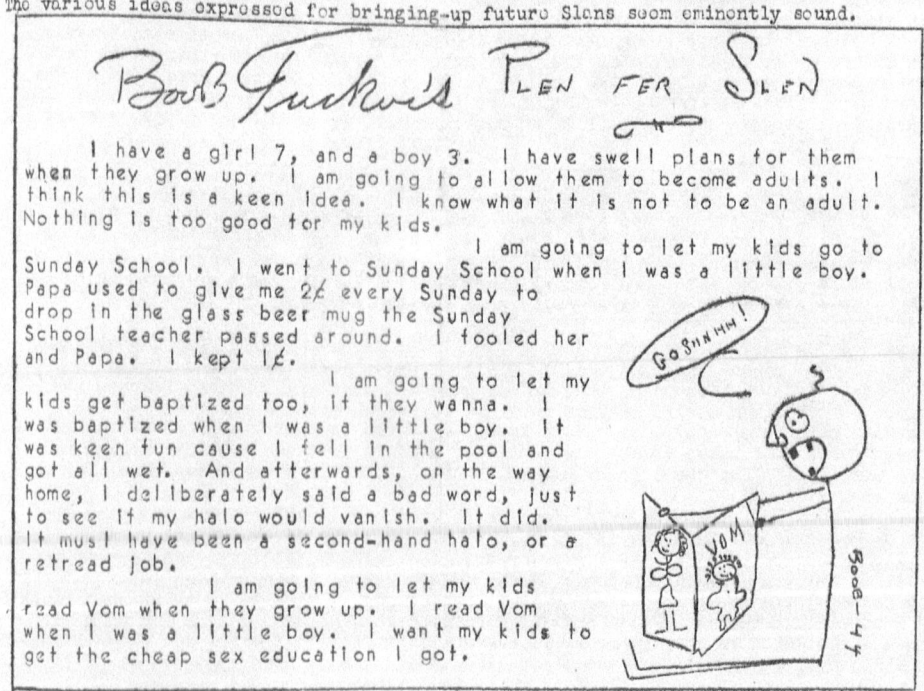

The various ideas expressed for bringing-up future Slans seem eminently sound.

Bob Tucker's Plen fer Slen

I have a girl 7, and a boy 3. I have swell plans for them when they grow up. I am going to allow them to become adults. I think this is a keen idea. I know what it is not to be an adult. Nothing is too good for my kids.

I am going to let my kids go to Sunday School. I went to Sunday School when I was a little boy. Papa used to give me 2¢ every Sunday to drop in the glass beer mug the Sunday School teacher passed around. I fooled her and Papa. I kept 1¢.

I am going to let my kids get baptized too, if they wanna. I was baptized when I was a little boy. It was keen fun cause I fell in the pool and got all wet. And afterwards, on the way home, I deliberately said a bad word, just to see if my halo would vanish. It did. It must have been a second-hand halo, or a retread job.

I am going to let my kids read Vom when they grow up. I read Vom when I was a little boy. I want my kids to get the cheap sex education I got.

VoMaidens Portfolio 2, c. 1944; ed. Forrest J Ackerman. "He lost his head over a snake charmer" art by Abby Lu Ashley. Ackerman's responses to complaints that there were too many nudes in *Voice of the Imagi-Nation* was *VoMaidens Portfolio* 1 and 2, and *VoMaiden Frolics*, all showcasing nudes only. Harry Warner on the subject: "Heck, if it's getting to be such an argument, let's have all the nude anyone wants: more space is wasted on arguing over them than they take up." (*Horizons* #12, 1942.)

ZINE LETTERS

Manly Banister (1914-1986) had a few stories published in WEIRD TALES, but of course was the editor/publisher of *Nekromantikon*. (See "An Amateur Ex-editor Speaks," pg. 122.) He began writing weird tales at thirteen and was a marine serving in the Pacific Theater during WWII. After the war he worked in advertising in Kansas City and published an sf novel *Conquest of Earth* in 1956. ¶ Comments within (( )) are from the zine editor Hoffman. —LO

Manly Banister

(from Quandry #15, Nov., 1951; ed. Lee Hoffman)

DEAR LEE:
Received and partially perused Annish of *Quandry*. This is terrific. This is wonderful. This is the reason I stopped publishing. Why should I have short fingernails and a frustration complex from bucking such competition as this?

I shan't comment on everything — I haven't read everything yet. But what I have read is commendable. Especially that Repeating Harp, Walter Willis. Walter, as you probably know, is the King-pin of Fandom in Ireland. This is an entirely just position for Walter to occupy, being the pin-headed descendant of a long line of Irish Kings. Briar Boru was that first King's named Briar Boru who invented the smoking pipe. This is attested to on every pipe you purchase. It says "Genuine Briar."

About Walter now, Walter has a wonderful flair for words (flair: from the French *flairer*, to smell). He is a great columnist. He does, however, have a miserable predilection toward lapsing into Gaelic at the most uncommon points in his narrative. I think it's Gaelic. I have culled some of these expressions from the reading matter, and a few of them are: *habe, IL, ans, temmis, yhos,* and many others. ((Many others sounds like English to me))

I, too, have a singular predilection toward grappling with culture in all its forms — blond forms, brunette forms, red-headed forms, and things like that. Anyway, I was fascinated by the facile Willis mind and pen. I desired to know the meaning of these Gaelic words, so I went down town and bought a Gaelic-Patagonian dictionary. Why not a Gaelic-English dictionary? I already have a Patagonian-English dictionary which I have never had occasion to use. It will now prove highly useful as a medium between me and the Gaelic-Patagonian dictionary.

However I could not find these Willis expressions in the Gaelic part of the dictionary. I couldn't even find them in the Patagonian half. Could these be Hoffmanisms, I ask myself? And, as I always demand answers to my questions, I return "Probably." If so, please translate them into Patagonian for me — I *will* use that Patagonian-English dictionary! ((Such Hoffmanisms are merely translations of Willisisms such as 'wrer, heesh, futire, and poctsarcd!))

Now, I am certain to have my doubts about this Willis chap. I am sure he is not even Irish. There isn't a trace of brogue in all that stuff he writes! I protest against this with every drop of Irish blood in me own veins. As I an one-eighth Irish one drop of blood out of every eight is making this uncommonly loud noise — I can hear them slushing through my veins even now, muttering "Begorra, begorra, begorra." There is no doubt at all that one-eighth of my blood is Irish blood. It won't associate with any of my other corpuscles, and I can show it to you any time you desire to open a vein and look. It is emerald green. And it circulates only in my left arm. I keep reaching on that side for shamrocks, Irish whisky, blondes and wheelbarrow handles. It is so full of blarney, you can't believe a word it says — I am writing this with my left hand.

Nonetheless, Walter is a great editor (next to Lee Hoffman, of course) and *Slant* is the greatest magazine in the world (in line after *Quandry*, to be sure. NOTE TO WALTER. Sorry old man, but I've got to get this published, you know. NOTE TO LEE HOFFMAN: Stop reading my mail!) I have a high estimation of *Slant* and have come to this esteem through research of the magazine's editorial content, judicious study of the situation, and recognition of the fact that Walter has lately taken to publishing some of my stuff. The last point, however, is redundant to the overall conclusion. No truly GREAT magazine would fail to publish my ju- literary effesions. (Are you listenin' Lee?)

I suppose Walter has fooled you all into thinking you know why he calls *Slant Slant*. Of course, that is not it. You see, Walter slants — 40 degrees from the perpendicular. At first, there were only two of them — Walter and James White. James slants at 38½ degrees, but, since Walter slants to the right and James slants to the left, the discrepancy is not sufficient to occasion architectural stress while they hold each other up.

The true fact of the matter is that, although the two managed to maintain equilibrium in a passive state, each supporting the other, positive locomotion was somewhat of a difficult feat, characterized by frequent dispersions upon their separate anterior physiognomial areas — falling flat on their faces, as the vernacular has it.

What luck, then, when they found Bob Shaw leaning one day against a light standard. Bob Shaw slants backward, of course; angle: 39 degrees. All things being equal, or nearly so as in this case, they now make like a wigwam and progress not only forward but backward with the greatest of ease.

This matter of slants is a very fortunate thing, indeed, as now all three face in the right direction when having their (if you'll pardon the expression) collective picture taken.

Such is the secret of *Slant*. I have said it and I am gla-a-ad!

Keep on with this good-looking *Quandry*.

Fanzine ad for *Voice of the Imagi-Nation* from *Le Zombie*, #35, Jan., 1941; art by Bill Evans and Damon Knight.

Ad Astra, vol. 1, #5, Jan., 1940; ed. Mark Reinsberg; cover by Julian S. Krupa (1913 - 1989), who did a lot of art for AMAZING STORIES and Ziff-Davis Publishing Company. Krupa was attending the Bauhaus School of Design in Chicago until WWII broke out and quickly found himself in uniform as a marine. His fanzine art (like Virgil Finlay's) was recycled illustrations from pro mags.

ZINE LETTERS

Sometimes the best part of a science fiction fanzine was the letters that came in. Fanzine editors begged and solicited them like panhandlers in Times Square. There were even entire fanzines made up of letters, like Ackerman's *VOM* (*Voice of the Imagi-Nation, 1939–1947*). For more on Moskowitz see "The Immortal Storm," pg. 176. ¶ Comments within (( )) are from the zine editor Hoffman. —LO

Sam Moskowitz

(from Quandry *#15, 1951; ed. Lee Hoffman)*

DEAR LEE:
Slightly staggered by the tremendous size of your first anniversary issue of *Quandry* ((grrr)). The flames of enthusiasm must be burning high in your case, for in the history of science fiction, publications of 100 pages or more have been few and far between and somewhat exulted. Certainly no one has produced a 100 page fan magazine in a single month! ((Us included))

Although I grow increasingly lethargic in recent times, the fuss about polls prompts me to raise a little finger of enlightenment.

Unlike Bob Tucker who subscribed to *The Time Traveler* and did not keep them, I did not subscribe to *The Time Traveller* and I kept them, therefore I am in a position to give a little information on the closest approximation they had to science fiction fan polls. In Vol. I No. 8, Sept., 1932 issue of *The Time Traveler* ("Science Fiction's Only Fan Magazine"), editor Allen Glasser in an editorial announced that on the last page of that issue the readers would find a coupon for listing the best science fiction stories of 1932. There were three categories: 1) Serial 2) Novelette 3) Short Story. This was to become a monthly feature of the magazine thereafter. Unfortunately, *The Time Traveller*, now sub-titled ("Science Fiction's First Fan Magazine"), lasted but one more issue before it combined with *Science Fiction Digest*. In this last issue dated Winter, 1933, the stories chosen by the readers as the "Best Science Fiction of 1932" were: Serial: When Worlds Collide by Edwin Balmer and Philip Wylie; Novelette: A Conquest of Two Worlds by Edmund Hamilton; Short Story: A Scientist Rises by D.W. Hall. No information on the number of votes cast was given. *The Time Traveler, The Science Fiction Digest* and *The Fantasy Fan* all carried short feature squibs by their readers titled: "My Favorite Science Fiction Story."

The Jules Verne Prize Club organized by Raymond A. Palmer was quite possibly inspired by *The Time Traveler*. Virtually on the heels of the appearance of the last number of *TTT* Palmer announced the set-up of a club to award prizes for the three best science fiction stories of the year, the winners to receive cups from the group in recognition of their achievement. Palmer intimated that prize-winning stories for 1933 had been chosen, but folded up the club due to lack of funds early in 1934. The winners, if actually voted on, were never made public.

The detailed expositions of Walter Willis remind me (sigh) of my own carefully detailed write-ups of every bottle of soda-pop consumed at a fan meeting, with every gurgle and slop fervently recorded for posterity. In a sense it really is the only way to get the true flavor of a fan meeting, because of this I read Willis's account with pleasure.

Yes, Sam Moskowitz's turgid prose could be funny, but usually not by design. *Void*, #22, May, 1960; cartoon by Andy Reiss. See "The Immortal Storm" page 176.

ZINE LETTERS

This letter is from the *Spacewarp* "Insurgent Issue" (see "The Deeper Significance of Science Fiction," pg. 202). I may be wrong but he vitriolic style appears to give it away as by editor Laney. —LO

Letter By A Guy Who Wishes To Remain Nameless

(from Spacewarp *#42, Sept., 1950; eds. Art Rapp, Charles Burbee, F.T. Laney)*

I THOT THE young fans went overboard in their enthusiasm for stf, but after all it's slightly excusable in them. But when middle-aged people talk about the stuff they write for pulps as if it were the finest literature ever written — ugh, it sickens me. I find it hard to believe that anyone who knows the stf field can't realize that if the whole thing were wiped out tomorrow no one else would give a damn.

Gahh, stf reading is supposed to teach you to think for yourself instead of accepting the opinions of others — and then everyone obediently swallows Hubbard's crackpot Dianetics simply because Campbell printed it in ASTOUNDING[71]. No wonder Palmer made a goldmine out of Shaverism — all you have to do is tell stfreaders that only the fine mind of a fan could grasp this particular bit of hogwash, and they suspend all critical judgement and swallow whatever they're told.

Hubbard might have something revolutionary, for all I know, but until he dishes out facts instead of propaganda, no one can judge. Yet most of fandom is already enthusiastically championing Dianetics without the faintest idea of what it's all about. I wonder what would have happened if Hubbard had sold his article to Palmer rather than Campbell? We'd probably have all the AMAZING readers boosting Dianetics and all other fans sneering.

Sometimes I think the hydrogen bomb might be a good way to round off this enlightened era.

---

71 Unknown to fans at the time, and outlined by Alec Nevaka-Lee in ***Astounding***, was that Campbell also collaborated with and helped Hubbard in creating Dianetics.

ZINE LETTERS

Rick Sneary (1927 –1990) could not spell to save his life. Walt Willis called him the "Great Illiterateur." He was a half-feral fan who did not let his limitations keep him from contributing to many fanzines and sf apas.[72] Most fans grew to love his inadvertent neologisms. In *Quandry* #15, 1951, he wrote, "I was unable to attend school, and not being an abnormally bright lad was not overly interested in learning. I had hoped that by writing a great deal that it would improve. But after calqulation the other day that I had written in the neighborhood of a million words, I see there is still much room to improve." He edited *Mi Skribas, Moonshade, Spiane* as well as a few issues of *Shangri L'Affaires*. ¶ Comments inside Double (( )) are by the editor Charles Burbee. —LO

Richard Sneary

(from Shangri L'affaires, *#20, Nov., 1944; ed. Charles Burbee)*

11:30 IS TOO LATE

DEAR EDITOR Burbee First let me thank you for puting me on your mailing list.

Second let me thank Walter Daugherty and apologize to. Thank him for passing my address on to you and to apologize for calling him Lorraine. I am *afraid* I cause him some embarrassment for which I am deeply sorry. The only reason I can give is that there was a Lorraine listed just above Walt and I may have copied it by mistake. If walt wants I will be glad to bang my head against the wall 100 times, the only thing is the dust comes out of the cotton pading and makes me sneeze.

And next I my sorry to say I will be unable to come to the meteing

---

72 See "What Makes A Fanzine Crud?" pg. 210.

as I live onehours by street car. Besides winter's coming on. One hour from Bixel St I live und 11.30 is no time for me to be out.

Why doesn't your club have branches in the smaller citys? ((We have one in N.Y. and one in Battle Creek — good enough?)) So the fans that live to far out can belong to the club even in a small way. No! I am not trying to change your swell club, just make it biger.

As for *Shangri-L'Affaires*, the best fanzine I have read and the first.

Cover is good but why not a flying eye? It is more appropriate.[73] Your editorial was swell. That one thing about a free fanzine you can tell your readers to go jump into space, if you fee like it.

The articles by Ebey, Daugherty and some one named Yobber were fine, swell.

Merlin Brown article was well writen but to long. Three pages! Nuts. I say Burbee you out to get a personnel manager to handle the troublesome help. Need I mention names? The fue letters you had were completely enjoyable, only they were way to fue. They sure are a hight type of fans. What do they drink to get so hight? ((Subject for a poll — somebody take it from here))

How about giveing my friend Benson Perry's new fanzine *Cygni* a plug. Allso wach *Cygni* for big news next ish. I mustent tell you what but be on the look out for it anyway. Sorry the letter looks a mess (I suppose you won't print it) but I don't have a typewriter.

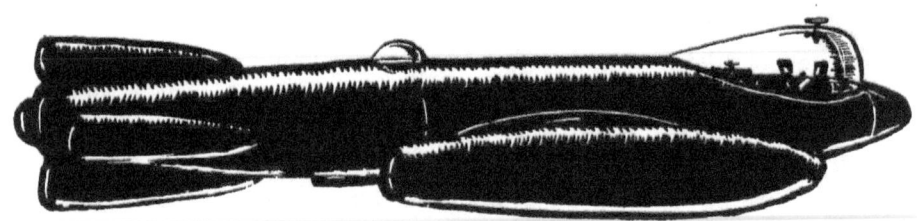

Science Fiction Newsletter #19, Mar., 1952; ed. Bob Tucker; art by Bill Rotsler.

---

73 The cover art to the previous issue showed a human ear butterfly thing, flying over an alien landscape, with no particular reason for it to be there.

Wild Hair, #3, December 1952; eds. Charles Burbee, Cy Condra, Roger Graham, F. Towner Laney, Sydney Stibbard, Art Vidner; cover art by Stibbard. According to its editorial this 36 page issue was created in 6 hours by the 6 editors.

FANZINE BITS & PIECES

Laney mocking the serious/constructive branch of sf fandom amounts to the traditional high school schism between nerds and jocks or in sf terms: "fandom is a way of life" compared to "fandom is just a goddamn hobby." *Wild Hair's* editors were part of the late 1940s L.A.-based insurgency group that believed in the latter, and took every opportunity to knock the Los Angeles Science Fantasy Society and its *de facto* leader Forrest J Ackerman. —LO

THE DEEPER SIGNIFICANCE OF SCIENCE FICTION

F. Towner Laney

(from Wild Hair #3, *December, 1952; eds. Charles Burbee, Cy Condra, Roger Graham, F. Towner Laney, Sydney Stibbard, Art Vidner)*

"I hope... that fans will get a more serious view of what stf is and what it can be. Too many, I'm afraid, fail to see any further than a hobby of collecting and writing letters. These things are very fine, but I want to underscore the deeper significance of it to those who consider stf a mere hobby."—Gwen Cunninghan, *Dawn* #2

HERE IN our midst is one of the leading authors of science fiction of our time —Roger P. Graham[74], who has written and sold more science fiction than most fans have read.

"Roger," I said, "What is the deeper significance of sf?"

"Science fiction," he said pensively, "is an escape used by escapists who are trying to escape from what they have escaped to."

---

74 Aka Rog Phillips (1909 –1966) a pro sf and mystery writer who also reviewed fanzines in "The Club House' column for *Amazing* that ran between 1948-1953.

FANZINES ARE FUN

This piece by Walt Willis attempts to mimic Ray A. Palmer's (RAP) hyperbolic editorial voice in AMAZING STORIES and OTHER WORLDS. Keep in mind that most of the names mentioned by Willis are known Palmer pseudonyms. (Palmer had the habit of filling his pro magazines with a lot of his own writing.) Of course, Richard Shaver (1907–1975) is a personality all his own, though Palmer claims to have rewritten Shaver's early work (see "The Palmer Hoax," pg. 152). Bea Mahaffey (1928–1987), mentioned by Willis, is also not RAP. She was a 1950s sf fan, who also happened to be a beauty with many male admirers in fandom. RAP hired her at the 1949 Worldcon, in Cincinnati, Ohio, as his assistant editor and for a while she became the pretty face of his sf magazines, and a voice of reason. —LO

THE FAN FROM TOMORROW

Walter A. Willis

(from Oopsla #9, Jan. 1953*)*

WELL, HERE we are again with another issue of your favorite magazine, and mine. Of course, yours must have been out for quite a while now, and mine is a bit late this year. Sorry about that, folks, but things have been kind of rough with your old pal RAP. First thing was, the Australians let off one of those phlogiston bombs of theirs and blew all my cows off their feet. That wasn't so bad, because the Russians let off another one and blew them all right way up again, and now I get my butter without having to churn it. But then the Chinese dropped a whole battery of bombs and blew all my carrots right up out of the ground. One of the really big ones came down again on Dick Shaver and hit him a terrible blow on the head. I'm afraid it's affected his brain, because he doesn't believe in the Shaver Mystery anymore.

And from that special issue of *Doubt*[75] that came out the other day it looks to me as if a couple of those carrots landed as far away as New York and hit Tiffany Thayer just as he was leaving a meeting of the Fortean Society. This sort of thing has got to stop. I want to say right here and now that I'm getting mighty tired of all these governments pushing my crops around, when I'm perfectly able to rotate them myself. I warn them frankly that they'd better stop right away or I'll do something drastic that'll shake them to their foundations. I might even publish another pocketbook. "The Coming Of The Carrots" maybe. It wasn't so bad when the Government just messed up the weather — nothing but rain or snow or clouds or sunshine all the time — but what am I going to do with all these carrots? I just don't know where to put them. Any suggestions?

I'll bet you took one look at that contents page and sat right back on your seat. Right? What a line-up — Robert N. Webster, Richard S. Shaver, Frank Patton, A. R. Steber, Wes Amherst, and C. H. Irwin! What more could you ask for? Well, some of you — maybe not more than a mere 99% but I want all you readers to feel you have a say in 'our' magazine — have been asking what about all those stuffed-shirt writers I used to run in OTHER WORLDS, people like Ted Sturgeon and Eric Frank Russell. I'm glad you asked me that. Some of you won't know the full story of why I left OTHER WORLDS and I'd like to straighten you out on it[76].

Well, first off I got to admit it was all my own fault. Palmer is willing to admit when he made a mistake and it was me and nobody else who promoted Bea Mahaffey to Associate Editor of OTHER WORLDS. I take full responsibility. Of course I should have known what would happen from the way she called me a liar about *The Demolished Man* in my own letter column. But at the same time it was the only way I could think of to keep her on the staff. As it was, I had to fight my way into my own office every morning through a crowd of fans all waiting to propose marriage or something to her. It was just a question of keeping the wolves from the door.

---

75 Subtitled *The Fortean Society Magazine* (covering pet ideas of Charles Fort)
76 Palmer began OTHER WORLDS in 1949, suspended it in 1953, then began SCIENCE STORIES, then brought out UNIVERSE SCIENCE FICTION, followed by OTHER WORLDS, then he changed the title to FLYING SAUCERS FROM OTHER WORLDS in 1957, and finally FLYING SAUCERS. Essentially they are all variations of the same magazine.

Then after I made her Associate Editor I made my second big mistake. I let her force me into signing an agreement which said that if I could reject any manuscript I didn't like, she could reject any manuscript she didn't like. Well, that seemed fair enough. It worked fine at first, and it sure did mean a big saving in trouble and money. But I guess it was too good to last. After six or seven issues, a few of the nosier readers began to notice there was something missing. They even began to write in about it, nasty sneering letters full of complaints, just because the magazine was all blank paper. They said they had always figured the best thing about OTHER WORLDS was that if they were stuck they could always read it as well. They said if I didn't start putting something to read on those blank pages pretty soon they'd go back to my old rival, Sears-Roebuck.

Well, I've made my reputation by playing both ends against the middle, and I knew that if I didn't put something on those blank pages soon nobody else would. I went along to Bea and showed her the letters. "Look, Bea," I said, "Read these letters. And think of Calkins and all those other poor letterhacks breaking their hearts trying to comment on the last issue so they can have an excuse to write to you. We just got to start printing stories and things again. I've got some terrific stuff here by Webster and Steber and Irwin. All good boys, and I happen to know they could use the money."

But she says no, if she printed that stuff she wouldn't be able to face the Beappreciation Society at the next Beacon. She'd got a position to keep up now. All these people looked up to her and she couldn't let them down. Then she produced a sheaf of manuscripts she'd been given at South Gate, all by stuffed-shirt writers like Van Vogt and Bradbury and Heinlein and Tucker and so on. I took a look at the manuscripts and saw at once that they wouldn't do for our magazine. You wouldn't have liked them. All dull heavy stuff, full of scientific jawbreakers. No caves, no heros, no half naked goddesses. In a word, no human interest. I tried to reason with Bea, but it was no good. I even called in Calkins and Burwell and Vick and Entrekin[77], but none of them could get anywhere with her. So I gave up and left *Other Worlds* to its fate and started my own magazine. And now *Other Worlds* has gone slick with four-color interior illustrations and John

---

77 Fanzine editors and fans Gregg Calkins, Henry W. Burwell Jr., Shelby Vick, and Bill Entrekin.

W. Campbell, Jr. as Assistant Editor. It isn't a fans' magazine any more.

You sure can't say that about our mag. This is a magazine for fans run by fan, and pretty soon I'll be crowding those snooty slicks off the newsstands. Just wait till you see some of the things I've got lined up for the next issue. Right now my co-editor R. J. Banks is scouring the country, using all his influence to pick up the very best material we can afford. Why, the other day he picked up twelve original cover paintings by Ralph Rayburn Phillips! Picked them up out of an ordinary garbage can. (We're pretty sure they're paintings and if they are they're certainly by Ralph Rayburn Phillips.) Not only that, but if things go the way we hope the next issue will have a three color cover, illustrating our new serial, "I was A Captive In A Flying Carrot." Hectographed of course but — hold on to your hats — the interior of the mag will be mimeographed! How about that? Surprised, eh? But that's the *Palmer Mystery Magazine*[78] for you. Yessir, whatever else you may say about it, it sure is a real fan zine!"

VOM #26, Nov., 1942; eds. Forrest J Ackerman & Morojo [Myrtle Douglas]; cartoon by Weaver Bronson riffing on the Charles Fort concept of humans as property belonging to an alien entity.

---

78 No such zine exists. Willis is joking about the *Shaver Mystery Magazine*. See "The Palmer Hoax," pg 152.

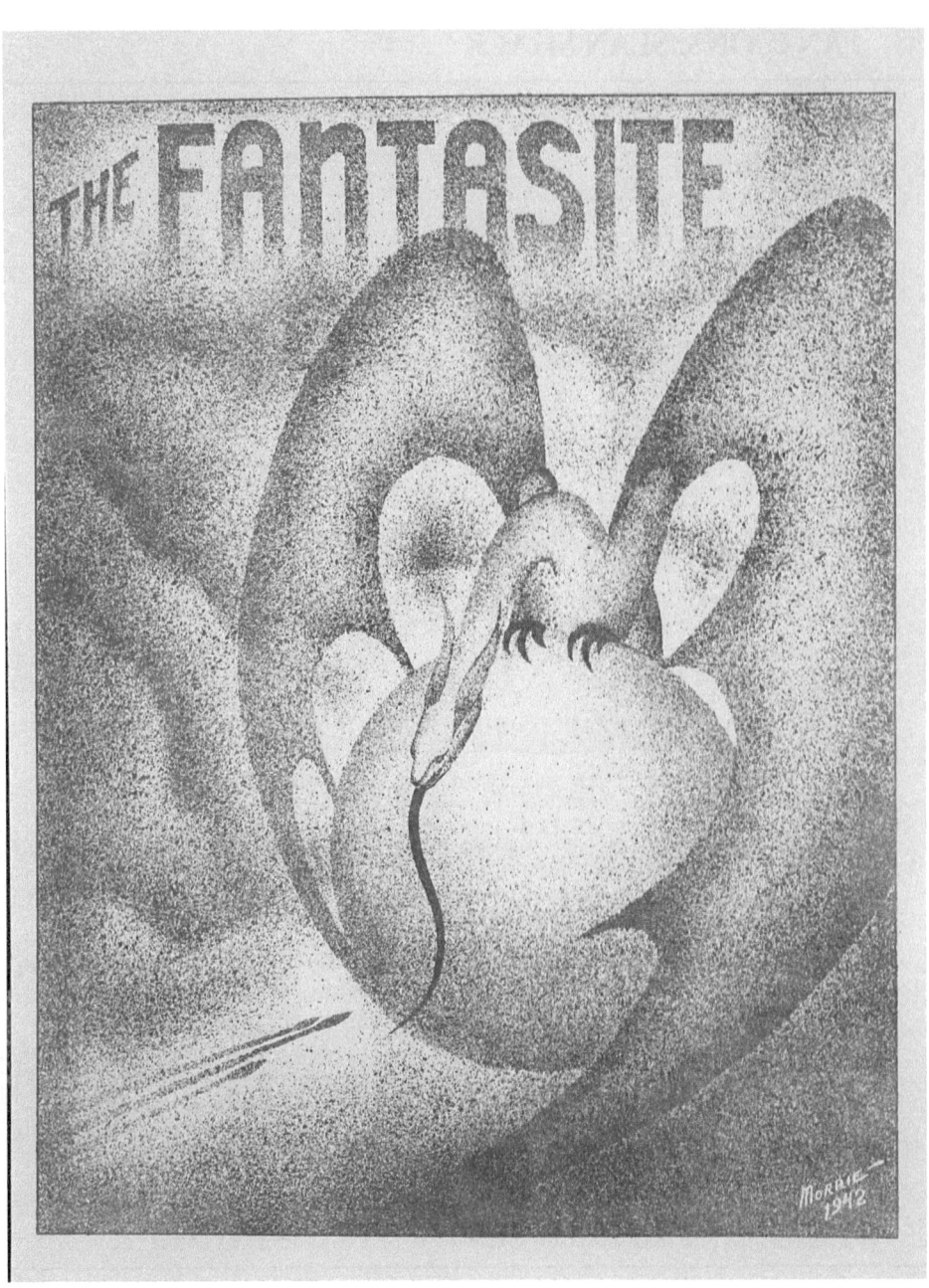
Fantasite, vol. 2, #3, whole #9, Aug.-Sept., 1942; cover art by Dollens.

FAN ICONS: SLAN SHACK

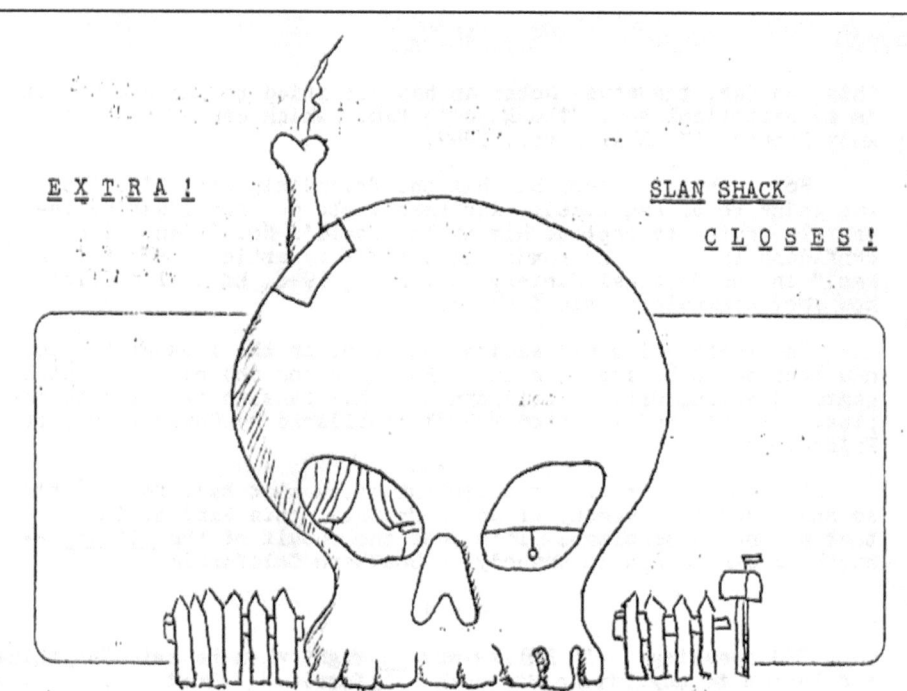

E X T R A !   SLAN SHACK
                                                     C L O S E S !

The apartment that has, for the last couple of years, been known as Slan Shack Pro-Tem is empty and no longer contains fen. One of the landmarks of Los Angeles Fandom is gone, swept away by these troubled times. In that apartment at 643 South Bixel Street where Myrtle R. Douglas (so well known to the fan world as the gracious "Morojo") lived for nearly ten years, from whose rooms dozens of issues of the famous "VoM" crept into the sunny Southern California daylight, to which in 1945 the Galactic Roamers of Michigan lost their mainstays of the Slan Shack there: Al Ashley, Walt Liebscher, Jack Wiedenbeck, and Abby Lu Ashley; has happened dozens of happy fan events, gatherings, parties, and kindred events oft reported in the fan press. From that address many fanzines have appeared, at least for part of their life: Vom, Guteto, Stefan, En Guarde, Chanticleer, Fantasy Advertiser, Slithy Toves, to name but a few. It has often proven a haven for out of town fen who enjoyed the hospitality of the sofa. Myrtle's hospitality and, later, Abby Lu's cooking were appreciated by literally scores. Such was the spot that is no more, its denizens scattered to the four quarters of Los Angeles and Phoenix, Ariz. Bow your heads, you Sons of Fantasmia, and cast a-moan for another of fandom's Shattered Institutions.

From *Shangri-LA* #6, May-June, 1948; ed. Dale Hart; art William Rotsler. A slan is a member of a race of super-humans in A. E. van Vogt's 1946 novel *Slan*. A favorite fan saying at the time was, "Fans are Slans!." A Slan Shack is a place where unrelated sf fans live or congregate together.

Inside and Science Fiction Advertiser, #17, Mar., 1957; ed. Ron Smith; cover art by Alan Hunter. **Next pg. top spread** *Vega,* #8, June, 1956; ed. Joel Nydahl; art by Margaret Dominic. *The Gorgon,* #9; 1948; ed. Stanley Mullen; art by Roy Hunt. *Spaceship,* #21, Apr., 1953; ed. Bob Silverberg; cover by Dean A. Grennell. *Science Fantasy Bulletin,* #7; 1952; ed. Harlan Ellison; art by Margaret Dominic.

THE HEART OF ZINES

Marion Zimmer Bradley (1930-1999) is better known for her fantasy fiction. She became popular enough to have a magazine named after her, MARION ZIMMER BRADLEY'S FANTASY MAGAZINE, but in the early 1950s she was contributing fiction and non-fiction, like the following, to various fanzines. One of her early fanzine stories, in *Spacewarp*, was later reprinted in AMAZING. She also put out a fanzine titled *Astra's Tower Leaflet* that was mostly written by her. This piece is from Joel Nydahl's famous last issue of *Vega*, (which was a 100 page annual, and one of the best — single-issue — fanzines of all time). See Harlan Ellison's "Joel Nydahl's *Vega*," pg. 296. —LO

WHAT MAKES A FANZINE CRUD?

Marion Zimmer Bradley

(from Vega, *#12, 1953; ed. Joel Nydahl)*

WHAT IS it—the intangible thing which makes one fanzine a thing of beauty and a joy to the mailbox, and the other one, which makes it simply fannish crud, to be tossed into the nearest wastebasket?

Let's explore that problem together... because, as I begin to write this article, I don't know, any better than you do, just what it is. I know that out of ten fanzines which land in my mailbox, perhaps four will be worth reading once, and one will be worth reading twice while in all my years of fandom—seven to be exact—I have seen perhaps fifteen fanzines worth a third reading after six months.

Is it neatness? No, I would say not. I can shuffle through almost any kind of snafu-jagged typing, sloppy hecto, fearful arrangement—if the fanzine has some quality which makes it worthy of the reading. Of course, neatness has value. No fanzine is much good unless one can read it. Of course there are some fanzines which would probably be better if they were illegible...*Incinerations*, for instance, would have saved itself some trouble, if it had been illegible enough to keep itself from being banned by the post-office[79]. The first four issues of *Spaceship* were illegible, but on reading them, the reader didn't have the feeling that he was missing anything when the mimeo ink faded out into a pale blur. But neatness in itself is not the criterion... I can remember issues of *Gorgon* which were so dimly dittoed that I literally had to read them with a magnifying glass, but when I finished, I felt they had been well worth the trouble. No, neatness and method of reproduction are not critical in fanzine-judging.

Is it the personal enjoyment of the subject matter? No. Definitely not. I have less than no interest in most fannish affairs, and yet I could always manage to read right through an issue of *Quandry*, and enjoy the reading, even thought I was not greatly interested in what was being said. On the other hand, in spite of my great interest in weird fiction, I was never able to struggle through an issue of *Nekromantikon* without yawning now and again. And *Nekro* came pretty close to being my idea of what a fanzine should be ... yet, on the other hand, it often teetered on the verge of crudship.

Is it editorial personality? No, I don't even think it's that, although doubtless that has something to do with it. I don't like either Hal Shapiro or Gregg Calkins, and they reciprocate most cordially, but the stray issues of *Ice* and *Oopsla* that I've read have always held my interest from the first page to the last... and although R.J. Banks is one of the nicest fans in fandom, I've never been able to read a copy of *Utopian* all the way through *yet*. Of course, *Utopian* is NOT crud.

Then what is it, that makes one fanzine crud and another fanzine a worthy project?

After thinking it over carefully, I believe the criterion is probably Sincerity.

Probably the best example, if you are an old fan, are the few fanzines which Rick Sneary published, back in 1941 and 1948. As you know, Snearyism has become synonymous with bad spelling. Rick couldn't spell cat—literally—he spelled it "cait." A semi-invalid, he didn't go to school, and although he was intelligent, he was almost wholly illiterate. And yet his fanzines, like his letters, had something

---

[79] See "Pure As New Fallen Slush," pg. 147.

in them which communicated itself to the reader. That communication, that empathy to use the psychological term, makes a fanzine readable and enjoyable; and without that *empathy* that power of establishing communication, the fanzine publisher might just as well burn his mimeograph and make a bonfire out of his stencils.

Let us have one thing understood before we go any father; personal enjoyment does not distinguish between a good fanzine and crud fanzine. Many fanzines which I have personally enjoyed, are readily distinguishable as crud; others, which I have genuinely despised, are sincere and honestly good fanzines.

Perhaps the best modern example is *Quandry*, *Quandry* was a good.... and almost all the fanzines spawned in its wake were the purest crud, reaching its lowest point in *Sol*. *Quandry* was a good fanzine, not a crud fanzine — at first, anyhow—because Lee was completely sincere. She was writing and publishing things which she enjoyed, and she had the power of making others like what she liked, while they were reading it anyhow. In other words; she had the power of communication, the power of *establishing* empathy.

The "Quandry-ish" or "Hoffmanesque" fanzines which began in

the period of fandom's Hoffmania, were good for nothing. I'm not saying Lee hadn't earned the egoboo. She deserved it, and imitation is the sincerest form of flattery. But during the period when all zines were judge by how they compared with *Quandry*, instead of on their own merits, fanzine publishing had begun to die on its feet. Because the editors, who were trying to publish the type of thing Lee published, because they thought that was what fandom wanted, were not establishing empathy. They were simply taking advantage of the empathy already established, the communication which Lee had set up with *her* readers, and therefore they were publishing crud. They may have liked Lee's stuff, and kidded themselves because they liked it, they were publishing what they liked. But a real fanzine must *break new ground*, and establish its *own* lines of communication with the reader. It can't follow in the footsteps where another fanzine has taken.

I'm not saying that every fanzine editor must think up some new "gimmick" for his fanzine. But he must find his own personal ground, his *querencia* from which to attack the public.

Perhaps the first fanzine to pump new life into the fanzine world which was dying of Hoffmania, was Norman Browne's *Vanations*.

Frankly, I didn't like *Vanations*; I thot it silly in the extreme. But Norman was at least using his own, personal ' ideas of what a fanzine should be. It was different—you could like it or dislike it—but you felt that Norman was doing something which was personally meaningful to him, and like or dislike it, *Vanations* was instantly recognized as a top and coming fanzine. "Promising" was the word used most, I think. And hard on its heels, the ice having been broken, came Harlan Ellison's *Science Fantasy Bulletin* and Joel Nydahl's *Vega*.

Why were these three liked? Because they instantly established their personal stand; because they had integrity... by which I mean that intangible thing which adepts a policy of its own and is not swayed by the taste or distaste of others.

A fanzine can say, as Harlan Ellison does, "My policy is to print what, fandom wants", and still can have integrity. Because, in Harlan's case, publishing what other people will like is *his* way of publishing what *he* likes. He has the newspaperman's or the professional editor's viewpoint; a sound respect for the written word, an ear for the public taste, and the ability to judge between the ephemeral and the enduring.

And on the other hand, a fan editor can blatantly declare, as at least one editor did in so many words, "I don't care what you say—this is my fanzine, dammit, and I'll print what I like," and still can have no integrity, since his blatant and belligerent "individuality" is a mask for an inferiority complex; he doesn't really know what he likes, and his vociferous statements that he will print what he damn well pleases, are simply another way of defending the unintegrated hodge-podge which he does print. He knows it is no good, but he yells loudly about his own personal taste and thinks to be acquitted that way.

What then, make a fanzine crud?

If the editor is printing his fanzine for the purpose of egoboo, or because everybody else is printing fanzines; if he wants to print a fanzine "like Joe Fann's", if he apologizes for his own enthusiasms, if he is ashamed to take publishing seriously, or uses phrases like "don't make such a damn crusade out of fandom", then the chances are that he is printing crud. Or if a fan editor calls his own work "crud" the chances are that he is right. Modesty is, of course, a virtue; but it is not modesty to disparage one's own honest effort. It is *true* modesty, when an editor states —either in so many words, or by his general policy—I've done the best I can. It may not be very good, because I don't know much about editing, and I'm too busy with other things to learn because I'm never going to be a professional editor; but I've published the things which I genuinely like, and that I think worth while, and I hope you'll like them too."

The fan editor who takes his work in that spirit, can never be accused of publishing crud. And, personally, I like to see a fan editor, or a fan, who will brag a little about his fanzine. It shows, at least, that he takes it seriously.

The real crud publisher is the one who states—either over his signature on the editorial page, or else by implication all over his fanzine... "Well, here's this crudsheet again. It isn't much good, but shucks, fandom isn't a crusade, I'm just doing this for the hell of it, and let's see you do better anyhow. Besides, this is my fanzine, I have a right to publish any kind of old crud I 'like, and if you don't like it, you don't have to read it, and most fans are so dumb they wouldn't know the difference anyhow."

Now sometimes this crud publisher is just young. He is terribly in earnest about his fanzine, but he hears older fans jeering about the "serious constructive fan" and so he hides his trembling earnestness under a mask of "I don't care whether you like it or not", so as not to be laughed at. I think the Insurgents have wrecked more prospective writers, by their jeers at seriousness, than any comparative group anywhere.

And, of course, sometimes the crud publisher is just a brainless, cynical egotist, who publishes just to make a splash, or for other reasons even less worthy—everybody likes egoboo, and nobody can be blamed for hunting a little of it—and so, in order to make his own version of crud defensible, he takes refuge in mocking his betters. After all, when he, in his cynical and pseudo-sophisticated fashion, has relegated the better fanzines to the realm of "that serious highbrow junk", the other fans who would *like* to be serious, but are still young and bashful, are going to be mighty shy about exposing themselves to Joe Crud Bigshot's scornful laughter. The psychology of the crud publisher, is similar to that of the smart guy who makes low grades in high school, and defends himself by jeering, "Look at all those greasy grinds! You don't catch *me* studying my ass (head) off just to get high marks! Nyaah .... all the honor students wear glasses and have pimples!"

Of course, this isn't true... any more that it is true that all Serious Constructive Fans are Degler-type fanatics, or that all serious fanzines are boring.

But you'd be surprised how many people believe *all* that stuff! As long as they do, high-school students will continue to neglect their studies for fear of being called "a grind", and fans will continue to publish crud for fear of being jeered at.

But as long as a few fanzines have integrity, we can always find wastebasket for the crudzines.

Vega, #10, 1953; art by Juanita R. Wellons (nowadays Juanita Coulson).

Art by Ralph Rayburn Phillips for Robert Bloch's "The Seven Ages of Fan." *The Fanscient* #6, Winter 1949.

LETTERS

The pseudonymous column "Stardust" by The Star Treader in Warner's *Spaceways* was written to create some turmoil and draw attention within fandom. The name behind the pseudonym, Jack Miske, had a reputation for making incendiary statements, "I think Ackerman is a nut. I know of no fan who ranks as 'intensely active' who is not some sort of disgusting character. I rank among them, so save the weeping and wailing."[80] Damon Knight (see "Snide," pg. 288) did not mince words in taking Miske to task for making asinine comments. Miske[81] co-edited some issues of the *Scienti-Snaps* (1938-1941) and *Bizarre* (1941) with Walter Marconette. —LO

THE READERS ALWAYS WRITE

Damon Knight

(from Spaceways #14, July 1940; ed. Harry Warner, Jr.)

I SHOULD LIKE to point out that Miske has made an ass of himself in that paragraf on fan mags (In *Spaceways* vol. 2, no. 4). His assertion that poorly duplicated, carelessly assembled mags with 50% poor material take the bread out of the mouths of such sterling publications as *Spaceways*, *Stardust*, et al. strike me as needing no comment other than a hearty snicker. Further, Mr. Miske overlooks the fact that some people are so low-brow, actually, as to *like* the mags he censures. Quite a lot of people, f'rinstance, have expressed a decided preference for Pong[82]. Another item that should be considered is the fact that most fans, on limited budgets, buy a fan mag — any fan mag — because they want to read it or collect it, or both. There are a few, like

---

80 His last Stardust column in *Spaceways*.
81 For more on Miske, see Harry Warner's "The Damn Thing," pg. 252.
82 A Bob Tucker pen name (Hoy Ping Pong) used in tongue-in-cheek writings.

4sj,[83] who send out five-dollar bills recklessly in all directions, just to help the new fan pub along; but not many. Hence, a magazine which goes on existing does so, either on its merits as a magazine or as a collector's item, or at its publisher's expense. What could be fairer? And in conclusion, fandom is not the exclusive club Miske, Moskowitz, and others assume it is. You don't have to take an entrance examination to become a fan; your name on list of members is not required to prove you are one; and, thank God, you can't be expelled from fandom by any royal decree. In short, fandom is not an organization; it is a state of mind. And the publication of a fan magazine is a matter among the publisher, his readers, and the postal authorities. Nobody else, not even Miske, has the right or power to "clean house."

"...Whaddya mean, which way is up?"

Jinx, vol. 1, #1, Dec. 1941; cover art by Damon Knight.

---

83 Forrest J Ackerman.

FANZINE PROFILES

Harry Warner, Jr. is back again with another forgotten fanzine from the days of yore. Quite a few pros published fanzines before becoming pros, but not many published a fanzine after becoming a pro. Jim Blish is one of the few. (Terry Carr and Bob Tucker also come to mind.) —LO

Harry Warner Jr.

(from Quip #9; July, 1968)

JIM BLISH has suddenly become a fanzine editor. A few extremely old fans who received the first Blish-edited issues of *Kalki* must have dug feebly into shaky old memory cells and produced eventually remembrance that this wasn't the first time that Blish had published a fanzine. His first was *The Planeteer*, issued during the middle 1930s. The majority of the fans who have emerged in the last decade or two must have wondered at the ease with which a filthy pro had suddenly assumed the fannish capacity. Hardly a fan now alive fits into a third group of reactors - those who remembered Jim Blish's most important fanzine, *Tumbrils*.

It must be the most obscure important fanzine. I haven't seen a reference to it in print for at least a dozen years, nobody ever reprints from it, and it's hardly known to the Fannish Index. Only one of its twenty-four issues is listed there. No conspiracy or other mysterious circumstances caused this forgetfulness to envelope *Tumbrils*. It had the misfortune to appear throughout its career in the Vanguard

Amateur Press Association[84] mailings. VAPA rarely had more than a couple of dozen participants, many of whom weren't fans in the usual sense, there seems to have been little distribution of *Tumbrils* outside the mailings, and even when it existed, *Tumbrils* was almost unknown to general fandom. But it would be indispensable reading for anyone who attempted a large-scale essay on Blish as a writer, some of its contents throw interesting sidelights on Blush's fiction because of the common subject matter, and *Tumbrils* provides the only large-scale look at Blish's mature non-critical non-fiction.

Understand, this was not a fundamentalist, sercon[85] fanzine. Blish would certainly have disdained to call it a fanzine when it was appearing from 1945 through 1950, and I've been afraid to ask him what he would call it today. It dealt occasionally with science fiction, more often with matters vaguely related to science fiction, sometimes with completely mundane things. In a file of *Tumbrils*, you would find only a couple of pieces of very brief fiction, a large quantity of poetry, mailing comments in its earlier issues, and imposing essays of every length. Blush usually wrote most or all of the contents, but occasionally published contributions by outsiders. Illustrations were rarities, and an issue might run from a half-dozen to more than 30 pages. If it had one typical attribute, it was the way it demanded the reader's closest attention. Blish didn't write down to his audience and obviously considered his readers as highly intelligent people capable of understanding big words and possessed of considerable basic knowledge in a wide variety of fields. His style in *Tumbrils* was not obscure or crabbed, but it had nothing in common with the sort of essays you found in your first grade reader.

This time I'll stick to *Tumbrils* as the sermon topic, but I should point out that this was not the only fanzine productivity from Blish of the 1940s. He published several issues of (. . .), devoted to mailing comments. I can't find it at all in the Fanzine Index, but maybe that's because I don't know where they put the publications whose titles

---

84 Fandom's second apa, a supposedly more intellectual spin-off from FAPA. It ran from 1945–1950. Members included: James Blish, Robert Bloch, Virginia Kidd Emden (later became Virginia Blish and then Virginia Kidd), Joe Kennedy, Damon Knight, Robert A. W. Lowndes, John Michel, Alva Rogers, Art Saha, Larry Shaw, Harry Warner, Jr., Bill Watson, Basil Wells, Don & Elsie Wollheim and Judy Zissman (later Judy Merril).
85 Serious constructive.

consist solely of punctuation marks. He also published occasional official VAPA publications and a few other less important apa titles.

One of the remarkable things about *Tumbrils* is the similarity of many topics in it to the matters that concern so many fans today. Do you think that Ayn Rand is a writer who has attracted fannish attention only within the past decade? You'd be dead wrong. Disguised as a letter to Chandler Davis, a long review of "The Fountainhead" appeared in the 11th issue, distributed in February 1947, with the 11th VAPA mailing. Blish said, in part:

> "It's not a great book, of course. By the nature of its thesis, it could not have been, because the great book on that thesis has already been written, and nobody in this stage of our culture can hope to do it again better than it was done in "Also Sprach Zarathustra" . . . . Ayn Rand may be a victim of a sort of philosophical Gernsback delusion, but she has sugar-coated one of the bitterest pills people like you will have to swallow in the coming years, which is a sort of service. If you like, you can see in "The Fountainhead" one of the great precepts made available to you by Goethe, Spengler, Korzybski, and a number of others. If you don't like it, you can blame Nietzsche, who has earned it; of course, if you do, credit Rand, who hasn't . . . It is "The Fountainhead"s thesis - not Ayn Rand's - that only the people who are good at doing certain things are good at doing them. Not everybody. Only those who are competent are competent. Psychology, as opposed to educational psychology, philosophy as opposed to sentimental economic theory; General Semantics, as opposed to maxims; these fields make of individual differences our major materiae logica. Science is a useful habit of mind, engaged in forcing similarity; but it all begins with the recognition that every person, every object, every event, is unique and like nothing else, any place, any time."

The same mailing distributed the 12th *Tumbrils*, whose lead article dealt with another topic that retains its prominence today; the draft and those who object to it. The article quoted a press release about a draft card burning demonstration in Washington "against the impending threat of peacetime conscription" and ended with Blish's own opinions about the effectiveness of statistically small protest movements:

> "This protest may not, probably will not, prevent universal military conscription from being enacted. It will pound home into the noggins of our military-headed State Department that an unknown proportion of its draft army is going to be disaffected, and that the draft army is to be a less reliable instrument of policy than they had hoped. A small result? Certainly. But it is of such paving-stones that the road to peace is made - not of pyramid-like blocks requiring thousands of people to move."

You don't normally think today of Blish as a person with strong interest in poetry. Of all the poets you might imagine him to write about, Clark Ashton Smith would require one of the greatest exertions of that imagination. But in the second *Tumbrils*, distributed in May, 1945, two pages are devoted to CAS's poetry. Blish recalls that Edwin Markham called Smith the greatest American poet, "and while it is obvious from internal evidence that 'The Man with the Hoe' was a fluke, it is possible for a man to be right twice in his life." Blish estimates that the wordage written about Smith must equal the output regarding Cabell, but finds barely 2,000 words of actual criticism of Smith in all the outpourings. He decides that "Smith has occasionally achieved some really moving effects with such eclectic material", and occasionally "the results are more unfortunate . . . to the sober reader merely the sewage of a plastic-and-chrome Eblis," Blish finds that Smith does not have full control of prose and chose deliberately a style and material that

> "Is incomprehensible and boring to the pulp readers whom he has — perhaps perforce - addressed most often. It is moribund and intolerably 'arty' to a literate reader. The best he can hope from it is that it will please the very tiny segment of the reading public that is made up of men like Derleth and Lovecraft, who, incapable of distinguishing the artistic from the arty, can pass it through their digestive tracts and absorb from it the little nourishment that it contains. As a product of irresistible influence and inclinations, it might have been forgivable. As the conscious choice of a man who has shown that he can do better, it is funny."

Blish's own preference in poetry seemed to favour quite advanced style and hard-to-extract inner meanings. I hesitate to quote from his own poetry in *Tumbrils*, since its effectiveness increases as you grow accustomed to a lot of it. If anyone must suffer, let it be an outside contributor, Ree Dragonette. "A Dedicated Poem" appeared in the 20th *Tumbrils*, distributed in February, 1949. Blish praised it highly, and it's typical of his preferences in this era:

>   Met to no burning point
>   At any day's encountered dark.
>   Touched somnolent recall
>   In monotones, of sun
>   Of frequent sky
>   From unfamiliar weather
>   Taught sudden modes
>   To quick, divergent light.
>   Paused;
>   Informed astonishment of answer
>   In ear grown conchoid Struck to resonance.

Better known today, because of his fiction, is Blish's interest in music. He once wrote a story in which Richard Strauss comes back to life. Only slightly less impressive is what Blish did about Richard Strauss in VAPA. He published some fifty pages of review and associated materials about one record album containing music by Strauss. In the late 1940s RCA Victor released in this country a 78 rpm album containing four twelve-inch records. They contained with a few cuts the final scenes from "Electra" conducted by Sir Thomas Beecham. This was only about forty minutes of music, but it was a tremendous event in that era, before the lp record caused the production of modern operas in uncut, complete form to become commonplace. The 21st *Tumbrils*, distributed in June 1949, consisted solely of a 32-page review of this album, delving deeply into the background of the music, its Freudian implications, and the Straussian composing methods in general. In the same mailing, Virginia Blish published her translation of the portion of the libretto contained in the Beecham album. As if this weren't enough, the next mailing provided VAPA members with ten pages of "appendices" to the foregoing: musical quotations to go with the prose and miscellaneous additional information. I feel quite certain that the "Electra" publishing must have consumed as much time as a short novel would have eaten up. The scholarship that went into it is almost frightening, dealing with this important opera in such depth and detail as nothing known to me in print in professional musicology even today. And it was almost completely wasted, as far as the readership was concerned. Perhaps five or six VAPA members were interested enough in music to be able to make sense of most of what Blish wrote, and I doubt that Blish circulated his accomplishment much outside the organization, because of copyright problems.

Less rarefied in subject was an essay in the sixth *Tumbrils*, which went out in January 1946. Francis T. Laney had been propagandizing for jazz in FAPA, and Blish thought that Laney was making too much of a kind of music that Blish enjoyed himself. Laney had remarked that jazz fans "are going to listen to the stuff that kicks us and to the devil with the rest of it." Blish took this as the text for his sermon:

> "It assumes that there is no way to judge a work of art — in any artform — except through the personal preference of the individual spectator or auditor, as Mr. Laney agrees in the next line of his essay. Actually it does not make any difference whether this is Mr. Laney's opinion, and the opinion of millions, or not; it does not happen to be fact. I propose a similar example; millions believe that the world is only as old as Bible concordances make it, a matter of some 8000 years; specialists in the subject know that this estimate is wrong, and very wrong at that. In exactly the same fashion, anyone who is thoroughly familiar with music as an art-form — a field involving vast areas of knowledge outside the emotional twinges of the uninstructed — is aware that there are definite standards of judgement in the weighing of a musical composition, which seldom change regardless of what Mr. Laney or anyone else happens to 'like'. Unfortunately Mr. Laney does not seem to know what these tastes and measurements are, let alone how they are applied; he has held the mirror of his personal preferences up between himself and music, and naturally cannot see any more therein than what he himself brings to the observing. The mirror itself is the multiplicand of his equation, and has flung back in his face, even in the course of this two-page essay, a whole series of contradictions; it has made it impossible for him to be faithful even

to the method he wants to use . . . . Jazz, like the pulp magazine idiom, continues to forge ahead in any number of directions at once, with the astonishing commercial vitality discoverable in any industry which manufactures a utilitarian product needed in the kitchen or by the kitchen-mechanic. It has about the same artistic standing as Lowndes'[86] love magazines or the two-in-one corkscrew. The cook may feel that the corkscrew is a very useful object and one hell of a lot nicer to have around than an Epstein bust, regardless of superficial similarities between the two objects. Mr. Laney, in his turn; prefers Jazz."

Despite the frightening thoroughness with which he sometimes considered a topic, Blish also had the knack of putting into compact and plain form quite difficult matters, when he felt in the mood. For instance, the fiction of James Joyce's later years. I haven't seen anywhere a better brief explanation of the reasons for its difficulties than a mailing comment in the 13th *Tumbrils*, in the September 1947 VAPA mailing:

"As for why a committee is needed to explicate *Finnegan* properly: Joyce spoke fluently every major language, including Russian, Norwegian, Latin, Greek, and Chinese. It had smatterings of other languages, including Sanskrit. He was a medical school graduate, with a continuing interest in the sciences. He had a good tenor voice and knew music from the technical as well as the listener's side. And so on; he was a flabbergastingly erudite man and evidenced an eidetic memory. He used everything he knew in writing the last novel, and the reader, lacking both Joyce's original information and the knowledge of where and how he used it in writing the book, is at a considerable disadvantage in explicating it. If you have on your committee another person who speaks fourteen languages — Pound say — then your language problem is pretty well solved; but most normal scholars rarely speak more than two languages well, so that's seven people necessary for your committee right there. Then, philology is a special science, rarely

---

86 Robert A. W. "Doc" Lowndes published the VAPA and FAPA zine *Agenbite of Inwit*. He became a pro editor for Columbia Publications through the 1940s and 1950s, and edited sf, western, crime fiction, sports fiction, and romance titles for them.

combined with, say, knowledge of music, in the same person. Two more committee members. And does anybody in the room know Dublin well enough to tell us which church in that city is known as St.-George-The-Greek, and on which street it is located? No? Well, we'll have to find one - and ask him if Eccles Street in Chapelizod runs as far as the house number 1132, while you're at it, and if so, whether or not the house is still there."

Then there were the occasional light-hearted moments in *Tumbrils*, not many of them, but worth the hunt. One page in the 16th *Tumbrils*, distributed in July 1948, would be a good candidate for reprinting intact someday, provided copyright permission can be obtained. Entitled "Bloody Pulp Stories", it takes the hero in a few hundred words through the pulp art forms of the sea story, African adventure, gothic mystery, sport epic, and horse opera, ending with the final section for which the reader was supposed to supply his own technicalities because "we've had a bad day":

> Maren looked at Fenwick, the _____ standing in her _____.
> He brushed her _____ gently with his, and took her little _____ in his huge one. Don't be _____, darling, he _____ softly.

This could go on and on. *Tumbrils* had splendid Eric Frank Russell articles, on Fortean theories and racism in science fiction; an extended series by Blish on the art of prosody that beats all hollow the explanations you read in college literature books; more musical material, like a long explanation of Vanguard Records, the fan-directed commercial recording firm, and an extensive commentary on Peter Grimes; a whole barrage of articles, comments, and replies devoted to another of Blish's favorites, Ezra Pound; philosophizing about the apa phenomenon in general and FAPA in particular; morsels of information about such recondite subjects as the art of silk-screening and a fantasy by James Fenimore Cooper; and, as the advertisements always say today, much more. A big anthology from *Tumbrils* is needed; until someone gets the ambition to publish one, keep your eyes open for the few surviving VAPA mailings, in case one should be offered for sale.

Dawn #5, Aug., 1949; interior art by Jeppi. A bit of suggestive art (for the time) illustrating a story titled "Queens of Space" by Basil Wells.

Masque, #7, 1950; cover art by William Rotsler. Someone commenting on issue #7 wrote: "From all the pictures of ripe females with swords, I'm beginning to think Rotsler's concept of sex goes along the lines of slicing a watermelon open." Rotsler replies: "...what more is there in life but a good fanzine and juicy, ripe watermelons?" (from *Masque* #9, Nov. 1953).

FANZINE NUTS & BOLTS

Charles Burbee's (1915 –1996) writings tended to mix sex and humor. He was another L.A.-based fan and edited *Shangri L'Affaires* for a short time. As an original member of the Insurgents he did not take sf fans or their activities too seriously (see "Fanzine Scope," pg. 58). You just know that Burbee had the last line firmly in mind when he started writing this piece. —LO

HOW TO STOP WRITING FOR FANZINES

Charles Burbee

(from Masque #7, vol. 2, #2, 1950; ed. William Rotsler)

IT BREAKS over you eventually – the realization that you are wasting too damned much time writing for fanzines, those ephemeral things read only by a few esoteric folk who believe only what they believe before they start reading your article. By god, if I were rewriting this I would change that sentence. I really would. If I were rewriting this article. But before I go any farther along this digression I'd better go back to my original clause or I'll find myself explaining how to write a fanzine article and this is meant to be an article on how to stop writing for fanzines except *Masque*.

It comes to you with compelling force that you are doing yourself little good banging out wordage for fanzines since your writings have little effect on the intelligentsia, though this may be explained perhaps by the lack of a fannish intelligentsia.

And so you stop writing for fanzines, except *Masque*. It is not easy to do, in a way, because once the brain is channeled to thinking along fan article lines, everything that happens is magically twisted and shaped into a fannish article. Whole paragraphs pop into your mind and you want to grab a typer or a pencil and jot them down before you forget them. And if you neglect to do this your trained mind goes right on developing the article, right down to supplying a solid punch line, something it usually doesn't do ahead of time. At a time like this the article writer is suffering the pangs of birth and simultaneous death. He longs both to bring his opus to print and the notice of a handful of esoteric eyes hidden for the most part behind lenses of varying thicknesses, and to slay the beastie before it gestates. This is the critical period. It is a towering monster of an impasse. The weapon to slay the dragon quight (Willie, leave that word alone) is to shrug and say, "Fugg it." Or, if you choose to lessen the shock of your capsule statement, you say, "The hell with it." And then you stride away, taking big steps, and leave the idea where you hatched it. If you're a big man, that is. If you're just an ordinary person such as I am, you just shove the idea aside and concentrate on something significant. This would depend on what sort of person you are and what you consider significant. For example, when I was plagued by the urge to write an article on the various methods of masturbation bragged about by members of the LASFS, I simply changed the subject and remembered the trouble a neighbor of mine had when his first-born learned to walk. Seems the child learned to walk by watching flies and his parents had to pick him from the ceiling to keep him from eating the light bulbs because broken glass is dangerous in the hands of small children.

So after a while your brain will no longer turn out fannish ideas for articles and you are comparatively safe, unless you know somebody like William Rotsler who is such a fine fellow withal that it is difficult to refuse him when he asks for material. But you buckle right down and say, The hell with you, Willie, don't you know I've stopped writing for fanzines? And so, by God, you write an article for *MASQUE* to show that you can stop writing fanzine articles any time you choose.

This is the first of a series

Science Fantasy News, #13, Aug., 1955; cartoon by Bill Price.

SF ZINE ICONS

What more can be said about Walt Willis (1919–1999)? His *Slant* (co-edited with James White) and *Hyphen* are the epitome of classically good science fiction fanzines. *Slant* was one of the few foreign zines to have an influence on American zines. It can also be said that Willis almost single-handedly put Irish Fandom on the world map. —LO

AUTOBIOGRAPHICAL NOTES

Walter A. Willis

(from CANFAN #25, June; 1955)

IF SOME enterprising hobbyist manufacturer ever starts manufacturing 'Fandom Kits' he can come to me for a testimonial. I can recommend the hobby to anyone with a surplus of mental energy, a sense of humor and an interest in people. (A liking for science fiction is no handicap.) It seems to me one of the few hobbies that give an actual and continual return commensurate with the energy expended. Admittedly if I had diverted the same amount of energy into dull mundane channels I should no doubt be earning a few pounds more a month and people would be able to find their way through my front garden without a compass, but then look at what I would have missed. As a result of having become involved in fandom I have learned to type; I have acquired an intimate knowledge of the reproductive processes (printing and duplicating I mean, not sex — though I could have learned about that too at some conventions); I have acquired a rudimentary facility for stringing words together; I have been to Oshkosh, Cheyenne and Tallahassee; I have introduced Lee Hoffman to Forry Ackerman, watched the latter sneer at the Grand Canyon as mere terrestrial scenery and taken the former to the Okefenokee Swamp; I have learned to drive a car; I have been offered the Associate Editorship of a leading pro mag; I have fixed the lock on the bathroom door (it would never have been done if Bea Mahaffey hadn't been coming to stay with us); and I have met some of the most likeable and interesting people in the world.

Thinking of all this, I sometimes wish it had occurred to me to write to the letter column of those ASTOUNDINGs I used to read in the early Thirties; I might so easily have entered fandom along with Bob Tucker. But for some reason I didn't, and in the late Thirties I stopped collecting pro mags and turned my attention to women. Fortunately I wasn't a completist. After a while I started going steady with one Madeleine Bryan. We'd been going together for quite a while when one day she darted in a news agent's shop. I followed her because I'd noticed a copy of ASTOUNDING in the window, and found she'd just bought it. She had, it turned out, been reading science fiction for years. It didn't seem so important or surprising at the time but as the newer Campbell authors, mainly Van Vogt, made their appearance our interest began to increase. By the time we were married (1945) we knew to the day when the next British Edition of ASTOUNDING was due out, and sometimes we used to read it together.

Then one day in early 1947 I came across, in a secondhand bookshop, a copy of the American Edition of ASTOUNDING SCIENCE FICTION for January of that year. I was shocked to the core. The last time I had seen the American edition of a science fiction magazine was in 1939, and I had innocently assumed that the miserable little British quarterly reprint was all there was of it. It hadn't occurred to me that there could exist any fiend so black-hearted as to suppress any of it, no matter how great the wartime paper shortage. But here was the evidence of the crime. This magazine was monthly, had twice the wordage of the BRE [British Reprint Edition], and had contained serials. Moreover this had been going on for years! Filled with a burning sense of injustice we embarked on a determined investigation of all the secondhand bookshops in Belfast. We didn't find any more *ASFs*, but we did find a copy of *Fantasy*, a short lived British pro mag, containing a letter from a James White of Belfast. I wrote inviting him to come and see us, mentioning casually my large collection of British Editions. We soon found that James was the reason we had never found any other American ones in the secondhand bookshops. James had been camping on their doorsteps for years and had acquired almost a dozen. We regarded with awe and envy this wealth beyond the dreams of avarice.

James and I at once joined forces, and for months our only interest was in furthering our collections. We wrote to all the dealers we could find, and joined Ken Slater's Operation Fantast[87]. At that time Ken was enclosing with his mailings various one-page fanzines by various fans. By now James and I had read each other's collections, had want lists written in blood with all the dealers, and had nothing left to do but gnaw our fingers. We got the idea of producing one of these fan magazines as part of our collecting drive. But we hadn't access to a typewriter or publishing equipment and after making enquiries from professional duplicators we rather lost interest in the idea. Then one day I happened to be in the loft of a shop where one of my friends worked. There, lying in a heap of junk was a curious looking machine. I asked what it was and was told it was a printing press the boss had got to print letterheads on and later thrown away. I smuggled it out under my coat and we started right away. We had only enough type to print about a third of a page, so we spread it out with em spaces between the words and James made woodcuts with plywood and a razor blade to fill the rest of the space. We called the magazine *Slant*. We sent out the first three issues free.

By the fourth issue, however, we had progressed to 42 pages, a subscription rate, and linocuts. James' work in this medium has never been surpassed in the history of fanmag art. Manly Banister, editor of *Necromantikon*, was so impressed that he crated up his old press, a massive brute of a thing, and shipped it off to us. When this arrived we really went to town, with photo-engravings and multicolored linocuts. But by now each issue was getting so ambitious that the intervals between them were getting to be something like six months. *Slant 6* was probably the most ambitious handset magazine ever printed and after it we felt we needed a rest. Besides James' eyesight was going and I'd found a new type of fanactivity. So far I's only written what I had to write to fill up blank pages in *Slant*, but recently I found I was tending to have several hundred words left over. It seemed to

---

[87] Organized in England to get around the restrictions on foreign magazines, and money, brought into the country just after World War II. It ran until 1955.

me it might be a good idea to foist them off on some other editor, so when a new mag called *Quandry* arrived I offered to do a column for it. Freed from the inhibitory feeling that every word I wrote would have to be set up in type I let myself go and spread myself over page after page of *Quandry*. Nevertheless the column turned out to be popular. So much so that within a year Shelby Vick of Florida had started a campaign to bring me over to the Chicon. By the middle of 1952 it had succeeded. I travelled about the States — New York, Chicago, Salt Lake City, Los Angeles, Kansas City, Panama City, Savannah — for a hectic four weeks. When I got home I was in a state of complete mental exhaustion, partly from the strain of the journey, and partly from the effort of all the fan writing I'd done in the previous months. But even during a long bout with pneumonia in the following Spring, I never really lost touch with fandom. For one thing it would have seemed ungrateful after all fandom had done for me. I soon became active again . . . but in a different way. It no longer seemed sensible to devote most of my spare time to pure drudgery like setting type. In the old days James and I had been quite happy to sit working all evening listening to symphony concerts on the radio, but now we had a third fan, Bob Shaw, and we kept putting down our composing sticks to talk. We did produce one more issue of *Slant*, Number 7, but it was mostly mimeographed and we didn't feel happy about it. And yet once having known the comparative luxury of duplicating, we could never go back to typesetting. So *Slant* fell into suspended animation. I egged James into starting his pro-writing career and in collaboration with my friend Chuck Harris of England started a new mimeoed mag called *Hyphen*, strictly for amusement only.

Which brings you more or less up to date. We have so much fun with *Hyphen* that I doubt if *Slant* will ever appear again, and yet I hate to proclaim it officially dead. I shall have to make up my mind about it one of these days. One thing I'm sure of, and that is that I'll stay in fandom. I have met more fans than probably anyone in the world except Forry Ackerman, and I'm still not disenchanted with them. They can be infuriating at times, but at least they're never dull.

Fantasy Times, #71, Nov., 1948; ed. James V. Taurasi; cover art by John Giunta.

The Little Monsters of America, #3, Apr., 1952; ed. Lynn Hickman, cover art by Ronald Clyne. This was a midwest clubzine edited by Lynn Hickman for people who were stared at "as though [they] were a little monster or something" when they left a newsstand carrying a science fiction magazine. Hickman later edited *J.D. Argassy*. Artist Clyne became a graphic designer of record albums, most notably for Folkway Records.

FANZINE NUTS & BOLTS

A QUESTION OF TITLE

Walter A. Willis

(from Wastebasket #3, 1951; *edited by Vernon L. McCain)*

IN QUANDRY 8 there was an article about fanmag names. The writer pointed out how lacking they were in originality and inspiration. He called for "sparkling, eye-catching titles." He rightly stigmatised as "dull and insipid" such titles as *Fantasy Review, Universe,* etc. Altogether there was nothing in the article to which any right-thinking fan could take exception.

But suppose the curious neofan notices the author's name — Bob Tucker. "Ah," he asks, "what then is the sparkling, eye-catching title this Mr. Tucker has chosen for his very own fanmag? What evocative, glamorous, semantically powerful name has his inventive genius conjured up?" The answer falls about his ears like a soggy rice pudding — *Science Fiction Newsletter.*

"No doubt," will say our warm-hearted neofan, "Mr. Tucker was stuck with this title before the light dawned on him, and fears to change it lest he lose his goodwill?" Alas, no. Bob Tucker has changed the name of his fanmag recently, but only like the man in the old joke who went to immense trouble to change his name from Joe Stensch to Harry Stensch. His mag used to be called 'Bloomington Newsletter'. Not an inspired title: it does not sparkle noticeably. But nevertheless it had some merit. It had local color. It was distinctive. One imagined the inhabitants of the quiet town of Bloomington sitting in their rose-covered cottages listening to the newsboys pattering up the street. "Newsletter ... Newsletter ... Boggs raps Campbell ... Vance is Kuttner[88] ... Read all about it ... All the news that's fit to photo-offset

---

[88] Some fans wrongly believed that Jack Vance early stories could not have come from a newbie author and were written by Henry Kuttner using a pseudonym.

... Extra ... Extra ... Vance not Kuttner ... Newsletter ... Newsletter ..." As the childish voices fade away into the distance the gentle people of Bloomington say to one another, "God bless Mr. Tucker for bringing such fame to our little town."

And then Bob ruthlessly wipes the colorful name of Bloomington off the map and substitutes the epicene words 'Science Fiction', as if he were afraid the readers might start looking for gossip about the Bloomington Sewing Circle. What possible justification can there have been for this? A small matter, you may think, but how superior was the old name to this new epitome of dullness and insipidity. *Bloomington Newsletter.* It rolled trippingly off the tongue. It was memorable. It had tradition. And furthermore, it started with the second letter of the alphabet.

This last is a very important fact, as all you Wilsons and Youngs will agree. If your name begins near the bottom of the alphabet your whole life is overshadowed. You sit in the back row at school. Your name is always at the end of lists. It is called last on every possible occasion, from viva voce examinations to firing squads. You follow where the Adams and Bonapartes lead. You assume the role of an onlooker. For your fanmag it is equally serious. If its name begins with a late letter it comes far down the review columns at a point where even Rog Phillips[89] is beginning to run short of superlatives, and where the inattentive reader has already started on the little advertisement offering fancy articles in plain envelopes.

Furthermore, take the case of the neofan sending out sample copies of the first issue of his fanmag. He starts at the top of the column and writes labels for every address. Then he begins to get tired. He starts missing out names. If he is a very innocent neofan he might even miss out Bob Tucker. There may come a day when a new fanmag of promise starts up and Bob doesn't know about it. That will be the beginning of the Dark Ages. If Bob Tucker doesn't know everything in SF, what security is there left in the world? No one will know where he is. The corner stone will have been removed. Fandom will fall into anarchy.

Well may you blench. I trust you now see the importance of having a name for your fanmag which starts near the beginning of the alphabet. And it's not difficult to choose one, when you remember that a fanmag name does not have to shout at the top of its voice

---

89 This is Roger Phillips Graham, fanzine reviewer for "The Club House" in AMAZING.

that it is connected with sf. No one will be in danger of thinking it is not a fanmag, for no one but a fan will ever hear about it, and he will always hear about it in circumstances that leave no doubt as to the type of magazine it is. No need to assume that your fanmag is going to be put on a newsstand and have to distinguish itself from the *Poultry Breeder's Gazette*.

So let us pick a few names from the first few pages of the dictionary. I hope you don't mind my throwing out a few suggested slogans too — by the looks of them I'm afraid they should have been thrown out long ago.

ABACUS — "The fanzine you can count on."
ABASEMENT — "A really low story every issue."
ABATTOIR — "This fanzine will slay you."
ABBESS — "The Superior fanzine."
ABDOMEN — "The fanzine with guts."
ABROAD — "The Femfanzine."
or even
ABSINTH — "Be conspicuous by your ABSINTH. The fanzine of spirit."

Had enough? But of course there are other things to consider when picking a name for your fanmag. For instance, the name should be very short so that irreverent fans can't make embarrassing abbreviations of it, and so that it doesn't take up space in your reviews which might have been filled by egoboo. It should also consist so far as possible of straight letters, which are far easier to draw and cut in lino.

So you want a short name, one with straight letters, and beginning as near the front of the alphabet as possible. Well, of course you could just call it 'AAA' ("The mag with the indefinite articles") but I feel that the ideal title should have a little more significance. You want a word that fulfills the three desiderata above, and also carries some suggestion of innovation, of mutancy, and if possible of fannishness, or some hint of some typical faned characteristic. There is only one word that answers all these requirements. I offer the ultimate in fanzine titles. The word 'AI'. I need hardly explain to all crossword puzzlers and Lexicon players that this is the name of a three-toed sloth, known for the "feeble plaintive cry which it utters while in search of its kind."

The Thing, #3, Summer 1946; eds. Helen Wesson & Burton Crane.

Psychotic, #19, April, 1955; ed. Richard E. Geis; art by Bob Kellogg. With the 21st issue the name was changed to *Science Fiction Review*.

BEHIND THE ZINE

Dick Geis's (1927–2013) *Psychotic* burst onto the sf scene in 1953, soon after the demise of *Vega*, and quickly became a focal point zine. His uniquely quirky editorial voice was felt throughout the zine, and included a running debate with himself via an "Alter Ego" antagonist. If any zine could be accused of muckraking in fandom it was *Psychotic*. In the 1960s Geis made a living from writing soft-core porn novels with titles like **Slum Virgin, The Mouth Girl, In Bed We Lie,** and **Call Me Nympho**. Geis has stated that he wrote over a hundred of these novels. He also authored **How to Write Porno Novels for Fun and Profit**.—LO

THE FANNISH AUTOBIOGRAPHY OF RICHARD ERWIN GEIS

Richard E. Geis

(from Abstract *#3; Jan., 1954; ed. Peter J. Vorzimer)*

I WAS BORN on a windy beach on the Oregon coast. I was nine years old at the time and seeking refuge from the flying sand under a thin blanket in the lee of a log. This is much better than the log of a lee. A friend had just deserted me in favor of the warm and sheltered comfort of the cabin our parents had rented during the summer vacation. So there I was alone. Alone with nothing to do but huddle and regard the view or huddle and regard my navel. I chose the former; I'd seen the latter many times while taking much hated baths. And in my calm and dispassionate regard of the view, I noticed a half-buried magazine a few feet away. One of the adults must have dropped it or even (horrible thot) left it to the mercy of the elements. I saved it from the incoming tide.

I don't recall the cover now, nor the stories, but I do know that I read it from cover to cover. I read it that afternoon, that night by the flare of the Coleman lamps, and the next morning. I was a slow reader at the time. But I finished it, and promptly started on another that was in the cabin. I interested my friend in the first one, and he started reading. He now has three kids and a pretty wife. I now have eleven issues of a fanzine and debts. But then, he doesn't read stf anymore. The fool. If he only knew what he was missing.

The next vivid memory I have of a stfish nature is of myself in the corner drugstore pawing over the magazine racks for more science fictionmags. One time I didn't have a dime and stole a copy of ASTONISHING STORIES. Put it under my belt as I remember and buttoned my jacket over it. Man, was my heart pounding! And I remember one particular story from that issue: it was about a pair of earth men who land on a planet and find a city that is populated, apparently, by multitude of air-borne crystals. They also find many, many different kinds of spaceships of alien designs. But every spaceship is deserted. They go from the landing field to a nearest building and discover that it is of an educational character. They learn from it and proceed to the next building. It is another step in their education. They go from building to building until they are so advanced that they have no use for their bodies. They then enter the final building. A tower, as I recall. When they come out they are greeted by myriads of flashing, many colored crystals and welcomed to their ultimate society. For now they are jewels too. I remember that story to this day. It made a tremendous impression on me.

I can remember buying, reading, collecting, and (sob) selling ASTOUNDING's and UNKNOWN's during my late grammar school days and early high school years. Had I but known.... I was a fan, but had not heard of fandom. Oh wasted youth. I can remember writing indignant letters to Sergeant Saturn complaining about the corn and juvenility of the letters in TWS and SS.

I can next remember reading with relish and awe the letters of Joe Kennedy and later Oliver and later still of Les and Es Cole. I even remember Rick Sneary. Pardon while I stroke my beard and mutter, "Ah.... those were the good old days." I was passive then. My few letters had not been printed. I never forgave Freind and Merwin. It is my secret shame.

I first came upon a fanzine in the Portland book store. I was in there hunting for a certain back issue of ASTOUNDING, when I saw on the counter next to the cash register, a pile of small half-sized booklets. They were copies of *The Fanscient*, and lucky for me they were volume one, number one. I bought one and enjoyed it very much. Every once in a while I returned to the bookstore to look for stf and to buy the latest issue of *The Fanscient*. I now have a complete collection of that most revered zine, and not once did I every go to a meeting of the PSFS[90] or attend the Norwescon. I wish now I had, but I was VERY shy and bashful then. For that matter, still am. However, I did manage to call up Jim Bradley one day and arranged to come to the organizational meeting of the ATOMBIES. That was the club which rose from the ashes of the PSFS after the Norwescon. Unfortunately, because of a lack of interest and older members, the Atombies soon died a death of indifference.

BUT.... I had a further taste of fanzines. At the meeting I was surrounded by shouting fans who flourished fanzines in my face and urged me to buy one.... buy one.... buy one.... I bought one. I bought a copy of *Destiny* and almost bought a copy of *Fungus*. And also I was introduced to the club newsletter.

A few months later I was feverishly writing fanstuff, sending for fanzines, and busily planning and dummying my first fanzine. This was in 1952. THAT at least is one date I'm sure of. I haven't been giving dates during the previous parts of this story because I wasn't sure of them; my memory is a real mixed-up mess.

So I was launched. Only one thing kept me from entering fandom with my zine at the time: reproduction. I COULD NOT MAKE A HECTOGRAPH WORK. I still can't. That was about two years ago, but today it seems like ancient history to me. Incidentally, the zines' name was not then *Psychotic*. Nope, it was *Aberrant*. I still like the name. I even suggested it to Tom Piper for his new zine when *Reason* folded, but he only used it for awhile. Now he used *Fascination*.

Then, in April of 1953, I saw in the window of a typer company a flat-bed ditto. I KNEW that would solve my problems. I walked in and mortgaged my soul. Two month later, in June, 1953, *Psychotic* #1 hit the mail. And to this day I don't know why you like *Psychotic* instead of *Aberrant*. Out of my mind one day in May popped *Psychotic*, and the

---

90 Portland Science Fiction Society.

whole zine just fell into place. The departmental names were naturals, and I was happy as a lark. I untied my straight jacket and ran off in search of egoboo. I'm still running.

The vital statistics are as follow: Height 6'; weight 160; Eyes, Brown; Hair, Dark Blond (when not gooped up with hair oil); hobbies, stf and nonsense, girls, and eating. I've had other hobbies in the past: stamp collecting, photography, and collecting pornography. The trouble with the latter is that once one has reached the point where Woodford[91] books no longer produced the desired effect there is no legal next step. Thus far I haven't met a purveyor of really lewd-and-lascivious-literature who really had what I wanted. Ahh, Well....

Ping-Pong anyone?

Art by Neil Austin for *Fantasy Advertiser* #4, Apr., 1955; eds. Gus Wilmorth & Roy Squires.

---

91 Jack Woodford, a pulp writer who late in his career wrote erotic novels bordering on what some critics called pornography. It is likely that Geis read Woodford's **Trial and Error: A Key to the Secret of Writing and Selling**, 1933, before embarking on his own "lewd and lascivious" books.

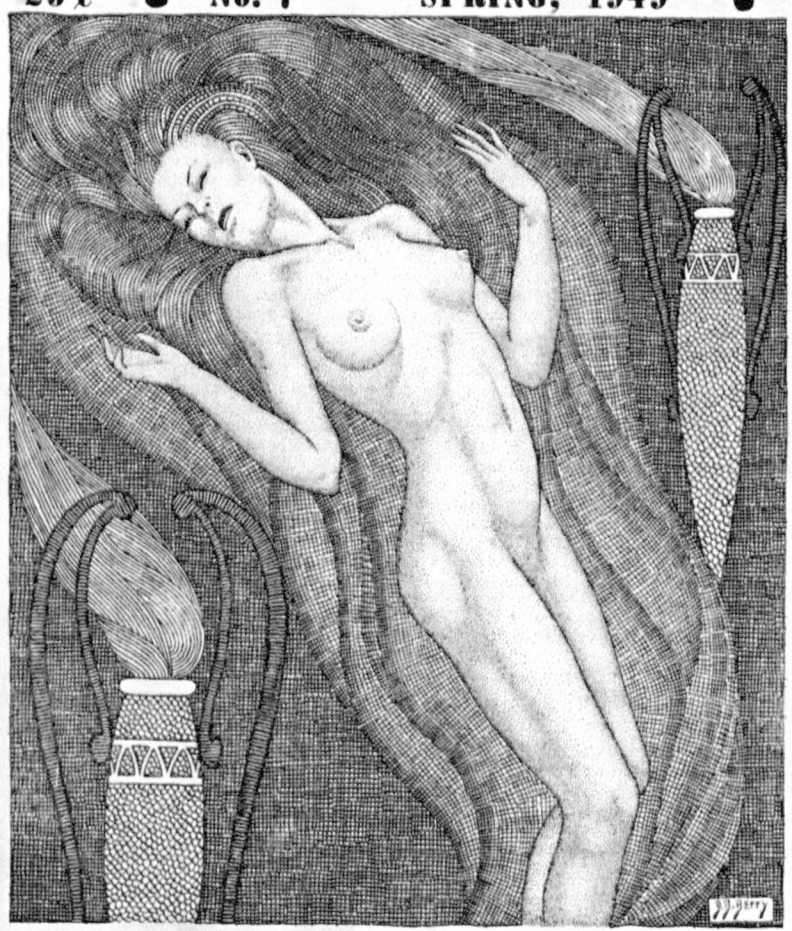

The Fanscient, #7, Spring 1949; cover art by D.V. Berry (1924–1998).

Peon, #35, May, 1955; cover art by Ed Emshwiller (EMSH), who was a pro artist working for many of the science fiction pro mags, but, like Robert Bloch, he was also a fan.

FANZINE BITS & PIECES

Yes, Harlan Ellison started as a fanzine editor/publisher — and, at a tender age, was already pissing people off. Charles Riddle was not amused by Ellison allowing fans to buy his fanzine by invitation only. Riddle was in the Navy for most of the time that he was publishing *Peon,* and moved around a lot. He was also married — with kids — and it was a wonder that he was able to produce a zine with the quality exhibited in *Peon.* He once confessed that he had a lot of help from his wife Rosella. —LO

Charles Lee Riddle

(from Peon, *May, 1955; ed. Charles Lee Riddle)*

THE LONG-PUBLICIZED, long-promised, and enormous second issue of *Dimensions* finally arrived via a staggering postman here in Norwich a week or so ago, but I'm afraid that I was terribly disappointed in it. Like the first issue, it just simply didn't live up to its advance publicity. Harlan has plenty of BNF and BNP[92] names represented in this issue; there are over 80 pages of material, but somehow it just don't jell completely. Perhaps the best explanation lies in the quote from Dick Geis[93] printed in this issue of *Dim* — "The total impression I received is that you are lost to us as an amateur publisher ... and undiscovered as yet by the profession publishers whom you want to edit for..." You have to be invited by Harlan to send 25 cents for this issue before you can get it, so if you don't get an invitation, you won't miss much.

---

92 Big Name Fans and Big Name Pros.
93 Known primarily as editor/publisher of *Psychotic* and *Science Fiction Review.*

Presenting Ronald Clyne, FAPA Mailing, Sept., 1943; ed. Paul Freehafer; art by R.C. Clyne. Drawing shows L.A. Fanzine editor Theodore Bruce Yerke (1923–1998). He was one of the founding editors, along with Ackerman, of *Imagination!*, and after its demise put out his own zines *The Knave* and *The Damn Thing*.

FANZINES IN PROFILE

The Damn Thing was another L.A. fanzine, and as we learn in this piece, printed a lot of Bradbury's early fiction and also some of his artwork. Forrest J Ackerman financed *The Damn Thing*, but had no editorial presence, and didn't want any, within the zine. He called himself a silent supporter, but admitted "I am the Patron Saint of the Damn Thing."[94]—LO

THE DAMN THING

Harry Warner Jr.

(from Focal Point *#28, April, 1971)*

I CAN PROVE that 1941 was a long time ago. First: a fanzine was considered magnificently daring when it was given the title The Damn Thing. Second: its editor introduced a story with a note which concluded "I've got to fill this mag with something," and the something was fiction by Ray Bradbury.

T. Bruce Yerke was editor of *The Damn Thing*, one of the earliest of the nose-thumbing, fannish fanzines. It emanated from Los Angeles, which normally emitted sercon publications, and very possibly it had a major influence on later fanzine editors like Charles Burbee and Francis T. Laney. Yerke didn't edit it nearly as long as Laney published *Fan-Dango* or Burb produced *Shaggy* [*Shangri-L'Affaires*], and its not as much fun to read as the later insurgent publications from Los Angeles. But its five and one half issues are notable for the instant nostalgia that they can evoke for lost people and times, and even though I've never seen a copy advertised for sale, I suspect that the Yerke fanzine would command a quite high figure nowadays from anyone collecting Bradburyana. There's something under his by-line in four of the five

---

94 *Voice of the Imagi-Nation* (VOM), #10, Dec., 1940.

complete issues, and its quite probable that he was also responsible for some of the pseudonymous material. Bradbury is also responsible for at least one of the covers, a head and shoulders cartoon that isn't bad at all, and appears to be in imitation of Virgil Parch, who contributed occasionally to fanzines of that era.

"I haven't bought or read a professional scienti-fiction magazine since the middle of 1939. They became so putrid I got sick," Tubby wrote in the editorial of the first issue, dated November, 1940. His outlook on golden age ASTOUNDING and certain other prozines highly respected today was matched by the way he felt towards some fans. A few of the milder remarks he directed toward the New York City-area fans who were acting as if they had planned a worldcon in 1941 in competition to the Denvention:

> "The same person who has done more agitation in the fan world, and caused more hard feelings and unfavorable publicity for science fiction in general, is now doing his latest dirty stunt... We trust that the bigots behind the idea are quite happy that they've been able to make things difficult for the more honourable faction of science fiction fan circles. The editor can express only the most detestable opinion for any group that would deliberately attempt to sabotage the activities of the majority of fans.... We trust that the blustering bulls and sour egotists of the Newark pushers will be told just where the hell they stand by the rest of U. S. fans..."

No, I don't know whom Yerke meant by the opening sentence quoted.

More interesting than the 15-line story in this first issue by Bradbury is a personality sketch by someone identified as Ben Dover Farr. At one time, Bradbury seems to have been very nearly the court jester in Los Angeles fandom. "Bradbury was neither a critique nor the Rabelanasian (sic) that he is now," good old Ben says. "He was simply a wacky student of Los Angeles High School. Then one night Bradbury came in and commenced to hold his nose, giving imitations of Franklin D., W. C. Fields, and Fred Allen. We all followed his example and held our noses. Ever since then we have been plagued by Bradbury's imitations... Today, Bradbury is a critique. He is an aristocrat. He is Rayoul Douglas Bradbury, a most unique individual... Rayoul attends all the latest affairs of Hollywood. He is on speaking terms with Jack Benny, with whom his father went to school in Waukegan... Rayoul is also acquainted with a number of Hollywoodians. His favorite hangout is the Brown Derby on Vine Street, though he gets his meals at Hugo's Hot Dog stand across the street. Here, in front of the Brown Derby, he points out (but never speaks to) all the celebrities to anyone who may be with him. And yet, Rayoul makes his living as a news hawker on 10th and Normandie! What we can't figure out is how in the devil he makes his ten dollars a week stretch like it does."

The Damn Thing, vol. 1, #2, Dec., 1940; art by Ray Bradbury.

Ray replied to this description in the second issue of *The Damn Thing*. Yerke, he wrote, "suggests to me an epileptic beer-barrel doing a jig in a delicate old Chinese print. But still, all those who know Bruce have grown to love him. Even Bobsy Heinlein loves Bruce. Even after that article which Bobsy made Brucey toss out of *The Damn Thing*... Brucey wanted to print an article in this issue telling all about Bobsy and his strange reasonings on Technocracy, only Bobsy dint have no sense of humour and he threatened to sue."

In this second issue, Bradbury had a longer story, "Genie Trouble!" It is notable mostly because of a passage that seems to have obsessed Ray at this time. It keeps turning up in one little story after another that he published in fanzines, usually with a change in noun. "There sat a genie. Not a BIG genie. That would be silly. But a little genie." It was a Martian, I believe, in a short-story he contributed to my fanzine, *Spaceways*.

A purely personal pang strikes me every time I look at an advertisement in the third issue. I had all sorts of trouble finding clear photographs to illustrate "All Our Yesterdays" and I quiver all over at the thoughts of what might have been if I'd somehow found someone with the pictures advertised for sale in this issue. Ackerman, Morojo, Bradbury, and Hornig standing in front of the former Futurian House. An early LA Halloween party including Heinlein, Daugherty in cowboy outfit, Ackerman and others. "Yerke having a fit over a stencil." Jack Williamson and Daugherty talking in Walt's car, guaranteed to be candid. "Nash breakdown on way to Pomona, showing Hornig, Bradbury & Nash." Film is prominent in another startling way elsewhere in this issue. Yerke wrote some paragraphs about fannish events in Los Angeles, and included some remarks about a then fan[95] who later had considerably more success with movies than on that night of January 9, 1941:

> "A brief intermission was held while an ancient and creaking movie projector which was being jointly operated by Ray Harryhausen, Arthur L. Joquel and Yerke, was stopped to permit it to cool. With a gigantic light in the lamphouse, there was no means of fanning it. The damn machine got so hot that people around it were moving

---

95 This would be Ray Harryhausen, who went on to win a special Oscar for his long career in movie special effects. His films include *The Seventh Voyage of Sinbad*, *Earth vs. The Flying Saucers*, *Mighty Joe Young*, and *One Million Years BC*.

away, and the insides of the thing were scorched. Not so funny was the danger of fire, and the old-fashioned film is the highly inflammable type. To act as a precaution, ten or twelve glasses of water were sitting beside the operators, and they weren't for drinking purposes. In case of emergency, Joquel was to pull the plug, Yerke pour water down the top of the opening, and Harryhausen attempt to extract the burning film."

And Yerke was still commenting on New York City area fandom: "Congratulations, Burford, for knocking Sykora half across the room, even if it did start a riot."

The Bradbury contribution to this issue is the closest so far to a real short story. 'How Am I Today, Doctor?' is described as similar to a story in THRILLING WONDER STORIES several years previously, although to me it sounds more like a short-short by Weinbaum which was published, as far as I know, only in *Fantasy Magazine*. It's about a hypochondriac who wants to live practically for ever and worries more and more as he feels better and better. Eventually his doctor gets tired of his patient, gives him a pill containing poison, and after the patient has asked the title question for the last time, the doctor tells him: "You were never better off than you are now."

Somewhere in the Ackermansion[96], I imagine, is a fabulously rare small piece of yellow paper which riled dreadfully yet another pseudonymous writer in the fifth issue of *The Damn Thing*. Here's a superb demonstration of how much fondness we can feel for the enemy after he no longer threatens us. Ackerman's home was the place where Claude Bloomer Quid had seen the note sent out with the Science Fiction League emblem by THRILLING WONDER STORIES. Here is the text of that note:

"Hi, Space Pilot! Red Spot of Jupiter, but here's that gold-plated SFL emblem your old Space Sarge has been telling you about on his etheradio. It's as rare as a Martian fire-opal, you can bet a sun against a meteor, and I had to comb the nine planets to find it. Well, Rocket Rookie, this button makes you a full-fledged space veteran. You're welcome now to passages on all voyages of the good ship THRILLING WONDER STORIES, STARTLING STORIES, and CAPTAIN FUTURE. And I'll be riding the space lanes with you in every issue.

---

96 Forrest J Ackerman's L.A. home, which contained a multitude of sf artifacts.

All the luck in the Universe. —Sergeant Saturn[97]

But some of the fun had gone out of *The Damn Thing* by the time this last complete issue was stencilled. The needling, the parody, and the slapstick humour of the earlier issues had begun to turn into more serious, sometimes nasty, fussing. As you might expect, a pen name was used for one of the blasts. I more or less agree with Fywert King, who wrote in defence of a conscientious objection, as far as his arguments are concerned. But some of his statements are quite as far below the belt blows as the paragraph by Jack Chapman Miske which set him off. Miske was scornful of several British fans who had refused to fight, whereupon King referred to Miske as an Aryan superman, described his mind as paranoid, described him as on a par with Hitler, and in general sounds as if he were John the Baptist preparing the way for the coming of Claude Degler[98]. Fitmore Katel (and you can guess the reality of that name) filled a page with an equally unsatisfactory criticism of FAPA, although the poor fellow couldn't have had the foresight to know that exactly the same faults would persist in the organization for another thirty years. "Fans are too lazy to put out a worthwhile mag for the FAPA. All they need is something in the mailing to maintain their membership... The avid collectors who want to get a copy of everything issued by fandom, continue their support and thus contribute to this disgrace to fan publishing and fandom in general." A shorter blast, this one at Damon Knight, directed this scornful insult at him: "Maybe you are going to turn professional." John B. Mitchel took out after Walt Daugherty, who had criticized some poetry by Robert W. Lowndes, mainly because of its erotic aspects. A sample of Michel as critic: "Pastels for Rosalind is a frankly sexual work which clearly tells the story of a frustrated lover rejecting the advances of the daughters

---

97 The in-house pseudonym, later attributed to Mort Weisinger, used for responding to readers in the letter columns, beginning 1941 for three sf pulp sister magazines — CAPTAIN FUTURE, STARTLING STORIES and THRILLING WONDER STORIES. The Sarge's tone was exceedingly juvenile and he went MIA in 1947. The first use of 'zine – albeit with apostrophe – in a pro magazine is credited to the Sarge in an early issue of STARTLING, and his column was the first, in a pro mag, to run fanzine reviews.

98 Degler had been confined in the Indiana Hospital for the Insane from 1936 to 1937, and was a contentious individual who spent most of WWII (he was classified 4F) organizing what he called cosmic-minded fans under the umbrella name Cosmic Circle. He published various fanzines advocating a super-race of fans. Ray Palmer decried this as Nazism and threaten to cut these fans off from AMAZING STORIES' support. Backlash from both sides revealed some of the paranoid elements of fandom.

of joy, simultaneously subtly imploring his loved one to assuage his passion. It is simple, direct, and true to life."

I don't know if the bad tempers exhibited in that issue formed a cause or a symptom of the approaching end of the fanzine. But the sixth issue never appeared in complete form. Yerke issues pages five through twelve as a separate publication. Most of it was quite different from previous issues, a conreport on the Denvention. Among the several thousand wild notions I've acquired over the years is to issue someday a worldcon history which would consist simply of the best conreport issued on each year's event. The six pages in this issue don't tell too much about the events in Denver, but they are crammed with what must have been the spirit of those pioneer worldcons. For instance:

> "That night at the party, a large keg of foaming stuff was placed in the kitchen. Fans sneaked cautiously around it. Leonard Jenkins, a Denver man, had a small pump, and promptly pumped up the pressure. Granny Widner led the fans in a devil dance around the sacred fluid, and Adam Lang (of no relation to Adam Link) turned the first tap. For the next hour we got nothing but foam. The party had to suffice on wine while McKeel, Martin, Wiggins, Madle and others bailed out the foam. Towards eleven, we began to get some liquid. But then it was past hotel drinking hours and the barrel was removed. Cries of anger and remorse. The kiddies being boisterous lay down on a rug in the lobby and whistled at the doormen. When they were kicked out, they took the rug with them and made an encampment on the street. All was going nicely when sirens were heard in the distance. Fortier wanted to know if they were blonde or brunette sirens, but when he was told they were sirens with red lights, he joined the rest of us in scattering down a side street. The fans reformed again, slightly above 17th Street on Broadway, and headed northwards looking for a bar."

Yerke, who wrote the conreport, was proud of the way the Los Angeles fans had made the LA-Denver trip in 36 hours with only two drivers. "This is as good as Lindbergh did."

Someone sent me a printed announcement not long ago which revealed Tubby to be still alive and well, holding some kind of function in a library in California. I hope he realizes how many forms of pioneering he did with his fanzine and his writing.

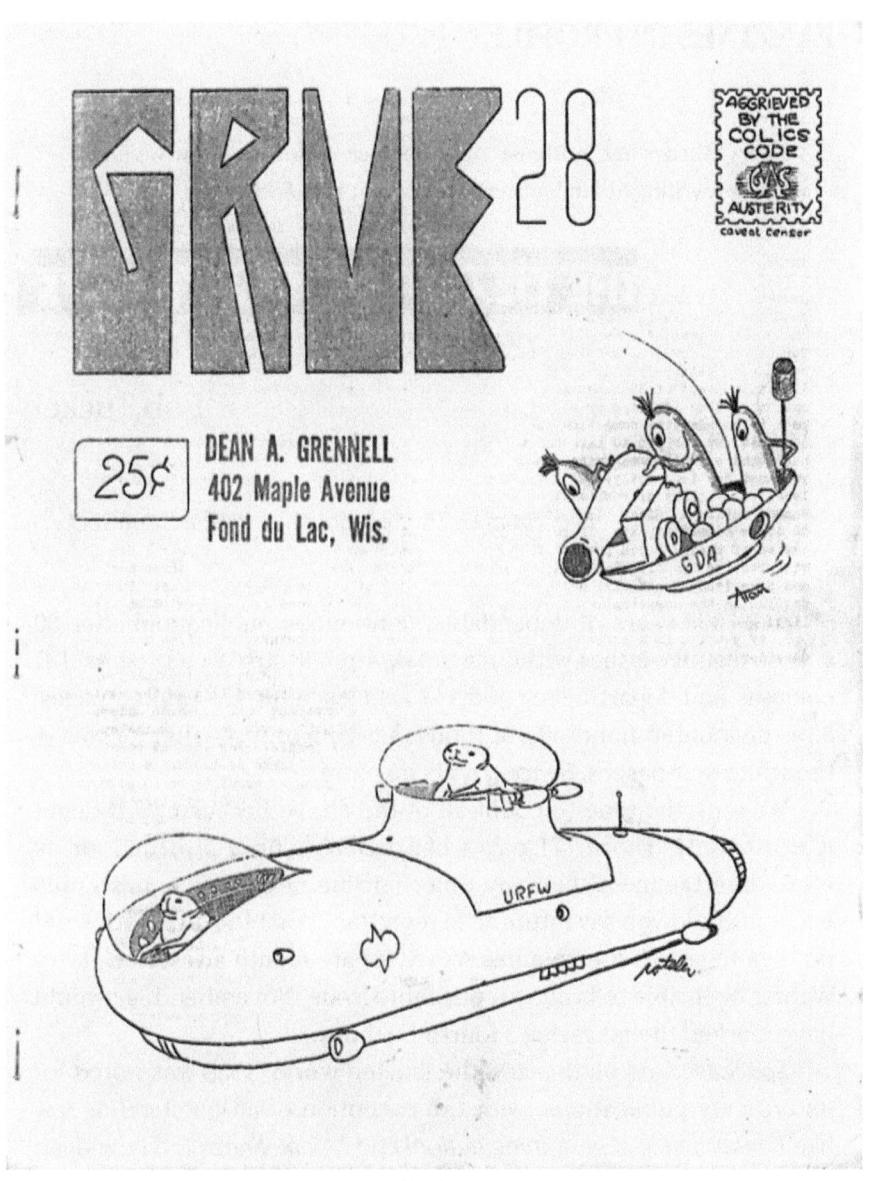

Grue, #28, May, 1956; edited by Dean Grennell, cover art by Bill Rotsler and ATom (Arthur Thompson). *Grue* began as a FAPA zine.

FANZINES IN PROFILE

Harry Warner has written about Bob Tucker fanzines. Now we find Tucker writing about Warner's focal point zine *Spaceways*. —LO

THE DEATH OF SPACEWAYS

Bob Tucker

(from Le Zombie *#50, Nov., 1942; ed. Bob Tucker)*

AFTER FOUR years of dependable, continuous publication; after 30 consecutive issues without a break; after 46 stories, 68 poems, 137 columns and departments, and 147 articles; after 771 printed pages; after uncounted hundreds of thousands of words — after all this — the white star passes. *Spaceways* is no more.

We took the time to count all of the above because we thought it worthwhile. Those 771 pages of *Spaceways* have provided for us more entertainment than any other fanzine in existence, past, present, and could you say future? It is regrettable that the publication did not live to see its fourth anniversary, a bare month away. Had Harry Warner been able to bring out one more issue, November, 1942 would have marked the magazine's fourth birthday.

Spaceways revolutionized the fanzine world. 1938 was noted for its crummy publications, with the exception of an outstanding few like *Fantascience Digest, Imagination!* and *Scienti-Snaps* (all now dead and gone, alas). *Spaceways* almost appeared in a hektographed format, but at the last moment the grape jelly failed, as is its habit, and we had the splendid mimeographed magazine of today .... or yesterday, rather. Undoubtedly the magazine's history would have been far different (and possibly much shorter) had it appeared hektographed. Warner has, for the greater part of the time, published it alone and unaided – either mechanically or financially.

Spaceways #8, Oct., 1939; cover art by John Giunta.

The circulation figure has always been a minor mystery, fanzine editors usually being as jealous of them as pro editors. It was the consensus of opinion that *Spaceways* led the parade merely because it was the most popular, but such is not the case. The first issue had a circulation of only 69 copies and the peak was 185. We know of 3 fanzines off hand which top that figure. It is Harry's opinion that not more than twenty complete files of the fanzine are in existence; Harry holds four sets; and we have one. Where are the remaining fifteen?

We personally thought a great deal of the magazine from beginning to end, and contributed to it accordingly. During the 30 issues, we're represented 28 times, and in one issue appeared four times under three names, We had articles in the first and last issues, as did only two others, Jack Speer and Larry Farsaci. The ironic payoff is this: in that last issue, number 30, is an article by Julius Unger, entitled: "Why Fanmags Fold Up."

Spectre, #5, July, 1959; ed. Bill Myers; ant art by Ray Nelson, who wrote pro fiction, but in fandom was mainly known as an artist.

ZINE LETTERS

E. Hoffman Price is mostly forgotten today, but he was a popular pulp writer of the 1930s and 1940s who specialised in adventure stories set in foreign lands, and exotic fantasies. Even then his fiction was considered at best second rate. If Price is remembered at all it is because of his face-to-face meetings, at different times and places, with Robert E. Howard, Clark Ashton Smith, and H.P. Lovecraft, the supreme trinity of WEIRD TALES. (Price wrote about these meetings in **Book of the Dead**.) The following piece is an example of professionals writing for fanzines that is somewhat different from the fannish writings of professionals like Robert Bloch who did not take sf fans and fanzines as seriously.[99] ¶The reputation of H.P. Lovecraft rests on a few top-notch works of fiction published in pulp magazines. In the 1940s, when his works were little known to the world at large — and seemed destined for obscurity — a few acolytes kept his name alive; of course Arkham House, with August Derleth as publisher, and *The Acolyte,* a zine dedicated to Lovecraft. – LO

SHOPTALK: LETTER TO THE ACOLYTE

E. Hoffman Price

(from Acolyte *#7, Summer 1944; eds. Francis T. Laney & Samuel D. Russel)*

WITHOUT INTENDING any disrespect to H. P. Lovecraft or to the tastes of his many admirers, I must say that I can go for "unnameable" stuff just so long. That I can read it at all is a supreme tribute to HPL as a craftsman. And on *top* of it all, he did create remarkably faithful and sound mundane backgrounds and personalities, I prefer the weird yarn which is keyed to earth's problems. That is, I am almost totally lacking in that sense of cosmic terror which is required either to write

---
[99] In fan talk "ser-con."

or to enjoy the type of yarn in which he specialized. I do not for a moment condemn or look down on those who do have a taste for cosmic horror — no more than does my color-blind buddy ridicule my taste for Persian carpets, of which I have a modest, yet diverse, collection.

HPL once asked me, "But don't you shudder and ask, can these things really be?" We'd been discussing Arthur Machen, cosmic horror, etc., in Providence, on July 5,1933. I said: "Frankly, no. I read Machen with interest, yes; I read your works with the keenest interest — because of the style, the settings, the personalities, the flavor, the workmanship — but I simply do not get anything resembling any sense of horror. I sincerely and deeply admire "Pickman's Model", I have re-read it many a time — but without a hint of a shiver, I've re-read "Cthulhu", enjoyed it each time, but no horror."

He gave up. I wasn't disparaging him or his ideal of fiction, and he never disparaged my aims. Neither of us could have been quite so silly and childish. He did disparage — in an impersonal and amiable way — *portions of one of my yarns, because the yarn –not a good example of its type*; just as I shook my head sadly at one of his, and on the same grounds. Not because it was a story of mood instead of a story of action, *but because it was not well done as a yarn of mood* — just as mine had been poorly done as a yarn of action. Neither disparaged the other's aim. Whatever infrequent and mild criticism — of the most impersonal sort — HPL and I exchanged, was leveled at that story in which the author had not achieved his aim. To belittle the author's aim is some thing else. The criterion we had was, *is this good for its kind?* Not, *is this a good kind?* Did the author achieve his purpose? Not, was his purpose right or wrong?

As a broad generality, I say that fans tend to bigotry, to self-centeredness, to setting up a one-man criterion of excellence, and then feeling that all other readers should accept the same criterion. Why that pontifical attitude which Fort terms "exclusionism"? The Christian faith has many splendid aspects — but its damning all other faiths and arrogantly presuming to "convert" the "heathen" is what makes it, to me, offensive. I greatly admire the Moslem faith, and find but one fault: the same one I charge to the Christian. If not converting infidels, then the sharp line of demarcation, the feeling of superiority to the infidel. Judaism — more of the same: the elect, and then the gentiles. All of a piece with Hitler and his *Herrenvolk*!

The Acolyte, #13, Winter 1946; eds. Francis T. Laney; cover art by E.T. Beaumont.

The Chinaman is the only civilized person extant. He doesn't believe that anything as personal as belief is worth arguing about! The Chinese are the only major group who have abstained from persecutions of a religious nature. Hinduism is as pernicious (far more so, in fact!) as Christianity, Islam, and Judaism in its exclusionistic arrogance. The Buddhists come closest to being free of that arrogance. We need more Buddhistic influence among our fans.

And these ratings which fan mags have published — what rot! A fair, impersonal display of discrimination, a detached attitude in making comparisons — that's splendid! But the belittling and disparaging, that's something else.

I read a lot of stuff I consider sheer drivel. OK. But other readers think it's enchanting. The editor would be a goddamn fool if he ignored those readers and bore down on just what *I* like. Who am I to want a mag made up 100% to my taste? Am I buying up the entire edition? If so, then I'd be entitled to demand 100% my pet yarn-styles.

Why don't fans strive to become connoisseurs and quit being enthusiasts? I use enthusiast in its original sense: a person who is dizzy, hopped up, obsessed with some notion — and with the implication that he's reached the point of incoherence and irrationality. He feels exalted and prophetic, usually with little justification.

I don't blame fans for being enthusiasts, understand. Any person of intense personality is bound to be an enthusiast, for a while. Finally he sobers up enough to become a connoisseur.

After all, it is twenty years this coming week since I wrote my first weird yarn. Naturally enough, I am no longer the enthusiast I was in those days, when I literally could not write anything but a weird yarn. However, my enthusiasm did not drive me to writing belittling letters about the work of some weird writer whose approach was not to my taste.

The hodgepodge of so-called "science" in science-fiction is certainly pathetic. I mean, taking it seriously is pathetic. Because there's no science, not a damn trace of real science, in a carload of sf. Why not consider the stuff, honestly, frankly, as entertaining whimsy, some of it worth while and well done, some of it sheer tripe, and let it go at that — enjoy much of it, but not make a cult of any of it? And quit crapping yourself about "thought-variants" (a one-time shibboleth) and the science content — there ain't any. Not that I am a scientist — hell, I am merely a B. S., and they have Ph.D.'s writing for sf mags. But I have a rudimentary acquaintance with science.

I like a science-fiction yarn *when it is a good yarn*; I like it because it is well done as a piece of story-telling, and not just because it has a dribble of science-so-called. After all, if I want some science, why not get a textbook on some branch of science and then sweat it out? Science-fiction, I think, is a hell of a lot more fun if you regard it frankly and honestly as make-believe, let's-play, just suppose – the Same way in which you read *The Arabian Nights, Alice in Wonderland* (a satire, by the way), or *Candide*. It'd seem silly to me to enter into ponderous scientific speculations about Alice's gambolings about, and try to devise some "law" of nature which "logically" permitted some of her experiences.

Atmosphere unnecessary to a story? Hell, how can you do a yarn without atmosphere? You can do a composition having a plot and no atmosphere, but is it a story? The big fallacy lies in trying to dissect a yarn. A story is an entity. Take a lot of anatomical parts and assemble them; does that give you a human being? A story is not simply so many parts plot, such-and-such percentage atmosphere, such-and-such amount of characterization, and so many percent theme. Any more than a strip-tease queen is summed up in such-and-such hip measure, such-and-such bust, etc.

Atmosphere, characterization, mood, plot, theme are so inextricably linked that you can't separate them as an assayer breaks down an ore specimen. They are all aspects of the same entity. True, some yarns devote more space to atmosphere and less to plot, and so forth in permutations and combinations. The predominance of one aspect and the subordination of the other aspects is not a matter of rule but rather a matter of *what effect author desire*, and *what purpose does he wish to achieve*? Whichever aspect-dominance best achieves his purpose is certainly the best one. But no two stories can or ought to have any arbitrarily assigned aspect-dominance.

The only answer to this matter of proportioning the "aspects" is this: it depends on your narrative purpose. The only time when one can be definite in condemnation is when a writer has, to the point of absurdity, squelched one of the aspects. He can suppress and emphasize within wide limits. If he knows his business, he knows just how and what and how much to suppress and to emphasize and overemphasize to get a true and valid story-entity. If he does not know his business, that is, if he lacks the instinct of dramatic rightness, all his babble about proportions is like a madman laughing into a well. He should stick to mathematics or something precise, and avoid pursuits where intuition dominates.

But please do convince your pals that there is absolutely no such thing as novelty of plot. All plots are banal and hackneyed. The personality of the characters is what carries a story; that, and suspense, arising not so much from wondering how it'll turn out, as from participating in the nature of the viewpoint-character to such an extent that the reader shares the hero's emotions through his sympathy for a fellow-human.

My best stories — that is, those sold for the most money, or sold to the more esteemed magazines, or those longest remembered by readers and friends — have been stories utterly lacking in plot novelty. What these stories did have was; (a) striking personalities, (b) colorful atmosphere, and (c) a theme whose truth and effectiveness had considerable in common with the Joe Doakes reader's daily life and problems.

I am always interested in glancing at a fan magazine, but it is only fair to confess that I do not keep in touch with the fan world. I wrote for *Diablerie* for fun and to humor Bill Watson, whose kind invitation to attend a conclave had to be declined. I've written just 25 weird yarns since "Spanish Vampire." Not many — and only that and Apprentice Magician" and "Khosru's Garden" appeared in *Weird Tales*. Since May 1932 I have done but 69 fantasy yarns; since my start in 1924, just a bit short of 100, including collaborations. Of my total of 454 yarns about 430 were done professionally, that is, since May 1932. Of professional stuff: 69 fantasies, 62 westerns, 137 adventures, and 131 detectives; the rest are miscellaneous. So you see why, perforce, I am not in touch with the fan world. Fantasy is a sort of hobby with me; I write a fantasy yarn only when I feel that fantasy is the ideal medium for a theme, or to depict some personality or situation. I don't write a fantasy just to be writing a fantasy (I used to do that, in 1932-33, until I got mortally sick of my own stuff!).

I am not remotely interested in fandom's classifyings, dogmatic cries, awards of crowns of dung and wreaths of orchids. To me, fantasy is something to enjoy, rather than to make into a cult. I enjoy writing. Why should I limit my writing to just one field? I meet all kinds of people, I've travelled considerably; I've moved in so many strata of life, . I have so many interests, that I imply could not cramp myself to doing just fantasy or just any other one kind of fiction. Doing nothing but fantasy is almost inconceivable! I can hardly imagine living all these years and seeing the world only in terms of cosmic terror, or as a setting for Gothic yarns, or in terms of science-fiction. As for those who can and do, all power to them.

On the other hand, I do not by any means dismiss the fans with a shrug. They are fellows who think along lines which I from time to time consider intently. We share a common taste. They are customers. But for their interest in fantasy—they, the great group of fans and mere purchasers—there'd have been nearly 100 yarns I could never have sold.

I do not contribute fiction to fan mags, simply because writing a story is work not merely splashing something off. And when I work, I expect to get paid. I can do only one grade of work: my best — that is, my best at that moment, and with respect to that theme or subject. My best brings an appreciable sum from a commercial publisher. Frankly I couldn't afford to hand a fanmag a MS. for which I can get, via return mail, $100 or $200 or $300. No fan mag editor would expect me to hand him even a $50 MS., though these days I don't warm up a typewriter for less than $100. As for dishing out a reject — no. If it were good, it would have sold for cash, if it's not worth selling, it's not worth anyone's acceptance as a gift.

True, I do write essays for fan mags. That is different. No problem of drama and structure is involved. It's relaxation, hobby writing, a bus-man's holiday! I enjoy it — in limited amounts.

A motor-racing fan mag—of all things, but why not?—once asked me if I had any motor-racing rejects. Oddly, I did have. I've followed racing, I've written articles on motoring, and fiction on racing. One bounced. But I turned the man down. If it wasn't good enough to sell, then it wasn't good enough to give away. Months later, a salvage editor bought it — cut rate, of course. But it was, after all, worth paying for. Fiction writing, while fun, is also work. Essays—well, that essay on rum in *Diablerie*: fun doing it. Relaxation, done after dinner, when I was burned out and couldn't write fiction. I did it instead of spending an hour in the darkroom tinkering with cameras. That very same kind of copy, not one bit better, not one bit worse, used to bring me $50 on the barrel head, in the days when I fooled around writing articles. For that matter, I sold some technical photographic articles last year; lost money on them, but did it just for fun. Bill Watson kindly said my article on rum was good enough for ESQUIRE. While

I've never sold to ESQUIRE, Bill was just about right. I have sold such copy to mags which had the Esquire approach-but-varied and came close to ESQUIRE rates.

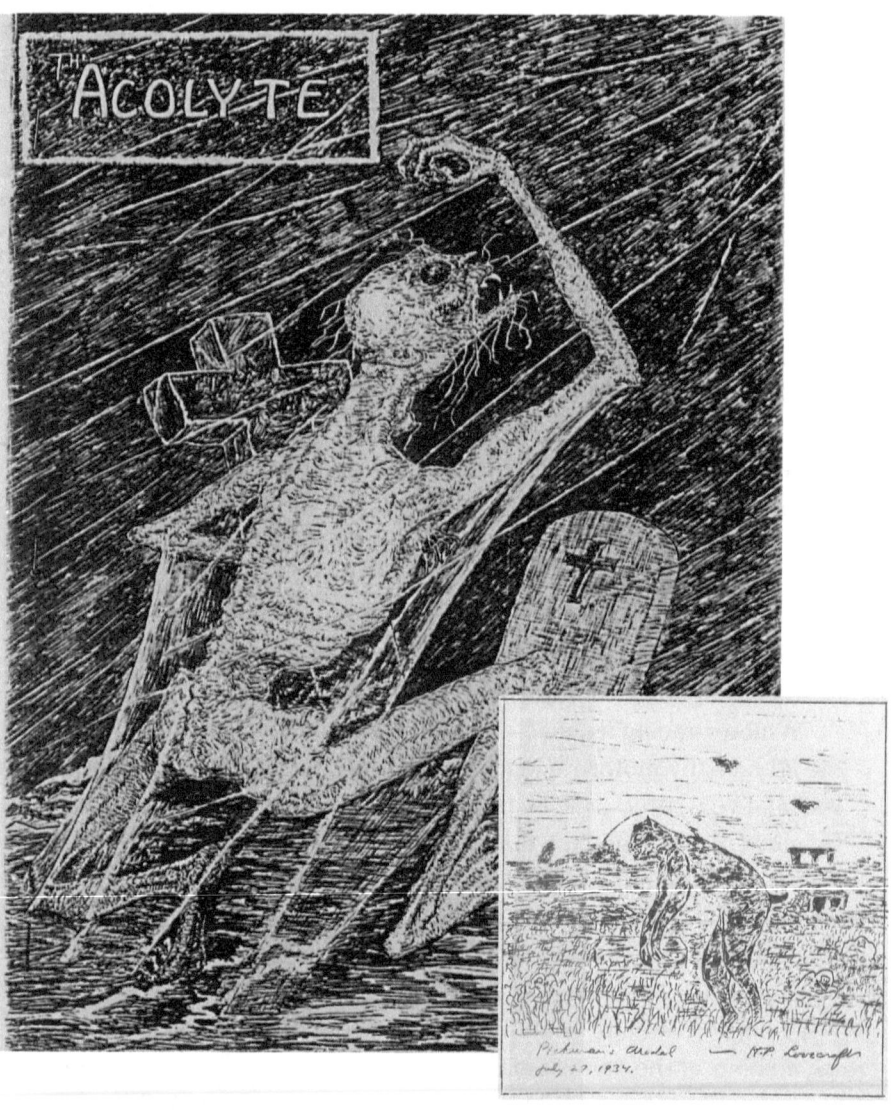

The Acolyte, #13, Winter 1946; cover art for H.P. Lovecraft's "Pickman's Model" by W. Robert Gibson. (**Insert**) "Lovecraft as an Illustrator" from *The Acolyte,* vol. 1, #4, Summer 1943. Showing Lovecraft's own depiction of the creature from "Pickman's Model." This was taken from a letter Lovecraft sent to Franklin Lee Baldwin.

FANZINE SCOPE

Francis Towner Laney (1914–1958) was of course behind *The Acolyte* and the autobiographical *Ah! Sweet Idiocy!* and edited *Wild Hair* and *Shangri L'Affaires*. Laney discribed himself once as "... militant, iconoclastic, cynical, sarcastic, and without reverence for anything or anyone."[100] ¶A snap-zine is a one page zine, quickly produced and mailed. —LO

CRACKLE: THE SNAP-ZINE

F. Towner Laney

(from Spacewarp *36, March, 1950, ed. Art Rapp)*

UNDER THIS title, an individual named Jay Gibson of 24 Kensington Ave., Jersey City 4, New Jersey, is putting out a single sheet item in an edition of one. Each comprises one page of typed text and one full-page ink drawing, and are supposed to be passed from hand to hand. I have just received issues #3 and #4, and find myself mildly obsessed by them.

In the first place, one wonders why Jay Gibson does not do her stuff in hekto. Hekto ink would work as well as what she is using for her drawing, and Coswal would no doubt publish it for her for a mere pittance. Then all of you could look askance and shake your heads!

I dunno.

Jay Gibson[101] says she is a girl, but Redd Boggs says "It is probable that Jay Gibson is not a femme at all." Not that it makes any difference, but that is his opinion, and I list it here so if heesh is unmasked and turns out to have a crew hair cut, gray mustache, and downward slanting eyes, we will know Redd for a false prophet.

---

100 *Fandango*, vol. 2, #3, whole #7, Winter 1944.
101 She was a hoax sister created by Joe Gibson.

The reason I'm mildly obsessed with *Crackle* is the innate fuggheadedness of the contents. #3 consists of an article — "Dear Fans and Gentle Egos: A Psycho Thesis on the Genus Stfanatic" — which tells us the Gibsonian ideas of what makes fans fan, and includes among other quotable lines the following gems: "It seems obvious to me that fans are just young people with fairly good, imaginative minds, who're living in an age when nothing is done to help them take advantage of that talent"; and after a couple of paragraphs typified by "Thus, a lot of us who might become well-trained specialists making good salaries miss our chance." Miss Gibson hits the high note: "And until the rest of the world catches up with us ... we'll just have to go along as wild stf fans and dreaming stf authors."

The cover of #3, incidentally, depicts a nude female figure with a rocket ship zipping between her spraddled out legs.

#4 follows up this theme with an article called "The Cautious Approach." Gibson gets in high gear about how she wants to take off in a spaceship with some boy and spend months hurtling across the galaxy ... As soon as I and this boy took off, the very first thing I'd do is strip naked! The second thing I'd do is strip him!" And so on and so on — almost like a female Crouch. In a footnote she apologizes: "if a bit sexy — why, I need some way to get that out of my system."

But here is the line that obsesses me: "I know I'd rather act sexy than sneak around and pretend to be angelic — *or submit myself greedily to worse things.*" (My underlining.) I dunno.

Vampire #8, Dec., 1946.

BEHIND THE ZINE

Fanzine editors developed all sorts of tricks to compensate for limitations of mimeo/hecto printing, and typographical shortcomings in using a typewriter. Interlineations were first used to delineate different stories and break up large blocks of copy in zines. In some cases one editor's typesetting trick is picked up by another editor and soon this turns into a standard. Interlineation was an example of stealing the best ideas from other editors. —LO

DELINEATING THE INTERLINEATION

Bob Tucker

(from Vega #8, 1952; ed. Joel Nydahl)

A PRACTICE LIMITED solely to fandom and fan magazines (so far) is a novel typing device know as an interlineation. This habit or practice was originated in almost pre-historic times by Mr. Jack Speer, a grandfather-type fan who introduced them into amateur journalistic circles in the late thirties. Quickly passing into public domain, interlineations were seized upon and eventually used by virtually every fan editor in the business. Doubtless Mr. Speer, viewing the results of his invention, wishes he had cut his throat instead.

Interlineations have evoked from the simple things they once were, much as fan magazines have evolved from the high-intentioned journals they used to be. In the beginning they were little more than a random comment by an editor; a comment perhaps caused by something he had read, or seen, and were placed in the fan magazine only to separate two articles on the same page. But this reserved comment did not last. Where Mr. Speer would say

but these were unfavorable mutations

the modern fan editor, having lost all sight of the original intentions, or even know of them, now bursts out with

> **"I said, Cheerio you son of a bitch, and shot him in the head."**

This is a most deplorable state of affairs, and occurs when some impetuous youth-type editor reads a story in some pro-magazine and become angry with it. Disliking the story and its author and the magazine and its editor, the young editor seizes upon the one line most offensive to him and gives it a temporary sort of immortality by interlineation. That this practice is a most dangerous one will readily be seen. Someday, some pro-magazine will publish in a story or article from a bit of obscenity which will be seized by the fan editor and reprinted in an interlineation. The post office of course will ban only the fan magazine, while the profession will reap the benefits of an enlarged circulation.

Another early practitioner of the fanly art of interlineation was Mr. Art Widner, who in his magazine, enlarged upon the early form and popularized direct quotes and bits of dialogue. After viewing a picture starring Crosby and Hope, he said

> **I'm glad you're a camel too, Gertie.**

and invited his many readers to guess the origin source of the lines — not revealing until later that they had been taken from the Crosby-Hope movie. As mentioned, this struck the fancy of his audience, and if the habit was a hesitant one before, it was off in full cry now. This led directly to the practices of today.

Today's fan editors however do not follow the same rules in interlineating; if indeed they follow any rules at all. Whereas one editor may choose to print a single line known to everyone:

> **Gosh-wow-boy-oh-boy-the-mosta-of-the-besta!**

the perverse or impish editor, cherishing private joke shared only by one of two other fans, will publish this intelligence:

Seeded shoulders

knowing that the one or two other readers who share the joke or the incident will be inwardly delighted to see it in print, and will afterward go about with the self-satisfied and smut expressions, looking down on the common reader who know not what it meant. Some readers to be sure, possessing suspicious or evil minds, will immediately attempt to read all manner of suggestive things into the interlineation, and perhaps go so far as to write the editor a letter demanding an explanation. The editor, smug and complacent, delighted with its success, replies in the next issue

Hah!

and nothing is resolved. By the time the reader, caught up in the middle of he knows-not-what (and by odd coincidence, publishing a magazine of his own) jumps into the queer verbal fray with

What do you mean by "Hah!" ??

which only compounds the felony because now a second magazine and a second set of readers are committed, and because much time has elapsed between respective issues, straining the memories of all concerned. But among that second set of readers will be a third inquiring fan and this third inquiring fan sakes in his magazine

What do yo mean by "What do you men by "'Hah!'" ???

and all the squirrels begin storing up nuts for the winter. It is obvious that the only winner in this lopsided exchange of nonsensical interlineations can be the origin fan editor who said

seeded shoulders

Because all or nearly all the varieties of contents of fan magazines were (like sin) invented years ago, the beginning fan of today who wishes to make a respectable mark in the fan field is hard put to find a new angle. It must be pointed out that the first fan fiction, the first amateurish attempts at pro fiction, the first illustration, the first article, the first news or gossip column, the first magazine, book or movie review all appeared twenty years ago in those pioneer fanzines; the great horde of fannish scribes who have followed after are no more than imitators of greater of lesser merit. To climb, a neofan must exploit something new, Obviously some fans have knowingly or unknowingly discovered that spark of originality and skyrocketed into fame — or its reviews. From LNFs they become BNFs almost over night. Degler discovered and promoted something he was please to call The Comic Circle; Laney discovered a third sex; Eisberry and Beale found themselves possessed of extremely sharp tongues; Hoffman discovered she was a woman; Ben Singer discovered Nancy. These and others have, in their individual ways, hit upon that spark of originality which caught the attention of the jaded masses. Neofans desiring fame and fortune in fandom might will study their examples.

It is astonishing that no one in the last fifteen years has seized upon Mr. Speer's remarkable invention, has thought to twist it to private use and thereby build a ladder to fannish glory! Beyond the occasional old-line hack who hammers out an article on interlineations, no one has seemed to realize that a solid-gold BNF reputation may easily be fabricated by using these interlineations in a truly startling and original manner! Banish all thoughts of becoming another columnist, another pundit, or another space-opera writer. Hundreds of competing fans flood the fanzines with drivel they term articles, stories, artwork, columns, poetry and reviews. But has any brilliant neofan yet conceived the truly original idea of writing interlineations? Of supplying them to fanzines in wholesales lots?

No.

A fruitful field of endeavor has been sadly neglected. Editors are, on the whole, tired old men and women who slave from dawn to duck cranking out each new issue, and then fall exhausted into bed. They have little or no time for the sublets of fan-magging, precious little time to devote to frivolities and trimmings of a well-founded fan publication. There is no duplicate Redd Boggs[102]. You have already noticed

---

102 Dean Walter (Redd) Boggs (1921–1996) edited the *1948 Fantasy Annual* and *Skyhook* (1948–1957).

that many of them are so hurried they lack time for correct spelling and typing; lack the time to correct the errors of their contributors. Therefore, they should welcome with open arms (and perhaps be willing to pay for) the fan who supplies manufactured interlineations in wholesale lots.

I this new and fertile field the neofan must write and submit with care, choosing this market as carefully as he would choose the pro-magazine to buy or submit this stories to. Exercising caution, he would take care not to send Shelby Vick[103] the line

---
Confusion confuses
---

although this subtle gem might so very well indeed in a competing fan magazine. The writer of enticing interlineations desiring to climb up in the fannish sky will study the moods of each editor, will note the amounts of blank space left over at the ends of pages, and will then carefully tailor his submissions to fit the mood and the space. He would do will to advertise in fandom

---
All the interlineations fit to print
---

and perhaps include that slogan on his letterheads. Complete pages of interlineations should be typed or mimeographed in neat, readable manner and then submitted to each editor. Sufficient blank space should be left between each interlineation so that the editor may clip out and use any one he desires, or any one that will readily fit the particular space remaining at the bottom of the page. A little practice, paying close attention to originality, wit, and humor, should soon place the neofan in an enviable position in the fan magazine world, and then he too may publish

---
Who sawed Courtney's boat?[104]

---

103 Editor of a zine called *Confusion*.
104 A once popular sf fanzine catchphrase, used as a non sequitur, that has nothing to do with sf or fandom, and refers to a sabotaged boat race. Charles Courtney was the rowing coach at Cornell University in the late 19th Century.

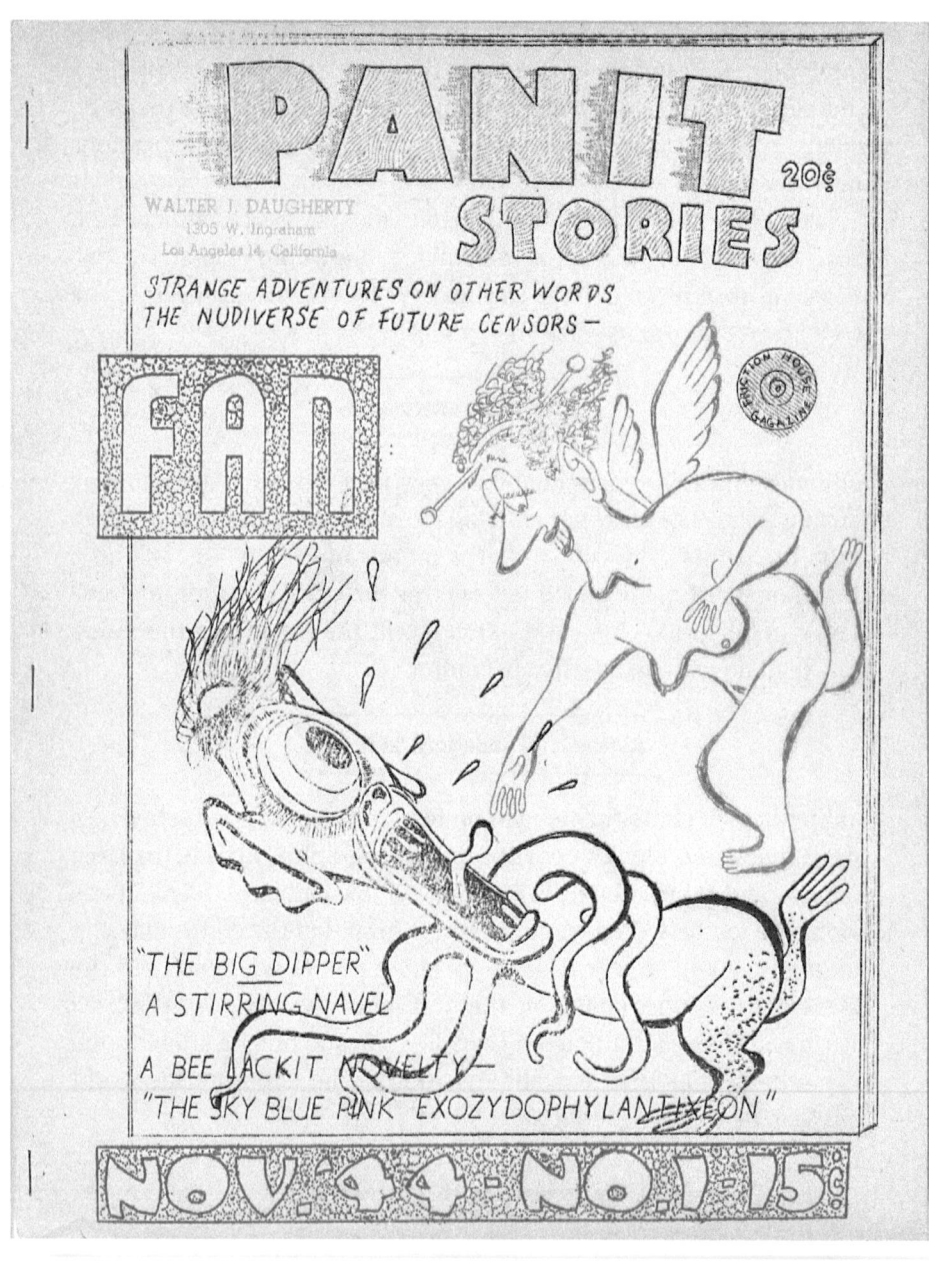

FAN (Panit Stories), #1, Nov., 1944; edited by Walt Daugherty. This issue is full of caricatures of LASFS member and fans by cartoonist Virgil Partch (VIP), who met Forrest J Ackerman while doing art for a Fort MacArthur Base Army newsletter Ackerman edited. *FAN* was a fanzine version of LIFE magazine, made up mostly of pictures and art work.

Vega, vol. 1, #12, 1953; ed. Joel Nydahl; art by Bob McMillan.

ZINE EDITORS

The following is of interest more for its rundown of focal point fanzines during the period under discussion rather than its attempt to outline the numbered cycles of sf fandom started by Jack Speer. (The cycles was a fannish affectation and most fans could care less.) White alludes to a tie-in between fanzines and different cycles. One can see how on many occasions the birth and death of a popular, or focal point, zine paralleled the birth and death cycles of sf fandom. The attempted *coup d'etat* in 1953, that became a pseudo-seventh fandom, led by a young Harlan Ellison, and coalescing after the demise of *Quandry*, got little, or negative, recognition by fans and led to Ellison's famous response, in *Psychotic* #15, about mad dogs and groins. ¶ This piece appeared in *Science-Fiction Five-Yearly*, which began in 1951 and actually came out every five years. Hoffman edited nine issues up to 1991, before turning it over to other hands. —LO

123456789? WHAT WAS THAT FANDOM I SAW YOU WITH...

Ted White

(from Science-Fiction Five-Yearly *#4, November 1966; ed. Lee Hoffman)*

TWO CYCLES seemed to go hand-in-hand. One is the cycle of fandoms[105]. The other is a cycle of speculation: What fandom are we in now?

When Bob Silverberg speculated in *Quandry* over the fandoms which had ensued since the original Speer article of over a decade earlier, he unwittingly set off a mad scramble which called itself

---

[105] In a nutshell: *Eofandom*: 1930–33; *First Fandom*: 1933–1936; *Second Fandom*: October 1937–October 1938; *Third Fandom*: September 1940– early 1944; *Fourth Fandom*: late 1944–1947; *Fifth Fandom*: 1947–mid-1950; *Sixth Fandom*: Early 1951– mid-1953. After this point things get murky.

Seventh Fandom. Since that time, fandom has not been the same. Periodically, prophets rise to announce the eminent demise of one fandom, or the Coming of the next. Different speculators have stated that we are currently in anything from Fifth to Tenth Fandom.

The average fan, old and tired perhaps, yawns knowingly, scratches his head, waves his arms, and says, "Whatinhell difference does it make?"

None, Charlie. But I want to write an article about it.

It seems to me that is wisest to accept the Silverberg thesis that Sixth Fandom began in the earliest fifties. If we want to go back to second-guessing before this point, we might as easily revise Speer while we're at it. And that could destroy the very foundations of First Fandom — they might end up having to admit fans from as recently as 1953 into that exclusive Order.

So let's assume that Sixth Fandom reached its first flower during the height of Q's popularity.

Silverberg felt that Q's death would signal the demise of Sixth Fandom, and a group of younger fans, triumphantly led by Harlan Ellison, eagerly awaited that death to announce their formation of Seventh Fandom.

For many fans of that period, the "Seventh Fandom Group" made up of such fen as Ian McCauley, John Magnus, Jack Harness, Joel Nydahl, Charles Watkins, Ellison and, while he wasn't looking, Dean Grennell, were a lot of noise and not much else. A couple of years later Harlan would utter, in *Psychotic*, his famous pronouncement that "the mad dogs have kneed us in the groin," but for the most part fandom just stood about and looked on, much as it would later do while Los Angeles fans romped about with swords and black uniforms. Seventh Fandom badges were in prominent display at the 1953 Phillycon and a FAPA was formed and produced perhaps four quarterly mailings or so, but fandom never took to the self-proclaimed "7th Fandom." It was indifference, not the frenzied knee-thrust of mad dogs, that killed the movement. Then, too, if one new generation of fans could announce the death of a "fandom", and the inauguration of their own, so could the next generation, following on their heels. At least one fanzine article named me as a leader of Eighth Fandom, and an issue of *Psychotic* carried the musings of two columnists on the subject of an "8th Fandom." This, no later than 1954 ...

If fandom was resolved that no upstart group of fans — no matter how talented — could announce itself to be the "next fandom", there was considerably less agreement over what had constituted a true Seventh Fandom, and gradually it seemed as though Harlan had won over the mad dogs after all — for fans, when speaking several years later, seemed to accept as *fait accompli* the existence of a Seventh Fandom in the 1953-54 period. They were wrong, of course.

If we accept Sixth Fandom's formation as concurrent with *Quandry*'s rise to dominance of the fanzine field, and the rise in popularity of Lee Hoffman and Walt Willis, together with the re-emergence of Tucker and Bloch, we will have a beginning. But it is wrong to assume the sixth fandom died with Q.

A pandemic is characterized by the quality of its kind of mortality rate. And the guns did not die. It peculiar qualities of both their mission as and staff now led a — bound up in the Rev. of wit and humor — which characterized six fandom during quandaries did not disappear when Q. did.

Just as Q was eking out its last issues, a young Michigan fan, Joel Nydahl, who, at the age of fourteen, had sold a story to IMAGINATION, began a hectographed fanzine called *Vega*. With its third issue, it went mimeo, and with its fifth or sixth, it became a very good fanzine. It was monthly and it quickly attracted columnists like Dean Grennell and Marion Bradley, and printed such milestone articles as Tucker's piece on interlineations[106] — which single-handedly revived the interlineation for a whole new generation of fans. The letter column was rarely lacking in letters from Grennell, Tucker and Bloch, an unholy trio that was as much as anything the most potent symbol of the melding of older fans with the new—for Dean Grennell was then a hyperactive fan whose explosion into fandom in late 1952 made him at once one of the most active of the "7th fandomites", and at the same time their patron, as his maturity naturally elevated him into the ranks of the ghods, Tucker, Bloch and Willis.

VEGA was a flash in the pan. Monthly until just before its last issue, the First Annish (which was mailed out in two fifty-page sections, months late), it went straight to the top of the heap and then winked out of existence. Its life span covered only the last quarter of 1952, and the year of 1953.

---

106 See "Delineating The Interlineation, pg. 273."

But, rising phoenix-like out of *Vega's* ashes, was Dick Geis' *Psychotic*. I've often wondered about the appropriateness of that title, in the light of Geis' later activities and proclivities, but in any event, here was a dittoed, monthly fanzine, to which The Clique quickly graduated. Its first issues appeared in the fall of 1953, and within the first half-dozen, *Psychotic* was The Fanzine. Geis was a sensible editor, and he embellished his pages with the columns of Vernon McCain, and the articles of Grennell, Tucker and all the rest. It was no coincidence that Harlan's last raspberry to the foes of "7th Fandom" appeared in *Psychotic* — this was the fanzine where it was happening, baby. Like *Vega* and *Quandry* before that, *Psychotic* carried the lifeblood of fandom within its pages, and most especially in its lettercolumn. There were no newszines of note then, but if you subscribed to *Psychotic*, you were up on everything, from the famous Door Incident[107] at the Midwescon, to the fights of the SFCon with the Hotel Sir Francis Drake.

The pace of publishing a monthly fanzine is wearying, though, and *Psychotic* began faltering after its first year. There was no fancy annish to destroy editor Geis in a burst of what was now called "Nydahl's Disease" but *Psychotic* began to become less and less regular, although compensated for by larger issues, and Geis was obviously looking for a new direction and new challenges. *Psychotic* went photo-offset and half-size "perhaps the only fanzine in this format that wasn't overwhelmed by the pretentiousness of it", then to Gestetner print, and finally to a name change— *Science Fiction Review*.

It was then quite dead as a focal point — and with it died, at last, Sixth Fandom. A neofan, Cliff Gould[108], tried to pick up the torch but was neither regular nor good enough.

Seventh Fandom did not rise immediately out of the ashes of Sixth. Sixth Fandom had not died a sudden death, but a gradual one, a death by attrition. By the time *Psychotic* had effectively folded, there were no notable genzines being published at all.

Where were the ghods? Along with everyone else, they were channelling their activity into the apas. Bob Tucker, Lee Hoffman,

---

107 Fannish lore has it that Jim Harmon was waterbagged by Harlan Ellison at the MidWestCon in 1954 and raced up to Ellison's room. When Ellison rolled a firecracker under the door, Harmon slammed his fist thru the door. Hotel management threatened arrest, but a collection was made by fans and pros to pay for the busted door.
108 Editor of the well regarded *Oblique*.

Dean Grennell, Robert Bloch — all were active almost exclusively in FAPA. Walt Willis was still publishing *Hyphen* — a beacon in the dark night of fandom — but irregularly. SAPS[109] was burgeoning. The Cult had been born in 1954, siphoning off the prodigious energies of the younger fans. And in England, in 1955, OMPA[110] was formed to perform an analogous function for British fandom.

I joined FAPA with the May, 1955 mailing. I had applied to Sec.-Treas. Redd Boggs in the fall of 1954, and had gotten only 2 FAs before I was invited to join. Two years later, the waiting list was climbing to unheard-of proportions, while at the same time, mailing after mailing, page records were being made and broken.

It was a time of a great migration into the apas. It would be neither the first, nor the last, but it had a great impact upon fandom, since for the first time, a vast majority of the best material in fandom was being published for exclusive groups and was unavailable to newer fans. The apas became the In place to be, and the greatest status was attached to FAPA. Even today, long after the high points in FAPA quality were edged away from, and the group became listless and lackluster, the waiting list remains of approximately the same size as the membership list.

But a turning point was reached. In 1958 several things happened. One was that after the abortive attempt by a triumvirate from New

Fanhistory, #2, March, 1956; ed. Lee Hoffman; cartoon by Harlan Ellison.

---

109 Spectator Amateur Press Society founded in 1947 and still around.
110 Offtrails Magazine Publishers Association (1954–1981).

York, London and Antwerp, to launch a newszine, *Contact*, Terry Carr and Ron Ellik waved the other wand, *Fanac*, and began a weekly newszine. Another motivating force was that the ten-year dream, "South Gate in '58", was being realized. It was four years since the last west coast worldcon, and twelve since the last in Southern California, and many fans seem to have been waiting to reappear from the woodwork of gafia[111].

Suddenly there were genzines all over the place, and plans for more. John Magnus was publishing *Rumble*. I was publishing a weekly *Gafia Newssheet*. Redd Boggs brought out *Bete Noir*. Later *Shaggy*[112] would be revived, and I would be publishing *Void* with Greg Benford. And in the meantime, Terry Carr was turning *Innuendo* into one of the finest fanzines of the period.

But *Fanac* was the focal point. It won a Hugo, and it consistently came in #1 on its own polls. As a newszine, it took the disparate threads of a fragmented fandom and wove them into a whole again, putting fans previously so isolated in their own lives that they'd never heard of each other before into communication. And it had news. Once again, there was a central clearing house for all the news and quasi-news, such as the furor over the WSFS, Inc.[113] and it's legal battles.

While Terry Carr published it, *Fanac*, although its schedule sometimes faltered, remained the guiding light of fandom. Its circulation huge with paid subscriptions in a time when fans were notorious for their refusal to pay money for fanzines, *Fanac* remained the center of fandom's paper universe, making and broadcasting the scoop on everything that was happening.

The original Speer Theory of Fandoms included the concept of interregnums — a period in which fandom is in a state of flux, during which there is no central point about which fans coalesce, a time between Fandoms. Silverberg did little with the idea, but I think it is one of the most valid aspect of Speer's structure. As I see it, Sixth Fandom lasted into 1954, lapsing with the death of *Psychotic* into an interregnum which itself lasted three years. True Seventh Fandom was born in early 1958, with *Fanac*, and persisted into 1961, and perhaps as late as the 1962 Chicon, carried on by *Axe*, and the fandom-wide interest

---

111 Fan term for *get away from it all*.
112 Nickname for *Shangri L'Affaires*, also titled *Shangri-LA*.
113 World Science Fiction Society.

in the second Willis trip.

After 1962? Another interregnum, and one which has persisted despite the attempts of various people, such as myself, to abate it. I published *Minac* in 1963 and 1964, and had plans for a monthly genzine which more or less died amidst the Boondoggle[114] unpleasantness. The period from 1962 on has been marked by another swing into the apas, a swing heightened by the advent, in 1964, of the local weekly apas like the late APA F and still functioning APA L. There are regional apas like the Southern Fandom, Cult-like apas like TAPS, and others, such as APA 45 and INTERAPA and N'APA, which have drawn off much of the younger talent, just as the Cult and WAPA did ten years before them. Some fans now move directly from stark neofandom into an apa without ever becoming aware of the history, traditions, or even existence of general fandom.

As for Eighth Fandom? It's been twelve years now, and we still ain't dere, Sharlie …

(Ellison smoking pipe)

Vega, #12, 1953; ed. Joel Nydahl; art by Juanita R. Wellons.

---

114 AKA the Breendoggle. This is complicated, and outside the scope of this book, but the gist of it was that in 1963 the SF Worldcon Committee announced that they were banning popular fan Walter Breen (who later married Marion Zimmer Bradley), an alleged pedophile at the time, from the con. Sides were taken and active fandom went to war. Breen died in prison in 1993.

Snide, #2, February, 1941; cover art Bill Evans and Damon Knight.

FANZINE PROFILE

Damon Knight (1922–2002) was an sf fan, author, and editor, toiling in the sf field through most of the latter half of the 20th century. Like many a pro he published a fanzine in his youth. (A very short list of this select group would include Ray Bradbury, Robert Silverberg, Harlan Ellison, Charles Beaumont, James Blish, Greg Benford, and Roger Ebert — yes that Roger Ebert, with two issues of the mimeographed *Stymie*.) Knight's first story, "The Itching Hour," appeared in the, Summer 1940, issue of Ray Bradbury's zine *Futuria Fantasia*. Knight exhibited a talent for art, which he never developed, and sold a cartoon to AMAZING STORIES when 17 years old. ¶ In this piece, from 1951, Harry Warner thought Knight showed some writing talent and wondered why Knight "… didn't go on to make a living by his pen." He spoke too soon. In 1994 the Science Fiction Writers of America named Knight a Grand Master.— LO

Harry Warner Jr.

(from Fanvariety #12, Sept., 1951)

THIS FANZINE was like most of the fanzines in history — its first issue had a cover containing a space ship blasting onward and upward. But unlike other fanzines this one also had on its cover a worried-looking little man in a business suit, lugging a briefcase, rushing toward the vessel which was just blasting off from earth, and yelling: "Hey, wait!" That was fandom's introduction to *Snide*.

I mentioned last time the new note that *Sweetness and Light* had struck in fandom. Fans had taken themselves rather seriously before the 40's, having a good time at conventions, occasionally cracking jokes in the fanzines, but rarely taking the attitude that science fiction might not be the most important thing in life. But *Sweetness and Light*, the return of Tucker, Bruce Yerke's *The Damn Thing*, and *Snide*, all came along within a couple of years, less successful imitators sprang up, and nothing was sacred in fandom from then on.

Damon Knight was responsible for *Snide*. (He still used capital letters on his name in those days.) He resided in an alleged place called Hood River, Ore., which no one had ever heard of before, and which has probably vanished from the face of the earth since he moved to New York. Why Damon didn't go on to make his living by his pen is one of fandom's unsolved mysteries. In those days, he seemed to have at least as much talent as Tucker, and definitely more than Bradbury. A little later he did sell an occasional yarn to the prozines, particularly to those edited by the New York Futurians group after he became closely associated with the Futurians in fan activities. He has also done some professional editing and agenting, I believe, but has turned out nothing to fulfil the promise of those issues of *Snide*.

One thing more about Damon, before we turn to *Snide* itself. Hardly a fan who is alive remembers that he is the guy who is responsible for the National Fantasy Fan Federation. Probably Damon himself has a whole chain of guilt complexes, caused by the outcome of his innocent suggestion. He wrote an article called "Unite for Fie" and submitted it to me while I was publishing *Spaceways*. It urged the creation of a national fan body. I rejected it, because I thought it would start a lot of discussion over the need for such a group, and didn't want to devote much space to such an abstract quality. Damon then sent it to Art Whiner, Jr., who published it in *Fanfare*. I was wrong. Fandom rallied around the idea without prodding, and the NFFF[115] was created. Damon himself never took much of a part in the organization, smart fellow. It's hard to tell what fandom would have been without that article. No doubt, a national group would have been successfully proposed by someone else, but it might have been a national group with different purposes and methods.

Snide began to appear in 1940 and lasted for a year or two. Bill Evans, then living near Damon, was a co-editor after the first issue, but I think he'll agree that the vital spark was furnished by Damon. The best material was written by Knight under pen names, and Knight did the illustrations that contributed so much to the magazine's fla-

---

115 National Fantasy Fan Federation, aka N3F, begun in 1941.

vour. It was one of the few fanzines, in those days with really free format — i.e. one in which a heading could be any prescribed size or shape, a format which permitted the page in the middle of an article to be broken by an illustration. Damon ranks in my books as the best cartoonist ever produced by fandom. Not the best artist, he didn't have the finest sense of humour, but he had the ability to weld a joke idea and a drawing inseparably together. Best of all, his cartoons were genuine stf jokes, not something borrowed from a magazine and twisted around into fantasy. They were inspired by situations, that could only occur in stf., like the most famous cartoon of all, the man in the space suit, trying to get rid of the fly perched on the tip of his nose. Or the breathtaking silk screen cover for the second *Snide* — silver, deep blue, and blazing red, on a pale blue background, depicting a spaceman shooting his futuristic gun, receiving the full effects of the blast in his posterior and saying: "Damn Einstein!"

Snide wasn't altogether humorous. Serious stuff was published, although you never knew how long it was going to stay serious, like the remark in the middle of a prozine review column: "Free life subscriptions to any of the publications listed here may be obtained by writing to their respective editors, enclosing a one-and-a-half-cent stamp."

However, satire, light-hearted fiction, and nose-thumbing at prozines were the lifeblood of the magazine. The fiction was typified by a Ray Bradbury story, "Tale of the Mangledomvritch." This was only two pages long (*Snide* was a half size publication, with 8½ by 11 pages folded down the short axis).

But I think the best thing in the first issues was "Via Totem Pole" and "Via Sweepstakes", a couple of parodies. It's an old thing, how a good parody can remain enjoyable, long after the thing it burlesques has been forgotten. Lewis Carroll's "You are Old, Father William", is a satire on a now forgotten poem, which lives in its own right. Similarly, Damon's parody is as fresh and delightful as ever, even though the inspiring stories are permanently buried in the files of THRILLING WONDER STORIES. Around 1939 or 1940, TWS was publishing a series of connected short stories, each of which had a title beginning with "Via", and all of which consisted of radio messages received from a pioneer space expedition. The author was listed as Gordon A. Giles, generally considered a pseudonym for someone, and while the adventures of these earth men on other planets were better than the average

TWS fiction, the series grew ridiculous, stretched out to such length.

In the first of the Knight parodies, Jupiter Expedition Number One is in a bad shape. The gravity on Jupiter is so strong that the metal in tin cans has been compressed, and so the cans can't be opened with the ice pick, and everyone is starving. The expedition has found life on Jupiter, although the natives are not considered very intelligent, because none of them has been seen to move yet, except for one that got knocked down a hill by a rolling stone. However, on the 2,348½th day of the expedition:

> "As I said yesterday, our food problem was solved. It happened this way. Ginerton was looking in a pile of trash for the ace of spades, when suddenly he came up with a small metallic object in his hand. It was a can opener. "Ginerton", said Captain Batwell, summing it up, "you have found a can-opener." And that's the way we all felt about it. We drank a piece of toast in honour of Ginerton's quick-witted act, (Toast is liquid on Jupiter, Ugh.)
>
> "Barnay and Paren have gone off together and are learning how to read. Barnay is cross-eyed, which complicates matters, Captain Batwell, Ginerton, and myself have done a little scouting around. Heavily loaded, we have staggered part way into the jungle. The pink elephants and alligators charged now and then, but we found a simple way to stop them. We quickly form a circle and feed each other seltzer tablets. Then they go away. Stilson is working out a new way to peel an orange from inside. He says the world of science will be astounded.
>
> "A little later, the men decided to explore a totem pole that was standing just outside the ship. Snarletti was anxious to get inside and look for records and things, so we walked all around it, looking for ladders. We found none. "Strange", mused Captain Batwell, impressively, as always. We gathered around him, shushing each other, while the great man thought. Finally he looked up, his face alight.
>
> "I have it!" He said, "There must be some other means of entrance!" We cheered. The captain had again saved the day. And sure enough, when we had looked unsuccessfully for elevators and fire escapes we found a door at the base of the huge monument. It was a triumph for human reason."

The expedition then tries to figure out why totem poles have been found on all the planets. The members decide that it was because the inhabitants liked to build totem poles.

On the long voyage home, the ship is polluted with Jovian bedbugs, so Captain Batwell sprayed everything with kerosene and lights a match. "For six years, on Jupiter, we had not known a temperature above a hundred," the narrator points out. Then the creeping cold of space sets in, while Parker calculates every half minute, with the space duodecant, because "The slightest error would land us inches and inches from our destination."

The narrator sums it all up by saying of the return trip: "I can't describe how we felt. Anyway why should I?"

Scienti-Comics, #2, Aug., 1940; art by Damon Knight.

FAN ICONS: BEANIE

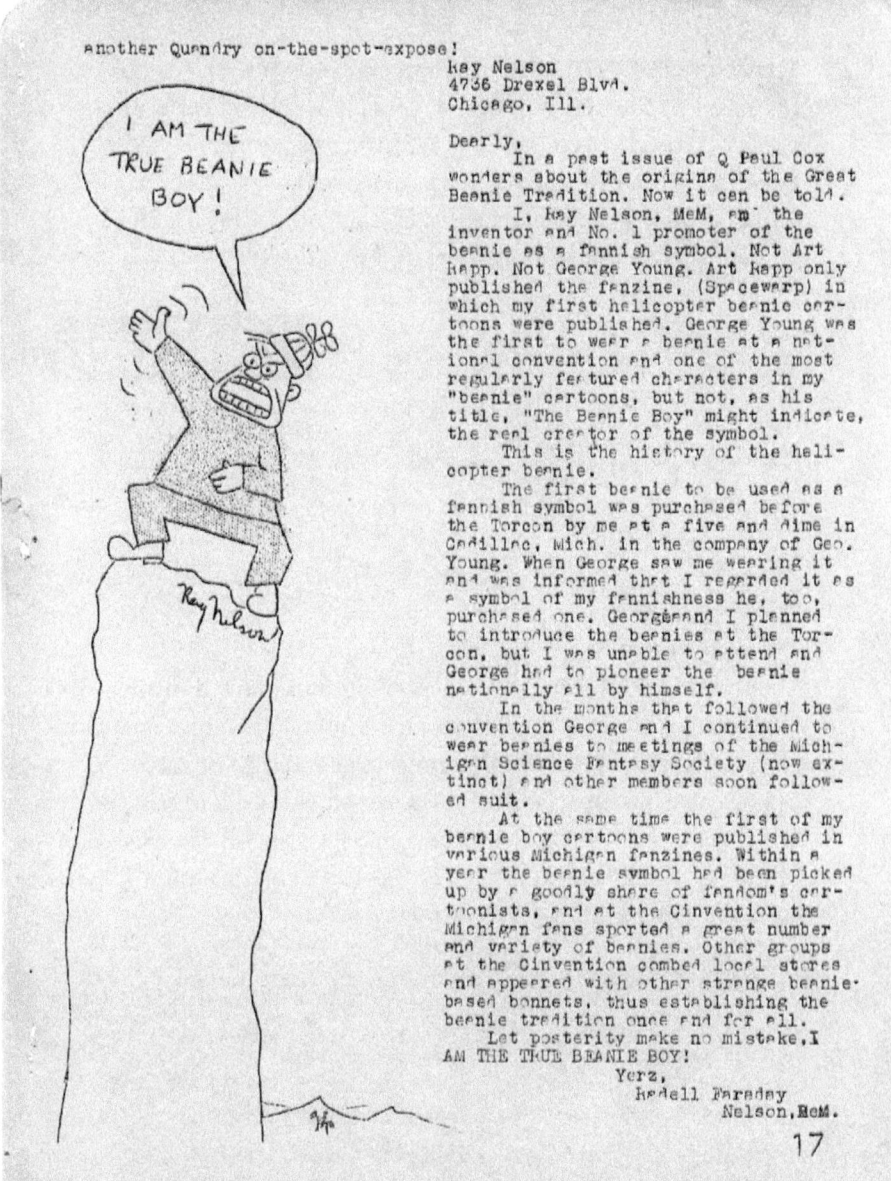

Quandry, #29, 1953; origin of the fan beanie by Ray Nelson. In an editorial to a zine he published in 2003 (*Uncle Smiley's Bookcase* vol.2 #1), Ray tells us that "the beanie has ventured forth into new realms, most notably the 'geek culture.' I have totally lost control of it & can no longer use it as a signature. With a sigh I release it to the universe."

FANZINE BITS & PIECES

Terry Carr (1937-1987) went on to become a pro editor and author. His fanzines *Fanac, Lighthouse,* and *Innuendo,* among others, were always top-notch. His earliest teenage writings appeared in Charles Lee Riddle's *Peon*. He was also the pseudonymous hoax black fan "Carl Brandon" (sometimes with Ron Ellik and others) behind the fan satires "The BNF of Iz" and "The Cacher of the Rye."—LO

Terry Carr

(from Peon, *vol. 6, #1, January, 1954; ed. Charles Lee Riddle)*

ITEM OF NO MOMENT: You may be interested to know that those 3-D viewers enclosed with the 3-D comics books (the latest fad) work wonders on many stf cover paintings. Particularly beautiful when viewed by these glasses are the Bok cover on FANTASY MAGAZINE #1 and the [Frank Kelly} Freas cover on TOPS IN SCIENCE FICTION #2 as the red areas shine with an eerie light as result of these new glasses, giving those covers quite a weird effect.

Skyhook, #18, Summer 1953; art by Ed Emshwiller

Vega, #12, 1953; ed. Joel Nydahl; art by Juanita R. Wellons.

FANZINES IN PROFILE

This was suppost to be the first in a series where a well-known fanzine editor wrote about "a mythical top ten of fanzinedom." Harlan Ellison (1934-2018) started the series in characteristic manner by ignoring all the requirements set forth by *Spaceship* editor Bob Silverberg. *Vega* was a lively, fun zine that lasted only a year and went out in a blaze of glory, and fannish lore, when its 12th issue, a 100 page tome, appeared to exhaust its teenage editor Joel Nydahl. Promptly thereafter Nydahl stopped all fanzine activities. The term "Nydahl's Disease" was soon coined to describe the scenario of zine editors overtaxing themselves to the point of no return. But, as we will see, there is more to this story. (Besides, of course, Silverberg and Ellison going on to fame and fortune as pro writers.) —LO

JOEL NYDAHL'S VEGA

Harlan Ellison

(from Spaceship *#22, July 1953; ed. Bob Silverberg)*

HERE INDEED was a problem. I was offered the opportunity to lead off a series of articles on the best fanzines. I was told I should not choose my own zine, nor could I choose *Spaceship* (not that there was the slightest chance of that, anyway) or any "dark horse" fanzine that few people knew about. I was then confronted with a more-or-less "approved" list of BNF fanzines including, roughly, *Slant*, *Opus*, *Quandry*, *Science Fiction Newsletter*, *SF Advertiser*, and a few other widely-circulated and obvious publications.

However, and here I must be firm, I don't find as much entertainment in the aforementioned magazines as I do in other, perhaps not as well known, but to me a great deal more delightful. Thus I have gone directly against Bob's orders and will hereby proceed to regale you with the finer points of a relatively new fanzine put out by one Joel Nydahl and titled, simply enough, *Vega*.

My first copy of *Vega* came unheralded. It was a fairly legible copy of Volume 1, Number 3 (I am, at times, thankful that I didn't receive numbers 1 and 2; they must have been horrors) and contained a motley collection of average fan stuff without much emphasis on any one facet of fandom. That is, there was no preponderance of the quasi-cure slop usual oozing over the pages in imitation of the Savannahoffman[116] humor. Nor was there a visible leaning towards the holier-than-thou deep stuff that peers at you from such august periodicals as *SF Advertiser* or *Rhodomagnetic Digest*. It was, obviously enough, the handiwork of a fan who was starting his first zine and hadn't had a) the nerve, b) the knowledge, or c) time to write an impressive list of BNF and have them write ream upon ream. It was unpretentious, promising little mag.

Why did I immediately take a liking to it?

Perhaps it was the very unassuming attitude of the mag that attracted me, or perhaps it was the neatness of the thing, or even, possibly, it was the way in which the editor was clearly struggling to issue an interesting, all-around, plodding-yet-getting-where-it-was-going zine. But I think that it was the identification I made with the early issues of my own mag that made me tilt my head to one side and say, "The boy's trying', that's all you can expect." So I began trading with *Vega*.

And I watched it for three issues, the magazine arriving at my address every month, just as Joel Nydahl had promised. By number four *Vega* had still retained its atrocious covers (done by Nydahl, for it appears he had no artists to bear the brunt of cover ills) but had improved tremendously on the inside. I've since learned that Nydahl is one of those people who don't do crawling to the Big Names to have them turn out stuff, because he feels it's degrading. Whether this might mount into a complex is neither here nor yonder, to mutilate a quotation, but it shows that what he has made of this zine he has done without any begging. However, issue four sported a column by Marian Cox which, though Cox denies it vehemently, is a perfect example of distaff thinking, and is something that fandom has needed: a feminine chitchat column with thought behind it, not a Louella

---

[116] Lee Hoffman, editor of *Quandry*, lived in Savannah, Georgia.

Parsons-type grab bag of puerility (such as many male columnists have been handling us lately.)

The zone also contained the first of a highly origin series by Marion Bradley on the phase of fandom so disruptive to those who last more than a week. The first was titled "What Every Young Fan Should know," and let me state unequivocally that they should. The next in the series was under the same title, and discussed fan clubs for the neofans. It is such a simply stated and forthright group of articles, it's a wonder the fan ranks have never been graced by such before.

Issue number five contained, with no more ballyhoo than an article by Fred Floopgruber, a short story by Mari Wolf entitled "Intelligence Test," which was of a high enough caliber to have appeared in any of the less specialized proziness without any trouble.

Perhaps I'm basing my judgments on fallacious frame of reference, but I judge a magazine on whether or not I feel the material therein is such that I would publish in my mag. If it is, as the case rarely is, then I feel I have enjoyed the magazine. If I can't see the stuff appearing in *Science Fantasy Bulletin*[117], then I'm inclined to believe the material is below my enjoyment level. This, of course, is my procedure with one or two exceptions. I can perhaps see a bit of semi-pornographic fan material as humorous, and still not want to publish it. But roughly, that's the way I work my rating of a zine.

And it seems that there is more printed in *Vega* that I would have liked to have written or published that in any other fanzine in the country now. Perhaps I'm being a bit inane about it, but I don't go for a zine that caters to cliques. I don't like one that tried to impress me with the subtlety or heavy-handedness of its concepts. I shun those who feature too-too cleverness. In short, I like fried shrimp and Tchaikovsky, but I also like hamburgers and Bop. I believe it was Vernon McCain and Barclay Johnson who recently (and, strangely enough, separately!) announced that they were sure *Vega* was going to be the focal point of next fandom. And I wouldn't doubt it.

Nydahl has the makings of a top-drawer editor. He is alert, quick to take a situation and make the best of it in *Vega*, and he know where he's going. Unlike some fan editors, he feels a sort of duty to his readers, and wants to entertain them with an all-around publication.

Joel's mimeograph has improved tremendously, his material is of

---

117 This is the zine that Ellison was editing at the time.

the highest quality (within fan boundaries, of course) and his painstaking neatness is exceptional in these days of crowded, sloppy, ill-printed and ill-spelled monstrosities. It is safe for me to say, I'm sure, that within a year, Joel Nydahl's *Vega* will be among the top five, not the top ten.

As a parting suggestion, may I induce you to drop the boy a line, send him a dime for the issue at hand and a nickel for postage, which is what you'd pay for any fanzine half as good, and mail it to Joel Nydahl in Marquette, Michigan. Fandom needs more Joel Nydahls, and fandom needs more mags like *Vega*.

Science Fantasy Bulletin, #12, Jan., 1953; ed. Harlan Ellison; art by Ed Emshwiller.

LOOKING BACK

Joel Nydahl discovered sf in December, 1951, when he picked up a copy of WORLDS BEYOND off the newsstand. Fifty years down the line a grown up Joel Nydahl speaks to the issue at hand and clears up some myths about the last issue of *Vega*. —LO

A POSTSCRIPT TO VEGA

Joel Nydahl

(from Trap Door, *#21, March, 2002; ed. Robert Lichtman)*

THE FIRST issue of *Vega* appeared in all of its naïve hectograph glory (ah! those purple, gelatinous days) in the fall of 1952. Since I was new to fandom, of necessity contributors were limited to those young souls with whom I had been corresponding.

By the time the third issue came out, my father—who financed the entire operation from paper to postage—had purchased a cheap mimeograph which printed all subsequent issues. Since I possess only a limited number of these (including the famous Vegannish[118]), my history of the fanzine must be vague and sometimes, I'm afraid, imprecise.

As the months wore on, I got additional subscribers, interest being fueled by a laudatory review in Mari Wolf's fanzine column in the same issue of IMAGINATION (May, 1953) which carried my short story. By the time the first four or five issues had appeared, I was receiving most of the fanzines in print and corresponding with their editors and with as many other fans as possible. Soon Dean A. Grennell (an "old guy" in his late twenties), Mari Wolf, Marion Zimmer Bradley, Harlan Ellison and Robert Silverberg (the last two only a few years older than I) were contributing on a regular basis. Then Redd Boggs, Robert Bloch and Bob Tucker joined in. What a thrill for a young edi-

---

118 This was the famous mammoth last issue, #12 — fan speak for an annual issue.

tor. From having to beg for contributions, I was receiving more columns, articles, fiction, and artwork than I could print. Suddenly, to the complete bafflement of my parents, I was a minor celebrity.

In my halcyon *Vega* days, I had one very negative experience—one that bothered me terribly at the time and still bothers me even now. For whatever reason, Marion Zimmer Bradley (who was, as I recall, not yet or only recently published) took a liking to me and offered (I may have asked her) to write a regular column. This she did for a number of issues. Then she wrote another piece—the nature of which I don't recall—but asked that it appear above a pen name and that I not reveal who the author was. This I agreed to do—and immediately broke my promise. Marion was furious, and I didn't blame her. I was mortified and have worn a hair shirt ever since. What a jerk I had been. As far as I know, Marion never revealed my betrayal to anyone, and for that I would thank her even now had she not passed on.

I vividly recall the experience of putting together the Vegannish—from rounding up a field of contributors that read like a Who's Who of Fandom, to typing the 100 mimeograph stencils (justifying the right-hand margins, as Harlan Ellison had been doing in his *Science Fantasy Bulletin*), to printing the gold-colored pages (the idea also copied from Ellison), to coordinating three runs (each of a different color) for the cover, to assembling the monster by walking around the dining room table (often with my mother) collating pages by hand, to mailing both parts (no staple would go through fifty sheets of paper).

There has been much speculation on the demise of *Vega* and on my subsequent disappearance from fandom. On a few of the matters, Harry Warner[119] is definitely wrong. He mentions financial problems as contributing to my decision not to publish a thirteenth issue; he even speculates that selling my short story to IMAGINATION helped finance *Vega*. Not true. Financial problems played no part at all in ceasing publication. Nor did "lowered grades in school." What probably happened (some incidents are vague here) were basketball and girls. It was about this time also that my family moved from our farm, about six miles outside of Marquette, Michigan, into town; there I was no longer isolated from high school social life and I had a chance to expand my horizons beyond my small upstairs farmhouse room.

The reason I stopped publishing *Vega* and dropped out of fan-

---

119 Warner talks about the demise of *Vega* in ***A Wealth of Fable***.

dom is terribly prosaic—hardly the stuff of legend. Suddenly and inexplicably I lost interest in both fandom and science fiction. "Burnout" might be an apt term to describe the final cause of my disappearance; but what caused the final cause is more problematic. I remember the excitement and energy which infused me over the twelve-month life span of *Vega*. I don't remember any gradual diminishment of that excitement and energy; I don't remember any warning signs. I remember only that once the Vegannish was in the mail, I had no interest in putting out a thirteenth issue; nor, strangely, did I have an urge to read any more science fiction.

> I feel that Redd's article deserves some sort of editorial comment but what to say. I can't say I agree with him, and yet I can't say that I disagree with him. I do think that an ann-ish can be a threat to the particular fanzine that's putting it out, but that doesn't mean that it will. A lot of zines have survived beautifully, Quandry and SCIENCE FANTASY BULLETIN to name two, and the latter has issued two ann-ishes. I will admit though that many zines have folded on account of the "dreaded" ann-ish, but VEGA won't be one of them. I'm going to set out to prove Redd wrong. And you fans can help too by writing me a nice letter of comment about thish. I don't expect you to comment on each item, but pick your favorite five and drop me a line about them. Of course, you can comment on the whole issue if you want....JN

Famous last words from Joel Nydahl, in the 12th (an "ann-ish"), and last issue of *Vega*, responding to an article by Redd Bogg on the growing menace of ann-ishes killing zines.

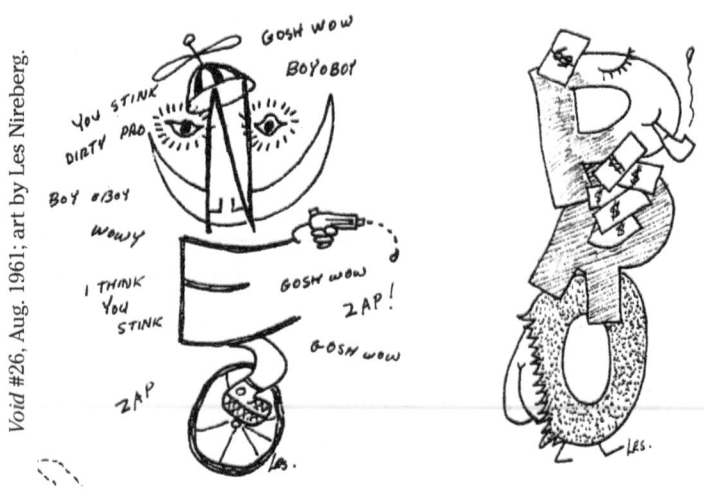

Void #26, Aug. 1961; art by Les Nireberg.

BEHIND THE ZINE

And as a coda to the preceding piece, here is Walt Willis's take on the fannish disease that he calls annishthesia — better known in fannish circles as Nydahl's Disease. ¶ Calkins managed to publish *Oopsla* even while on duty in the Marine Corps.—LO

UP THE GARDEN PATHOLOGY

Walter A. Willis

(from OOPSLA #12, March/April, 1954; ed. Gregg Calkins)

HAVE YOU noticed how short-lived BNFs are nowadays? In the old days three years was considered the normal life cycle of a fan, from serious constructivism through BNFdom to permanent gafia, but these Seventh Fandomers seem to have speeded the process up. Nowadays us old timers sit back dazed as a bewildering succession of BNFs flash past us almost as suddenly as they appeared. From comet to comatose, you might say.

I have studied this phenomenon and I have come to the conclusion that it's largely the result of a new disease which I have called annishthesia. I know that Professor Boggs in the Vegannish pointed out that annishes are a plague, but as Dean Grennell is my witness I thought of it first, and as the discoverer of Stigwort's Disease[120] I feel that my researches go more deeply into this vital matter.

Annishthesia attacks fans in the prime of life and is so much more deadly on that account, wreaking as it does such havoc among the very flower of fandom. There are two forms of it, primary annishthesia and secondary annishthesia, but the first symptoms are identical. The young and enthusiastic fan publishes several promising issues of his fanzine and a type of euphoria sets in, indicated by an insatiable

---
[120] A disease which displays no symptoms until the patient dies.

thirst for egoboo. This in itself is not a serious complaint, being almost endemic in fandom. But often a young fan neglects the most obvious precautions and with a reckless expenditure of energy begins to produce more and more ambitious issues, like a child throwing stones into a pond to make splashes. This can have only one result — annishthesia sets in. He decides to publish a hundred-page annish.

In primary annishthesia, which is almost invariably fatal, the effort is too much for him and after a short fever he succumbs to permanent gafia. Those with stronger constitutions survive and eventually publish their annish. Haggard, wan, his fingers bleeding from misguided staples, his back stooped from gathering, his pores stopped up with mimeo ink, in advanced malnutrition through poverty brought on by the high cost of paper, the fan stumbles to the mailbox and mails his annish. In his ignorance he thinks his troubles are over. But no, secondary annishthesia has still to strike.

Back at home, the fan eagerly awaits the plaudits of fandom, the prospect which has given him strength to carry on through all these months of toil and strain. He half expects to receive that very same afternoon an enthusiastic telegram from the Postal Inspector. But the days pass and there is utter silence from fandom. But the poor wretch is not dismayed — rather he is awed at the effect he has produced. Obviously, he thinks, fandom is stunned. All over the world fans are sitting around open-mouthed, numbed with admiration, refusing meals, neglecting their families and jobs while they gaze and marvel at the wondrous thing he has wrought. It is just a matter of waiting until they recover enough strength to crawl to their typers and airmail paeon after paeon of praise. But no. The days, weeks go by, and still no paeon. (That's why it's called annishthesia — there's no paeon.) Finally, just as he has wildly decided that the Postmaster General is in the pay of rival faneds, two letters arrive. One is from Dave Ish, who says it's not a patch on the Quannish. The other is from Redd Boggs, who says it's not as good as the Insurgent issue of *Spacewarp*. In another week or so he gets a letter from Vince Clarke saying it's not to be compared with the November 1945 issue of *Zenith*. He refuses to open the letter from Bob Tucker.

This is the crisis. If the fan survives this he will slowly recover. The treatment is complete rest and frequent injections of egoboo. It must also be patiently explained to him that he has unwittingly run counter to one of the fundamental laws of Fannish Thermodynamics, that comment always flows from a cold fanzine to a hot one. He has made the terrible mistake of publishing something which is too big to be read at one sitting, a zine that fans will tend to put aside to read and comment on adequately later. By which time its priority has been yielded to the latest oneshot.

However recent research has shown that there is new hope for the victim of annishthesia. In the first place, any victim who emerges from the ordeal is the stronger for it. In the second place, it seems clear now that the amount of egoboo resulting from an annish is not in fact less than it deserves. It may even be greater. What happens is that its impact is temporally as well as spatially dispersed. For one thing, dozens of fans now have guilt complexes about not praising his annish. This, like murder, will out; and over the years those fans will keep alluding to his annish in their articles, columns and editorials. It will become a legend. And in a few years he will have the joy of knowing that at this very moment some poor Neofan is being made wretched by being told that his annish "is quite good but . . . ."

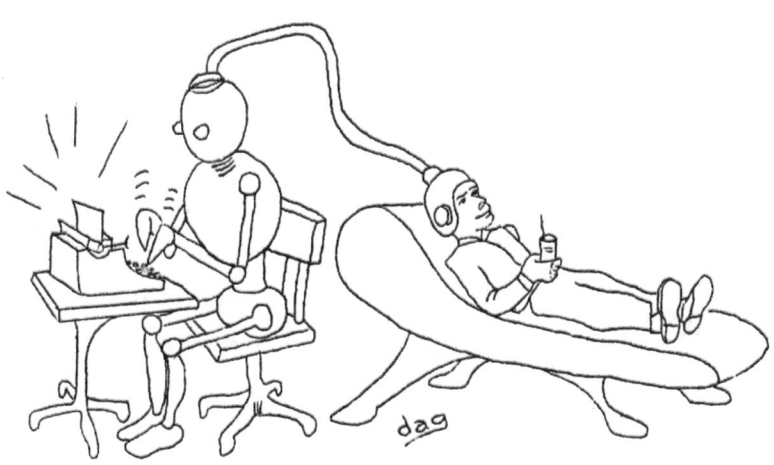

HOW TO EDIT AN ANN-ISH.

Vega, #12; cartoon by Dean A. Grennell.

Cry of the Nameless, #143, Oct., 1960; eds. F.M. & Elinor Busby; art by Betty JoAnne (Bjo)Trimble (née McCarthy). *Cry* was a clubzine that started in 1950. Linked with "The Nameless Ones," a Seattle, Washington-based fan group, before it left the nest in the late 1950s, *Cry* received the Hugo Award for Best Fanzine at the 1960 World Science Fiction Convention in Pittsburgh.

THE FANZINE LIFE

Charles Burbee's (1915–1996) fan writings came off as a more mordant Bob Tucker. He was another L.A. fan, and was best friends with F. Towner Laney. (See "Fanzine Scope", pg. 58.) —LO

SLAVE OF THE PIXIE

Charles Burbee

(Cry of the Nameless, #143; eds. F.M. & Elinor Busby; Oct., 1960)

I AM NOW a staff writer for *Shangre-L'Affaires* and I love it. This incredible situation came about because I was outsmarted and bewitched. I must have been, because why should I love this curious fanzine? I think I've got it pretty well figured out. I'll explain in a moment.

A few months ago, I didn't care at all whether or not *Shangre-L'Affaires* was being published, and if the LASFS got so hard up they had to use material by some of their own members it was of little consequence to me.

But now I feel I am under a geas, a happy compulsion, to write something for each and every issue of this sterling fanzine. I have a personal interest in it. I will be very disappointed if it doesn't make its scheduled publication date. I would not be surprised if some day I even show up to help run off and assembled the darned thing.

Oh, but think I've got it pretty well figured, as I said. This thing was accomplished by a read headed pixie name of Bjo.

Bjo. For a long time after she assumed ownership and operation of Southern California Fandom I did not see her. Her center of operations was the LASFS and I haven't been to a LASFS meeting since 1947. But I had heard of her. Fanzines come to my door and all of them are scrutinized carefully. In these pages of shimmering mimeography there appeared many cartoons by Bjo.

They were striking, captivating cartoons. Here was a rare bird, a woman with a wonderful sense of the ridiculous. I knew after a time that here was the most sparkling fan ever to hit the area. The only person I could think of who could match her for impact was F.T. Laney. If Laney and Bjo had ever met, Laney might have fallen madly in love with her; all of his four wives were redheads. Of course he seemed to prefer women older than himself, and for this Bjo would not qualify. She doesn't even look more than eighteen.

So there was this fabulous Bjo, a glorious gift to fandom. Somehow she snagged the hearts and minds of all who knew her, and her dedicated followers fell into two categories; the Mountain Movers and the Hired Guns. The Mountain Movers, I learned, did the heavy, unimaginative work like helping Burbee clean up his garage, and the Hired Guns did the more urbane, sophisticated sort of stuff like shooting people.

I do not mean to imply that she is slinky, or wears tight-fitting satin gowns, or smokes Turkish cigarettes in a long jeweled holder, or stands on a shiny dais under a baby spot singing "That Old Black Magic." She take over hearts and minds in her own special way, which is probably blended with magic because there seems no special reason for her powers.

It naturally came about that one day I met her. She came to my house to a party. She didn't look much to me. Maybe 5'1" tall and no spectacular measurements. Red headed and freckled. Pixie face. She didn't even seem at ease in my presence.

I must have chuckled silently to myself. I could see at once that I was immune to this one. "After all," I said to myself, "I am Burbee." This remark seemed at the time to be quite sensible, complete, and satisfactory. I know now that it was stupid.

Let the others fall for her, I thought. Even Willie Rotsler by this time was hooked on Bjo. He tried to simplify the whole thing by saying that she controlled all the fellows by the use of "thinly-veiled sex promises." I didn't give it any thought but assumed idly that maybe this was a good enough explanation.

One day I said to her, "Bjo, make me a thinly veiled sex promise." She sort of lowered here lids and slunk up to me (well, *this* time she slunk) and said in a low sexy voice (ever see a sexy pixie?), "That sort of thing works on boys, but for a mature man like you, I'd need something else."

She left me speechless. Big Mouth Burbee for once had nothing to say. I wonder what the "something else" was?

Well, if she was going to conquer me she certainly couldn't use sex because everybody knows I have no interest in sex. Besides that, I am hard-headed, stupid, suspicious, crude, mean, boorish, unjust, and intemperate, with no capacity for love of anything except homebrew and ragtime player pianos. I must have presented a challenge to the young lady, for she outflanked me.

One day one of her agents smashed my typewriter.

I thought nothing of that. I was rather relieved. Now I had a fine excuse never to write for fanzines again. I could even quit FAPA. I could stop writing letters.

Then, a few weeks after the typer was broken, Christmas came. (Later, as I recapped, I had the mad notion for one fleeting moment that Bjo had invented Christmas for the occasion). Bjo, through her disciples, gifted me with this very typer.

I fell in love instantly with it. I laid my fingers gently on the keys and all sorts of fine stuff typed itself out. I had a ball, at first. I thought for a time I was really living. Why, it would even be fun to write fan material, I thought.

I was softening, like a dead fish in the sun.

Next time I saw Bjo, she didn't seem to say anything of great significance, but when she was gone I found I had a sort of inner craving to write untold amounts of material for *Shangre-L'Affaires*. Without even thinking I told her that if Gordon Dewey wrote her an article I would write a companion piece, even titling it "Companion Piece" (Or: "How to Lay a Friend"). Just saying that exhilarated me.

When I saw her again the spell was somehow completed. I was completely englamored. I don't know what class of magic she used. There was no sex in it and surely she doesn't resemble a ragtime player piano but the whole thing was strong, valid stuff. I instantly wrote an article for that curious fanzine, and I am Bjo's slave just like all those other guys I used to chuckle about, and this mad happy compulsion to write and write and write will not wear off until this typewriter ribbon wears out.

Then I'll be my own man again. I'll be free.

But what is there left in the world for a man who is not Bjo's slave?

ODD, #1, 1949; cover art by Jack Gaughan, which is a self-portrait. Gaughan would become a prolific pro artist in the 1960s and 1970s. (**next pg. top left**) *Fan Slants,* vol.1 #1, Sept., 1943; cover art by Ronald Clyne. (**top right**); *Void,* #2, July, 1955; cover art by Jim Benford. (**bottom left**) *Quandry,* #5, Dec., 1950; cover by Lee Hoffman. (**bottom right**) *Rhodomagnetic Digest,* #21, 1952; cover art by Kenn Davis.

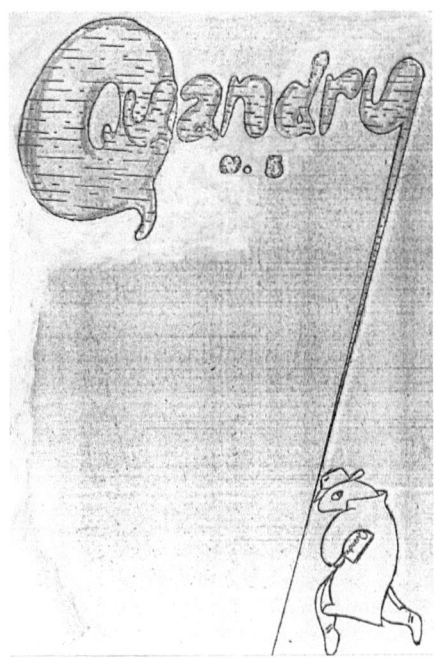
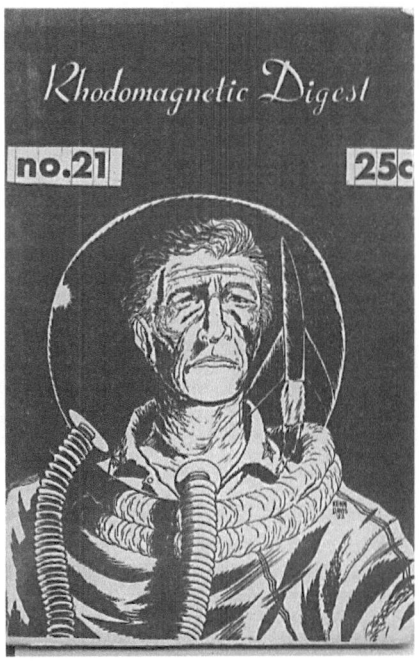

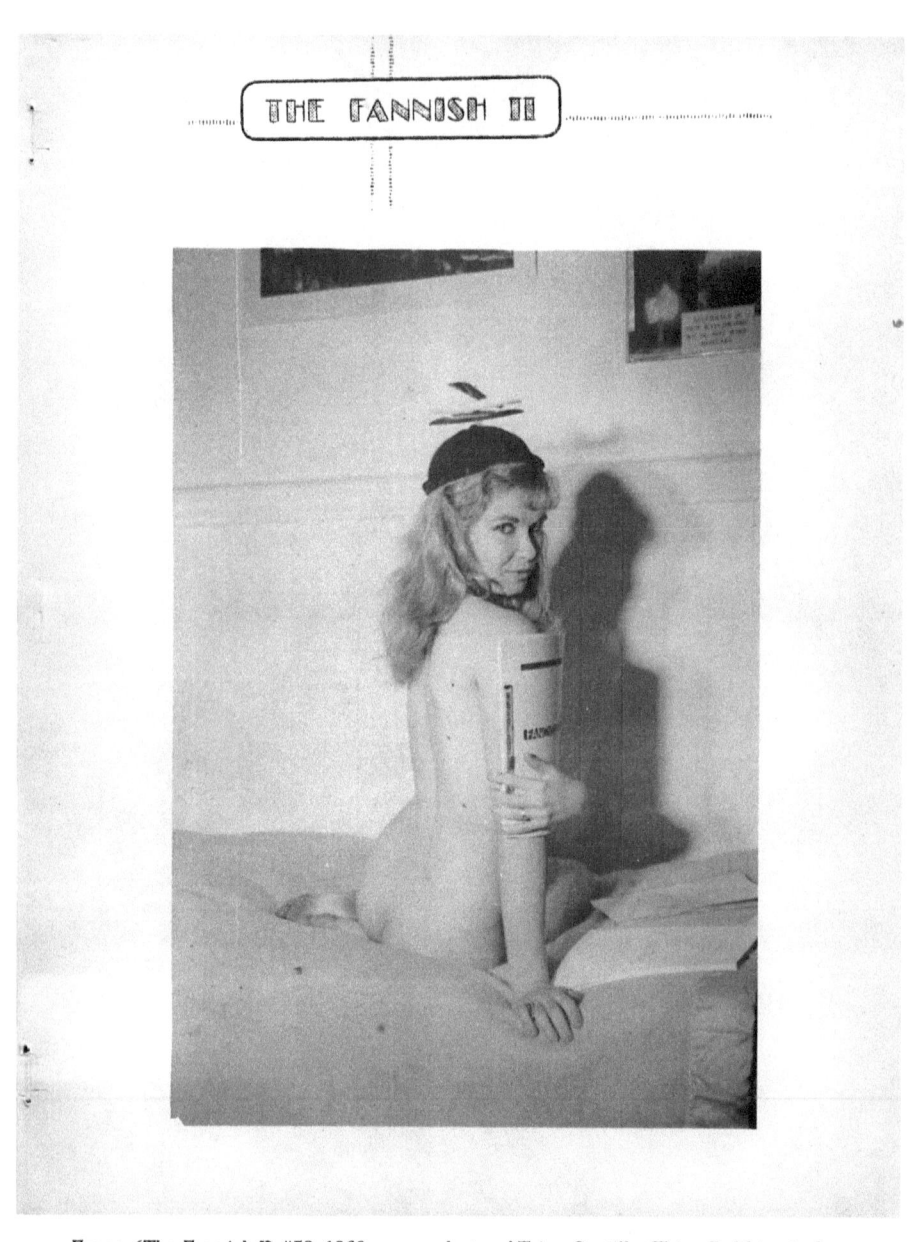

Fanac, (*The Fannish II*) #53, 1960; cover photo of Trina Castillo (Trina Robbins today, though she was not legally married at the time) holding a copy of *Fanclyclopedia II*, photographed by "husband" Art Castillo. Trina was introduced to nude modeling for men's magazines by Forrest J Ackerman, who became her agent. She also dated Harlan Ellison for a while in the 1950s, and was a real sf fan, not just a fellow-traveler girlfriend or wife. Today she is better known as a cartoonist and comic art historian.

ZINE FICTION

There has been a lot of fan fiction published in sf fanzines, most of it bad. Much "faan fiction" is about fans and their antics within a sf universe. I have generally avoided fiction for this book, but I am making an exception for the following piece. Bob Tucker was there at the dawn of sf fandom and fanzines (publishing *The Planetoid*, 1932; *Le Zombie*, 1938-1975; *Science Fiction Newsletter*, 1945-1953; *The Neofan's Guide*, 1955) and continued as a fanzine contributor until his death in 2006. He always injected humor into his fanzine writings. The idea behind "The Iron Curtain Drops" originated with a news bit, brought to Tucker's attention by Jack Speer, that the then-communist government of Czechoslovakia was mandating the licensing of all mimeographs in that country. — LO

THE IRON CURTAIN DROPS

Bob Tucker

(from Oopsla *#9, January, 1953; ed. Greg Calkins)*

Mr. Handel C. Ranker
Minister of Mimeographs
Prague, Czech.

Dear Mr. Ranker:
A couple of weeks ago I sent 10¢ (American) to Imovar Slobarish who lives at 101 Wagnerstrasse, in Prague, for a copy of his fanzine PLEIADES PIMPLES but he ain't never sent it or sent my money (American) back. Please do something about this.

- **Joe Fann**

Box 702
Minneapolis, Minnesota

Dear Mr. Fann:
Imovar Slobarish doesn't seem to exist.

- Handel C. Ranker

Mr. Handel C. Ranker
Minister of Mimeographs
Prague, Czech.

Dear Mr. Ranker:
Imovar Slobarish exists all right, because the same day I got your letter I finally got my copy of PLEIADES PIMPLES from him. But I guess he doesn't live at 101 Wagnerstrasse anymore because in his editorial he said he was going underground, so I suppose that means in a bomb shelter or whatever you people are building over there.

- Joe Fann

Mr. Josef Fann
Box 702
Minneapolis, Minnesota

Dear Mr. Fann:
I am delighted to hear that at last you have received the publication for which you waited. We in this country strive at all times to cooperate with our friends in the western democracies. In order that I may assist Mr. Slobarish in the future production of PLEIADES PIMPLES, will you please send me the address from which it was mailed?

- Handel C. Ranker

Mr. Handel C. Ranker
Minister of Mimeographs
Prague, Czech.

Dear Mr. Ranker:

That's pretty good of you to help out fanzine editors and I'll bet Imovar will be pleased and surprised when you drop in on him. The fanzine was mailed from the White Horse Inn, Upper Newtownards Road, Brunn, Moravia. I liked PLEIADES PIMPLES so much I've sent Imovar $1 (American) for a year's subscription. Give good old Imovar a shot in the arm so he can start work on the next issue.

— **Joe Fann**

Mr. Josef Fann
Box 702
Minneapolis, Minnesota

Dear Mr. Fann:

Imovar Slobarish doesn't seem to exist anymore. I'm sorry we can not refund your subscription, but apparently no records were kept.

— **Handel C. Ranker**

Which bill do we pay this month, dear, the baby or the mimeo?

Mr. Handel C. Ranker
Minister of Mimeographs
Prague, Czech.

Dear Mr. Ranker:
Sorry, but you're wrong again, old boy. No snide cracks intended, but I guess bureaucrats are the same the world over. Good old Slobarish is still cranking them out and the latest issue arrived today — and a crackerjack number it is, too! Just about the best he's done, although the ink was a little thin in spots. In case you don't know it, Imovar is the number-one humorist of fandom and the lead article in this issue proves it. He has a three-page article on the difficulties of producing PLEIADES PIMPLES and you'd split your sides laughing when he tells about bootleg fanzines, forged licenses, and smuggling copies over the border to be mailed. Why doesn't your office get behind this boy and give him a boost?

- **Joe Fann**

Mr. Josef Fann
Box 702
Minneapolis, Minnesota

Dear Mr. Fann:
I was pleased to receive your letter and very glad to learn that Imovar Slobarish is still publishing. Believe me, this office wants very much to locate Mr. Slobarish and offer him our services. I would appreciate your sending me his newest address.

- **Handel C. Ranker**

Mr. Handel C. Ranker
Minister of Mimeographs
Prague, Czech.

Dear Mr. Ranker:
I'd be glad to do a good turn for Imovar. The last copy came from 2215 Benjaminstrasse, Holmes-on-the-Seacoast, Bohemia. And listen, take along a couple of cans of mimeograph ink for him, will you?

There were some thin spots in the last issue.

- Joe Fann

Mr. Josef Fann
Box 702
Minneapolis, Minnesota

Dear Mr. Fann:
It becomes my sad duty to inform you that Mr. Imovar Slobarish no longer seems to exist. We at this office shall miss his sprightly wit and his publication.

- Handel C. Ranker

Mr. Handel C. Ranker
Minister of Mimeographs
Prague, Czech.

Dear Mr. Ranker:
Say, what's got into you guys anyway? Believe me, we wouldn't tolerate such ignorance and inefficiency here in this country! Imovar ain't dead — he sent me another issue just a few days ago. But he certainly is having a hard time of it, and your office doesn't seem to be shooting him any help. Why, would you believe it, this new issue was cranked out in the back of a truck! Imovar said in his editorial that he was on the move again and apologized for the sloppy mimeo work, but it couldn't be helped because this truck was rolling pretty fast and it bounced around a lot. Although he didn't explain, I got the impression that he was forced to move and so he turned out the issue during the trip. Why doesn't your office find this boy a permanent place to live? PLEIADES PIMPLES could be so much better then!

- Joe Fann

Mr. Josef Fann
Box 702
Minneapolis, Minnesota

Dear Mr. Fann:

I have taken the matter of Imovar Slobarish and his publication to my superior officers, and we all now agree that the enterprising fellow deserves our closest attention. He has been given a priority, as you Americans would say, and we are leaving no stone unturned in the search for him. You will also be happy to know that Mr. Gregory Ratchet, our Prefect of Police, has prepared a permanent home for him when he can be found. In view of all this, I am sure you will send me his new address when next you hear from him, so that we can make him safe and comfortable as quickly as possible.

- **Handel C. Ranker**

Mr. Handel C. Ranker
Minister of Mimeographs
Prague, Czech.

Dear Mr. Ranker:

Well, I've heard from good old Imovar again, but I don't think it will be much help to you or him. He didn't send a copy of PLEIADES PIMPLES this time — he said all his equipment had been seized. He dug up an old hektograph somewhere and printed this little one-shot while he was waiting for a boat, there on the seacoast of Bohemia. Imovar seemed rather unhappy about things — he's moving out of the country and wants to come to America. He said there was too much regimentation in his own country — you had to have a license for this and a license for that. And too, some stool-pigeon has been making it tough for him these last few months, forcing him to be on the move all the time. The hektograph sheet wasn't too clear, but I gathered he was pretty sore about everything. I guess your office was too slow in helping him out.

- **Joe Fann**

Mr. Josef Fann
Box 702
Minneapolis, Minnesota

Dear Mr. Fann:
Please rush me by airmail special delivery the name of the town where Imovar Slobarish is awaiting a ship. Perhaps it still isn't too late.

- **Handel C. Ranker**

Mr. Handel C. Ranker
Minister of Mimeographs
Prague, Czech.

Dear Mr. Ranker:
It becomes my sad duty to inform you that Mr. Josef Fann no longer seems to exist.

- **Imovar Slobarish**

Hyphen, #6, Jan., 1954. Header for "Grunch" column by A. Vincent Clarke. Artist unknown.

Neophyte, vol. 1, #1, Jan., 1948; ed. and art by Bill Rotsler. A one-shot FAPA zine.

SEX AND THE SINGLE FANZINE

Bill Rotsler (1926–1997) was a man of many talents: zine editor, artist, cartoonist, author, photographer, filmmaker, "pornographer" (though not even close by today's standards), and all-around sf fan *bon vivant*. He began appearing in fanzines in 1944 and joined FAPA around 1947.—LO

I THINK STF HEROES ARE QUEER

William Rotsler

(from Masque *#7, 1950; ed. William Rotsler)*

I'M FOR more sex in science fiction
   Yes, I'm for more sex in that unusually sexless brand of so-called writing labeled science fiction. May Ceres have mercy on them!
   For crying out loud, people do have sex don't they? And I mean heterosexual sex, too. StF heroes rush around from galaxy to galaxy (planet-to-planet stories being milk runs nowadays) with their hyper-beautiful-scientist's daughter and never so much as hold hands much less shove them into a bed — tho they do give them a brotherly peck just before they think all is to be lost. So I offer the theory that the bulk of stf heroes are as queer as the Mercury day is long.
   Proof? Do stf heroes ever have any thing but tender anti-sepic affections towards their alabaster, case-hardened female companions? Do they ever take their heroines by the lily whites and go out into the airlock to neck? Are there ever any marriages? Any children or any menstruations? And does anyone ever go to the toilet?
   No.
   With this kind of a setup an abortionist would starve to death.
   So the heroes must be queer (note: it is more polite in artier circles to say "gay" or in bad cases, "Swish") 'cause they never have a

lustful thought in their heads. And that is the same head that brought fort the idea for the Intergalactic Geodesic-neuphyline Sub-atomic Converter, the mind books, the Hyper-speed-sub-space motor and the meterless time machine.

More proof: Ndia and Steve, in "Spacehounds of IPC", cast away on Ganymede, do not have sex. Easy choice for Steve of course.

Oh, there have been a few attempts towards sex — quickly throttled before they got out of hand (and exposed a new way of life)... Generally the hero cuts his way trough a planet full of seven-armed, eyeless Tetrohydras (armed with mind-armor and electroneural blasters) to rescue Lurali, then sit at her feet toying with an atomic motor or a universal communicator.

Maybe we should all join Eney's sexocrats and have orgasms on a monthly schedule.

Maybe the authors are a bit off, I dunno. Seem all so damned atisetic and platonic somehow. The sexiest people ever get is being married for years before the story opens. Oh, I'm not for a Spicy Space Stories — just a normal, heterosexual life.

This new magazine GALAXY show great promise, and not only erotically speaking, but with some good ASTOUNDING level stories. I understand that old AMAZING is getting rocky too.

Guess I'm just a crude, dirty boy.....

Masque, #7, 1950; editor and artist Bill Rotsler.

HOAXES, DIGRESSIONS & FEUDS

Dianetics became a legitimate fan — and fanzine — concern when it was first introduced in the ASTOUNDING issues of Dec, 1949, and May, 1950. John W. Campbell, the editor of ASTOUNDING, and science fiction's potentate at the time, had it in the back of his mind that his magazine could also function as a quasi-scientific journal for avant-science, though all of his "scientific" breakthroughs were at best half-cocked. Fans always thought that Ray Palmer was a bit crazy, pushing flying saucers and the Shaver Cult, but expected more sanity from Campbell. Many fans also saw Lafayette Ronald Hubbard as a fraudster, and Campbell as an abettor who gave Dianetics a lot of free publicity at the start. The following two pieces give us some of the early debate on Dianetics taking place in fanzines. ¶ Boggs was a well know zine writer and editor of *Skyhook*. —LO

FILE 13: DIANETICS – FAD OR SCIENCE?

Redd Boggs

(from Spacewarp *#42, Sept., 1950; eds. Art Rapp, Charles Burbee, F.T. Laney)*

JAMES BLISH submits the following rebuttal to my remarks in *Science Fiction News Letter* (July 1950) concerning dianetics. If you read *SFNL* — and you should, because it has a lot more in it besides my column — you may remember I accused *aSF* [ASTOUNDING SCIENCE FICTION magazine] editor John W. Campbell of publishing Hubbard's "Dianetics" article in order to produce a Sensation "by adopting the READER'S DIGEST method — seeking the verdict of the uninformed public before submitting the work to psychology experts for the 'ruthless criticism and cross-checking that is the very life-blood of science.'"

I concluded by remarking that the possibility of "a hack writer's 'new science,' presented full-blown to the world in a two-bit pulp, will revolutionize psychotherapy," is a wild dream. Here is Jim's rebuttal:

> "Your comment on Campbell's publication of Hubbard's dianetics article has some limitations about which your readers should know. It is; first of all, the comment of a man who has not read Hubbard's book (**Dianetics**, Hermitage House, N. Y., $4). Secondly, it is the comment of a man who lives in Minneapolis and who has hence been unable to run any kind of check upon Hubbard's, Campbell's, and Winter's claims for dianetics. Third, it uses push-button terms which do not reflect the actual situation.
>
> "Point (1) I leave to your innate honesty. If it moves you to go and get the book and read it, if only to give the chance to say you have too read it, it will have accomplished its purpose.
>
> "(2) Admittedly it is most difficult to check many of the claims made by the dianetics boys; they are being very cagey about the question of formal evidence, despite their talk about rigid examination of the claims. I think it germane to note, however, that I first tackled Hubbard's book for laughs, from the point of view of a dogmatic, classical Freudian; that since that time I have managed, despite considerable evasive action on the part of the dianetics people, to check some of their most extravagant claims, as well as some of their minor ones; and that thus far the claims check with the facts. My checking includes, as might be expected, practice of dianetic therapy upon myself, my wife, and friends. It also includes, however, specific checks of clinical evidence from good sources unconnected with Hubbard, Winter or Campbell. (Details on request.) Did you attempt to make any such checks?
>
> "(3) Your description of Hubbard as a 'hack writer' and of *aSF* as a 'two-bit pulp magazine' brings up the question of the reputation of the parties involved. As a question, it is not asked very well, and so pre-determines a bad answer. Hubbard is inarguably a hack writer, especially these days, but if the claims made for dianetics check all the way out to the end, he is also an original thinker of staggering gifts. I do not yet make the latter claim for Hubbard, but I observe that these two categories are not mutually exclusive, and that no one can rule out the latter without examining critically

and intensively what Hubbard says he has accomplished. As for aSF, it is to be sure a magazine costing 25¢, printed on something rather unlike pulp paper, and containing stories something like those printed in less toney pulp magazines. It also has an audience rated as the most intelligent and the most technically knowledgeable of any general magazine in this country — by which I mean to exclude only actual technical magazines and the literary quarterlies — surely the most remarkable audience ever commanded by a mass magazine. Whether or not an audience which greets articles on the mechanisms of electronic computers with interest is a bad introduction to dianetics is not, after all, a very open question. When you observe, furthermore, that the article was deliberately delayed pending the publication of the book, which contained a great deal of material aimed directly at specialists in the field of psychotherapy, the analogy with *Reader's Digest* practice breaks down with great rapidity. (There is, I will add, still some justice in the analogy; I object to it only as a quarter-truth, with the qualification that there were serious, considerable motives behind Campbell's and Hubbard's proceeding as they did.)

"If the question of reputation is to enter into our discussion, then we can't stop at labeling the reputation of Hubbard and *aSF*, however. We have to ask: what is the reputation of Campbell? of Dr. Joseph A. Winter? of Hermitage House? of Nancy Roodenberg? What is the reputation of the psychosomatic clinic of New York's Presbyterian Medical Center, which vouches for a specific, spectacular success for dianetic therapy? of the two oculists who have reported with amazement that they have had to revise their patients' glasses formulae upwards? (One of my own checks.)

"Moreover, we have to ask: just how pertinent is this whole question of reputation. The reaction of an established authority to any teetotally revolutionary discipline is historically predictable. The reputation, for instance, of Dr. Winter really proves nothing, no matter how good it is (and it's plenty damned good.) The reputation of Dr. Frederick Wertham, also damned good, is also no guarantee, whether he's for or agin dianetics (he's violently agin.)

"The question is, DOES IT WORK? If it does, I don't care whether Hubbard is Christ or Barrabas. And I'm irritated by your prejudging an idea by the reputation of the man who advance it. Why not check first? Not the reputations, that's worthless. Check the idea."

Which ends Jim Blish's remarks.

Admittedly, my remarks in the *SFNL* column were those of one who has not read Hubbard's book, and for that matter read Hubbard's *aSF* article with much mental confusion. But that fact, I think, merely points up my whole argument: that Hubbard's "new science" has been given to the uninformed public rather than to the scientists. Granted that *aSF* has an intelligent, technically trained faction in its audience. It also has a plethora of readers like me — moderately intelligent, technically untrained guys, whose wide-eyed acceptance of such a "science" (which is clearly but perhaps not correctly labeled "world-shaking") is the same sort of half-witted "fad" as General Semantics degenerated into. The spectacle of a bunch of fuggheaded juveniles loudly mouthing dianetical catch-phrases can do LRH's idea no good.

Dianetics has two strikes against it already: it has been immoderately publicized in a "two-bit pulp" — a term I used deliberately in the original article, not to mirror my own thoughts, but to show how a lot of non-stf-reading scientists will and do regard *aSF* — and it has been proposed by a man who has absolutely no standing in psychological or psychiatric fields at all, and is, in their eyes, merely a "hack writer of pseudo-science." That Hubbard's livelihood is based, in part, on pulp writing cannot be helped, of course, and I agree that it bears no direct relation to his ability as a thinker. But since this one fact — who it was that formulated dianetics — is unalterable, I see no reason for making his "science" endure the added onus of pulp presentation and a "fad" status among brainless juveniles. No reason, that is, except one of publicity. Of course, publicity of the sort Campbell has given dianetics may help the "new science" just as much as it helped *aSF*. But is enough good to come from that publicity to outweigh the above-mentioned bad points?

My reaction to reports so far concerning the "success" of dianetics is merely "So what?" Unless testimony is once again, after so long, considered an infallible source of psychological information, then we'll have to discount most of the present reports on dianetical "successes." Experimental investigation is necessary to establish dianetics on a scientific basis, and this will be done by scientists who know what they are about, and not by dewy-eyed amateurs who rush to

LASFS or ESFA meetings to report their "successes in the same irresponsible way that Shaverites report their occult experiences. After all Coueism[121] "worked," too; it even had some psychological basis; but I never heard of a psychologist who believed Coueism was a universal cure-all merely because a bunch of harebrained people said, By god, I am getting better and better!

You're right: the question is, does dianetics work? But it needs a chance to prove itself. It needs the serious attention of psychology for the next 10 or 50 years, just as such a revolutionary "science" as psychoanalysis did. It doesn't need publicity among uninformed people such as *aSF* readers. Is dianetics to be a cultish fad, or a science? The way it has developed so far, I foresee ads of the Dianetics Research Foundation occupying the same place that Rosicrucian ads do today, while psychology, the well-grounded science of behavior, carried on as before. After all, psychology is now a pretty sound science, and its successes, if not spectacular like dianetics, are at least decisive enough to show that it's on the right track.

I plead innocent to "prejudging" dianetics as far as its value is concerned. As someone points out in the current *aSF*, anyone would be crazy not to want to believe it. I hope that it is all that Hubbard claims. But I am from Hannibal — I want to be shown. I don't want the anecdotes of fad-happy juveniles. I want the results of experimental investigation, showing a correlation of plus .80. Is that too much to ask?

Art by Ralph Rayburn Phillips for *Fantasy Advertiser*, vol. 3, #3. Dec., 1948.

---

121 A method of self-help using auto-suggestion, popular c. 1920. It used the slogan "Day by day in every way I am getting better and better."

HOAXES, DIGRESSIONS & FEUDS

John Larkins

(from Rhodomagnetic Digest *#17, Nov.-Dec., 1951; ed. Don Fabun)*

THE CASE of L. Ron Hubbard, discoverer and chief Prophet of 'Dianetics — the modern science of mental health,' is to the well-known semanticist S. I. Hayakawa an almost unparalleled illustration of the principle long-held by writers in the field of general semantics that language habits tend to become internalized — i.e. one's evaluations and method of thinking reflect the structure of the language one speaks.

Hubbard has been an extremely prolific contributor to science fiction and other magazines. According to his own account of himself in the 1942-43 edition of Who's Who in the East he has had five million words published under six names — and he has substantially added to that total since. Hayakawa considers it inevitable that anyone writing several million words of fantasy and science fiction should ultimately begin to internalize the assumptions underlying that verbiage, and he maintains that exactly this has happened in the case of Hubbard and Dianetics.

"The slick craftsman of mass-production science-fiction, mustering his talents and energies for a supreme effort, produces — and what could be more reasonable? — a fictional science."

Hayakawa considers the art of science fiction writing to consist in "concealing from the reader, for novelistic purposes, the distinctions between established scientific facts, almost-established scientific hypotheses, scientific conjectures, and imaginative extrapolations far beyond what has even been conjectured." The danger of this technique is that if the writer of science fiction writes too much of it too fast and is not endowed with a high degree of consciousness of his own abstraction, he may eventually succeed in concealing the distinction between his facts and his imaginings from himself. The men of Mars may acquire so vivid a verbal existence that they may, to the writer, seem to have 'actual' existence. Like Willy Loman in *The Death of a Salesman*, he may eventually fall for his own pitch.

Hayakawa has no bone to pick with literary imaginings as such. To the contrary, he writes:

"Had dianetics been presented as fiction it might have been like other ingenious science-fiction, good entertainment. But in the book DIANETICS, Hubbard does not write as a novelist. He is, he says, a scientist. He has discovered — nay, created — a new science of the human mind which, in one fell swoop, renders obsolete the psychological groupings of Wundt, James, Pavlov, Kraepelin, Charcot, Janet, Freud, Jung, Adler, Lewin, Thorndike, Kohler, Moreno, Reik, Menninger, Masserman, Rogers, and all the work of the neuropsychologists to boot."

(Two of the first three sentences in Hubbard's book proclaim: "The hidden source of all psychosomatic ills and human aberration had been discovered and skills have been developed for their invariable cure. The creation of dianetics is a milestone for Man comparable to his discovery of fire and superior to his inventions of the wheel and the arch.")

To Hayakawa the expository technique of DIANETICS is straight out of science fiction. First, there is the elementary device of taking for granted the existence of things which do not exist, and then making assertions about them. ("The reactive mind is the entire source of aberration. It can be proved and has been repeatedly proven that there is no other, for when that engram bank is discharged, all undesirable symptoms vanish and a man begins to operate on his optimum pattern.") There are innumerable references to 'research' and 'tests' which 'have been' performed. ("A series of severely controlled dianetic experiments over a much longer period demonstrated that the law of affinity, as applicable to psychosomatic illness, was more powerful than fear and antagonism by a very wide margin. So great is this margin that it could be compared as the strength of a steel girder to a straw.")

Hayakawa mentions also the use of "vivid narratives (i.e. 'case histories') by means of which that which is assumed to be so is transmuted into that which is felt to be so. References are made to unspecified 'laboratories' and 'clinics' where zealous (and unnamed) teams of 'dianeticists' are busy refining the 'techniques' and 'basic postulates.' Occasionally, he (Hubbard) goes through the motions of distinguishing between 'fact' and 'theory' and abstemiously denies himself, as a scientist, the self-indulgence of proceeding on mere theories. ("As an organized body of scientific knowledge, dianetics can only draw the conclusions which it observes in the laboratory.") And, of course, there is an occasional mathematical-looking equation or graph, extremely impressive except to those who can read them."

The special and compelling feature of Hubbard's talent in science fiction is vocabulary. In the main the vocabulary used in DIANETICS is his own invention — an invention inspired by some acquaintance with the literature of cybernetics. His technical jargon is marvelously suggestive at once of both electrical and psychological phenomena, which, says Hayakawa, although no doubt ultimately related, are certainly not related in the way Hubbard describes.

"The fact that startling analogies between 'thinking machines' and the human mind can be shown is beyond question. But, at present, we don't know how far this analogy can be legitimately carried. The existence of such a scientific No Man's Land is exactly the condition under which the science-fiction writer is stimulated to his best work: dazzling new scientific miracles seem to be around the corner, while enough news of current developments has appeared in popular science literature to arouse public interest and curiosity."

Hubbard speaks of dianetics as an 'engineering' science. The 'analytical mind' or 'analyzer' is 'not just a good computer, it is a perfect computer.' Past experience is stored and filed in 'memory banks.' Of the 'Analytical mind' Hubbard asks: Would you leave its delicate circuits prey to every overload, or would you install a fuse system? . . . Any computer would be so safeguarded." Pain results, by definition, in the 'shutting off' of the 'analyzer,' which state is, by definition, 'unconsciousness.' The 'engram' is "a series of impressions such as a needle might make on wax."

They may be 'keyed in' by 'restimulators' causing 'demon circuits'. Such aberrations are the cause of 'all neuroses, psychoses, insanities' and also (by definition) of all psychosomatic illnesses. Therapy is accomplished by 'discharging' and 'erasing' the 'demon circuits.' The 'auditor' sends the patient back on his 'time track' so that he may 'run through' the 'engramatic' painful episodes and eventually become a 'clear'.

Hayakawa points out that Hubbard is not so flat-footed as to introduce in so many words the assertion, "the mind is a computing machine." Indeed, such an assertion would have only the effect of causing the reader to wonder about the degree to which this might be true.

"Hubbard introduces the computing machine analogy explicitly as an analogy, but he hastens to state that the analogy has shortcomings only because the mind is a better machine. The effectiveness of this statement, in its context, lies in the fact that it is, in some respects, true. Nevertheless, the unique abilities of the human brain are of a different order than those of the machine. No computing machine has so far invented so much as a pocket abacus. If this difference of order is ignored — from that point on, the language does your thinking for you. Hubbard does not have to convince the reader who let the metaphor slip under his guard; the reader convinces himself."

"The difference between the humbuggery of dianetics and the rich scientific and humanistic promise of cybernetics is a measure of the difference between linguistic naiveté and full semantic awareness. I know of no contrast in recent literature which shows more vividly or dramatically the importance of what Korzybski called 'consciousness of abstracting' — the disastrous results when it is absent, and the rich consequences when it is there."

Despite the devastating criticism which can be, and has been, leveled at Hubbard's new science of mental health, it has gained a tremendous following. Why? Hayakawa sees two answers to this question. The first and obvious answer is that thousands of people today are looking for help in emotional problem solving, and dianetics purports to offer a technique for self-help. But this appeal to economic self-interest is not sufficient in itself, he feels, to explain the sudden spread of dianetics. There is something more: the unusually successful use of mechanical analogies.

What about the oft-made claim that, regardless of its theory, dianetics works? That it has actually cured psychosomatics and produced 'clears'? Hayakawa replies:

Macabre #2, June, 1948; art by DeHerty.

"Sometimes I ask myself,'where's it all going to end?'"

"All this computing-machine mumbo-jumbo is only a small part of the incredible nonsense to be found in dianetics. Before going into a discussion of the rest of the chaff, let me state my position at once: there is no wheat. Even if dianetic 'processing' produces, as Hubbard predicts, cures or apparent cures of neuroses, ulcers, falling hair, or diabetes, such results do not 'prove' a single item of dianetics doctrine. I say this on the basis of a simple distinction, familiar in general semantics literature, between kinds of predictions. There is a world of difference between predictions which cannot effect the outcome, and predictions which themselves are part of the outcome."

A prediction that two cannon balls of different sizes dropped from a tower will hit the ground at the same time cannot be overheard by the cannon balls and hence cannot affect the outcome of the experiment. On the other hand, recently a manager of a big-league baseball team nearing a pennant remarked scornfully of a tail-end club, "Are they still in the league?" The semantic reaction of the last-place club was to decisively defeat the league leaders in the last few days of the season, depriving them of the pennant.

"The testimony of any number of individuals who, having been told they will be helped, later claim to be helped by dianetic processing cannot constitute proof of the dianetics theory. Every therapeutic theory (psychiatric or medical) that has ever been believed in has worked to some degree, and sometimes to a spectacular degree (witness the rows of crutches at miracle-working shrines), for the people who have believed in it."

There is one further reason for the 'evidence' that dianetics 'works.' Emotional disturbances are basically failures in inter-personal relations. Thus it is apparent that if a man and his wife read in DIANETICS the technique of 'auditing' and are persuaded to try it, the effects can be those of an improved social structure. The husband no longer listens to his wife in his mind as he waits for an opportunity to break in to her conversation the cutting and unassailable retort. He is now an 'auditor' and must be attentive, non-judgmental, and permissive. The same will be true of the wife.

"With the alleviation of the misunderstandings and the dismissal of suspicions now seem to have been unwarranted, there may arise warmth and pleasure. Headaches and fatigue, and possibly more serious ailments may be relieved. The appalling thing revealed by dianetics about our culture is that it takes a 452 page book of balderdash to get some people to sit down and seriously listen to each other!"

In conclusion, Hayakawa warns that even the limited good that dianetics may do by introducing a single, narrowly-defined role-playing technique into interpersonal relations is probably more than offset by the damage it can do with its accompanying pretensions and nonsensical doctrines:

"Those who are helped by dianetics will necessarily be kept at a low level of intellectual and emotional maturity by the nonsense they have absorbed in order to be helped. The lure of the pseudoscientific vocabulary and promises of dianetics cannot but condemn thousands who are beginning to emerge from scientific illiteracy to a continuation of their susceptibility to word-magic and semantic hash."

As an epilogue, it might be suggested that the danger of internalizing the assumptions of science fiction faces not only the writer, but also the constant reader of science fiction. If the reader is aware of the abstractions being made — if he keeps in mind the fact that an analogy is an analogy and that there is a distinct difference in the genera to which Mark III and Mark Anthony belong — the process of abstraction can be extremely provocative and enlightening. This is one of the great values of science fiction. But if, on the other hand, the reader accepts analogy for reality and metaphorical thinking for logic — he is likely to carry this same method of evaluation over into the realm of non-fictional problems and become ripe for enmeshment in the coils of some new irrational 'science' such as dianetics. Science fiction enthusiasts deserve a kinder fate.

1 Elsewhere Hayakawa mentions that "good science-fiction is not too common. Much of it today is written hastily and according to formula, to meet the unceasing demands of pulps." (Amen)
2 "One swell foop" in the original — which was, perhaps, even more expressive.
3 Hayakawa describes the 'case histories' as "so rich in absurdity, so preposterously and awkwardly obscene." In a footnote he remarks: "Hubbard's hatred and contempt of women is quite intense; His 'case histories' betray a remarkable obsession with 'AA' (Attempted Abortion) and female adultery.
4 Hubbard is carefully unspecific as to how this recording is made; "Engrams are not memories but cellular level recordings. Therefore, the child needs no eardrums to record an engram."
5 Anyone can become an expert auditor, says Hubbard: "The auditor can do everything backwards, upside down and utterly wrong and the patient will still be better."
6 Not to mention science-fiction editors: John W. Campbell being one case in point, and — if one can believe in the sincerity of his comments during AMAZING's publication of the Shaver Mysteries — Howard Browne another.

Next Pg. *Spacewarp,* #41, Aug., 1950; ed. Art Rapp & Charles Burbee. *Twig,* #8, April, 1958; ed. Guy Terwilleger; art by Dan Adkins. *Science Fiction Review,* #21 (the first 20 issues were titled *Psychotic*), 1955; ed. Richard E. Geis; cover art by Bill Kellogg. *Vertigo,* #1, June, 1944; ed. Donald A Wollheim.

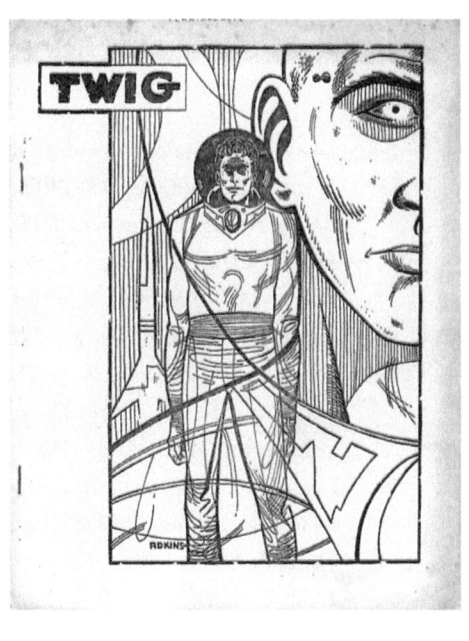

ZINES ARE FUN

Okay, to get the players straight in the following piece, Ray Palmer is the editor of OTHER WORLDS and FATE, Anthony Boucher is half of the editing team of THE MAGAZINE OF FANTASY & SCIENCE FICTION, the other half is J. Francis McComas. John W. Campbell, Jr. edits ASTOUNDING, and Horace Gold edits GALAXY. Paul W. Fairman edits IF, and Howard Browne is the editor behind AMAZING STORIES and FANTASTIC ADVENTURES — all professional science fiction magazines. Rog Phillips's "Clubhouse" is the fanzine review column for OTHER WORLDS, and Don Day is a fanzine editor (*The Fanscient*, 1947–1951) who also produced the *Index to Science Fiction Magazines* in 1952. The end of Willis's piece brings up Shaverism (see "The Palmer Hoax," pg. 152). Good, now continue reading please. —LO (Who took a while to get the title, being a city boy.) —LO

LOVE IN THE CORNFIELD

Walter A. Willis

(from Spaceship #17, April, 1952; ed. Bob Silverberg)

SOMETIMES THERE doesn't seem to be much hope for the world. Europe is full of Old World suspicions and New World atomic bomb bases. In Asia the great powers are defending democracy and justice to the last private soldier. South America is whirling around at thirty revolutions a minute. Everything is in a hell of a mess. Nearly everyone hates nearly everyone, and the newspapers are working on the rest. But in all this animosity there recently appeared one tiny gleam of hope, one oasis of loving kindness. A group of men who had apparently been natural enemies suddenly turned to one another with innocent affection. Pulp editors began to love one another. They greeted each other like long lost brothers. They fell weeping on each other's necks. It was touching. People began to point them out to the UN.

It was Palmer who started it. One day he came right out and threw his readers into a dead faint with the news that there were other sf mags in existence besides his own. Recklessly he went on to blurt out that some of them sometimes printed good stories. All over the country, readers with weak hearts went blue in the face and died with staring eyes. The other editors rubbed their hands and gloated. This was the end of Palmer. Years of editing FATE had finally had their inevitable result. Palmer had joined the ranks of the coverlet pluckers. But no. Palmer seemed to be no crazier than he ever had been. His mag survived. It didn't exactly go from strength to strength — it wasn't in a position to — but it seemed to be doing all right. The other editors were heartily ashamed of themselves. They began to fill their editorials with glowing tributes to other magazines. It got so you hardly knew what mag you were reading. Sometimes you felt like sending it back and asking the publishers to change it for one of the others, if they were so damned good; this one certainly wasn't up to much.

You half expected to see Rog Phillips start reviewing prozines in the "Clubhouse." "Now here's a very interesting little mag from a young fellow in California called Anthony Boucher. Tony has started this mag with a young fellow-pro called McComas and they are doing a very fine job. In fact, I'd like all of you to dig into your pockets and send these two young fellows a couple of hundred dollars to help them with this fine job they're doing. I know you won't regret it. I don't think I've ever seen a better mag since the one I reviewed just above. The printing is just fine — I don't know how they find the time — and the stories are just tops. Some of these pro-authors, I think, could teach us fans a thing or two about writing. In fact, I wouldn't be surprised to see some of them in fanzines one of these days. The paper these lads use in their mag is very white and the printing comes out nice and black. There isn't too much artwork inside, which will please people who don't like too much artwork in magazines, but what there is is very fine and it must cost them a lot of money. With this issue I got a nice letter from Tony telling me that my sub was overdue and I had better renew it. I'm certainly going to do that, and I think all of you should write to Tony for a copy of this very fine magazine of his and see just what these pro-editors can do. If you haven't seen one of these prozines for a long time you don't know what you have been missing."

But this happy state of affairs was too good to last. Somebody had to come along and spoil it. First, those two unscrupulous scoundrels, Campbell and Gold, preferred producing good magazines of their own instead of praising everyone else's. Now they're even insulting one another in public, just as if they were more interested in pleasing the public than in scratching one another's backs. Let us hope such selfishness will not lead other editors to take an unfair advantage of their brothers by printing good stories, and similar underhanded tricks.

And now here's Mr. Fairman. No one can accuse him of these unethical practices, but he leans too far in the other extreme. He strikes an even worse blow at the mutual admiration society movement. He goes too far. He is destroying public confidence in the sincerity of the praise editors bestow on one another. Look at this in the first IF: 'No greater boost could be given an infant publication than Howard Browne's name on the cover.' Offhand I could think of quite a few names that would be better infant-boosters, but I don't suppose Bob [Silverberg] wants this annish devoted to a reprint of the author's index of the Don Day checklist. 'AMAZING is the best science fiction your money could buy.' You talk for your own money, Mr. Fairman. I've no doubt Browne could lay his hand on his pocketbook and swear that his mag has the biggest circulation, but to say it is a good magazine is like calling 'Chopsticks' the greatest piece of music ever written. People run shouting down the streets when AMAZING prints a good story. The rest of this ridiculous blurb is devoted to Mr. Browne himself. Devoted? It's crazy about him. Apparently he's an "astounding ((he means amazing)) mixture of Balzac, a ten-ton dynamo, and Peter Pan." Fairman doesn't say what attributes he has of each, but he insists he's a "great guy." Also that when he does a thing he does it in a big way. Certainly it seems that when he writes a bad story he writes a real stinker, and when he makes a fool of himself he does that in a big way too, as when he threw his 150,000 circulation into a lone fight with little *Fanvariety*. But the real case against Fairman's Mr. Browne is this quotation from Fenster's Norwescon Report in *Incinerations* No. 4:

"Howard Browne, editor of AMAZING STORIES, was approached by Jerry Waible with: 'Say, I've got a really hot idea for some of your authors to get to work on. The earth is full of big caves, see, and these caves have sub-human monsters living in them that cause all the trouble up here on the surface by using rays — why, you could work up a whole series, and — ' But Browne had turned away, saying to Dorothy de Courcy, 'Somebody ought to bring this boy up to date.' He wasn't smiling."[122]

These last three words are the most damning indictment I ever heard.

Fanac, #70, Jan., 1961; cartoon by Ray Nelson. John W. Campbell, of course, was the editor of ASTOUNDING.

---

122 See "The Palmer Hoax," pg. 152.

Void, vol. 1, #4, Nov., 1955; cover art by Jim Benford.

LOOKING BACK

Here are Greg Benford's reminisces of *Void*, the NYC mimeo shop called Towner Hall run by Ted White, and a simpler time. Greg began *Void,* a fannish centric zine like Willis's *Hyphen*, with his twin brother Jim in 1954. Jim eventually dropped out and Terry Carr, Pete Graham and Ted White came on — but here's Greg to tell the story of *Void.* —LO

TOWNER HALL, VOID, ADOLESCENCE AND ALL THAT

Gregory Benford

IT IS an odd and strangely echoing thought: those days of the early 1960s, when *Void* jetted forth with almost frightening regularity and there seemed to be a distant and Oz-like place called Towner Hall.

I never saw it. For me the whole *Void* experience was a matter of the printed word. Some history: my brother Jim and I edited and published *Void* for issues 1 through 13, ending in Fall of 1958. Something came over us then. Our best friend in fandom was a burgeoning talent named Kent Moomaw. Kent came to stay with us in Summer 1958, when we were living in Dallas. I'd just finished my junior year in high school and my interest in mathematics and science was emerging strongly. I spent much of that summer reading the biography of Enrico Fermi, *Atoms in the Family*, and thinking about physics and the serene joys that field promised. This was a departure for me, because until then I had thought I would be a writer. But physics seemed to have more substance and weight in the world, and the "Sputnik" crisis underlined the importance of that exact, quantitative world.

While I was studying Newtonian mechanics and watching the space program slouch into existence, Kent Moomaw came. We went to the Southwestercon, "the con which killed Texas fandom", as Kent was later to label it. And Kent went home to write a devastating piece on the con, which we published in the last all-Benford issue of *Void* (#13). Our career as fanzine writers and editors had been successful, and we had a good place in the litany of top fanzines of the time.

But increasingly mathematics interested me. I thought I would become an engineer. And then news came in Fall 1958, from Kent's mother, that he had gone to a draft board interview, and had been told that he would be drafted immediately (a false scare tactic, I knew; my father was an Army Lt. Col.). He then had left that place and gone down to a drugstore nearby and bought a straight razor, and gone into a city park, and cut his wrists—and then, impossibly, seeing the blood, had gone on to cut his own throat, most methodically—and been discovered by a passerby a short while later.

Something happened to me then, and I never published a fanzine again. I did not think it through clearly, but for me a thing went out of fandom at that moment, reading the letter from his mother, and it has never come back into that paper universe we all inhabit. Jim and I had shared the work of *Void*, with me doing the typing and writing, Jim the mimeo. Somehow the incursion of the 1950s reality—Sputnik, draft, suicide at the thought of going into the Army, mathematics; an odd mixture, to be sure—silenced forever our urge to communicate, to publish a fanzine and announce ourselves to the world.

So in the winter, when Ted White wrote to suggest a coedited *Void*, Jim immediately said no. And he has never appeared in fanzines again. I pondered the point, and agreed. It seemed a good way to keep in touch with the people I still loved and listened to, the voices who came through those mimeo'd pages with a mirth and insurgence that I, in my rather strict high school role, relished. So I agreed, and Ted became the principal momentum behind a new kind of *Void* which quickly grew a personality of its own, one neither Ted nor I had ever manifested before. The chitterchatter embodies it: irreverent, wry, affectionate in a warm but not fulsome way. It is a spirit I can still recapture by rereading those pages.

So *Void* took off, making its monthly schedule for an astonishing time, and then Ted moved to NYC and things slowed. I contributed editorials and suggestions, but the momentum was clearly his, and you could see in his letters (alas, now destroyed; I saved little then) a curious alchemy as he found an outlet for the natural mordant wit he has. His piece on Calvin Thomas Beck, his somewhat cynical asides—these were perfectly done, and fit the mood of fandom at the time remarkably well. He had never given of himself this way in *Stellar*, his bigtime genzine. And then Pete Graham joined, and Terry Carr. By then I had taken a four year scholarship at the University of Oklahoma. (I based my decision on money rather than prestige, and the decision seems amazing to me now; I could have done much better at Caltech, or MIT, or Berkeley). I wrote editorials and wondered what it was really like back there. And I think I got the voice right. Listen to this piece from a typical Benford editorial—by then called "Happy Benford Chatter" after someone's lettercol comment—in which I clearly try on the Towner Hall mannerisms:

Void, #21, April, 1960; art by Andy Reiss.

WE ARE FOUR

Some of you have commented on the vast editorial staff which *Void* now supports, and I'm happy to say there has been general approval. I'm rather glad it happened myself. At least we might be able to get the zine out regularly now. Of course, we realize that we will be breaking a tradition in fandom if *Void* come out more often than every once is a while, but we are adamant. "On to punctuality!" is our cry.

I'm so pleased to this addition to the *Void* staff that I've been considering doing more of the same. Why, we can make it an honor in fandom to become a Void coeditor. There can be a regular little club, sort of like the N3F or Foreman Scotty's Space Patrol. We can have a special Void Coeditor's handshake and secret signal ring (with a picture of one of the First Four inside which lights up in the dark so you can recognise one of us if you chance to meet us in a back alley somewhere—it's that sort of sf club) and all sorts of other things to induce people to join. All you have to do is send in a regular little column about Dallas fandom or one of the other 3 coeditors. Ted White will run it off and put your name in the colophon (it's his fanzine and we're all just sort of columnists, you know) and you'll be in.

Does anyone want to join?

It's a mistake to think of *Void* as an arena for harmless jokes, chatter and empty mirth, though. We all took some remarkably savage digs at high-profile targets: LASFS, Seth Johnson (now dead), Cal Thos Beck[123], and certainly: Dallas.

Something strange had happened to me in fandom. I think the sense of isolation I had while living in Germany, where my father was commander of a field artillery battalion, contributed to it. I didn't like the Army kids and I felt a tug toward the verbal universe of fandom. It was all I had, nearly. So I adopted a mannerism which has become a character trait: a certain distance, an easy cynicism, a biting tongue. These are with me to this day and I don't regard them as welcome assets. I think I got crippled back there, in ways I don't understand even now. Perhaps fandom itself had something to do with this process. The hallowed Names in that era were the biting humorists: Burbee, Laney, Red Boggs, Boyd Raeburn. I liked them, I copied them. And so I put a lot of weight on the putdown, the cutting remark, the making of others a convenient butt of a sly joke. I'm not proud of this; I think it became a habit I cannot now cast off. I think, listening to my younger voice through these issues of *Void*, that I hear the sound of thwarted idealism in these writings. Here was a boy on the way to becoming a man, and around him there seemed many highblown visions, many empty exhortations. He saw this as phony 1950s rhetoric, and I think it made him forever cynical about the world. In some ways he was dead right. But there is a cost for such caution, for such noninvolve-

---

123 See "A Day with Calvin Thomas Beck," pg. 353.

ment, and I think it is rather a high cost. Anyway, listen to the piece which brings this out best from my *Void* editorials:

GREG BENFORD HAPPY BENFORD CHATTER
A PARTY FOR DALLAS

"Come on over!", Tom Reamy said, "we're having a party for Dallas." I thought about that for a minute. It does not do to say the obvious thing that pops immediately into your head when dealing with Dallas fans, for that is almost always the wrong thing to say. "Are you sure you can get them all in?" I replied. "Oh", he said, "I mean all the Dallas fans. We're going to have a little party for them."

And so it came to pass that I attended my only fannish party in Dallas. I asked Jim if he wanted to go, but he demurred, saying he wanted to do something constructive, like sleeping. Later he arranged a date, explaining that this was more constructive in the long run, so I was forced to go alone. I contemplated taking a date along, but I realized that taking a girl to a place full of science fiction fans would probably be frowned upon, if not by the girl at least by the fans.

The Dallas slan shack, where Reamy, Dale Hart and one or two others lived was a bit depressing as seen from the street, obscured as it was by an overgrowth of shrubs and weeds. The interior was crowded with people, though, all talking at a furious pace and running back and forth to the kitchen for drinks. I immediately spotted Richard Koogle (who has no middle name) holding forth in the center of a group of fine minds, and insinuated myself into the outer regions of the circle. I stood there for a while, letting the words wash over me and ripple into the surrounding people, until Koogle noticed me. "This certainly is a great party, isn't it, Greg?" He burbled. "We don't have these often, but when we do they're good."

"Yes," I said, "standing here and listening to you talking and the hifi wafting music over our heads, it's almost possible to believe I'm among real people." He beamed at me and called over Reamy, who took me out to the kitchen to get a drink.

We went out on the back porch so Reamy could show me the

surrounding undergrowth and get some fresh air. The porch was the starting line in a furious race for survival on the part of local weed-dom, for the back yard was one great mass of greenish growth. I broached the subject of yard upkeep (which I loath) to Reamy. "Have the neighbors gotten up a petition yet?" I asked. In the conversation which ensued, Reamy mentioned that his landlord didn't especially want the weeds rolled back because the remains of a stolen car of doubtful age were hidden somewhere in it.

Coming back in I noticed one woman there of largish proportions who was circulating around collecting signatures in favor of Dallas getting the worldcon. I signed. What the hell, I was getting free drinks. Actually, the only remarkable thing which occurred during the evening was my accidental discovery of a fan who had been fairly active in Dallas a few years back but had since dropped out of sight. I can't tell you his name because Rich Koogle was trying to sell me part of his fanzine collection (over 100 separate and distinct fanzines) and I couldn't hear over the general noise level. The oldtime fan seemed like a normal, intelligent person, though, unpolluted by his surroundings. He told me about meetings of the Dallas Futurian Society at which Mosher would go out on the street and pull in passers-by in hopes of enlarging the membership. At the time the meetings were being held in a cafe, and whenever the club had a guest speaker Mosher would round up a number of panhandlers, promising them a cup of coffee, in order to present a large membership to the speaker. "Did he find many science fiction fans among the bums and loafers?" I asked, but since Mosher was not there at the moment, I could not find out. Considering recent issues of *Habakkuk*, perhaps the answer would have been a little surprising.

Shortly after this one character came wandering through the rooms moodily staring into peoples' faces and mumbling a few greetings. I asked Reamy who he was. He was identified as Dale Hart, who was currently running the plans for the Southwestercon VI (the convention that killed southwestern fandom). "Say, would you like to join the committee to work on publicity for the con?" Reamy asked as Hart drew nearer. I looked over at Hart. I looked back at Reamy. I went out to get another drink.

"I'm not worried about a war at all," one of the regular members said a few minutes later. "I've got my plan all worked out."

"What?" I said, taken aback. "Well," he gestured, "if we have a war they'll be sure to drop a bomb on downtown Dallas and then my troubles will be over." I thought he was probably right, but I wouldn't have been so foolhardy about it.

"The draft board is right in the middle of town, and if they drop any bombs my records will be destroyed. Then if anyone comes around trying to get me in the Army I'll tell them I've already done my time." The group around him fell silent.

"Don't you think if we have a war they'll just draft everybody in sight and not worry about the records?" someone else asked. "No", the planner said, "I'll appeal to Congress and by the time that gets through the war will be over."

"Well then", I said, "we'll all do that and there wont be any more war and we won't have to fight." The fan who had his future all mapped out in his head thought a moment to himself. "I don't think that will work. Somebody has got to defend the country in times of peril." At this time I was relatively new to Dallas Fandom so I ignored the opportunity to say something nasty and true. But my infinite patience and understanding for people has withered somewhat since then, which is why you're reading this article.

I was walking into the stf room of the slan shack when Reamy, who is a little on the heavy side, turned to me and said, "What do you think of that?"

"I think you're wrong", I said automatically. Usually that works pretty well. "You're always talking about how science can give everybody a better way of doing something. Tell me how I can lose weight without dieting." He stood there waiting for my answer. "Close your mouth", I said.

Rich Koogle was there, looking through the ASTOUNDING collection. He was still enthusiastic about the party. "It's just like last summer", he said, waiving an ASF at me, "when we had all our parties out at our swimming pool." I asked him what he meant. "One of the members of the club had a pool in his back yard and he invited the club over every week to have a meeting and talk by the pool."

"Why, that's fine", I said. "That's the best thing I've ever heard about Dallas fandom. It sounds like quite a change from just sitting around and reading old fanzines during meetings. I can hardly imagine a Dallas fan club meeting where you could lie around in the sun and swim."

"Oh", he said, "we didn't do that. None of us could swim."

In a little while the resources of the club began to evaporate and someone had to go out and replenish the food and drink. The oldtime fan whose name I never learned was driving, so I decided to go with him; as we were going out the front door Reamy, fearing that someone was leaving the party early, came over and told us to stay for the later festivities. "It's all right", I told him. "I just wanted to go out for awhile and see some real people."

I can see that there are good bits in this, some all-too-true aspects of fandom carefully outlined. Indeed, this piece is absolutely factual. The party did occur, all these things happened, and I felt pretty much that way about them. I didn't write it up until years later, though (notice it occurs before the Southwestercon), and here's why: I felt myself rid of these people by then, and I felt a real disdain for the world of fandom. I wanted to keep it at a distance, and cutting humor is a fierce defense. That was the mechanism I had developed for many of life's encumbrances: wit. And fandom seemed to reward such writing well, so I did it. And I felt the distant presence of Towner Hall through all this: older figures, better known, whom I wanted to resemble. So I wrote with a scalpel's edge, and the readers seemed to like it.

This piece about Dallas is the most savage I ever wrote. There's a lot in it that may not make much sense now: Bill Donaho's *Habakkuk* had recently detailed the incredible piggish behavior of the NYC crowd. Dale Hart was a well known alcoholic, and in fact died of it. And Tom Reamy. It seems astonishing, now, to realize that such a major talent was hidden beneath that calm, reserved exterior. There was a lot of the good ole boy in Tom, and I took him to be the best figure in the Dallas crowd, deeper than the rest, but hard to reach. He was mostly interested in graphics then and seemed curiously taken by the art of Morris Scott Dollens. A lot of his overlay graphic work ran to brawny men set before background moonscapes or rocket ships. I assumed, without pondering the point much, that he was gay. He never seemed very interested in women—there were nearly none in Dallas fandom— and had the retiring lifestyle I had learned to associate with gays. I think now I was wrong and that Tom was simply a fairly common type in fandom, not highly sexual, but not interested in concealing the fact. I liked him but, as my interests in physics increased, I saw little of him. Once I left Dallas for Oklahoma, I didn't see him again, beyond a few evenings, until California in the early 1970s.

Void (incorporating *Innuendo*), #26, Aug., 1961; eds. Terry Carr, Greg Benford, Pete Graham and Ted White; art by Bhob Stewart.

In the four years I spent in Oklahoma I wrote editorials and listened to the voices out of Towner Hall, but of course it was a paper universe. I met none of my coeditors until the long phase of *Void* was finished. Ted and Terry I saw first at the 1964 worldcon; Pete I never met. So, as my in-person contact with fandom dwindled, I adopted a mannered voice and posture in fandom. The "We Are Four" piece above is a perfect example of aping the *Void* voice. There are certain tics I picked up from Laney, and a deliberate lift from Willis, and overall a miasma of controlled style which I learned from my coeditors. I think I picked up my concern for compression of style in those years, too: fanzine editorials, and particularly those which seek to be witty, cannot drag on for long.

So in my *Void* work you see the mannerisms of others cloaking my own concerns. It was my only hobby; I was a ferocious worker, living a life stuffed with physics and mathematics, reading little sf (for in truth I've never read much of it; my secret vice) and thinking much about that sf world without knowing much of what went on in distant places where sophisticates talked in witty, stylish ways. Terry and Ted and Pete were all older than me, and I tried to write up to their standard. But I didn't have the immediate material from life at hand, so I delved into my own past, and made much of the apparently smallest incident. Witness this piece which started the then-famous running joke about a hapless minor Dallas fan:

> FABULOUS DALLAS FANDOM got quite a jolt late last August. Everyone had sort of mutually agreed that no expedition to Detroit would be planned, mostly because we were all going to be going to school or working or something. Then too, after last year's Southwestercon, we weren't too hot on conventions.
>
> Actually, I had advance warning. Two days before, I had received a letter from Marion Zimmer Bradley in which she asked: "Do you happen to know a Texas fan named Marland Frenzel?" and went on to describe how Marland had written her, asking if she were going to drive to Detroit and could he go and if not, could she spread the word? I briefly skipped over the passage, and forgot about it. Two days later, at 12:30 AM, the telephone rang.
>
> Now, I was getting up early for work. Working ten hours a day, I needed all the sleep I could get, especially since it's a half hour

drive to where I worked and I can't doze at the wheel. Therefore, people calling at odd hours of the night were most unwelcome. I picked up the phone.

"Hello, Greg. Remember, a fan in need is a fan indeed!" Came a voice. Mighod, I thought. "I'm Marland Frenzeland I'm down here at the bus station. I just got in here and come on down and-pick me up before the cops do." I must have made some sort of astonished noise, because he repeated the statement. I told him I didn't have room, and Jim was in the hospital (he was) so everything was a bit fouled up and it would be difficult to put him up for the night. What's more, it was late.

"Oh, I'm going to stay in Dallas for three or four days and visit all the fans," he said. I was suddenly immensely glad that we didn't have room. Perhaps, said Marland, I didn't know who he was. "I had an article published in *Cry of the Nameless* once," he said confidently. I reassured him that I did not know who he was. He hesitated for a moment and asked me for the names of some Dallas fans. I remarked on the impossibility of finding lodgings at this hour of the morning, but gave him the names, hung up, and went back to sleep. At 3:00 AM the phone rang.

"I couldn't get Albert Jackson or Jim Hitt," said Marland, and asked again if I could rush down and pick him up. I gave him Randy Brown's name, George Jennings' and Koogle's. I went back to sleep. At 6:30 AM, as I was preparing to leave for work, the phone rang.

"Jennings didn't answer," he said. (Jennings was vacationing in Colorado.) "I called Hitt and got no answer, and Koogle said he couldn't arrange to put me up for that long." (I later learned that Koogle had answered the phone, listened to the request, shouted something into the receiver, and hung up.) Marland mentioned that he couldn't afford to go to a hotel, and he really did want to see some fans. I told him the YMCA would be fairly cheap if he didn't mind living among the smells of disinfectant and old meals, but it brought no response. He talked a little about his plans of hitchhiking to Detroit, stopping over at fan centers on the way. "I'd hoped to get in with the fan caravan," he explained.

That afternoon, Randy Brown called, asking what the hell was going on. He said he'd been awakened at some unghodly hour of the morning, heard a tweaky voice at the other end talking about fandom, and hung up without a word. I detailed my own experiences and we laughed a little about it. Koogle called, as did Hitt and Jackson. We all wondered out loud what kind of fan would drop into a strange city late at night and expect people who had never heard of him to put him up for a few days.

Since then, every time a Dallas fan has called me, he has said, "Hello, Greg. Remember, a fan in need is a fan indeed!" in a high-pitched voice. Did Marland Frenzel really get to Detroit, Ted White?"

I admit, I would use anyone as the butt of a cool, mannered piece of editorial. I don't think it ever harmed anyone—I remember Reamy telling me he rather liked seeing Dallas fandom made a more interesting place than it really was—but it did put a certain cast on my work. I continued with this point of view in my later fanzine writing for *Frap* (which I coedited with the now-vanished Bob Lichtman[124]) and then beyond.

Was there anything wrong with this approach? I could, after all, have taken the gentle humor of Willis as a model. But I doubt I could have written that way (though Tom Perry has managed to do quite well at it since). I saw the stylized Void-boy way of writing as a form to adopt, and I worked what mirth I could from it. It was a useful exercise in assuming a voice when the roots of it are not in fact your own, and I think it helped in my later work in fiction. I now use whatever narrative approach seems warranted by the material, and this, too, is a skill that can be learned.

Void in the coeditor phase became vastly successful. It did have a certain something, I can sense it even now as I page through it. Copies of the coedited *Void* now command enormous prices among fmz collectors. (Even the strictly Benford *Voids* are worth a fair amount; they did have their moments.) I remember that era as a warm and happy one, despite the apparent cynicism of much of my work from that age. I hope that feeling comes through to the reader who chances upon an old copy, today, in some well-thumbed and fraying collection. It certainly was a wonderful thing, Meyer[125].

---

124 Lichtman's fanzine is *Trap Door*.
125 A sort of catch phrase used by Charles Burbee.

ZINE PEOPLE

I first discovered Calvin Thomas Beck (1929–1989) in the newsstand magazine called CASTLE OF FRANKENSTEIN, which he used to publish and edit, intermittently, from the 1960s into the early 1970s. *CoF* was a more adult version of Ackerman's FAMOUS MONSTERS OF FILMLAND. Before *CoF* there was JOURNAL OF FRANKENSTEIN. It has been long rumored in fandom that Beck was the model for Norman Bates in Robert Bloch's *Psycho*. It is unknown if Bloch ever met Beck, but Bloch certainly heard the many stories about Beck that were bantered around fandom. We remember the Bates character as played in the original film by a young, thin Anthony Perkins, but in the book the physical description of Bates fits Beck to a "T." Then there is the "mother thing." ¶ White's first zine, *Zip* (1953), was printed on a Sears & Roebuck postcard mimeo. It later went fullsize and became *Stellar*, which was later combined with Harlan Ellison's defunct *Dimensions*. Then it became *Gafia*, then *Gambit*, with some *Whammys* in there, though I may have missed some metamorphoses. All of White's later zines were also stellar. White went on to edit AMAZING STORIES and HEAVY METAL.—LO

A DAY WITH CALVIN THOS. BECK

Ted White

(from Void *#21, April, 1960; eds. Ted White & Greg Benford)*

I SPEND A day with Calvin Thomas Beck — twenty-four hours — yes. I did, actually and literally.

Now, long before we moved to New York, I had heard stories about Beck; stories which grew long and fabulous in the retelling. Stories about Calvin Thomas Beck and his mother, without whom he was never without... And since coming to New York, it had crossed my mind several times that here at long last was a chance to lay a legend, to see if the Beck Mythos was only that, or whether there was a flesh and blood substantiation to the stories I had heard.

Luck was with me in the person of Larry Ivie, a fringe fan and professional artist, and a long-time EC fan. Larry Ivie had found himself doing the layout for the second issue of Calvin T. Beck's prozine, THE JOURNAL OF FRANKENSTEIN.[126] For a week, Ivie had been taking the bus over to New Jersey to the Beck's home early each morning, worked a long day, and returned late at night and whenever he had a chance, he would regale me with stories about the Becks. Finally I could stand it no longer. I asked Larry if I might go along with him to meet these fabulous people.

"Well, it's your life..." is the way he put it. "But I could use someone to run interference; the way they keep wanting to talk to me all the time I never can get any work done." So, it was agreed. Sunday morning at 9:00 I would meet Ivie at the Port Authority Bus Terminal, and we would ride out together to North Berger, New Jersey.

The Beck house is a duplex, with the Becks on the left side. It is in effect a two-story, with a "basement" on the ground floor, and a "first floor" which is reached by climbing half a flight of outside steps to the porch. Fortunately, the house is about three doors away from the bus stop. The neighborhood is a seedy residential one, made up of lover-middle-class homes and cheap housing projects, with a run-down "business section" of a couple of blocks a half mile away. Like most of New Jersey, it is singularly depressing.

Larry knocked several times on the door, and finally it was opened by a small, plump, grey-haired woman in a house-coat. It seemed the Becks had just arisen. We entered through a crowded living room with an unmade studio couch-bed and two large bird cages, and Larry introduced me to Mrs. Beck. "This is Ted White," he said. "He came along to help me, since we're pushing so close to the deadline."

"Oh, yes," Mrs. Beck said, not for an instant questioning my qualifications, but simply accepting me. "Hello, Teddy." She said to me with a strange chirping-bird sort of accents. (Later I asked Calvin, who said it was a mixture of French and Greek accent.) I was to be "Teddy" for the rest of my stay. We were then ushered down into the "basement" where Larry began showing me what had been done, while the

---

126 Beck's first zine was *Science and Science Fantasy Fiction Review* in 1950.

Becks presumably prepared themselves for the day.

The basement had been newly done over, into what amounted to an apartment, with separate (but equal) kitchen and bathroom facilities. (Calvin later said they intend to rent it as an apartment come spring. Here's a great opportunity for someone who wants to do a psychological study, close-up...) It was light and attractive and spread out all over the main room floor were layout sheets. "It was the only place where we had room." Larry explained, and started showing me what he had done. The layouts were rather good, I thought, but conventional and not very world-shaking. Larry had done lots of picture paste-ups, montages, etc., and a fair amount of title lettering. The latter I nearly uniformly deplored. (Later, Larry agreed: "I'm an artist, not a letterer. I don't know why people think artists make good letterers."

The deal was this: the first issue of THE JOURNAL OF FRANKENSTEIN had been a serious "work of love", and looked pretty lousy. It had also received lousy distribution, and lost money. But Beck (who also publishes various cheap physical culture magazines —"Queer-bait." Larry calls them; he will have nothing to do with them) managed to find a better distributor: the one who handles *Playboy*. The distributor wanted something to compete with Ackerman's mag [FAMOUS MONSTERS OF FILMLAND], so the slant of the mag was being changed 190 degrees. It was also getting better printing and would at least not look like a scrapbook, as the first issue had. The catch at this point was that the distributor wanted to see the final preliminary dummy the next day. And the issue was only half completed. Larry was still explaining this when we were called up for coffee.

"Coffee" turned out to be "Coffee with." In this case, with two fried eggs and loads of unevenly burned toast, plus cheese sauce. It happens that I am not an egg fan, and have only learned how to eat (and enjoy that is) hard-boiled eggs and deviled eggs in the last year, and had never attempted fried eggs. Manfully, with a great spirits of adventure, and mindful of the fact that I had not eaten since rising that morning, I ate the two fried eggs.

I am still not a fried egg fan.

We were joined at this breakfast by Calvin Thomas himself, who turned out to be thirty-ish, plump, medium height, dark, and rather pleasant. It is difficult to imagine a man at thirty still bound to his mother as Calvin is, but the marvel is that Calvin seems to have adjusted to this as a life-long fact, and has accepted it with remarkable humor.(He often kids his mother, and puts her down, but still refers to her with child-like affection.) Calvin strikes me as a shy man, introverted, weak-willed, and aware of it. Much of this can be credited to is mother's dominance.

Strangely (particularly in light of reports I'd heard), I found neither Beck unpleasant, but in the long run only wearing. Yet, Mrs. Beck has certainly some very strange attitudes, which came out during the hour-long discussion we held as we ate. The Becks were pumping me of course, about my background, so I played my bearded role to the hilt with such remarks as, "I had to leave Washington DC of course. It is a beautiful town, but so *dull*. There are no real opportunities, and nothing ever happens there;there's nothing to *do*." I was actually referring to career opportunities in writing and editing, but Mrs. Beck took this as a comment on social life — which it could also easily be. "Well," she said, "I should think a man of letters would not mind that. It is not good to leave the home too much."

The Mama Beck philosophy seems to be one of Staying Behind Locked Doors, one which was to bear itself out several times later. Larry had earlier in the week told me her rather interesting views on social life between the sexes: "You know what boys and girls do now?" They *date*. If *I* had a daughter and she told me she wanted to *go out on a date*, you know what I would do? I would hit her over the head and put some sense into her! Of course, I have never had that problem with Calvin... He used to go to the YMCA. But finally he was going to the YMCA too much, and we had to move out here to New Jersey." Mrs. Beck still thinks highly of the YMCA however. "You know the 23rd St. YMCA?"[127] (Larry had lived there a short time before he found an apartment —"The queers scrawl messages and advertisements on the walls in the halls!") "That's a very good place for boys, you know?" She nodded her head in approval.

The effect this has had on Calvin, a very malleable individual with apparently a very malleable sex-drive, was to drive him into the introvert's fascination for sexological studies, and a vicarious approach to what in his house is an unapproachable subject. He told a rather funny story (funny more in the way he told it than for its intrinsic humor)

---

[127] In the 21st Century the McBurney Y on 23rd Street moved south from its 100 year old building to brand new digs on West 14th Street.

about how at one time he had published a pseudo-SEXOLOGY type magazine, and George Wetzel, who had decided he no longer liked Beck, complained to the FBI that Beck was a publisher of pornography.

"These two men came around one day from the FBI, and demanded to see my magazine. I stalled them a bit, and told them I didn't have any copies of it around, because I didn't like their methods, but I was pretty nervous, because it isn't every day you're visited by the FBI. They said that if I didn't produce a copy immediately, they'd get a search warrant. Of course immediately I get them a copy, because I didn't want them looking around through everything. You see, er, ha-ha, I did have one little item of pornography in the house; something I'd just picked up for curiosity, of course. I had it in my files, under 'P'..."

Little indications of Mama Beck's strong will and natural determination to take care of *everything* were amusing. For instance, she added milk and sugar to our coffee before serving it, and without asking if we wanted it. When I asked for salt, she salted my eggs (and Larry's, too, before he could object) herself. Later on in the day, when we were again having coffee when it is hot. Calvin relayed the request, and back from the kitchen came, "What does he want a spoon for? I have already stirred the sugar and milk!"

Past reports (including the one of when Mama Beck, having decided that Calvin had spent too much time in a men's room, charged in after him, calling "Caaal-vin, where are you?" — which I can easily believe) of Mrs. Beck activities have been pretty incredible, usually amusing if they don't involve you, and almost always indicative of the sort of busy-body-ish, PTA-ish, American "Mom" you'd love to hate. Mrs. Beck in person does not measure up to this. In person she is humorously pathetic, plaintive, insisting, ingenuous stereotype of the Old World Mama, a simple person bound up in the success of her son. Unfortunately, in this case, someone forgot to cut the umbilical cord.

We didn't see much of Mrs. Beck as we worked, which surprised Larry, who said she was in the habit of bringing him coffee every ten minutes on previous days. "No kidding. I couldn't drink it all, and at one point I had lined up along one-wall ten cups full of cold coffee. And every little while, she'd come down with another cup of the stuff."

When we returned to the basement, Larry began to letter a thing which read "Zachereley's Wife Contest." When he had finished, after a couple of brief minutes, I said, slowly, "Larry… that looks terrible."[128]

"Yes," he agreed. "Now that you mention it, it does." The outcome of this was that I found myself re-lettering the page and handling nearly all of the remaining title lettering. I'm not that proud of it — it was done for same-size reproduction, which I though was a mistake, and was a little uneven — but it was reasonable esthetically pleasing to the eye. (Especially at a distance. The further away one holds it, the better it looks… two block away seems about best, and I recommend it.)

The way we operated was that Calvin T. would type up some text on his electric IBM, and bring it down and Larry would cut it to fit and past it up into a layout with photo and I would letter in the titles, usually hand lettering but sometime using artype. (I'm rather proud of the one I did with artype for the "Hound of the Baskerville" — you'd think it has appeared in *Fantastic Universe*…) Unfortunately, it was difficult to keep Calvin upstairs and banging away at this typewriter. After we had run out of material to past up, and had ushered him upstairs to compose some more deathless prose, we would almost immediately hear this sound like two large barrels falling down the steps, and there would be Calvin, with a question, a joke, or two unusable lines of captions for a photo we'd previously decided not to use. This cause a considerable bottleneck, and was apparently the main

---

128 Ivie would, a few years later, publish his own newsstand magazine called MONSTERS & HEROES. He was still doing his own lettering and it had not improved noticeably, so that MONSTERS & HEROES looked and read more like a fanzine than a pro mag.

reason for the previous week's slow progress.

In all fairness to Calvin, however, I should point out that he was apparently starved for fannish news of any sort, and seemed really very lonely. I was a new contact to the fandom he'd lost touch with — Larry had mentioned that I put out a fanzine, remaining purposefully vague — and he wanted to soak up all the news he could. Most of the fans he asked about have since departed the scene, although we did discuss in detail the Wetzel mess[129]. Beck had at one time been friendly with Wetzel, like many other well-meaning people, because Wetzel and he shared an interest in fantasy ad supernatural fiction. Beck had been one of those whom Wetzel had used to mail off letters with other cities postmarks on them. One day Beck had investigated one of these letters and found it to be a poison pen letter to a friend of his, and had broken off relations with Wetzel. Shortly thereafter came the FBI episode.

Around mid afternoon, we ran out of india ink. Calvin wanted us to try water colors which we patiently informed him would not flow well through a pen, and black fountain-pen ink, which worked extremely badly, so finally we decided in desperation to set out and try to find a place which sold india ink, despite the fact that it was Sunday.

We were just climbing the stairs from the basement ("But why does Teddy want to go with you, Larry?" Asked Mama Beck; "I take him round with me for good luck," Larry replied, truthfully) when we made an astounding discovery! *We discovered Mr. Beck!* I had asked Larry earlier if there was a Mr. Beck, and he said he assumed that if there ever was one, he'd since been swallowed up by the earth, since he'd not heard a word or reference to any such person.

But there at the top of the stairs, shuffling about aimlessly in the hall in front of us was a tall, thin, aging man whom we could only glimpse, as through a dimensional rift, before Mrs. Beck, who had been ahead of us, hurriedly ushered him into a room.

"Mr. Beck has hurt himself," we were told. "He tried to gut a corn off his foot with a razor blade, which he had no business doing, and now it is bleeding, so please get for me also a—a—a— bandage, you know?"

"A band-aid?" I asked.

---

[129] George Wetzel's behavior in fandom was bad enough that few fans, even the most open and accepting, did not condemn him.

"No, no, no! A—a—" and again the inability to communicate. Inspiration suddenly struck, and she said, "Like this!" and pressed into my hand an extremely filthy, used band-aid.

"Yeah, band-aids." I said.

New Jersey had Sunday Blue Laws, and as I've pointed out, today was Sunday. We trudged over most of North Bergen's dumpy "business section," finding open only one drugstore, which had no india ink, and probably couldn't have sold it even if it had. We did get the band-aids, however.

So, after about an hour, we returned to the Becks, Larry betting that Calvin would have accomplished nothing during our absence (he won the bet), and there the decision was made to get out the car and drive around looking for a place which sold india ink. By now we sere all very hung up on india ink.

Mrs. Beck was not going to be left behind, so she followed the three of us back out of the house. I watched in amazement as she took a small padlock from off a hook and padlocked the door shut from the outside, leaving Mr. Beck locked inside! (To enlighten you about Mr. Beck, I later pieced together enough information to discover that he was connected with a restaurant somewhere, and came home only one day a week, during which he was kept in his room. It sort of fits in to the Beck Mythos after all...)

The four of us set off in the Beck's 1955 Buick and after searching most of New Jersey in vain, Calvin muttering all the while about how things were far worse than he had imagined — "I haven't been out on Sunday in four or five years..." —we finally headed over the George Washington Bridge to uptown Manhattan. On the way we talked about various things inspired by the subject of Blue Laws, finally settling upon a discussion of the Mormon control of Utah (Larry's home state) which is so strong that bus passengers passing through the state must stop smoking at the state line, and the morals of Salt Lake City's youth. Their morals turned out to be rather good, and I jokingly said, in a semi-non-sequiteur, "I don't know about their morals, but the girls in Salt Lake City are prettier than in any other city I've ever travelled through." (The Society of American Girl Watchers and Letchers, formed by Bob Pavlat and myself on our various long trips to conventions several years back, using a one-to-five star rating system for the incidence of pretty girls observed in various cities passe through, gave Salt Lake City forty-eight stars!) Mama Beck took this to mean that I though pretty girls were immoral, and over the protest of Calvin, Larry and myself, she lectured us on the morality of beauty, and how it was immoral to keep a beautiful girl locked up inside a house were no could see and admire her beauty. We didn't think, then, to question this in light of some of Mrs. Beck's other statements.

We found ink in Manhattan without difficulty, and finally returned to New Jersey, Mrs. Beck pointing out "scenic vistas" every time the car rounded a turn and a new garbage dump was visible, and soon we back at the Beck's.

From there on, it was work, work, work. Fortunately, when necessary, I could talk to Calvin Thomas and work at the same time, thus keeping him off Larry's back. I also freed Ivie from the drudgery of lettering, and thus speeded up his other work. By this point we were working on the latter portion of the mag, where a number of stills from a horror movie, plus captions, will be run, one movie to a page or two. Thus, I was really grinding out titles, like "Have Rocket — Will Travel," "The Woman Eater," and "Horror Film Cavalcade."

The magazine calls for a humorous approach, ala Ackerman, and Beck certainly has a weird and corny sense of humor. One of his "better" jokes was to name the magazine's new club the National Frankenstein Fan Federation, or N3F for short... I began riding him about this, making caustic jokes about some of his worst attempts, and I think this upset him a bit, but it did prod him into a slightly more productive vein... it also kept him out of our hair and at his typewriter where he belonged.

Around eight o'clock, we were called up at long last for dinner. We had had no lunch and were famished, but the food was plentiful enough to quell our hunger. It consisted of a plate for each of us heaped perilously high with potatoes cooked with still-raw onions, navy beans, and overcooked lamb. It was fairly tasty, albeit overstocked on carbohydrates.

After dinner we hit the final stretch, monotonously pasting up photos and captions, and lettering titles. "My layout is going to pieces," Larry said. When you have to create a new layout every page for twenty pages or so, it is impossible to keep them consistent to each other and make them all good. We were also getting tired (it hadn't helped that Larry, Sylvia and I had been up till two or so Sunday morning watching old films over at Dave Foley's, and had thus gotten rather little sleep before coming up to the Becks'...), and feeling less creative.

It was a rather momentous occasion, then, when Calvin T. said quietly, "I think this will be enough." We were finally through! I glanced at my watch... it was four a.m.?! "The buses have stopped running," Calvin said brightly. "They don't start again till six. And look! It's snowing!" Yes, it was. And that precluded any chance of Calvin — who was as tired as we were anyway — driving us to New York. We decided to wait the two hours till six, and then catch a bus. The Becks offered us a single narrow cot to sleep on, but somehow Larry and I both thought we'd prefer to sleep in our own beds at home. So we sat around, those two hours long and indeterminable, filled with aimless talking and over-powering drowsiness. Finally six came, and we were ushered out the front door into the still-falling snow by the still up and awake Mrs. Beck, and after three minutes or less we were on a bus to New York.

From there on, the trip assumed a surrealistic quality. Safely on our way, we relaxed, but could not sleep. We took the A train uptown from the Port Authority Terminal, and split up at Columbus Circle, where Larry changed to the AA local, and I transferred to the downtown local IRT train. I boarded it with a crowd of bright, almost cheerful looking people who had just risen and were on their way to work. I slumped down in my parka in my seat and regarded them fuzzily through my tangled beard, and reflected upon the difference between us. I preferred it my way. I had put in my own hours, and now I was free for as long as I wished. I was going home and to bed, and would probably sleep for a good twelve hours; and they, poor slobs, were off to work, probably still not recuperating from their weekends, and with eight hours of boredom, drudgery, or hard work ahead of them.

At 42nd St., four or five college types got on, carrying a six-pack of beer. Here were people who were marginally my kind, still drunk (not yet even hung over) and returning from a weekend not yet quite finished. They split up and drank the beer and sang songs to each other at the top of their lungs all the way down to 14th St., where one of them exclaimed, "Boy! You know I gotta make it home and change my clothes and be at work in two hours —!" I sympathized with him, but I don't think he made it... Especially since they were all on the wrong train, and thought they were getting off at Union Square, which is on East 14th St., and this was West 14th... The other passenger made an interesting study, as they attempted to ignore the college types (it has been said that if you disrobe on the subway, no one would stare directly at you, and probably most people would not notice),who made a little too much noise to be easily ignored. The whole scene — particularly when one fellow offered another passenger a can of beer (which was turned down) — furnished me with enough amusement to keep me awake until we reached the Christopher St., stop, and regained the street, where it was still snowing lightly. The sky was grey and darkly overcast, and I was still in a sleepy mood. I entered the apartment quietly, and surreptitiously slipped into bed, so as not to awaken Sylvia.

It was the end of a long day.

An amusing aftermath occurred when Larry Ivie and I were discussing that day several days later. "You know, I had noticed that door to the room where they keep Mr. Beck but I hadn't known he was there. It's real funny, though; the door opens inwards, and they have a rope tied to it from the outside, so that no one can open it without untying all these knots and everything."

"How strange." I said. How strange indeed.

Void, #21, April, 1960; art by Andy Reiss.

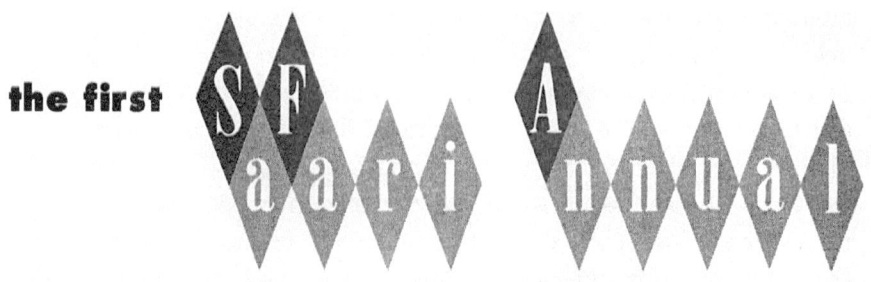

SaFari Annual: Who Killed Science Fiction?, April, 1960; ed. Earl and Nancy Kemp; cover art by Ed Emshwiller.

WHO KILLED SCIENCE FICTION?

When Earl and Nancy Kemp published the *Who Killed Science Fiction?* issue of *SaFari*, science fiction was going through a bad time. At the end of the 1950s one of the biggest newsstand distributors in the country had gone under and left many sf magazines without access to newsstands. Quite a few magazines had to take bad deals from other distributors or decided to throw in the towel. It seemed like the bottom had fallen out of the sf field. So in time-honored fanzine tradition Kemp began sending out questionnaires to pro editors, writers and big name fans, asking the questions then on many sf fans' minds: **1**. Do you feel that magazine science fiction is dead? **2**. Do you feel that any single person, incident, *et cetera* is responsible for the present situation? If not, what is responsible? **3**. What can we do to correct it? **4**. Should we look to the original paperback as a point of salvation? **5**. What additional remarks would you like to contribute? ¶ In his introduction to the zine Kemp wrote: "The title of the study itself bears little or no relationship to the actual five points under observation. It was merely to serve as splash — fuel to light the fire that would get the five questions answered. Apparently it worked, because there were some "whos" named." There were 71 contributors to WKSF? — many names we still recognize today. In answer to the first question, out of 71 contributors, 2 said YES — with 11 replies, stating either "yes" or definitely dying already — 51 said NO, and the rest were non-commital. —LO

Kurt Vonnegut, Jr.

(from SaFari Annual: Who Killed Science Fiction? *April, 1960; ed. Earl Kemp)*

NOBODY KILLED science fiction. Science fiction is not dead. More money will be spent on stories with science in them during the next year than in any year in history — will be spent by magazines, television, radio, book publishers, movies, and even Broadway.

So what is the beef?

The pulp writers can't make a living any more? *Tant pis.* They made intelligent readers want to throw up.

Anybody who announces that he is a science fiction writer is announcing that he is in damn bad company financially and artistically.

You are trying to conduct a post-mortem without a corpse. I would love to provide you with one. I would love to see the expression science fiction butchered this very minute in order that stories with science in them not be identified, in the minds of intelligent readers, with pulpers, beginners, and hacks.

AFTERTHOUGHTS:

(from SaFari, *#6; July 15, 1960; ed. Earl Kemp)*

THANKS FOR the handsome present [contributor copy of *Who Killed Science Fiction?*]... My own contribution was irresponsible, and I'm sorry for it.

What it expressed more than anything else was my own isolation. I don't know anybody else in the field, not even fans, and so I tend to think of the field as something far far away and belonging to strangers. That is self-pitying thinking without merit...

There seems to be fair agreement as to what the best pieces of work in the field have been. It might be interesting to make a list of those best pieces, a hundred of them, say — and, after each title, to name the thing most attacked, the thing most praised, and, in the barest possible terms, the intended moral. You might discover in that way the spiritual basis of the almost crazy affection many intelligent people have for the artificial category of writing known as science fiction...

All the shoptalk by ink-stained wretches leads nowhere. Underneath all that shoptalk something very important spiritually may be going on. I hope so....

WHO KILLED SCIENCE FICTION?

Earl Kemp's (1929–) previous fanzine had been *Destiny*, which he edited for its last five issues, 1953-1954. *Who Killed Science Fiction?* won the best fanzine Hugo in 1961. During the 1960s and 1970s, Kemp edited several lines of erotic paperback novels for William L. Hamling, who was a fanzine publisher who graduated to the pros (from *Stardust* to AMAZING STORIES and ROGUE; see "The Palmer Hoax"). Earl returned to fanzine publishing, producing 60 issues of the excellent online zine *el* from 2002 to 2012. Here is Ray Palmer's contribution to WKSF? He was one of the two respondents to give a definite "yes" for the first question.—LO

Raymond A. Palmer

1) **YES,** I feel that magazine science fiction is dead.

2) No, I do not feel that any single person, action, incident, etc., is responsible. Actual events today are more amazing. Also a reaction to "fiction" is very violent in all fields, but particularly science fiction.

4) Looking to original paperbacks, and books, for fans is the only answer—and there will be a market.

5) Why doesn't Fandom—(next convention) take up the subject of forming a book club of their own, publish and buy their own selection of science fiction book manuscripts, and use the profits to finance future conventions? Two thousand members who agree to buy four books a year at $3.50 can thus salvage all good science fiction written today!

Count on me as a life member!

WHO KILLED SCIENCE FICTION?

After fannish beginnings, Wollheim (see "Early FAPA," pg. 84 and pg. 90) became an editor of note in the sf field, especially while working at Ace Books during the 1960s, where he started Edgar Rice Burroughs and J.R.R. Tolkien booms, and published the early works of Ursula LeGuin, Roger Zelazny, Samuel Delany, Thomas Disch, and Phillip K. Dick. He also hired Terry Carr to assist him. Carr talked Wollheim into taking a chance with the paperback rights to a novel called *Dune* by Frank Herbert. The book became a runaway best seller. After leaving Ace Books in 1971 Wollheim and his wife Elsie started DAW Books. —LO

Donald A. Wollheim

I HAVE finally gotten around to your letter asking opinions on "Who Killed Science Fiction?" So, to answer your questions:

1) I don't think magazine science fiction is dead. Of course not. It is just going through one of its regular setbacks, which happen continually because the field is not and never was quite as big as publishers suppose. It can't support two dozen magazines and when an imaginary book causes the band wagon to get overloaded, it's got to break down. The breaking down must and does damage all magazines alike. Magazine science fiction is a vital necessity to the field. It serves as the breeding ground of new writers, the womb of new science fiction ideas and themes. It's the proper entry port for fandom and those enthusiasts who form the living guts of science fiction readerhood. It is the easiest market for the embryonic writer to break into—and that's damned important.

2) But why did the magazine field break down? Primarily as I said before because the field is not that general in interest to support

too many magazines at once. Every now and then news begins to seep through the magazine publishing field to the effect that such and such a theme is selling like crazy. When that happens, there are always a dozen marginal operators who will hasten to leap on the rising rocket. If TRUE magazine sells, suddenly there are several dozen men's magazines—and the others must and do get cruder and cruder as they try to shortcut the means to success by boiling out all but the most elementary factors in that success. If MAD moves, bingo, a dozen imitators (which die fast, as you can find out) in a field which never could support more than one such satire. If PLAYBOY starts, again the mad rush to get rich quick—a hundred magazines becoming more and more salacious and cheaper.

Hence the recent boom in science fiction, which broke down. SATURN, which I edited because requested to do so by just such a marginal producer, had fairly good short stories in it, even though they were the selections from everyone's rejections. But I know they had at least some taste and passable quality. However, look at the overall appearance of the magazine—the cheapest printer in the trade, the shoddiest proofreading, the sloppiest art work. Likewise the rest of the fly-by-night science fiction titles of that boom ... Some were better printed than SATURN, but they were still inferior to GALAXY, ASTOUNDING, and THE MAGAZINE OF FANTASY & SCIENCE FICTION. So every time a fan, or a reader, who didn't happen to be a millionaire, bought one of these johnny-come-lately products, he just possibly didn't buy one of the better magazines that month. Hence the circulation of all was hurt. Since the field wasn't that big, it was simply spreading its limited readership thinner, to everyone's hurt.

Now this isn't a crime—it happens to be the way any business is conducted today. It happens continually in all fields of publishing, and of manufacturing also. Sometimes the field has really expanded, but often it's an illusion. It will happen again, too, in science fiction. I don't known when, but it surely will. And the same results....

(And I won't hesitate to edit a magazine similar to SATURN when next it happens, even though the end product may be the same. It's money in my pocket—and if I don't do it, someone with even less fan taste will surely do it . . . You may be interested to know that even with this alleged bust, I am advised by SATURN's publisher that the five science fiction issues did not lose money! Each and every one of them cleared a profit . . . but a small one. However, the detective SATURNS cleared a bigger profit for a while.

Now, besides the above, is there a single element we can say ruined our gal? I have a feeling there may be . . . and I'd say that the idiotic "psi"[130] stuff initiated by Campbell (whom I regard otherwise as the best man in this science fiction magazine business) was a big factor in undermining the basic foundations of good science fiction. "Psi" is just the occult under pseudo-scientific terminology. You couldn't even peddle the occult to WEIRD TALES readers . . . Mr. Campbell is a wizard at understanding real science, but unfortunately he is so woefully, boneheadedly ignorant about anything outside of the physical sciences that he falls into the first trap any hokum artist hands him in psychology, sociology, or theology. (Remember Dianetics?)

Because I know that when plowing through the slush rejected by the biggies for SATURN I ran into an awful lot of psi material. Hence, when someone desperate for material on a low budget is scraping the barrel, he must take some of this simply because it may be readable and better written than other stuff, even if he disagrees with it. Hence the low quality of his new magazine gets even lower by real science fiction reader tastes.

3) What can be done? Nothing, I suppose. We can't shoot Campbell—he's too darn good and we shall have to put up with his foibles and hope the rest of the field doesn't follow him. And when somebody goes nosing around the New York publishers that "Oh boy, oh boy, GALAXY just tripled its circulation . . . " the boom will be on again.

4) No, we should not look to the original paperback as a point of salvation. The original paperback is a fine source of novel-length fiction, but I don't think it properly replaces magazine science fiction. Besides it tends to be too big a financial risk to allow a publisher (or his editor) to experiment too widely—and science fiction needs some medium for experimentation.

Besides, if science fiction is reduced to nothing but paperback novel publishing, it will mean the end of fandom. Because readers of paperbacks do not write letters—not to the editors and certainly not to each other.

---

130 Mental phenomena that include telepathy, ESP, precognition, and telekinetics.

Ace Books does about two or more science fiction novels a month, and must reach as many people regularly as the best and biggest magazines, yet our mail commenting on the science fiction we publish is nil. No comments, no mail.

How can you hold up fandom on that? How can an editor know the difference between a good original science fiction novel and a poor one if nobody writes to comment—and it may take a year to get any kind of a circulation report—and since each book is different, the policy line of the company is a lot less clearly defined than that of a periodical.

5) I guess I've said as much as I ought to.

Cry of the Nameless, #133, Nov., 1959; eds. F.M. & Elinor Busby, art Trina Robbins. In Terry Carr's "Fandom Havest" piece he tell us: "The heading illo for the column this month is a sketch that Trina did last time she came to visit. Every time a cartoonist comes by to visit I try to put him or her to work drawing cartoons for us. Once Bjo came to visit Ron Ellik and me ... she said 'Phooey, look at me — here I've come over four hundred miles to visit two young men in a college dorm, and all that happens is that I end up drawing cartoons!'"

WHO KILLED SCIENCE FICTION?

> Silverberg made the jump from fanzine editor/publisher of *Spaceship* (a fanzine he began before he ever saw a fanzine), to pro writer very quickly, and as a young pro writer initially depended on sf for his livelihood. With the late 1950s crash of newsstand sf magazines, he turned to other markets and landed on his feet, but things were pretty dicey there for a while. Silverberg has said that his opinion back in 1960 may no longer be valid.— LO

Robert Silverberg

(from SaFari Annual: Who Killed Science Fiction? *April, 1960; ed. Earl Kemp)*

1) **YES,** I think magazine science fiction is dead—even though the corpse is still moving. There are nine magazines right now, of which only one (ASTOUNDING) offers any sort of attractive rate to its writers, and of which only three (ASTOUNDING and the Ziff-Davis mags) pay its writers promptly. A field which cannot afford to pay on acceptance, or to pay much more than a cent a word, is a pretty feeble one from the writer's viewpoint—and more and more writers are deserting the science fiction mags as a result, preferring to earn their livings in fields where the pay is higher and faster and where the market is not quite so thin. Furthermore, of the nine magazines, only ASTOUNDING and THE MAGAZINE OF FANTASY & SCIENCE FICTION seem reasonably secure; folding rumors surround each of the other seven constantly, and within a month's time all seven could easily be blown away. A field with only two magazines in it is not a living field. And the prospects of new titles entering are slim—there hasn't been a new title since 1957.

2) What is responsible? Neither Russia's space tactics nor the editorial crochets of individual editors nor the high cost of living. The trouble, simply, is distribution. The collapse of the ANC[131] signaled the

---
131 American News Corp., a newsstand distributor that went out of business in 1957.

collapse of science fiction. Only ASF gets adequate distribution today, and they aren't totally pleased. The public can't buy magazines it can't find. The editor of today's weakest-selling science fiction magazine told me that in those areas where his magazine is sold, it does extremely well. But if your magazine only reaches half the outlets of the country, it has to come pretty close to selling out in order to break even.

3) What can we do to correct it? Not a damned thing, except form our own distributing company. Distribution now is a monopoly of arrogant petty potentates who can't be bothered putting such low-return items as fiction magazines on the stands. Science fiction in magazine form will survive only if we distribute them ourselves—and that's one company I wouldn't care to invest much in.

4) Yes, I think the original paperback is the chief chance of survival for science fiction. The paperback houses have good distribution, in the main, and their books can remain on sale indefinitely. Ace has shown that there is a month-in, month-out market for science fiction paperbacks, and most of the other companies have committed themselves to at least three or four books a year. Of course, this might mean the end of the science fiction short story—but the short western and the short detective story are similarly at the edge of extinction.

5) Additional remarks? Not many from here; it's an unpleasant situation, both for the fans and for the people who, like me, once earned most or all of their living from writing science fiction. After a nasty period of conversion, I'm now busily at work in other fields, and will be writing science fiction — only when and if I have some free time and an irresistible idea. (I'll continue to write science fiction novels, though.) I think science fiction has reached the peak of its curve of popularity, and, strangely by the distributors, will drop back to become once again the arcane thing it was in 1948—except for the crud so-called science fiction in the movies and on television, which will remain to haunt us. From a fan's point of view, the best thing to do seems to be to retire to the study and spend the rest of their days with back issues; the science fiction magazines of the future, bouncing along with their penny-a-word rates, will only attract amateur writers, and the prospect of future classics is thin. But there's always **Adventures in Time and Space** to return to, and the large-size ASTOUNDINGS, and the early GALAXYs—rearward march, full speed behind!

AFTERTHOUGHTS:

(from SaFari, #6; *July 15, 1960, ed. Earl Kemp)*

WHO KILLED *Science Fiction?* is certainly a monumental job, and I want to express appreciation for it; it's a handsome volume, compiled with obvious care (imagine—an index!) and will certainly stand as a definitive statement of what people were thinking about sf in 1959. I have but one major and one minor regret about the whole undertaking—the major regret being that it should have been necessary at all to conduct a symposium on such a topic, the minor one being that some of your remarks in back appeared to lower the generally lofty and serious tone of the rest of the book, as well as taking unfair advantage of the contributors. Your comments might well have been better placed in a supplementary volume that would contain everyone else's comments as well. And it really was tasteless to reply to Sid Coleman's thoughtful article that way; local fannish pranks and jabs can be fun, but they shouldn't be immortalized in works of serious intent. None of us were fooling around up front; why drag the whole thing down to the level of an apazine in the back?

Otherwise, though, a swell job, beautifully produced. I don't find myself with any specific comments on the individual contributions, though I do feel a number of folks are off beam in places. The fellow who dropped F&SF because, quote, it had four terrible stories in the annish, deserves some sort of fugghead award, though. My God, when a magazine publishes one good story an issue these days it deserves loud applause! And F&SF certainly manages to achieve that... The field is certainly a lot deader than it was when you sent your questionnaire out. Six magazines now, and only four editors. The loss of FUTURE, SCIENCE FICTION STORIES, and FANTASTIC UNIVERSE will have a crippling effect rarely considered; these three magazines, low-paying though they were, served as salvage markets for excellent but unconventional stories that lay outside the rather narrow requirements of the Big Three. A fiction field must have such salvage markets. The way we're heading, we'll soon be down just to our Big Three, each of which has very definite ideas about what it wants to print. Even if they paid 10¢ a word, they wouldn't attract many writers. In the past, I could aim a story at the top ranks and, even if I missed, could be sure of getting at least a penny a word for my time. Without the salvage markets I can't take the risk of rejection, not while I can have a 100% sales record in other fields. A 6,000-word story submitted to Campbell might take a week to write, and might get bounced, but at least I could be sure of getting $60 for it someplace. Not much for a week's work, but at least it covered expenses.

Today, if I sat down to do a story for John Campbell, I'd be faced with the situation of getting either $180 for it or nothing at all. This all-or-nothing deal is hardly attractive, and so, even though Campbell's rates are as high as they ever were, the lack of salvage markets is costing him writers. A situation like this feeds on itself. Writers either leave sf completely, as so many have done, or, if they remain, concentrate on writing sure-shot bell-ringers. They concentrate very hard indeed on writing a story that will satisfy Campbell, Gold, or Mills—usually by writing one just like stories Campbell, Gold, or Mills have already published. This produces a lot of safe little stories, and allows the writers to keep clothed and fed, but is hardly going to result in classics. When INFINITY and FUTURE and FANTASTIC UNIVERSE were around, a writer could stick his neck out, experiment, and (if he had any ability) could be fairly sure of some return for his trouble...

When there's no incentive to experiment, a fiction field dies fast. Even the most talented newcomer needs a sympathetic low-paying market to help him along. In today's all-or-nothing situation, sf in the short form is just about doomed. Since novel-writing has always been an all-or-nothing proposition, nothing much has changed there, and several active salvage markets do exist for the offbeat novel, for the experiment that fails to please Doubleday or Simon & Schuster, or Ballantine or Avon...Let's all be grateful that we've been such diligent collectors in the past. As I said in my article, we can always go back to the juicy years of not too long ago. Matter of fact, there's a yarn in a '49 THRILLING WONDER STORY I've been meaning to get down from the shelf for a while; now's as good a time as any....

WHO KILLED SCIENCE FICTION?

Bob "Doc" Lowndes (1916–1998) published *Science Fiction Weekly* and *Le Vombeiteur* (1938–1941) as a fan, and as a pro edited FUTURE SCIENCE FICTION, SCIENCE FICTION, DYNAMIC SCIENCE FICTION, SCIENCE FICTION STORIES, and SCIENCE FICTION QUARTERLY for Columbia Publications. With the MAGAZINE OF HORROR (1963–1971) Lowndes attempted to follow in WEIRD TALES' footsteps, and did a good job at it, considering the limited resources that he had—including a tiny budget to buy stories. Lowndes gives an experienced editor's take on the sf magazine field. —LO

Robert A.W. Lowndes

1) **NOT** dead, but possibly dying in the sense that all popular magazine fiction may be dying. By "popular magazine fiction" I refer to the type of magazine that was once known as the "pulps" and remains with us in digest-size publications. The sports and western titles have gone. The detective titles are mostly gone, and of these we have mostly ultra-cheap, sensational, sadistic crime fiction which has nothing to do with the classic detective story. The remainder consists of publications that are split between reprints of the better (purportedly) stories published in the last decades and new material mostly by authors who made their name in the "good old days."

2) There are two elements necessary to a continuing audience for any type of fiction: (1) The steady reader. (2) The new reader. No publication can endure very many years on the basis of "steady readers"; there is a considerable turnover going on all the time, and even in that category of the enthusiasts, any given individual is likely to lose interest for a time, or, for a time be forced to discontinue regular support. I myself have gone through periods when I was "fed up" with sci-

ence fiction. I've always come back, and usually tried to collect and catch up on the issues of the better magazines that I missed, but that doesn't replace the sales that were lost during my apostasy. Multiply that by "n" and you can see why "constant reader" just doesn't form a strong enough backbone.

The "new reader" may be a transient who picks up one issue only, or who, having been satisfied once will try again months later when he's in the mood for more, and a certain percentage of these transients will subscribe or become regular customers. But what has supported the magazines for years has been the flesh of transients upon the bone of the regulars.

What has happened? For the most part, the volume of transients has fallen to a very low figure—not enough to support adequately even the few remaining titles in the science fiction field. The disappearance of competition—or some competition—can, at times, help the remnant, providing that the reason for the death of a competitor signifies no more than distaste for that particular brand of science fiction. Unfortunately, this is not universally the case. While some may buy Abstract Science Fiction once Abstruse Science Fiction no longer appears on the stands, most likely others will not be interested in the Abstract brand—and others will have been repelled from science fiction completely because of dissatisfaction with what they found in the now-defunct magazine.

Without defining "good" and "bad" in this frame, it is still a truism that good competition helps a magazine, while bad competition injures it. A good competitor will leave a reader in a friendly frame of mind toward the field—and maybe next month he'll buy your magazine, too; and maybe he'll add it to his list or switch to you. Bad competition drives him away; he won't look at any science fiction magazine again, even a good one like yours. (This isn't 100% but describes what has happened in many instances. Bad movies and TV science fiction have also hurt good science fiction magazines in the same way.)

There is further a special situation in the field of distribution. When American News went out of the magazine distribution business, a gap appeared that hasn't been filled. Most of the science fiction titles had to find new vehicles of distribution—and found themselves up against individual, independent wholesalers who were not interested in handling these magazines and refused to take them or to do much of anything with them when they did. (This hit the detective titles in the same way.) Result: In many of the big cities, various science fiction titles cannot be found at any newsstand. We have received a steady flow of letters from readers of all our publications who have not been able to find our magazines. They asked their dealers; the dealers contacted the wholesaler—to be told that "we don't handle these books." Finis. Some have subscribed, but only a small percentage do that—after all, there is a difference between laying out 35¢, 40¢, or 50¢ once a month, or once every other month, and laying out the cost of a year's subscription all at once. And a large percentage of readership lay amongst people for whom subscribing was difficult. The real enthusiasts, of course, get their subscriptions in; but the larger number isn't that determined. In this frame, it makes no difference how "good" a good magazine was; if it doesn't get to the newsstand, then it doesn't matter what is inside those covers that no one sees.

General interest in science fiction waxes and wanes. There was a "fad" for awhile, and that could recur, theoretically. But my feeling remains that there is an audience for a certain number of good titles (at all levels of science fiction), titles which can make a profit (though not a fortune) if the books can get on the newsstands. Television has hurt magazine sales in general and I would say to the extent that there is no longer big money to be made in popular magazines as there was back in the days of the great pulp empires.

3) Who is—or are—"we?" I don't think that "we" are in a position to do anything about it—except to make sure that we buy our copies each issue, subscribing if necessary, and show a tolerant understanding of the difficulties the magazines are laboring under when "we" write to editors. (By "tolerant understanding" I do not mean pulling punches about what "we" may not like, or think bad—positively not that—but in the tone of the criticism and complaints.) And by letting editors know "we" are still with them even though less than radiantly satisfied.

4) What do you mean? Should we (ah, this vague "we" again!) forget about the magazines and just buy pocketbooks? You don't expect me

to say "yes" to that, do you? But seriously, I think that "salvation" in the sense of a continuing supply of science fiction—and a possibility for good science fiction—is more likely to come through the pocketbooks than the magazines. I'll continue to hope for the magazines as long as there are any left, and suggest that "we" continue to support them up to the end—hoping that we don't see the end. The situation doesn't look promising but, as I indicated above, I do not think that "we" can do anything significant about it. But what's it going to cost us to try? Nothing shattering—and if, concurrently with "our" support, the magazine field picks up, we can always enjoy the somewhat irrational but satisfying feeling that our efforts helped.

5) No additional remarks at present. See forthcoming editorials in FUTURE and SCIENCE FICTION STORIES.[132]

Void, #26, Aug., 1961; art by Les Nireberg.

---

132 As noted in the previous "Afterthoughts" by Silverberg, Lowndes' remaining two pro sf magazines were dead by the time *Who Killed Science Fiction?* came out.

FANZINES IN PROFILE

Lee Hoffman (1932-2007) was the darling of sf fandom during the early 1950s — that is, after it was discovered that she was a girl. Her birth certificate name was Shirley Bell Hoffman. Lee had three rules for publishing a successful fanzine: 1) Make it legible; 2) Make it frequent; 3) Get Walt Willis as lead columnist. There had been fanzines edited by fem fans before, but Hoffman's *Quandry* was the first fem-published fanzine to become a focal point in fandom.[133] Lee went on to publish four sf novels, but perhaps more impressively, 17 westerns, one of which won the Spur award, as well as numerous pseudonymous romances.—LO

MIMEO INK, FANAC, AND PAPERBACKS

Lee Hoffman

THERE IS something magical about the written word. It hooks a lot of people — as readers, printers, writers, publishers or some combination there of. From the time I learned to read, I had been an avid reader. My first venture into publishing came when I was around nine. It was a one-page newspaper produced by pencil in an edition of one, in large block letters. It had one-sentence items of news about WWII, swiped from the news reports I heard on radio. Later, I graduated to carbon paper and the old Underwood typewriter in our attic. The boy next door and I put out a cookbook in an edition of two. For content, we got a few recipes from our mothers. We charged ten cents a copy and sold out the whole edition, one to each of our mothers.

The first attempt I recall at creative composition was when, as a pre-schooler, instead of getting my mother to tell me a kiddy story, I

---

[133] *Fanhistorica* #1, May, 1976; eds. Joe D. Siclari & Gary Farber.

told her one. All I remember about it was that it involved Popeye. In the sixth grade, inspired by Nancy Drew mysteries, I started work on a whodunit, but gave up about a half page into the tale. However, in the seventh grade I wrote any number of two or three page adventure stories inspired by the Westerns and war movies I saw regularly. (I probably looked like a conscientious student making notes about the lectures as I sat there in class scribbling away.)

In grammar school, I watched a teacher put a purple drawing of a bird face down on a pan of jelly, carefully lift it and put down a blank sheet of paper. Most amazingly, when she lifted that one there was a replica of the purple bird on it. She did one of these for each of us in the class. It wasn't til I was in high school that I found out the wonderful pan of jelly was called a hectograph. I asked for one for Christmas, and I got it.

Three high school friends, Albert Freundt, Louis Snyder and Bob Noble, and I set out to publish a class newssheet. Instead we ended up destroying the hectograph. Undeterred, we got to school early the next day and chalked our newssheet on the end panel of the blackboard. Our teacher didn't object so we did this until we tired of it.

When I was in high school my uncle, Herschel, was living in Savannah. He had a friend whose hobby was printing and had a job press in his garage. They decided to start a magazine they called *Savannah All-Amusement Monthly*. They paid me five dollars to write two brief articles for the first issue. There never was a second issue.

Oddly, I never got involved with the high school newspaper, or with the student publications when I was in college. Instead I got into science-fiction fandom. I'd been reading science-fiction for years. Then one day in 1950, while I was a stagehand with the college-community theater, the production manager, Walt Kessel, showed me a short poem in a little mimeographed magazine titled *Cosmic Dust*. The magazine intrigued me. I asked him about it. He said he'd lend me something that would explain it all if I'd absolutely promise to give it back. What he loaned me was the original Fancyclopedia . This was a mimeographed book compiled in encyclopedia form, giving the history and lore of science-fiction fandom from its inception in the 1920s til 1944, when the *Fancyclopedia* was published. It was fascinating.

Fandom then consisted of just a few hundred people who read science-fiction and communicated mostly by letter and by amateur publications called "fanzines." While the main focus was science-fiction, they wrote about anything and everything that interested them. That covered a lot of subjects.

I found a column of fanzine reviews by Rog Phillips in the pulp magazine AMAZING STORIES. Most were offered for ten cents a copy. I sent off for a bunch of them. One of the first to arrive was *Spaceship*, published by a teenager named Bob Silverberg. Another was Art Rapp's *Spacewarp* .

I got really caught up by the whole business. Within a couple of months, the desire to publish my own zine overwhelmed me. I found out where I could beg the use of a mimeograph. I got some paper and stencils, and dragged out the old typewriter in the attic. I produced a fanzine of my own. Considering the quality of the material, which I wrote myself, it was good fortune that I didn't know much about mimeography. That issue came out nearly illegible. Even so, I mailed off copies to the fans for whom I could find addresses. And some of them wrote back.

I called my fanzine *Quandry*. Some time earlier, I'd come across a paperback by Robert Benchley titled *My Ten Years In A Quandary*. I'd had to ask my mother what "quandary" meant. She explained and I liked the idea. But I mispronounced the word. When I titled my fanzine, I spelled it the way I said it. Surprisingly few people pointed out my error but I was embarrassed by the ones who did, and considered correcting the title. However I liked the look of the word "Quandry" and I thought "Quandary" rather ugly. I stuck with what I had.

Walt Kessel was astonished by my sudden publication. Before he'd done his hitch in the service, he had been an active fan and had published his own fanzine, *Cosmic Dust*. He had recognized that I was an incipient fan, but hadn't expected me to erupt into fan activity so quickly. If that's what I wanted to do, he was willing to help. He gave me a stack of old fanzines he'd received when he was active, some material he'd never gotten the chance to publish, and some mimeographing supplies, such as lettering guides and shading plates. He created a cover for me that became the basic design for every issue. And he taught me to operate a mimeograph properly.

There was an old A.B. Dick mimeo stored in the basement of the college administration building. We got permission to clean it up and use it. I soon got the hang of turning out reasonably legible copy and

I was producing my zine monthly. Quick publication appealed to writers. Some of the best writers in fandom began sending me material. I got regular columns from Bob Silverberg and from Walt Willis.

Walt was one of "The Wheels of IF", a small group of fans in Northern Ireland. Walt's brilliant witty writing won him a wide following in fandom. In the letters I exchanged with Shelby Vick, a close fannish friend in Florida, we got to talking about how great it would be if Walt could come to a convention in the U.S. and we could meet him. But in those days transatlantic travel was expensive, and the U.K. was still suffering WWII-induced austerity. Shelby came up with the idea of starting a fund to finance a trip over for him, and a slogan for the campaign, "WAW with the crew in '52."

This was an awesome project. It took a lot of courage to even tackle it, and a lot of work to actually pull it off. Shelby did it, actually getting Walt to the convention. And in doing it, he initiated a fannish practice that has continued these many years. His project was the inspiration for TAFF, the Transatlantic Fan Fund, which alternately brought a U.K. fan to the U.S. or sent a U.S. fan to the U.K. for an annual convention, and for other funds for getting fans one place or another.

I was always Shirley to my parents, but when I discovered fandom, I learned that fans made a lot of fuss about the dearth of females among their ranks at the time. I wanted my zine to stand on its own, without readers being prejudiced one way or the other because the editor was female. I decided I wanted a unisex name to publish under. My mother suggested Lee.

In my fannish writings, I managed to avoid mentioning my gender. Shelby, who came to Savannah a couple of times, was in on my secret. Robert Bloch guessed from my writing style, and a couple of other fans found out when they visited Savannah, but kept quiet about it.

Then came the NolaCon — the World Science Fiction Convention in New Orleans in 1951. I went, and fandom discovered I was a female. By then it didn't matter. My fanzine was well-established.

Fans who'd been around for years sent me old fanzines for my collection, and I read them avidly. I felt I needed a mimeograph of my own. The local A.B. Dick dealer had become interested in this project I kept buying paper and stencils for, and I'd been giving him copies of *Q* (but never hooked him into fandom. I guess he just wasn't the type.). I'd saved up $35 after the New Orleans convention, and I asked him if I could get a mimeo for that. He said he didn't even have a used one that cheap, but he thought maybe he could put something together for me out of parts from junked trade-ins. He did. It was a Speed-O-Print Model L, a crude, cranky, hand-cranked piece of machinery that took up residence in my attic.

My fanac peaked in the year that followed. I kept turning out *Quandry* monthly. Early on, I had joined FAPA-the Fantasy Amateur Press Association — a group of sixty-five fans who put out small personal zines for each other. I used a number of different titles on those.

Walt Willis and James White were putting out a small zine titled *Slant*. It was printed on a battered old tabletop letterpress. When they produced a rainbow-colored segment on a cover, I was impressed and intrigued. I got some colored inks and adapted Walt's technique to mimeo. *Quandry* #10 came out with a rainbow-colored cover.

Bob Tucker commented that I had not yet done anything comparable to an old zine called *Pluto*, which had used copious color. Although I had never seen *Pluto*, I decided to try meeting his challenge. For the November 1951 mailing, I did the first issue of *Science-Fiction Five-Yearly*. The title was inspired by such prozines as *Science Fiction Quarterly* and the British *Science Fiction Fortnightly*. My ambitions exceeded the technology I had available. I tried to do an eight color cover with some of the colors in register. This called for running the cover through the mimeo five times. The Speedy-L just wasn't up to the accuracy I was after, but about half the covers were usable. I sprinkled the interior with colored spot illustrations which were a lot easier. Bob Tucker conceded that I'd met his challenge. Even the A.B. Dick man was surprised by the color work I managed to pull off my battered Speed-O-Print. As Sam Johnson would have said if he'd seen it, it was "like a dog walking on its hind legs. You do not expect it to be done well, the wonder is that it is done at all."

It was while working on *SFFY* that I learned the importance of making sure screw-on lids were snugged down before shaking containers of liquids. I did manage to clean up most of the yellow ink that spattered over the attic, but some faint stains persisted.

The WorldCon, in Chicago, was to have a masquerade, so I mimeographed myself a costume. *Quandry* appeared on paper in various pastel colors so I located some plain cotton fabric in similar colors, cut out pieces the size of pages and ran them through the mimeo, then stitched them together into a tunic that I wore over slacks. I accessorized it with a belt of paper clips and a mimeo stylus with a pin back glued on.

Shelby Vick's campaign to bring Walt Willis to the convention had been a success. After the convention, Walt did a tour of the U.S. visiting various fans. He came to Savannah for a while. Other fans dropped in on me. I went to the next Midwescon.

Late in the summer, I saw a help-wanted ad for someone, preferably with printing experience, to work a few days. I phoned the given number and said I didn't have printing experience, but I had plenty with a mimeograph. I was given an appointment for an interview. I suspect I was the only one who called. I got the job.

The printing department of the local Vocational School was ready to produce a batch of student record cards for the fall term, and the printer needed an assistant. The print shop was an interesting place with frames of type on one side and two big cast-iron C&P Gordon job presses on the other. It smelled of oiled machinery and printer's ink. The presses had been electrified, but had to be hand-fed. Each had a flat platen, on which the blank stock went. A roller ran up over an inked disk, then spread the ink it had picked up over the set type in the form. Platen and form clammed together and the stock was printed. My job was to remove the printed piece of card stock with my left hand, while I put a fresh piece in place with my right hand before the press could bite my fingers. Surprisingly, I succeeded.

I thought a letterpress would be a really neat thing to have, but one was far beyond my resources. I continued turning out *Quandry* by mimeo for 29 issues. By then I was working in the family store and had acquired a horse. My enthusiasm for *Q* had begun to wane. But a new young fan, Charles Wells, had appeared to take over the banner of Savannah fandom. I gave him the job of turning out the final issue. Number 30 bore a black border.

For a couple of years, instead of using my vacation time to attend science-fiction conventions, I went to ranches in Colorado. I drifted away from fanac but never gave it up completely. I continued my membership in FAPA and kept turning out small personal zines.

By 1955 I had orbited back within the gravitational field of fandom. I went to the World Science Fiction Convention in Cleveland.

There I met the man I was to marry. Fannishly enthusiastic, I turned out three issues of a zine called *Fanhistory*.

I moved to New York and married Larry Shaw early in 1956. Larry was the editor of INFINITY SF magazine and was a long-time fan as well. I'd been nominated for the 1956 TAFF trip and had won. Larry and I ended up combining a honeymoon with the trip to England. We were able to pay our own way, so it just didn't seem fair to take the donated funds. I turned the money back to TAFF and we went on our own.

I was always prone to air sickness. On the flight over, I was zonked on anti-sea sickness pills and never knew we'd had a fire in one engine til later when we were on the ground.

The visit was a mad whirl. In London we stayed with Pamela and Ken Bulmer. I remember a gang of us in London dining in the Elizabethan Room of the Gore Hotel, where I encountered someone I'd been in high school with. I remember that we took a bottle of mead back to Bulmer's and got sauced in their kitchen. I remember Hampton Court.

Of the actual convention, it's all a blur.

We visited Madeleine and Walt Willis in Belfast. I remember the men having a tea-drinking contest at Willis's. Walt and Madeleine took us to visit ancient sites, and arranged for me to enjoy a horseback ride in the hills. We went to Smithfield Market where we loaded up on old books, and an out-of-the-way antique shop where we bought odd bits of aged arms and armor.

On the return flight I was so air sick that when we set down at Gander a stewardess came and asked me to try looking as healthy as I could, lest the doctor who was coming on board to check us out quarantine the plane.

At some time or another Larry and I produced a couple or three issues of another fanzine, *Excelsior*, which seems to have been totally forgettable. For years, I forgot I'd done it. I barely remember it now and can't recall what was in it.

In the fall of '56 we turned out the second issue of *Science-Fiction Five-Yearly*. By the time for the third issue, Larry and I had separated. So had the Speed-O-Print and I. It was still working, but showing its age when Bob Silverberg moved and offered me the mimeo he'd published his zine, *Spaceship* on. It was the same style as the Speedy, but bore a "Pilot" label. It was in better condition than my Speedy.

I'd long been a folk music buff. In New York, I became involved with the folknik crowd. In the summer of 1957, I started a folk music fanzine called *Caravan*. Meanwhile I continued turning out personal zines for FAPA.

It wasn't until I moved to New York that I got involved with professional publishing. For a short while, I read slush for *Infinity* and *Science Fiction Adventures*, the SF magazines my husband edited. I got credit as an assistant editor.

After Larry and I split up, I went to work for *MD Magazine*, but my job wasn't in the publishing end. I simply handled sending reprints of articles from the magazine to pharmaceutical houses that wanted them for advertising purposes. However a couple of jobs later, I went to work for a large letterpress printer and began to learn printing production, a job I loved. It didn't last, but I was determined that I would stay in printing. I went work for a typographer, and finally for a lithographer.

The 1961 issue of *SFFY* I produced was not so fancy as the preceding ones. The new style mimeos were phasing out the old ones, and it was getting hard to find colored liquid inks. I managed to obtain the primary colors, but not the white toner I had been using. I knew that Bill Danner, an amateur printer and fan, had made himself a flatbed mimeo out of an old pair of pajamas, and was making his own ink. I don't recall his formula, but it involved pigment and corn oil. Inspired by him, I managed to fabricate some white toner for that issue from artists' titanium white oil paint, Naptha and cooking oil.

1962 was the tenth anniversary of Shelby Vick's campaign to bring Walt Willis to the WorldCon in Chicago. The WorldCon was to be in Chicago again. Larry Shaw and his new wife, Noreen, headed a campaign to bring Madeleine and Walt to it. I went to the parties to welcome Madeleine and Walt and went to the convention.

Fandom caught me back into its gravitational field. I joined the New York fan groups, *Fanoclasts* and *FISTFA*[134]. These met on alternate Friday evenings. *FISTFA* was hosted by Mike MacInerny and rich brown, two very personable young fans with great senses of humor who attracted crowds that made their meetings like parties. *Fanoclasts* meetings were held at Ted White's in Brooklyn and were limited to mem-

---

134 Fannish and Insurgent Scientifictional Association, a sister club to the Fanoclasts that, unlike the latter, had open membership.

bers of the group. These included Mike and rich and a bunch of the other FISTFAns. The groups were not competitive but complementary.

Ted became a very good friend. He was great company, interested in just about everything. He was an excellent artist and an expert in jazz and comic books as well as any number of other subjects. He'd started writing science-fiction professionally, and shared his enthusiasm, inspiring me to try writing a book myself. A Western came most naturally to me. It was a typical horse opera very much in the tradition of the Western paperbacks I'd enjoyed for so long. Don & Jo Meisner critiqued the manuscript for me. Ted read it and encouraged me to submit it.

Another friend, Terry Carr, was assistant to the editor, Don Wollheim, at Ace books. Ace had a reputation for giving new writers a break. I submitted my manuscript to Terry. I hadn't yet gotten a response on it, when Terry phoned and asked me if I "had time" to write a comic Western. I had plenty of time, but wasn't sure I had the ability. Terry had faith that I did. I wrote some chapters and an outline. Ace bought it, and published it ahead of the action Western I'd done first. I couldn't think of titles, so Terry provided names for both of them, *The Legend of Blackjack Sam* for the comic one, and *Gunfight at Laramie* for the horse opera.

The literary agent, Henry Morrison, was a long time fan. He handled Ted White and some other friends who had become professional writers. He accepted me as a client. With two sales, and another book in the works I quit working regular hours for other people. That meant I could take the time off to join a group of fans travelling to the Westercon in San Diego in 1966, by way of the Midwescon, and then to visit various West Coast fans, promoting New York's bid for the WorldCon in 1967. There were eight of us on the Trek (Ted and Robin White, Dave Van Arnam, Cindy Heap, Mike MacInerney, Arnie Katz, Andy Porter and me) divided between a car and a van. I saw a lot of interesting places on that trip and I got to meet a lot of great people on the west coast. New York won the convention bid and I was listed as a member of the Convention Committee, though I didn't really contribute. Despite all my other activities, in 1966 I turned out another issue of *SFFY* on schedule.

I met Bob Toomey at the St. Louis WorldCon in 1969. He was an aspiring young writer just finishing up the final draft of his first book, and looking to move to New York. Apartments in New York were hard to find, so when the one across the hall from me became available, I told him, and he grabbed it. Bob and I collaborated on a story that we sold to Damon Knight for *Orbit 9*, and critiqued each other's book manuscripts.

My parents had retired to Port Charlotte on the west coast of Florida. In 1971, I bought a house near them, and arranged for Bob to drive a U-Haul truck loaded with my belongings down for me. He stayed in town a couple of months and together we turned out the 1971 issue of *SFFY*. Supplies for my mimeo were even harder to get in Port Charlotte than in NYC, so this was the first all black& white issue.

In Florida, I reached the apogee of my fannish orbit. I had a house of my own to keep up, my parents took a lot of my attention, and I was trying to make a living writing. I maintained my FAPA membership a while longer, then gave it up completely.

I still wanted to keep *SFFY* going but the old mimeo was wearing out and I couldn't get the replacement impression roller it needed. Without the repair parts, the other supplies, or the time to worry about it, I looked for some other way to produce *SFFY*.

I was still in touch with a few fans, including Terry Hughes, who was publishing the very fine fanzine *Mota*. I conscripted him to edit and publish the 1976 issues of *SFFY* for me. That proved such an easy lazy satisfying way to put out a fanzine that I roped in Dan Steffen and Ted White to do the next one. The following lustrum Patrick and Theresa Nielsen-Hayden did it. Then Geri Sullivan and Jeff Schalles took over and Geri's been in charge of it ever since. As publisher-emeritus I sat back on my laurels.

I didn't completely give up fandom. After I dropped out of FAPA, I got into a very small private group in which a member only had to send in one copy, and the Official Editor photo-copied enough for everyone. I'm still in it. And I went through a new incarnation as a convention-fan.

Until my aging eyes started complaining, I was still an avid reader. I'd been in publishing and I'd been in printing. And I'd been writing for a living. As I said, there is something magical about the written word. It hooks a lot of people as readers, printers, writers, publishers or some combination thereof.

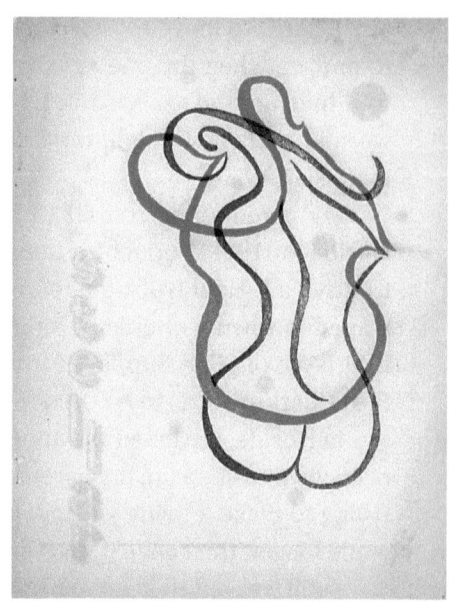

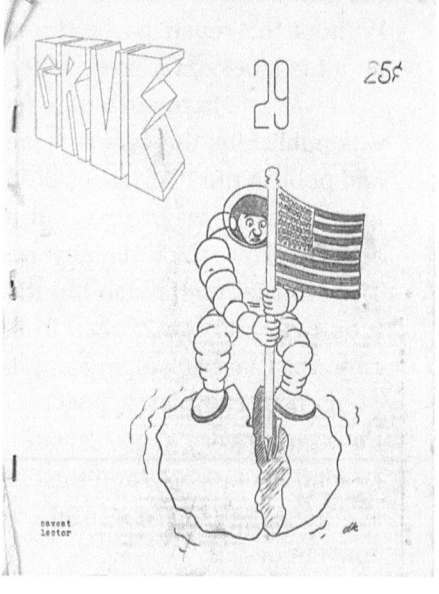

This Pg. *Innuendo*, #4, 1958; eds. Terry Carr & Dave Rike. *Stellar*, #14, 1957; ed. Ted White; art by Fred North. *JD-Argassy*, #54, April, 1960; ed. Lynn Hickman; art George Barr. *Grue* #29; April, 1958; ed. Dean A. Grennell. **Next Pg.** *Shangri-La*, #44; July, 1959; ed. Al Lewis; art by Lou Goldstone. *Vulcan*, #5, Jan., 1944. *Hyphen*, #3; Sept., 1953; ed. Walt Willis; art by Bob Shaw. *A Bas*, #5, 1955; Canadian fanzine edited by Boyd Raeburn.

ZINE POETRY CORNER: DAMON KNIGHT

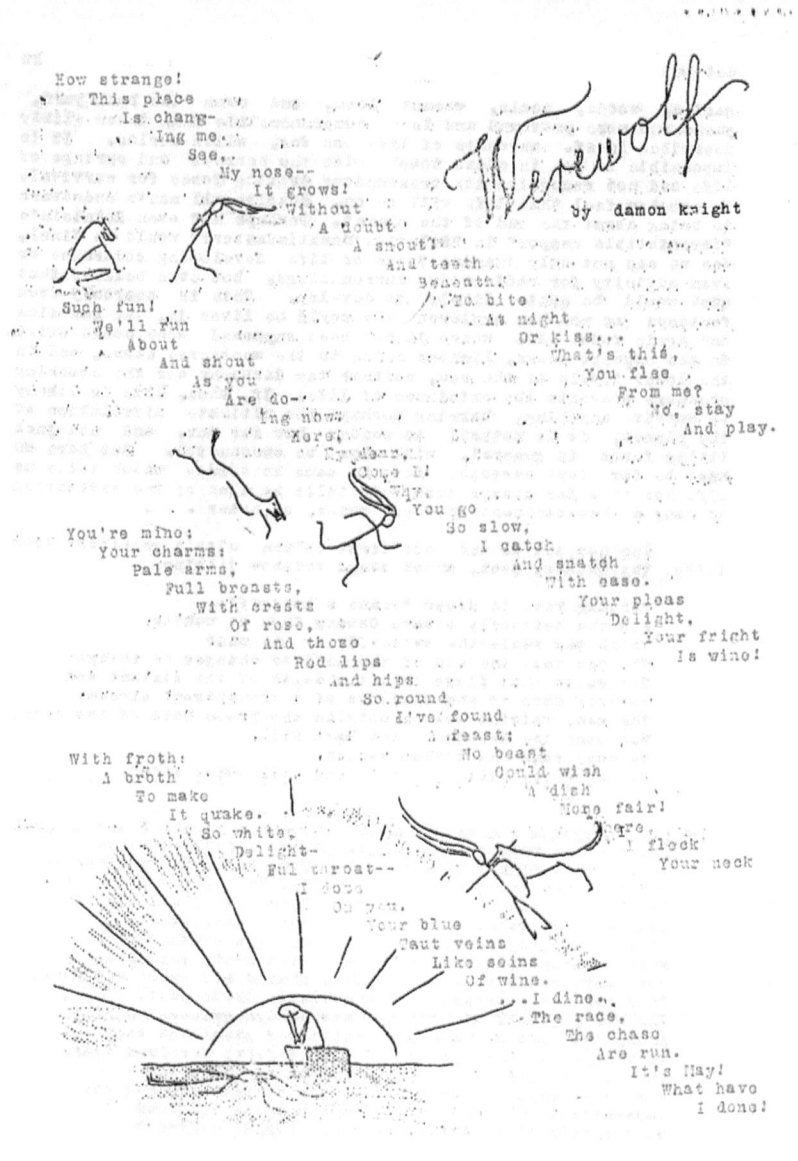

Fanfare, #8, Feb., 1942; poem and art by Damon Knight.

PRO & CONS

For a pro, Robert Bloch did a lot of fanzine writing. His approach was humorous and many a fanzine editor was deliriously happy after receiving a piece from Bloch. This was a sign that your fanzine had arrived. Bloch could also be serious. He ended one fanzine article, "How do I manage to get hornswoggled into writing this stuff? You'd think after 40 years or so I'd have enough sense to stop." ¶ If you have been paying attention so far, you should be able to get most of the references and allusions that Bloch makes here. —LO

Robert Bloch

(from Oopsla *#24; Jan., 1958; ed. Gregg Calkins)*

"ROBERT BLOCH SOUNDS TO ME LIKE AN OLD FAN GROWING SOUR." — RANDY BROWN, *OOPSLA* **#24**

THERE IS probably no more horrifying a phenomenon than the sound of an old fan growing sour. Those who have been so unfortunate as to have heard it will never forget the experience. For sheer soul-rending terror, it has country music beat a mile.

Sadly enough, we few old fans who still remain in the thin grey ranks are usually unable to detect our own decadence in terms of decibels. Our senile senses, raddled by long exposure to fannish outcries and deafened by the war whoops of younger and more vigorous enthusiasts, fail to respond. Besides, we are too close to ourselves; like many an old dog, we can't see the forest for the trees.

I am indebted, therefore, to Randy Brown for thus forcibly calling this matter to my attention, and I cannot hesitate to admit the soft impeachment.

Alas, it is all too true. I am an old fan growing sour. Once upon a time I was filled with a sparkling elixir, compounded of two familiar substances; now, one of them has evaporated and all that is left is the vinegar. But lest Randy be inclined to think too harshly of me for my cranky, morbid, SerCon[135] mutterings about fannish affairs, I hasten to raise my feeble voice in a word of explanation.

I know young folks like Randy are naturally impatient with us old gaffers and our continual ill-tempered outbursts and pointless reminiscences, but I'm asking his indulgence here. Forgive an old man his memories, Randy, and I'll try to tell you just what has soured me so dreadfully on fandom, and why I write such nasty, abusive articles as the one which recently aroused your critical perceptivity in *Oopsla*.

Actually, Randy, it's all a matter of disappointment. A man can take just so much frustration in the course of a lifetime, and when you reach my age (if you ever do; should you boys down in Texas actually get a World Convention, you'll find it will shorten your life expectancy considerably), you'll realize that long years of fanning will take their inevitable toll.

Fandom, to me, has been a source of endless disappointment and disillusion. Consider just a few of the disenchantments I've suffered through the years:

They lied to me about my birth. Yes, that's right, Randy; shortly after the time I entered fandom, one of the most prominent fans proclaimed that we lovers of science-fiction were star-begotten. Innocent youth that I was, I proudly rushed in and told this news to my parents. They promptly showed me (a) my birth certificate, and (b) the door. The same fan wanted me to sign up for an organization of super-fen known as the Cosmic Circle, but this proved to be pretty much of a bust. I didn't even get to spend a vacation in the Love Camp in the Ozarks.

They lied to me about ruling the world. All during the late Thirties a group of prominent New York fans were banded together in the belief that science fiction was a great potential political force. By advancing social and economic doctrines, fans were to assume power in the future. While it is true that a number of these fans have risen to positions of virtual dictatorship (they're magazine editors), I haven't

---

135 Serious constructive.

even been able to get a job as dog-catcher.

They lied to me about themselves. During the ages that I've been a fan, I've been the victim of countless deceptions perpetrated by other fans. They told me, for example, that Tucker was dead. Not once, but twice! If this is actually the case, then I sure would like to know who it was that won $1.32 from me at poker in Cincinnati last year. They told me there was a beautiful young femme-fan named Joan Carr, and she turned out to be a rough, tough, brutal Army Sergeant over in England. Still worse, they told me that Boyd Raeburn was a hoax and — cruel and bitter disappointment! — he actually exists.

They lied to me about England. No less a fan than Bea Mahaffey reported to me on how hospitably she had been received during a visit to the London Convention some years ago. She said that all the men had lined up to kiss her. Well, as you know, last year a whole plane-full of American fans went over there for a Convention. I checked recently with Bob Silverberg, who attended the Con, and he swears up and down that those hospitality reports are a lie – not a single man even offered to kiss him.

They lie about everything. As a faithful reader of science-fiction, I read everything Richard Shaver wrote and not once was I able to remember Lemuria, nor have I so much as seen a single Dero (except, of course, at Conventions). I studied Dianetics, but I never became a one-shot clear – in fact, I can still drink as many as ten shots and all that happens is I get foggier than ever. I bought a Hieronymous Machine[136], but it isn't even sticky enough to seal envelopes with.

No, an elderly fan like myself can endure only so much without cracking. After all, I'm a mere mortal, not a Texan. And thus it is, when confronted with the fakery and falsity of fandom, I totter to my feet, brandish my truss, and croak: "Fandom? Bah! Humbug!"

---

136 John Campbell, Jr. (1910–1971), the editor of ASTOUNDING SCIENCE FICTION, for all his scientific know-how (he was educated at M.I.T.) and story-telling savvy, fell for a lot of pseudo-scientific claptrap. Most famously Dianetics followed by the Hieronymous Machine, a sort of ore analyzing machine that you didn't even have to build — a diagram of the machine on paper could do the job of the machine as well — all that was necessary was a human nervous system that could sense the "tingling" or "stickiness" when energy was detected. Another one of Campbell's bizarre promos was the Dean Drive (an antigravity device). There are other dubious inventions/ideas that Campbell pushed in ASTOUNDING, but we don't have the space here to list them all. His biographer Alec Nevala-Lee called him a " . . . big man in a tiny office". Nevala-Lee was being literal, though I did not read it that way.

FANAC, #70; Jan., 15, 1961; eds. Terry & Miriam Carr; cartoon by Ray Nelson. See footnote on previous page for background.

Cartoon by Bill Rotsler from *Masque,* #13, 1961. Rotsler's cartoon was inspiration, in small part, for Harlan Ellison famous 1967 story, which used the caption as its title.

Diaspar, #9, Aug., 1958; a FAPA zine, ed. Terry Carr; art by Ray Nelson.

COPYRIGHT ACKNOWLEDGMENTS

This is a continuation of the copyright page.
While every attempt has been made to trace authors and artists, outside of public domain, or their heirs or executors, the following list of acknowledgements is necessarily incomplete. Apologies are offered for any omissions which have resulted from the publication deadline. Corrections will be made in future editions/printings.

WHEN TIME WAS NEW ©2019 Luis Ortiz

TOWNER HALL, VOID, ADOLESCENCE AND ALL THAT
©2019 Gregory Benford

POSTSCIPT TO VEGA ©2019 Joel Nydahl, reprinted by permission of the author

CONFESSIONS OF A FANZINE REVIEWER and
BAH! HUMBUG! ©2019 Estate of Robert Bloch, reprinted with permission

MY PAL JOHNNY ©2019 Robert A. Madle, reprinted by permission of the author

DEADLINE JOB ©2019 Estate of Frank Kelly Freas, reprinted by permission of Laura Freas Beraha

123456789? WHAT WAS THAT FANDOM I SAW YOU WITH… and
A DAY WITH CALVIN THOS. BECK ©2019 Ted White, reprinted by permission of the author

WHO KILLED SCIENCE FICTION? ©2019 Robert Silverberg/Agberg, Ltd., reprinted by permission of the author

MIMEO INK, FANAC, AND PAPERBACKS ©2019 Gary Ross Hoffman, reprinted with permission

Index (names and zines)

A

A Bas 108, 111, 390
Abstract 132, 133, 139, 244, 377
Ackerman, Alden Lorraine 120
Ackerman, Forrest J 3, 4, 12, 14, 18, 19, 20, 22, 32, 33, 40, 45, 53, 54, 59, 60, 69, 72, 75, 76, 79, 80, 81, 86, 91, 97, 118, 119, 120, 143, 145, 153, 171, 177, 179, 183, 189, 190, 191, 196, 202, 206, 218, 219, 233, 236, 251, 252, 255, 256, 278, 312, 353, 355, 361
Acolyte, The 13, 58, 101, 263, 265, 270, 271
Ad Astra 16, 114, 195
Agenbite of Inwit 226
Agnew, Jack 36, 37, 41, 51
Ah! Sweet Idiocy! 58, 117, 118, 271
Alchemist, The 181
Amateur Correspondent 14
Arcturus 27
Arfstrom, Joe 57
Ashley, Al & Abby Lu 17, 91, 180, 191, 208
Astonishing Stories 27
Astra's Tower Leaflet 210
Atheling, Jr., William (James Blish) 43
Austin, Neil 162, 165, 247
Axe 286

B

Baltadonis, John 27, 28, 35, 37, 38, 39, 40, 41, 51, 81
Banister, Manly 77, 121, 122, 192, 235
Beaumont, Charles (Charles McNutt) 18, 71, 265, 288
Beaumont, E.T. (Wilma Bellingham & Charles McNutt) 71, 265
Beck, Calvin Thomas 343, 344, 353
Benford, Greg 18, 285, 288, 341, 345, 349, 353
Benford, Jim 310, 340
Berry, D. Bruce 57
Bete Noir 285
Binder, Eando 54
Bixby, Jerome 166, 167, 168
Bizarre 34, 218
Bjo (Betty JoAnne Trimble) 150, 306, 307, 308, 309, 371
Black & White 91, 95, 100, 101

Blish, James 18, 26, 27, 42, 43, 44, 220, 221, 222, 223, 224, 225, 226, 227, 288, 323, 326
Bloch, Robert 16, 23, 69, 109, 171, 176, 217, 221, 249, 263, 282, 284, 300, 353, 383, 394
Boggs, Redd 138, 239, 271, 276, 284, 285, 300, 303, 304, 323, 344
Bok, Hannes 18, 31, 32, 33, 34, 57, 92, 102, 103, 106, 116, 171, 294
Bosh 70
Boucher, Anthony 166, 167, 336, 337
Bradbury, Ray 18, 22, 23, 31, 32, 40, 75, 76, 102, 103, 104, 105, 106, 107, 112, 171, 205, 252, 253, 254, 255, 256, 288, 289, 290
Bradley, Marion Zimmer 9, 14, 16, 18, 122, 138, 210, 246, 282, 298, 300, 301, 350
Bradley, Jim 246
Breen, Walter 286
Brooklyn Reporter, The 27
Brown, Randy 351, 394
Browne, Howard 159, 334, 336, 338, 339
Browne, Norman 213
Budrys, Algis 18
Bulletin of the Terrestrial Fantascience Guild, The 28
Bunch, David R. 122
Burbee, Charles 60, 86, 198, 199, 200, 201, 202, 230, 252, 307–309, 323, 334, 344, 352
Burroughs, Edgar Rice 36, 47, 118, 155, 368
Busby, F.M. & Elinor 306, 307, 371

C

Calkins, Gregg 205, 211, 303, 313, 393, 394
Campbell Jr., John W. 12, 13, 17, 22, 24, 32, 56, 113, 135, 160, 198, 205, 234, 239, 323, 324, 325, 326, 334, 336, 338, 339, 370, 375, 396
CANFAN 233
Carnell, Ted 81, 171
Carr, Terry 16, 18, 58, 63, 220, 285, 294, 341, 343, 349, 368, 371, 388, 390, 397
Carter, Lin 168
Centauri 71
Charles Wells 385
Chauvenet, Louis Russell 10 78
Clarke, A. Vincent 319
Clyne, Ronald 170, 171, 238, 251, 310
Cobb, Ron 132
Cole, Les & Es 245
Comet, The 10, 22, 25, 29

399

Conover, WIllis 28
Cosmag 140
Cosmology 10, 27, 50, 153
Cox, Marian 297
Crane, Burton 242
Crawford, William 27, 52, 90
Crozetti, Lora 14, 74, 143, 183
Cry of the Nameless, The 306, 307, 351
Cummings, Ray 88
Curious Stories 44, 90

D

D'Journal 27
Daugherty, Walter 10, 73, 76, 199, 200, 255, 257, 278
Damn Thing, The 75, 218, 251, 252, 254, 255, 256, 257, 289
Dawn 147, 202, 228
Day, Don 336, 338
Degler, Claude 179, 216, 257, 276
Destiny 77, 167, 246, 367
Diablerie 75, 268, 269
Dikty, Ted 171
Dockweiler, Harry 28
Doings of the Lincoln 28
Douglas, Myrtle (Morojo) 14, 72, 73, 75, 92, 119, 145, 190, 206, 255
Dollens, Morris 28, 29, 37, 38, 39, 207, 348
Dominic, Margaret 209
Dunkelberger, Walt 118

E

Ebert, Roger 288
Ellik, Ron 285, 294, 371
Ellison, Harlan 18, 22, 133, 209, 210, 214, 250, 280, 281, 283, 284, 288, 296, 298, 299, 300, 301, 312, 353, 397
Emshwiller, Ed 249, 294, 299, 364, 404
En Garde! 91, 208
Escape 81
Estes, Jr., O.G. 184
Evans, Bill 194, 287, 289
Eyde, Edythe (Tigrina) 14, 118-120

F

Fabun, Don 140, 166, 328
Fairman, Paul W. 166, 336
Fan 278
Fan Faire 167
Fan Slants 310
Fan-Dango 58, 61, 101, 252, 271

Fanac 13, 149, 150, 285, 286, 294, 312, 315, 339
Fanciful Tales 27, 143
Fanclyclopedia 312
Fanews 118
Fanfare 17, 164, 289, 392
Fanhistorical 58
Fanscient 22, 217, 246, 248, 336
Fantascience Digest 28, 35, 37, 51, 81, 260
Fantasia (Lou Goldstone) 31, 32, 33, 34, 76, 102, 103, 104, 106, 107, 116, 186, 188, 288
Fantasia (Geo. R. Hahn) 28
Fantasite 61, 207
Fantast 116, 143, 235
Fantastic Worlds 165, 166, 168
Fantasy Advertiser 160, 162, 167, 181, 184, 208, 247, 327
Fantasy Amateur 12, 84, 85, 90, 384
Fantasy Book 143
Fantasy Digest 78
Fantasy Fan 13, 19, 197, 289
Fantasy Fiction Telegram 27, 35, 38
Fantasy Magazine 13, 25, 27, 37, 52, 53, 54, 55, 56, 59, 63, 69, 81, 82, 128, 153, 256
Fantasy News 81, 232
Fantasy Review 152, 239
Fantasy Scout 81
Fanvariety 84, 103, 146, 147, 148, 149, 150, 288, 338
FAPA 3, 12, 18, 53, 58, 60, 61, 82, 84, 85, 86, 89, 90, 91, 95, 115, 221, 225, 226, 227, 251, 257, 259, 281, 284, 309, 320, 321, 368, 384, 385, 386, 389
Farley, Ralph Milne 56
Fascination 139
Fearn, John Russell 54
Finlay, Virgil 33, 92, 106, 151, 195
First Fandom Magazine 47
Focal Point 252
Fort, Charles 204, 206
Fourteen Leaflet, The 26, 28
Freas, Frank Kelly 185, 294
Freehafer, Paul 76, 116, 251
Futura Fantasia 31, 34
Futurart 82

G

Gafia Newssheet 285
Gaughan, Jack 18, 57, 160, 162, 310
Geis, Richard 16, 163, 243, 244, 247, 250, 283, 334
Gernsback, Hugo 13, 22, 36, 46, 49, 67, 76, 152, 176, 222

Gillespie, Jack 80
Gillings, Walter H. 28, 54, 152
Giunta, John 237, 261
Glasser, Allen 10, 23, 24, 27, 47, 48, 50, 58, 95, 196
Gold, Horace 12, 166, 167, 169, 336, 338, 375
Golden Atom 54
Goldstone, Lou 186, 187, 188, 189, 390
Gorgon, The 209, 211
Grennell, Dean 111, 133, 138, 148, 209, 259, 281, 282, 283, 284, 300, 303, 305, 390
Grossman, John 45, 57
Grotesque 29, 44
Grue 111, 133, 135, 148, 259, 390

H

HA! 139
Hamling, William L. 166, 181, 367
Harmon, Jim 283
Harris, Chuck 131, 236
Harryhausen, Ray 75, 143, 255, 256
Heinlein, Robert 19, 72, 75, 94, 97, 107, 205, 255
Helios 28, 43, 65, 143, 176
Hickman, Lynn 238, 390
Hodge-Podge 111
Hoffman, Lee 9, 12, 14, 20, 130, 141, 147, 168, 171, 192, 193, 196, 233, 263, 276, 280, 282, 284, 297, 310, 380
Holmberg, John-Henri 9, 20
Horizons 53, 101, 191
Hornig, Charles 13, 18, 76, 88, 171, 255
Howard, Robert E. 13, 23, 54, 55, 263
Hubbard, L. Ron 198, 323, 324, 325, 326, 327, 328, 329, 330, 331, 332, 334
Hughes, Terry 389
Hunter, Alan 209
Hutchison, Don 127
Hyphen 13, 70, 113, 131, 233, 236, 284, 319, 341, 390

I

Imagination! 13, 19, 22, 46, 72, 75, 81, 102, 251, 260
Imaginative Fiction 37
Incinerations 147, 148, 211, 338
Ink Blot 28
Innuendo 13, 63, 285, 294, 349, 390
Inside 51, 111, 209
International Observer 28, 44

J

James, WIlliam 397

J.D. Argassy 238
Jinx 219

K

Kalki 220
Keasler, Max 103, 146, 147
Kessel, Walt 208, 381, 382
Keller, David H. 23, 24
Kellogg, Bob 243, 334
Kemp, Earl 12, 13, 16, 18, 20, 364, 365, 366, 367, 372, 374, 404
Kemp, Nancy 364, 365
Kennedy, Joe 168, 208, 221, 245
Kepner, Jim 75, 117
Knight, Damon 10, 18, 107, 171, 181, 194, 218, 219, 221, 257, 287, 288, 289, 291, 292, 388, 392
Kornbluth, Cyril 82, 171
Korshak, Erle 171
Krucher, Joe 57, 68
Krupa, Julian 195
Kuttner, Henry 65, 75, 86, 104, 107, 239
Kyle, David 28, 171, 181

L

Laney, F. Towner 58, 60, 101, 202, 271, 307
Le Vombeiteur 376
Le Zombie 11, 13, 14, 32, 72, 73, 116, 149, 170, 171, 175, 176, 194, 260, 313
Leer 109
Leinster, Murray 13
Lewis, Al 390
Lichtman, Robert 20, 300, 352
Little Monsters of America, The 238
Lovecraft, H.P. 11, 13, 18, 29, 23, 44, 54, 55, 58, 101, 107, 109, 164, 223, 263, 270,
Lowndes, Robert A.W. 16, 18, 40, 68, 80, 82, 114, 171, 179, 221, 226, 257, 376

M

Macabre 127, 332
Madle, Robert 2, 35, 38, 39, 40, 50, 51, 81, 258
Magnitude 181
Mahaffey, Bea 203, 204, 234, 396
Marconette, Walter E. 34, 62, 63, 78, 218
Marvel Tales 27, 52
Masque 60, 229, 230, 231, 321, 322, 397
McComas, J. Francis 166, 336
McMillan, Bob 279
McNutt, Charles 71

Merritt, Abe 13
Michel, John B. 28, 81, 82, 221, 257
Mimosa 35
Miske, Jack Chapman 34, 66, 82, 218, 219, 257
Moffat, Len 9, 168
Morojo (Myrtle Douglas)14, 72, 73, 75, 92, 119, 145, 190, 206, 208, 255
Moskowitz, Sam 14, 15, 18, 28, 38, 40, 41, 43, 58, 63, 65, 79, 82, 143, 171, 176, 177, 178, 179, 196, 197, 219
Mutant, The 28

N

Nekromantikon, The 121, 122, 123, 125, 192, 211
Nelson, Ray ((R. Faraday Nelson), 22, 146, 149, 262, 293, 339, 397
Nelson, Perdita 146
Neophyte 320
New Fandom 177, 179
Nireberg, Les 302, 379
Nova 17, 29, 44, 91, 95, 180
Novae Terrae 28, 82
Nydahl, Joel 2, 20, 210, 214, 273, 281, 282, 283, 295, 296, 297, 298, 299, 300, 302, 303

O

ODD 147, 310
Oopsla 141, 203, 211, 303, 313, 393, 394, 395
Orb 77
Osterlund, Arthur H. 61

P

Palmer, Ray 10, 12, 13, 18, 53, 54, 55, 56, 69, 80, 151, 152, 153, 154, 155, 156, 157, 158, 159, 160, 161, 166, 179, 197, 198, 203, 204, 206, 257, 323, 336, 337, 339, 367
Panit Stories 278
Paul, Frank R. 36, 37, 46
Peon 13, 111, 167, 249, 250, 294
Perri, Leslie (Doris Baumgardt) 80
Phanny 83, 100
Phantagraph, The 28, 90
Phantastique 28
Phantasy World 28, 181
Phillips, Ralph Rayburn 57, 206, 217, 327
Phillips, Rog 141, 157, 160, 161, 202, 240, 336, 337, 381
Piper, Tom 246

Planet, The 10, 22, 47, 50
Planeteer, The 27, 42, 43, 44, 90, 220
Pohl, Frederik 18, 40, 44, 76, 80, 82, 171
Polaris 76, 116
Polymorphanucleated Leucocyte 27
Pragnell, Festus 54
Price, Bill 232
Price, E.Hoffmann 56
Psychotic 13, 139, 163, 243, 244, 246, 250, 280, 281, 283, 285, 334
Purple Flash 28

Q

Quandry 13, 130, 140, 141, 147, 167, 171, 173, 192, 193, 194, 196, 199, 211, 212, 213, 236, 239, 280, 282, 283, 293, 296, 297, 310, 380, 382, 384, 385

R

Raeburn, Boyd 108, 344, 390, 396
Rapp, Arthur 58, 198, 271, 323, 334, 382
Reamy, Tom 345, 348
Reiss, Andy 197, 343, 363
Rhodomagnetic Digest 140, 166, 167, 297, 310, 328
Riddle, Charles Lee 109, 250, 294
Rike, Dave 315, 390
Robbins, Trina 312, 371
Rocket, The 76
Rogers, Alva 221
Rogers, James M. 30
Rothman, Milton 36, 37, 40, 82, 171
Rotsler, William 14, 16, 60, 148, 149, 163, 200, 208, 229, 230, 231, 259, 308, 320, 321, 322, 393, 397
Ruppert, Conrad H. 27, 52

S

S-F Review 28
SaFari Annual: Who Killed Science Fiction? 364, 365, 372
Saha, Art 221
Schwartz 18, 23, 27, 50, 54, 55, 58, 69, 153
Science and Science Fantasy Fiction Review 354
Science Fantasy Bulletin, The 209, 214, 298, 299, 301
Science Fantasy Movie Review 86
Science Fiction Check-list 80, 82, 88
Science Fiction Critic 28, 67
Science Fiction Digest 13, 25, 27, 28, 53, 59, 153, 176, 197

Science Fiction Fan 8, 28, 30, 37, 44, 82, 178
Science Fiction News 27, 323
Science Fiction Newsletter 13, 167, 200, 239, 296, 313
Science Fiction World 28
Science-Fantasy Correspondent 28
Science-Fiction Five-Yearly 280, 386
Scienti-Comics 9, 292
Scienti-Snaps 13, 34, 62, 63, 64, 65, 67, 218, 260
ScientiFantasy 51, 57
Scientifiction 28
Shangri-L'Affaires (Shaggy) 74, 149, 200, 208, 252, 285
Shangri-LA 13, 45, 74, 75, 117, 120, 285
Shaver, Richard 151, 152, 153, 155, 156, 157, 158, 159, 160, 161, 203, 204, 206, 323, 334, 396
Shaver Mystery Magazine 151, 161, 206
Shaw, Bob 18, 194, 236
Shaw, Larry 18, 171, 221, 385, 387
Shuster, Joe 21, 25, 27
Siclari, Joe 20, 58
Siegel, Jerry 14, 21, 25, 27
Silverberg, Robert 2, 18, 20, 63, 84, 140, 168, 209, 280, 281, 285, 288, 296, 300, 336, 338, 372, 382, 386, 396, 404
Skyhook 13, 64, 111, 133, 138, 276, 294
Slant 9, 13, 122, 124, 125, 128, 129, 130, 167, 193, 194, 233, 235, 236, 296, 384, 402
Sloane, T. O'Conner 173
Smith, Clark Ashton 13, 19, 44, 55, 56, 223, 263
Sneary, Rick 199, 211, 245
Snide 10, 107, 218, 287, 288, 289, 290
Spaceship 63, 140, 209, 211, 296, 336, 372, 382, 386
Spacewarp 13, 58, 149, 198, 210, 271, 304, 323, 334, 382, 397
Spaceways 13, 17, 53, 79, 80, 81, 115, 155, 218, 255, 260, 261, 289
Spectre 262
Speer, Jack 12, 64, 79, 81, 82, 91, 92, 93, 94, 95, 100, 101, 177, 262, 273, 276, 280, 281, 285, 313
Spillane, Mickey 15, 63
Stardust 154, 156, 181, 218, 367
Stellar 343, 353, 390
Stewart, Bhob 349
Stibbard, Sydney 201, 202
Sun Spots 17, 99
Sweetness and Light 60, 76, 82, 86, 87, 116, 288, 289
Swisher, Robert 82, 85, 86, 88

T

Taurasi, James V. 80, 81, 82, 85, 157, 177, 237
Terwilleger, Guy 334
Tessaract 28
Thing, The (fanzine) 242
Thompson, D.B. 4, 100
Thompson, Arthur (ATom) 131, 259
Tigrina (Edythe Eyde) 14, 58, 117, 118, 119, 120
Time Traveller, The 10, 13, 21, 23, 25, 27, 47, 58, 59, 60, 90, 196
Timebinder 100
Toward Tomorrow 117
Train, Oswald 37, 38
Trap Door 300
Trimble, Betty JoAnne (Bjo) 150, 306, 307, 308, 309, 371
Tucker, Bob 3, 4, 5, 6, 11, 14, 15, 16, 18, 27, 32, 40, 69, 72, 73, 80, 81, 85, 88, 113, 122, 171, 190, 196, 200, 205, 218, 220, 234, 239, 240, 260, 273, 282, 283, 284, 289, 300, 304, 307, 313, 384, 396
Tumbrils 220, 221, 222, 223, 224, 225, 226, 227
Twig 334

U

Unusual Stories 27, 52, 86
Utopian 211

V

Vampire 13, 177, 208, 272
van Vogt, A.E. 187
Vanations 213, 214
Vance, Jack 239
VAPA 221, 222, 224, 225, 226, 227
Vega 13, 209, 210, 214, 216, 244, 273, 279, 282, 283, 286, 295, 296, 297, 298, 299, 300, 301, 302, 305
Venus 104, 160, 183
Vertigo 334
Vice Versa 14, 118
Vice, Shelby 20, 236, 277, 383, 384, 387
Virgil Partch 278
Virginia Anderson 89
Voice of the Imagi-Nation (VOM) 13, 20, 22, 32, 46, 73–75, 118, 119, 143, 145, 187, 189, 190, 191, 194, 196, 206, 208, 252
Void 13, 146, 197, 285, 302, 310, 340, 341, 342, 343, 344, 345, 349, 350, 352, 353, 363, 379

Vogt, A.E. van 187, 205, 208, 234
VoMaidens Portfolio 191
Vonnegut, Jr., Kurt 18, 365
Vorzimer. Peter J. 132, 133, 244
Vulcan 390

W

Warner Jr., Harry 2, 3, 4, 5, 6, 15, 18, 41, 53, 58, 63, 79, 80, 84, 101, 103, 146, 171, 191, 218, 220, 221, 252, 260, 288, 301
Wastebasket 239
Watkins, Russell K. 147, 149, 281
Weinbaum, Stanley G. 54, 56, 153, 155, 256
Weisinger, Mortimer 23, 32, 49, 50, 54, 59, 60, 153, 257
Wellons, Juanita R. 216, 286, 295
Wells, Basil 221, 228
Wells, H.G. 47, 54, 72
Wesson, Helen 242
White, James 124, 128, 129, 130, 194, 233, 234, 384
White, Ted 2, 16, 18, 20, 280, 341, 342, 344, 349, 352, 353, 354, 387, 388, 389, 390
Widner, Art 60, 72, 89, 164, 258, 274
Wiggins, Olon F. 8, 28, 30, 80, 178, 258
Wild Hair 58, 201, 202, 271
Williams, Paul 9
Williams, Vincent 94
Williamson, Jack 54, 75, 140, 255
Willis, Madeleine Bryan 234
Willis, Walter 4, 5, 6, 9, 10, 14, 16, 28, 69, 70, 113, 122, 124, 128, 130, 167, 168, 192, 193, 197, 199, 203, 206, 233, 239, 282, 284, 286, 303, 336, 341, 350, 352, 382, 384, 386, 387, 390
Wilson, Dick 65, 80, 86
Wolf, Mari 298, 300
Wollheim, Donald 12, 17, 18, 27, 28, 38, 40, 44, 47, 81, 82, 84, 86, 90, 143, 177, 179, 221, 334, 368, 388
Wood, Ed 176
Woolf, Virginia 11
Wright, Farnsworth 32, 33, 56, 173, 189

Y

Yandro 13
Yerke, T. Bruce 75, 251, 252, 253, 255, 256, 258, 289
YHOS 89

Z

Z.Z. Zug's Gazette 88
Zenith 304

Flyleaf art from *Amateur Correspondent*, vol. 2, #2, Sept-Oct., 1937.

OTHER BOOKS BY LUIS ORTIZ

NONFICTION

Arts Unknown: The Life & Art of Lee Brown Coye

ॐ

**Emshwiller: Infinity x Two:
The Art & Life of Ed & Carol Emshwiller**

ॐ

Outermost: The Art + Life of Jack Gaughan

EDITOR

**Cult Magazines: From A to Z:
A Compendium of Culturally Obsessive
& Curiously Expressive Publications**
with Earl Kemp

ॐ

Why New Yorkers Smoke

ॐ

The Monkey's Other Paw

ॐ

The Nonstop Book Of Fantastika Tattoo Designs

ॐ

Robert Silverberg: Other Spaces, Other Times

ARTIST

The Steampunk Coloring Book